Object-Oriented Programming
with Turbo C++®

Object-Oriented Programming with Turbo C++®

Keith Weiskamp

Loren Heiny

Bryan Flamig

John Wiley & Sons, Inc.

New York • Chichester • Brisbane • Toronto • Singapore

Turbo C++® is a registered trademark of Borland International, Inc.

Library of Congress Cataloging-in-Publication Data

Weiskamp, Keith.
 Object-oriented programming with Turbo C++ / Keith Weiskamp, Loren Heiny, Bryan Flamig.
  p. cm.
 Includes bibliographical references.
 ISBN 0-471-52466-2 (acid-free paper)
 1. Object-oriented programming. 2. C++ (Computer program language)
3. Turbo C++ (Computer program) I. Heiny, Loren.
II. Flamig, Bryan. III. Title.
QA76.64.W46 1991
005.1--dc20

Printed in the United States of America
91 92 10 9 8 7 6 5 4 3 2

Contents

Preface   **xv**

   Who Should Read This Book   xv
   What You'll Need   xvi

Chapter 1   Getting Started with Object-Oriented Programming   **1**

   The Evolution of Computer Languages   1
   What Is OOP?   2
   The OOP Viewpoint   3
      OOP Is Good Design   4
   Components of OOP   5
      Classes and Objects   5
   The Two Faces of OOP   6
      Encapsulation   6
      Inheritance   8
   Turning Theory into Practice   10
      From Structures to Objects   10
      The Object-Oriented Travel Expense Program   13
      What about Inheritance?   15
   Summary   20

Chapter 2   Writing an Object-Oriented Programming Application   21

The File Browser	21
How the File Browser Works	23
What's Under the Hood?	24
Working with Buffers	26
Working with the Screen	27
The Complete File Browser Program	29
Listing 2.1 browse.c	29
A Second Look at the Browse Program	35
Thinking with Objects	35
Browser Objects	36
The Screen Class	38
The File Buffer Classes	39
A Little Bit of Inheritance	41
Using the Objects	42
The Object-Oriented Browser	44
Listing 2.2 browse2.cpp	44
Code Critique	55

Chapter 3   Screen and Keyboard Tools   57

Overview of the Screen Objects	57
Inside the PC's Text Screen	58
A Virtual Screen Class	60
Buffer Initialization	62
Writing to the Screen	64
Moving Screen Memory	65
Miscellaneous Screen Tools	67
Working with the Keyboard	69
Testing the Screen and Keyboard	70
Listing 3.1 txunit.h	73
Listing 3.2 txunit.cpp	74
Listing 3.3 scrnsty.h	79
Listing 3.4 scrnsty.cpp	80
Listing 3.5 keybrd.h	81
Listing 3.6 keybrd.cpp	82

Chapter 4 An Object-Oriented Mouse Toolkit — 85

Overview of the Mouse Toolkit — 85
Working with the Mouse — 86
The Mouse Object — 87
   Communicating with the Mouse Driver — 88
   Declaring and Using a Mouse Object — 89
   Detecting the Mouse — 90
   Configuring the Mouse — 90
   Controlling the Mouse Cursor — 92
   Using Mouse Coordinates — 92
   Moving the Mouse — 93
   Working with Mouse Buttons — 94
   Working with Mouse Events — 96
A Mouse Test Program — 98
The Mouse in Graphics Mode — 100
   The Two Cursor Masks — 100
   Setting the Graphics Cursor — 102
   Testing the Graphics Cursor — 103
Code Critique — 105
   Abstract Classes — 105
   Event Handling — 106
   Listing 4.1   msmouse.h — 106
   Listing 4.2   msmouse.cpp — 108
   Listing 4.3   mcursor.cpp — 113

Chapter 5 Setting the Stage for Windows and Menus — 115

One World, Many Objects — 115
What Are Screen Objects? — 116
The Master Plan — 116
   The Secret Is Inheritance — 118
Starting with Rectangles — 120
   Clipping Rectangular Regions — 121
   Intersecting Rectangles — 122
The Rectangular Screen Object Class — 124
Moving Toward Text: The Trso Class — 125

Combining Multiple Objects   127
Adding Text and Borders   128
Copying and Swapping Images   130
Using the Trso Class   131
Code Critique   134
Adding a Clear Function   134
Supporting Text Cursors   134
Combining Classes   134
Listing 5.1   rsounit.h   135
Listing 5.2   rsounit.cpp   136
Listing 5.3   trsounit.h   138
Listing 5.4   trsounit.cpp   138

Chapter 6   Creating Framed Screen Objects   143

Framed Screen Objects   143
Testing Coordinate Status   147
Working with Screen Images and Shadows   148
Working with Attributes and Colors   148
The Tfso Class   150
Swapping Objects and Drawing Shadows   153
Determining the Size of Text Strings   156
Displaying Windows   156
Skeletons in the Closet   160
The Tskel Member Functions   162
Code Critique   162
Changing Frames   163
Adding Titles   163
Restricting Member Function Access   163
Tips on Creating General Classes   163
Listing 6.1   fsounit.h   164
Listing 6.2   fsounit.cpp   165
Listing 6.3   tfsounit.h   167
Listing 6.4   tfsounit.cpp   168

Chapter 7   Interactive Screen Objects   175

Supporting Multiple Screen Objects   175
The Interactive Screen Object Hierarchy   177
   The Iso Class   177
   The Screen Object Stack   181
   Initializing an Iso   183
   Sizing and Positioning Isos   185
   Opening and Closing Isos   186
   Drawing Isos   187
   Moving and Stretching Objects   188
The Event Handling System   189
   The Message Passing System   190
   What's in an Event?   190
   Keyboard Events   192
Every Screen Object Needs a Manager   192
   Event Loops   193
   Cycling through Screen Objects   194
Creating Text Windows   194
Supporting Text Screens   196
Putting the Wso Class to Work   197
Overriding Member Functions   200
Making Button Objects   201
Code Critique   205
   The Cycling System   205
   The Grouping Feature   205
   Writing to Windows   206
   Message Passing System   206
   Adding Extensions   206
   Listing 7.1   isounit.h   207
   Listing 7.2   isounit.cpp   209
   Listing 7.3   twsounit.h   223
   Listing 7.4   twsounit.cpp   223
   Listing 7.5   wsotxscr.h   225
   Listing 7.6   wsotxscr.cpp   225

Chapter 8 Building Pull-Down Menus   227

An Overview of Menus   227
Overview of the Menu Classes   229
   Working with msounit: Text or Graphics?   230
   Starting with Menu Entries   231
   Assigning Menu Actions   232
The Menu List Class   233
The Mso Class   234
   Setting Up Menus   236
   Overriding Member Functions   240
A Menu Example   241
Creating Pull-Down Menus   243
   The Pmso Class   245
   Building the Pull-Down Menu Bar   246
   Representing Drop Menus   246
A Pull-Down Menu System Example   247
Code Critique   251
   Graphics Menus   251
   Classes with Multiple Parents   251
   Typecasts   252
   Using Arrow Keys   253
   Rectangular Menus   253
   Listing 8.1   msounit.h   254
   Listing 8.2   msounit.cpp   256

Chapter 9 Putting Text Screen Objects to Work   265

Scrollable Windows   265
   Scroll Bars   267
   A Slider Class   269
Creating a Scroll Bar   271
   The Mouse in Action   272
   Communicating with Other Objects   273
Receiving Messages   275
A Generic Scrollable Window Class   276
A Scrollable Window Class   278

Dialog Boxes   283
  A General Dialog Box Class   284
  A Message Box   285
  Dialog Boxes with Options   287
Code Critique   290
  Flexible Scroll Windows   290
  Scrollable Window Objects   291
  Grouping Objects   291
  Communicating between Objects   291
  Listing 9.1   txscroll.h   292
  Listing 9.2   txscroll.cpp   293
  Listing 9.3   dialogue.h   300
  Listing 9.4   dialogue.cpp   300

Chapter 10   Graphics Screen Objects   **303**

From Text to Graphics   303
An Overview of the Graphics Classes   305
  Working with Graphics   306
  Rectangles in Graphics   307
  Initializing Grso Objects   307
  Working with Pixels   308
  Working with Window Styles   309
  Writing Strings   310
  Fill Operations   310
  Drawing a Rectangle   311
The Gfso Class   313
  Initializing a Gfso Object   314
  Drawing Gfso Objects   315
  Moving Gfso Objects   316
Revisiting Skeletons   316
The Wso Class   318
  The Wso Member Functions   318
Graphics Mode Tools   319
A Simple Example   320
A Menu Example   322

Code Critique   326
    Faster Swap Routines   326
    Providing Larger Swap Buffers   326
    Using Multiple Fonts   326
    Adding Fill Patterns   326
    Other Features   327
    Listing 10.1   grsounit.h   327
    Listing 10.2   grsounit.cpp   327
    Listing 10.3   gfsounit.h   330
    Listing 10.4   gfsounit.cpp   330
    Listing 10.5   gwsounit.h   334
    Listing 10.6   gwsounit.cpp   335
    Listing 10.7   grphscrn.h   336
    Listing 10.8   grphscrn.cpp   337

Chapter 11   Interactive Graphics Objects   339

Making Graphics Objects   339
Deriving Selection Buttons   339
Deriving Icons   342
A Button Test Program   344
Windows with Scroll Bars   346
    Scroll Bars in Graphics Mode   346
    Scroll Bar Overview   348
The ScrollBar Class   350
    Initializing Scroll Bars   351
    Scroll Bar Mouse Action   352
    ScrollBar Messages   353
Windows with Scroll Bars   354
A Sample Scrollable Window   355
    Handling Keyboard Input   357
    Sending Messages   358
The Main Program   359
Code Critique   363
    Merging Text and Graphics Scroll Windows   363
    Using Scroll Bars with Other Objects   363

Scroll Bars as Input Devices   364
Listing 11.1   gbutton.h   364
Listing 11.2   gbutton.cpp   365
Listing 11.3   gscroll.h   367
Listing 11.4   gscroll.cpp   368

Appendix   A Turbo C++ Survival Guide   **373**

Defining Classes   373
Implementing Member Functions   374
Creating and Using Objects   375
Understanding the this Parameter   376
Using Constructors and Destructors   377
Creating Dynamic Objects   378
Deriving New Classes   379
Polymorphism   381
Virtual Functions   382
    Using Parameters in Virtual Functions   383
Looking Inside Objects   383
Assignment Compatibility between Objects   385
Passing Objects as Parameters   386
Parameter Passing and Polymorphism   387
Typecasting Pointers to Objects   388
Calling Inherited Functions   389
Determining Which Inherited Function Is Called   390
Using Constructors in Derived Classes   391
Using Data Hiding with Inheritance   392
Using Arrays of Objects   393
Using Composite Objects   394
Different Types of Inheritance   395
Using Classes in Header Files   396

Index   **399**

Preface

 This book will remove the mystery of object-oriented programming (OOP) and show you that OOP is a natural way to design and write code, not an esoteric programmer's cult. If like most serious programmers you want to know how to apply OOP techniques, you will want a source of information that provides a hands-on approach to the art of developing object-oriented tools and applications. To fill this need, *Object-Oriented Programming with Turbo C++* takes you inside Turbo C++'s powerful object-oriented features and provides you with numerous useful programs.

Some of the major features presented in this book are:

- Coverage of the basic OOP techniques such as message passing, inheritance, polymorphism, and encapsulation

- Hands-on approach to building object-oriented tools

- Techniques for designing user interfaces

- Code critiques that explain how the tools and applications presented can be extended

- Tools and applications that will work in both text and graphics modes

Who Should Read This Book

If you want to learn how to create useful programs with Turbo C++ and it's object-oriented features, you'll enjoy this book. Whether you're new to OOP or experienced with its fundamentals, this book shows you how to design tools and applications including windows, menus, buttons, dialog boxes, scroll bars, and much more.

What You'll Need

To use this book you'll need Turbo C++ 1.0, as well as an IBM PC, XT, AT, PS/2, or a compatible computer system capable of displaying graphics. All the graphics programs are designed to work with the Enhanced Graphics Adapter (EGA) or the Virtual Graphics Array (VGA).

Contacting the Authors

Whether you program with C++ for business or for pleasure, we'd love to hear from you. One of the reasons this book keeps growing is because of the valuable comments we get. If you have a suggestion or a problem with C++ and OOP, send us electronic or postal mail and we'll try to help you out. You can reach us by mail at *PC TECHNIQUES* Magazine, 7721 E. Gray Rd., Suite 204, Scottsdale, AZ 85260. If you have access to CompuServe, you can reach Keith Weiskamp at 72561,1536, Loren Heiny at 73527,2365, and Bryan Flamig at 73057,3172.

Getting Started with Object-Oriented Programming

 Programming can be a messy job. The problem is that programs don't just sit on diskettes after they are written (at least the good ones don't). The more a program is used, the greater the odds are that users will request changes and new features. Unfortunately, it's usually more difficult to change a program after it has been written. With Turbo C++ and object-oriented programming (OOP) techniques, this situation can be greatly improved because objects allow us to design more extendable and reusable code.

In this chapter you will be introduced to most of the important concepts involved in OOP. First, the history of OOP will be discussed and then some key OOP design issues will be presented. Next, basic OOP terminology will be covered including *classes*, *objects*, *instance variables*, and *methods*. Some time will also be spent explaining the two main properties of OOP: *encapsulation* and *inheritance*. Finally, the chapter ends by taking an introductory look at how OOP is implemented in Turbo C++.

The Evolution of Computer Languages

Programming techniques have come a long way since the computer's introduction. As Figure 1.1 shows, programming first emerged in the Age of Chaos when programs were hacked together using low-level instructions and branch statements such as "ADD AX,5" and "JMP Error." Needless to say, the Age of Chaos didn't last very long and most programmers welcomed with open arms the revolution that began in the 1960s—the Age of Structure. This new era introduced programming languages—such as Pascal, C, and Ada—and other tools that helped to bring order to programmers' chaotic programming activities.

We're now on the threshold of another new era—the Age of Objects and OOP—an era which promises to be as innovative and important as the Age of Structure. The goal of OOP is simple: make programming easier. As users demand programs with increasingly more features and greater program complexity, the need for better programming tools becomes more important each day. That is where object-oriented languages such as Turbo C++ enter the picture.

What Is OOP?

In simple terms, OOP is programming with *objects*. However, what are objects? Objects are an evolutionary extension of the concept of *records* that enable us to organize data into packages. Objects allow us to combine both data *and* code into a single package. Simply stated, an object is a language construct that ties data with the functions that operate on the data. You can think of an object as a C structure that can contain code. However, don't be misled by this simple comparison. Objects are much more powerful than this lets on. Namely, objects can be extended to incorporate new data elements and functions by using the property of *inheritance*. We'll explain more about this property later.

Because objects contain both code and data, they are like miniature, self-contained programs. This allows them to be used as building blocks to create more complex objects, much like transistors and switches are used to build an electronic circuit.

For example, assume you need to create a word processor application. Rather than arranging the program as a set of functions to handle the required tasks, you

1950s–1960s **Age of Chaos**	1970s–1980s **Age of Structure**	1990s→ **Age of Objects**
jumps, gotos unstructured variables "variables scattered throughout the program"	if-then-else blocks records while loops	objects messages methods inheritance

Figure 1.1   The programming timeline from Chaos to Objects

could create a set of objects. Figure 1.2 shows one possible arrangement. The program is divided into objects such as a low-level screen object, window object, file management object, and so on. What is the advantage of this type of representation? Major operations of a program can easily be isolated. Because objects can be designed so that they work independently of each other, it's much easier to maintain programs that are built from collections of objects instead of simple functions whose organization makes them hard to maintain and modify. However, notice that some of the objects, such as the low-level screen object and the keyboard control object, are used to create other objects. This helps to hide the details of the lower-level objects and allows us to snap together objects in building-block fashion.

The OOP Viewpoint

To take advantage of the flexibility and power that OOP offers, you'll need to change your programming approach. Figure 1.3 illustrates the key difference between the traditional function-oriented approach to programming and the object-oriented approach. Note that the main difference between OOP and the traditional programming approach has to do with the way code and data are packaged and organized. Some other important differences that you should be aware of are:

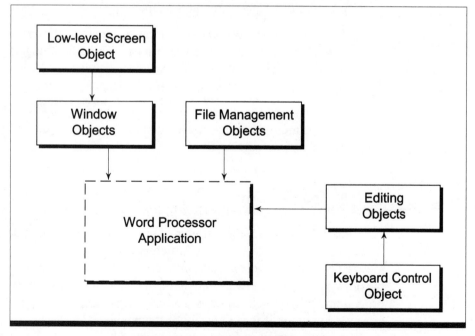

Figure 1.2   Working with objects

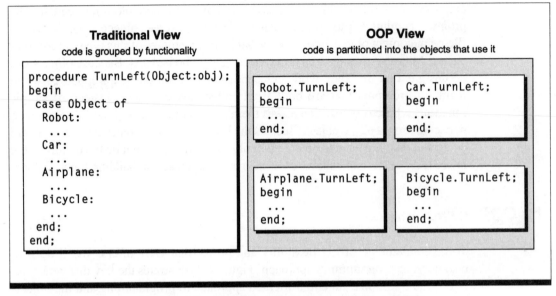

Figure 1.3   Traditional programming vs OOP

1. In the traditional view, functions are the most important. All the code in a program is designed around the functions.

2. In the OOP view, objects are the most important. Programs are designed around objects; functions are secondary. This role change reveals itself in the way objects are used. Rather than simply *passing* objects (data) to functions, objects are used to *call* functions.

3. Programs can avoid large functions that contain logic for multiple cases. Instead, multiple objects are created to represent the different logical components of a program.

OOP Is Good Design

For the last decade or so, programming languages and tools have been designed to take advantage of the concepts of structured design. However, in many respects these languages and tools haven't provided enough flexibility to handle the complexities of modern software requirements. Certainly, structured languages and programming tools help us to write more organized code, but what good is a structured program if it can't easily be maintained?

The question now is: Can OOP techniques help us write better programs that are also easier to maintain and modify? The answer is: Yes. In addition, OOP provides the support needed to help us become better program designers. As you work through this book, you'll start to see how objects are used as building blocks for developing code that can be easily adapted to different situations. For example, interface tools will be created that will work with both text and graphics modes (not an easy feat!). With each program and tool developed, we'll spend as much time as possible exploring the key design issues to emphasize the important relationship between OOP and program design.

Components of OOP

Although Turbo C++ is a complex language, there are essentially only four key OOP components of the language that are probably new to you. They are:

- Classes

- Objects

- Instance variables

- Methods

The first hurdle in learning how to program in the object-oriented style involves learning the differences between classes and objects. When objects were introduced in the previous section, the term *object* was used rather loosely.

Classes and Objects

A *class* is a template that is used to define an *object*. As Figure 1.4 illustrates, a class is a type and an object is an instance of a class. For example, when interface objects are created later in this book, a set of classes will be defined so that we can group the common features of the different objects. An example of such a grouping is a general screen class that defines the data elements and operations needed to process a rectangular screen region so that windows and menus can be displayed and moved.

A class contains two types of components: *instance variables* and *methods*. An instance variable serves as a data element and a method is a function. In one sense, the instance variables define the internal data state of an object and the methods define an object's behavior, that is, the actions that the object can perform.

Actually, in order to be more consistent with common C++ terminology the term *data member* will be used to refer to instance variables and the term *member functions* to refer to methods.

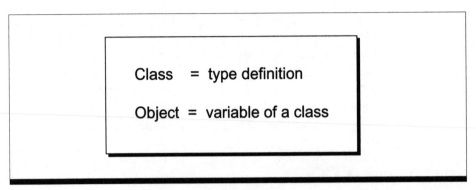

Figure 1.4   Difference between a class and an object

The Two Faces of OOP

When programming with C++'s object-oriented features, you'll discover that there are two underlying properties that surface again and again:

1. Encapsulation

2. Inheritance

Briefly, *encapsulation* is the technique of combining data and the operations needed to process the data under one roof. Encapsulation is what gives objects their building block flavor. *Inheritance* is the technique of taking classes you already have, and extending them to do new things. The following sections explore both encapsulation and inheritance in more detail.

Encapsulation

Encapsulation provides two important features:

1. Puts data and functions under one roof

2. Provides data hiding capabilities

We constantly rely on the principle of encapsulation in our daily lives—particularly when dealing with complex machines. For example, driving a car. When you're driving, you don't need to know whether your car has front- or rear-wheel drive. You only need to know that when you step on the gas pedal the car moves. (Of course, it helps to know how to steer and use the brakes!)

When using OOP techniques in our programs, the same principle applies. For example, if we develop a database object, we don't really want to know how the object is stored in the database system. The only thing we want to know is which routines to call to access the object.

Generally, encapsulation serves three purposes. First, it protects an object's data from getting too much exposure, since the data is usually only accessed through the functions that are defined within the object. Second, encapsulation makes it easier to use the object's data since all actions take place through a well-defined interface (once again, through the operations associated with the object). Finally, encapsulation can be used to hide the details of how data is stored or implemented, as Figure 1.5 shows.

Figure 1.5 Encapsulation can be used to hide details

Inheritance

Inheritance enables one to derive a new class from an existing class. As a result, you can:

- Add data and code to a class without having to change the original class
- Reuse code
- Change the behavior of a class

Let's return to our car example to see how inheritance works. Imagine an assembly line that produces a generic car equipped only with the essentials. You can think of this car as the low-end model—the car most of us could afford. Now with a few enhancements—a 200-watt stereo, crushed-velvet upholstery, and chrome wheels—the manufacturer can turn this basic car into a luxury automobile. Alternatively, its standard engine might be replaced with a souped-up, high-performance racing engine that transforms the budget model into a racer's dream.

As Figure 1.6 shows, we can use the basic assembly line to derive other assembly lines to create the fancier cars. These assembly lines show inheritance at work because they make it possible for the car manufacturer to build several specific cars by starting with one generic car as a base. Of course, the car maker really benefits from this manufacturing process because extensive resources don't have to be committed to build three completely different cars.

The important point to keep in mind about our assembly-line example is that we're using part of one assembly line to create other assembly lines—nothing useful is wasted. This sharing of resources leads to better tools and more profitable products. And that's what we'll be doing with the object-oriented programs

Figure 1.6   Assembly-line manufacturing often takes advantage of resource sharing

that we write. We'll build classes and keep reusing them so that we don't have to reinvent the wheel each time a new application is written.

Another useful feature of inheritance involves the ability to modify a class of an existing object to make a new class that has a slightly different personality. In this way, we can use inheritance to create multiple objects that perform different actions even though the objects are derived from the same stock.

For a brief example, let's return again to the automobile example. We can use inheritance to derive different styles of cars from the basic economy model. In addition to providing these different styles, we can make cars *behave* differently. For instance, think about what happens when you press on the gas pedal while driving each of these cars. The economy model will most likely be sluggish as we press down on the pedal, whereas the high performance model will take off like a rocket as soon as its turbo charger kicks in.

This last technique, of changing the behavior of a component that is shared by different objects, is important enough to warrant special attention. What our cars are exploiting in the gas pedal example is the property of *polymorphism*, which is Greek for "many shapes." In other words, the gas pedal is taking on the ability to act differently although it appears the same. As object-oriented programmers, we'll be using inheritance and polymorphism to create families of objects that are related yet perform a little differently.

One important aspect of polymorphism is that each object in the family can have methods with the same names, but the code for each object's methods can be entirely different. Figure 1.7 summarizes the operation of polymorphism. Note that when the air traffic controller sends out the message "Climb and maintain

Figure 1.7   Polymorphism in action

10,000 feet," each of the objects behaves a little differently. The air traffic controller sending the message doesn't necessarily know what kind of object is receiving the message. In fact, he doesn't know if the UFO has an engine or is powered by pedals. The controller just expects the message to be carried out, regardless of who the recipient is.

To see polymorphism at work, assume that we have a general window class that serves as the starting point for two more specific window classes that work in text and graphics mode, respectively. The general class might have a member function called **Draw()** which is used to draw a window on the screen. The text and graphics window versions of the classes would override, or modify the method in order to accomplish the drawing differently. A text window object would do its drawing using characters. A graphics window object, however, would use pixels. In either case, the net effect is that a window is drawn.

Turning Theory into Practice

Now that the basic principles of OOP have been covered, let's look at OOP through the eyes of C++ as we turn the concepts of OOP into code. In particular, we'll walk through a simple program as it progresses from a simple structured program to an object-oriented application. This example will introduce you to the key OOP features that Turbo C++ provides.

From Structures to Objects

Earlier we discussed the programming evolution—from chaos to structures to objects—that has been taking place over the past 30 years. A good way to see how a C++ object-oriented program is written is to view a program from this evolutionary perspective. Assume that we need a program to keep track of the expenses that employees incur from business trips. Let's start by exploring how we might write such a program using the common components of a structured language such as C.

First, we would define the data structures needed to support the tasks the program must perform. For our example, we might define the following structure to hold relevant trip information for each employee:

```
struct ExpenseRec { /* The trip expense structure */
  char TripName[80], Date[80];
  float Mileage, Cost, Fringe;
};
```

Next, we must develop a team of functions that interact with the user and manipulate this data structure. One such complete program is:

```c
/* expense1.c: A structured version of the trip expense program */

#include <stdio.h>
#include <string.h>

struct ExpenseRec { /* The trip expense record */
  char TripName[80], Date[80];
  int Mileage, Cost, Fringe;
};

void CheckWithBoss(struct ExpenseRec ExRec)
/* The boss is very tough. He won't approve every trip. */
{
  if (!stricmp(ExRec.TripName, "Hawaii") ||
     !stricmp(ExRec.TripName, "Tahiti"))
    printf("%s: You are fired for trying to sneak this one by\n",
           ExRec.TripName);
  else if (ExRec.Cost/4 < ExRec.Fringe)
    printf("The fringe expenses for the %s trip are too high\n",
           ExRec.TripName);
  else printf("The %s trip is ok\n", ExRec.TripName);
}

int I, ExCount;
struct ExpenseRec ExRec[20];  /* A list of employee records */

main()
{
  printf("How many trips did you take? ");
  scanf("%d", &ExCount);
  for (I=0; I<ExCount; I++) {
    printf("Please enter the name of your trip: ");
    scanf("%s", ExRec[I].TripName);
    printf("Which date did you leave (mo/day/year)? ");
    scanf("%s", ExRec[I].Date);
    printf("Enter the number of miles for your trip: ");
    scanf("%d", &ExRec[I].Mileage);
    printf("Enter the cost of your trip: ");
    scanf("%d", &ExRec[I].Cost);
    printf("Enter the cost of your meals and entertainment: ");
    scanf("%d", &ExRec[I].Fringe);
  }
  for (I=0; I<ExCount; I++) CheckWithBoss(ExRec[I]);
  return 0;
}
```

The program's primary job is to record information about a trip and then call the **CheckWithBoss()** function to see if the trip will be approved by the boss. Of course, the advantage of using a **struct** data type is that all of the related data can be combined under one roof. However, there still isn't any integration between the data structure and the code that operates on the data. This is where objects come in since objects allow us to combine both data and operations into one neat package.

With this in mind, we can easily turn our expense records into objects. An example is:

```
struct Expense {                    // The trip expense class
  char TripName[80], Date[80];
  int Mileage, Cost, Fringe;
  void AskQuestions(void);
  void CheckWithBoss(void);
};
```

This code looks like the **struct** definition we used earlier except for one very important difference: It contains function prototypes. These prototypes specify the *methods* or *member functions* built into the object. In this case, the member functions of the **Expense** object type are **AskQuestions()** and **CheckWithBoss()**.

The variables in the **struct** definition, such as **TripName**, **Date**, **Mileage**, and so on, are the *instance variables* or in C++ terminology the *data members* of the class. The data members can be any standard C++ data type such as **int**, **char**, **float**, **double**, or a user-defined type, including another class.

As mentioned earlier, the functions referenced in the **Expense** structure are only function prototypes. The code for the functions resides outside the **struct** definition. For example, here's the **AskQuestions()** member function:

```
void Expense::AskQuestions(void)
// This function gathers data for the expense object
{
  printf("Please enter the name of your trip: ");
  scanf("%s", TripName);
  printf("Which date did you leave (mo/day/year)? ");
  scanf("%s", Date);
  printf("Enter the number of miles for your trip: ");
  scanf("%d", &Mileage);
  printf("Enter the cost of your trip: ");
  scanf("%d", &Cost);
  printf("Enter the cost of your meals and entertainment: ");
  scanf("%d", &Fringe);
}
```

Note how the function header is constructed. It consists of the class name **Expense** as well as the function name **AskQuestions**. The two names are separated by a '::' which tells the compiler that the function **AskQuestions()** belongs to the **Expense** class.

Another thing to notice is how **AskQuestions()** directly references the data members of the **Expense** class. This is indicative of the tight coupling between the code in the member functions and the data in the structure. If we were to try to access one of the object's data members outside of its member functions we would need to also use the object's name, much like we would with a regular structure.

Remember that one of the benefits of grouping functions and data under one roof is that we can design the functions so that they provide the only way to manipulate the data. As a result, it's often possible to hide the details of the data's implementation. This is the essence of encapsulation.

Actually, we can go further to protect the members of an object. Turbo C++ also provides the **public**, **private**, and **protected** keywords to specify which data or function members are accessible by other parts of the program. For instance, to prevent access to any of the data in the **Expense** class, but still allow access to its member functions, we could use:

```
struct Expense {                 // The trip expense object type
private:
  char TripName[80], Date[80];
  int Mileage, Cost, Fringe;
public:
  void AskQuestions(void);
  void CheckWithBoss(void);
};
```

To aid in restricting access to object members, Turbo C++ also provides the **class** keyword that can be used in place of **struct**. Although it is used in the same way to define objects, by default all of its members are not accessible outside of the object; they are private members. Note that a class with all private members is almost useless since the program cannot access its data as well as its member functions! As a result, you'll need the **public** keyword somewhere in the **class** definition in order to make the class useful.

Although we could use the **struct** keyword to define our classes, we will be using the **class** keyword throughout the remainder of the book. This will help to emphasize the fact that we are using objects and not simple structures. In fact, if you look at the definition of the **Expense** class in the object-oriented version of the program, shown in the next section, you'll see that this is the format we will use.

Thus how do we declare an object? We only need a statement such as:

```
Expense ExpObj;
```

In this case the object **ExpObj** is declared as an instance of the class **Expense**.

The Object-Oriented Travel Expense Program

We're now ready to finish the conversion of our trip expense program from a structured program to its OOP counterpart. Before presenting the new program we need to explain how an object is used to access its function and data members. This is done by combining the name of the object along with the member function or data member name. For example, to call the **CheckWithBoss()** member function in the **ExpObj** object we can use:

```
ExpObj.CheckWithBoss();
```

If we were using traditional OOP terminology, we would say that the message **CheckWithBoss** is being passed to the object **ExpObj**.

We've now covered the basics. The new version of the travel expense program is:

```
// expense2.cpp — The object-oriented version of the travel
// expense program
#include <stdio.h>
#include <string.h>

class Expense {              // The trip expense class
public:
  char TripName[80], Date[80];
  int Mileage, Cost, Fringe;
  void AskQuestions(void);
  void CheckWithBoss(void);
};

Expense ExRec[20];
int ExCount, I;

void Expense::AskQuestions(void)
// This function gathers data for the expense object
{
  printf("Please enter the name of your trip: ");
  scanf("%s", TripName);
  printf("Which date did you leave (mo/day/year)? ");
  scanf("%s", Date);
  printf("Enter the number of miles for your trip: ");
  scanf("%d", &Mileage);
  printf("Enter the cost of your trip: ");
  scanf("%d", &Cost);
  printf("Enter the cost of your meals and entertainment: ");
  scanf("%d", &Fringe);
}

void Expense::CheckWithBoss(void)
// The boss is very tough. He won't approve every trip.
{
  if (!stricmp(TripName,"Hawaii") || !stricmp(TripName,"Tahiti"))
    printf("%s: You are fired for trying to sneak this one by\n",
           TripName);
  else if (Cost/4 < Fringe)
    printf("The fringe expenses for the %s trip are too high\n",
           TripName);
```

```
  else
    printf("The %s trip is ok\n", TripName);
}

int main(int, char *)
{
  printf("How many trips did you take? ");
  scanf("%d", &ExCount);
  for (I=0; I<ExCount; I++)    // Get expense data for each employee
    ExRec[I].AskQuestions();
  for (I=0; I<ExCount; I++)    // Write out the boss's response
    ExRec[I].CheckWithBoss();
  return 0;
}
```

Notice the size of the main program body. Because all of the code needed to process a trip expense object has been reorganized and assigned to the **Expense** class, the main program has become much simpler. Also note that we don't need to pass a structure parameter to the **CheckWithBoss()** function like we had to in the original version of this program. That's because **CheckWithBoss()** is now a member function, and member functions have direct access to the data components of objects. Note how we're accessing **TripName, Cost**, and **Fringe** directly in **Check-WithBoss()**.

You may be wondering: How does a member function know which object to access? It's simple—the one that called the function. For example, if **CheckWithBoss()** is called with the statement:

```
MyExpenseAcct.CheckWithBoss();
```

then the member function uses the data from the object **MyExpenseAcct**. Had the call been:

```
YourExpenseAcct.CheckWithBoss();
```

then the function would have used the data from the object **YourExpenseAcct**.

What about Inheritance?

Earlier in this chapter it was mentioned that inheritance was a key feature of OOP, but this property was not in the previous program. Inheritance is applied when we want to extend or modify the behavior of a class, but don't want to alter the original code. Let's see how we can apply inheritance to our previous example.

Assume that we want to change the trip expense program so that expenses can also be kept for executive employees. We'll need to program in the fact that executives are treated differently from other employees because they are allowed more expenses. To support this change, we'll need to modify how the **CheckWithBoss()** member function works. As we make this one change, we'll also add a new variable so that executives can rate their business trip. Instead of changing the original **Expense** class we can use inheritance and derive a new class that is based on the **Expense** class. This can be done as follows:

```
class ExecutiveExp : public Expense {
public:
  int Rating;
  virtual void AskQuestions(void);
  virtual void CheckWithBoss(void);
};
```

The statement to the right of the colon, **public Expense**, tells the compiler that the new object type contains the function and data members from the **Expense** class. The new class, **ExecutiveExp**, also contains the data and function members listed in the new definition. It is referred to as the *derived* class and the **Expense** class as the *base* class. These terms will be used repeatedly as we explain our object hierarchies.

Note that we've added a new data member called **Rating**. We've also included the member functions **AskQuestions()** and **CheckWithBoss()** again, but notice the **virtual** keyword listed before their declarations. The **virtual** keyword indicates that these functions have new definitions that override the definitions from the inherited class **Expense**. Actually, we've also had to modify the original **Expense** class and add the **virtual** keywords to **AskQuestions()** and **CheckWithBoss()**:

```
class Expense {              // The trip expense object type
public:
  char TripName[80], Date[80];
  int Mileage, Cost, Fringe;
  virtual void AskQuestions(void);
  virtual void CheckWithBoss(void);
};
```

The placement of the **virtual** keywords here tells the compiler that new functions for these routines may be provided in derived classes. Normally we wouldn't have to modify the base class like we've had to do here. We could have anticipated that we would be overriding these functions and declared them virtual in the first place. It pays to plan ahead.

Note that using the **virtual** keyword in the derived classes—in this case **ExecutiveExp**—is optional, but useful since it helps to remind us that a function is virtual. Here are the new versions of these member functions:

```
void ExecutiveExp::AskQuestions(void)
// This function gathers data for the executive expense object
{
   Expense::AskQuestions();    // Call the inherited version
   printf("How would you rate the trip ");
   scanf("%d", &Rating);
}

void ExecutiveExp::CheckWithBoss(void)
// The boss is very easy on executives
{
   if (Cost / 2 < Fringe)
      printf("Watch it. You're not having enough fun!\n");
}
```

Let's take a look at the **AskQuestions()** member function. Notice the function call inside it:

```
Expense::AskQuestions();
```

There's some new syntax here. Recall that **Expense** is a class definition, not an object. Member functions are normally called from objects, but we're not doing a normal member function call here. We're calling the inherited version of the member function—that is, the **Expense** version of **AskQuestions()**. The double colon is a scoping operator that tells the compiler to use the **AskQuestions()** member function contained in the specified class, in this example the **Expense** class.

We're doing this to reuse the code of the inherited function, so that **AskQuestions()** will ask all the questions for a normal expense account, and then it will ask an additional question about how well the user rates the trip.

This type of function call, where we're calling an inherited function, is known as method chaining. It's one way that we can achieve code reusability with OOP. For example, if we declare an **ExecutiveExp** object:

```
ExecutiveExp ExecObj;
```

and then call the **AskQuestions()** member function for that object:

```
ExecObj.AskQuestions();
```

then all the questions for a regular expense account will be asked, as well as the new trip rating question.

The **CheckWithBoss()** member function uses a different approach. Rather than reusing the code from the **Expense** class, we're completely overriding the function. Note that there's no call back to the inherited function.

In both of these cases we have overridden the original member functions and supplied new ones to be used by an **ExecutiveExp** object. Both of these functions illustrate the property of polymorphism. We can use the same function name, either **AskQuestions()** or **CheckWithBoss()**, to achieve two different actions in the two object types. Actually, we can make the polymorphism even more powerful. By design we can reference classes derived from the same base class using a base class pointer. In other words, if we had the pointer:

```
Expense *ExpensePtr;
```

we could assign it to either an **Expense** object or a **ExecutiveExp** object. Then if the pointer were assigned to an **Expense** or **ExecutiveExp** object, we could call one of their common member functions using the exact same statement. For instance, to call **AskQuestions()** we could use:

```
ExpensePtr->AskQuestions();
```

Which member function gets called depends on what the type is of the object the pointer is pointing at. Before going on, note that pointer notation must be used here to access one of the members of the object. This notation is the same as it would be if simple structures were used.

Now let's rewrite the expense program so that it uses this more powerful form of polymorphism. First, we'll redefine our array of objects as pointers to the base class **Expense** and we'll allocate memory for the objects dynamically. The new array declaration is:

```
Expense *ExRec[20];
```

Then to allocate one of the objects we'll use C++'s **new** operator, which is specifically designed for dynamically allocating objects. For example, to allocate and assign an **ExecutiveExp** object to the beginning of the **ExRec** array we can use the statement:

```
ExRec[0] = new ExecutiveExp;
```

Putting all this together, the new expense program asks the user to specify which type of objects are to be used, either **Expense** or **ExecutiveExp**. Then it allocates the number of objects required and calls the **AskQuestions()** and **CheckWithBoss()** functions for each of these objects. Once again, note that the call to these member functions is identical for the two types of objects since these are overloaded functions with the same base class.

The revised program is:

```
// expense3.cpp - The object-oriented version of the travel
// expense program that uses inheritance to handle executive
// employees differently
```

```c
#include <stdio.h>
#include <string.h>
#include <ctype.h>
#include <conio.h>

class Expense {                    // The trip expense class
public:
  char TripName[80], Date[80];
  int Mileage, Cost, Fringe;
  virtual void AskQuestions(void);   // Use virtual because we'll
  virtual void CheckWithBoss(void);  // override in ExecutiveExp
};

class ExecutiveExp : public Expense {
public:
  int Rating;
  virtual void AskQuestions(void);   // The virtual keyword is
  virtual void CheckWithBoss(void);  // optional here
};

void Expense::AskQuestions(void)
// This function gathers data for the expense object
{
  printf("Please enter the name of your trip: ");
  scanf("%s", TripName);
  printf("Which date did you leave (mo/day/year)? ");
  scanf("%s", Date);
  printf("Enter the number of miles for your trip: ");
  scanf("%d", &Mileage);
  printf("Enter the cost of your trip: ");
  scanf("%d", &Cost);
  printf("Enter the cost of your meals and entertainment: ");
  scanf("%d", &Fringe);
}

void Expense::CheckWithBoss(void)
// The boss is very tough. He won't approve every trip.
{
  if (!stricmp(TripName,"Hawaii") || !stricmp(TripName,"Tahiti"))
    printf("%s: You are fired for trying to sneak this one by\n",
           TripName);
  else if (Cost / 4 < Fringe)
    printf("The fringe expenses for the %s trip are too high\n",
           TripName);
  else
    printf("The %s trip is ok\n", TripName);
}

void ExecutiveExp::AskQuestions(void)
// This function gathers data for the executive expense object
{
  Expense::AskQuestions();   // Call the inherited version
  printf("How would you rate the trip (0-10)? ");
```

```
    scanf("%d", &Rating);
}

void ExecutiveExp::CheckWithBoss(void)
// The boss is very easy on executives
{
  if (Cost / 2 < Fringe)
    printf("Watch it. You're not having enough fun!\n");
}

Expense *ExRec[20];      // Array of pointers to base class type
int ExCount, I;
unsigned char Executive; // True if user is an executive

int main(int, char *)
{
  // Determine if the user is an executive or not. If so,
  // use the ExecutiveExp class.
  printf("Are you an executive (y/n) ");
  if (toupper(getch()) == 'Y') Executive = 1; else Executive = 0;
  printf("\nHow many trips did you take? ");
  scanf("%d", &ExCount);
  // Allocate enough objects, of the correct type, for the
  // number of trips taken. Which objects get placed in the
  // array depend on whether the user is an executive or not.
  for (I=0; I<ExCount; I++)
    if (Executive)
      ExRec[I] = new ExecutiveExp;
    else
      ExRec[I] = new Expense;
  // The following are polymorphic calls. We use the same
  // call to reference ExecutiveExp and Expense objects.
  for (I=0; I<ExCount; I++)   // Get expense data for each object
    ExRec[I]->AskQuestions();
  for (I=0; I<ExCount; I++)   // Write out the boss's response
    ExRec[I]->CheckWithBoss();
  return 0;
}
```

Summary

In this chapter most of the basic concepts of OOP were introduced and we saw how they are implemented in C++. It's doubtful that OOP will completely replace the way we program computers. Instead, it's more likely that OOP techniques will merge with traditional structured programming techniques to give us more programming power. As you learn and experiment with Turbo C++, you'll find that you don't have to throw away everything you know in order to make good use of object-oriented features. As emphasized earlier in this chapter, the most important issue has to do with program design.

Writing an Object-Oriented Programming Application

You probably have a number of tools and application programs stored away that you'd like to rewrite as object-oriented programs. Where's the best place to start? Unfortunately, there's no simple answer to this question. There are, however, some guidelines to follow to make the transition to OOP. The best way to see how these guidelines apply is to work through a realistic example.

In this chapter, a file browser program will be developed that can be used to view text files. First, we'll write the program without using object-oriented techniques. Then, we'll take you through the process of converting the program to an object-oriented application. With this approach, you can discover firsthand the basic steps involved in crafting an object-oriented program. You'll also learn how your programs can be improved by writing them in the object-oriented style. Of course, keep in mind that OOP is certainly no panacea. In fact, you'll see that, as we convert the procedural file browser program to its object-oriented counterpart, the program will increase in size. Most programmers would agree, however, that the size increase is a small price to pay for the power and flexibility that objects bring to the craft of programming.

The File Browser

Some applications are a snap to write in the object-oriented style. For example, a CAD program is well suited for OOP because the components in the program, such as the drawing shapes (lines, arcs, rectangles, polygons, and so on), can easily be represented as objects. Unfortunately, not all programs you write will be as good a fit. In fact, the application that we're about to develop is one such stickler. We've chosen this application to show you that, with a little bit of work and clever design, most programs can benefit from the new OOP features and techniques.

Figure 2.1 shows a sample screen generated by the file browser. The top line of the screen presents information about the file being viewed such as its name, date, size, and attributes. At the bottom, an information bar is displayed which lists the input keys that can be used to control the browser. The file itself is displayed in a scrolling region between rows 2 and 24. As you'll see in an up-coming section, text lines of the file are written directly to screen memory to speed up file viewing. This is particularly important when scrolling through the file.

```
File: browse.pas       Date: 8-17-1989        Size: 7922     Attr: R-W
  UpKey   = #72;
  DnKey   = #80;
  Alt_S   = #31;        { The search key }

type
  Texel = record        { Record used for direct screen access }
    Ch   : char;
    Attr : byte;        { Character attribute }
  end;
  ScreenArea = array[0..24,0..79] of Texel;

  FileBuf = array[1..BufSize] of char;

var
  InFile        : file;
  ScreenPtr     : ^ScreenArea;
  Attr,NoBytes  : word;
  Time,Size     : longint;
  BufPtr        : ^FileBuf;
  LinePtr       : array[1..2000] of integer; { Line pointers }
  I,Lc,Bot      : integer;
  Ch            : char;
  Done          : Boolean;
 <Home=Top>  <End=Bot>  <PgUp=Prev>  <PgDn=Next>  <Alt-S=Search>  <Esc=Quit>
```

Figure 2.1   Sample screen of the file browser

How the File Browser Works

Figure 2.2 is a conceptual view showing how the file browser works. After you call up the file browser with the command

```
Browse filename
```

the file that you specify is read into memory and the first 23 lines of the file are displayed. (Remember that the file is displayed from rows 2 to 24.) The file's data is stored in a dynamic buffer that is accessed using array notation. Because the buffer system we are using is the most complex component of the file browser, later we'll spend some time looking at how it is implemented and accessed. (When we make the conversion to the object-oriented version, we'll show you how inheritance techniques can be used to derive different types of buffers so that file data can be displayed in different formats.) Before we get too far ahead of ourselves, let's return to our basic program.

After the file is read into the buffer, you can then use any of the input keys listed in Table 2.1 to examine the file. Note that the browser also contains a searching feature. If you press Alt-S, the following prompt will be displayed at the last screen row:

```
Search for:
```

You can then enter a search string that the browser will attempt to locate. The search always starts with the first line listed in the browser window. For example, if you have scrolled through the file by pressing the PgDn key a few times and line

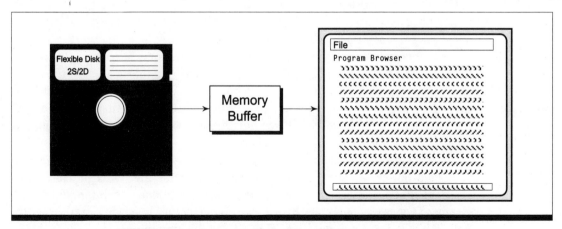

Figure 2.2   An overview of the file browser program

Table 2.1   The browser input keys

Key	Action
PgUp	Scrolls the file up one page
PgDn	Scrolls the file down one page
Home	Advances to the top of the file
End	Advances to the end of the file
Up Arrow	Scrolls the file up one line
Down Arrow	Scrolls the file down one line
Alt-S	Searches for text string
Esc	Quits the browser

60 is the first line displayed in the browser window (screen row 2), the search will start at line 60 after you press Alt-S. When using the search feature, remember that it doesn't allow you to search for multiple occurrences of a string.

What's Under the Hood?

To create the file browser, the set of functions listed in Table 2.2 will be used. The main function for updating the screen and displaying text lines is **ShowScreen()**. Each time one of the file scrolling keys is pressed, **ShowScreen()** is called to up-date the screen and to display new lines of text. To support the browser, three independent data structures will be used called **ScreenArea**, **TextBuff**, and **LinePtr**. What roles do they play?

The **ScreenArea** array is used to access screen memory, **TextBuff** is the buffer that stores the file's raw data, and **LinePtr** is the array used to access the file's raw data as text lines. As the different components are explored, we'll explain how these data structures are represented and accessed. Once the first version of the file browser is completed, you'll see how these data structures will become the building blocks for the object-oriented version.

The main program shown in Listing 2.1 is easy to follow. It processes the command-line arguments, opens and reads the input file, calls the functions **DisplayFStat()** and **DisplayCommands()** to display the file information and command bar, respectively, and then initializes the internal line index array, **LinePtr**. After the initialization tasks are performed, the function **main()** sits in a **do-while** loop to process the input keys.

Table 2.2   The functions used to create the browser

Function	Description
GetStr()	Returns a string entered by the user
SelectMonitor()	Returns the address of the screen
DisplayFStat()	Displays status bar of the browser
DisplayCommands()	Displays the command options
ShowScreen()	Displays the text of a file
FileSearch()	Searches the file for a string
ProcessInput()	Processes the command entered

Reading and processing the supported input keys requires a two-step process. The **getch()** function provided with Turbo C++ is called to read an input key. If the key pressed is an extended key, such as PgDn, PgUp, Home, and so on, **getch()** returns a value of 0 and then the first case of the following **switch** statement is executed.

```
do {
  Ch - getch();
  switch (Ch) {
    case 0:              /* Extended key pressed */
      Ch - getch();
      ProcessInput(Ch); /* Perform operation */
      break;
    case EscKey: break; /* Do nothing for now */
    default: putch(7);  /* Illegal key; sound the bell */
  }
} while (Ch !- EscKey);
```

Note that the **ProcessInput()** routine is called when an extended key is pressed. This function acts as the switching station for the program. Review its code in Listing 2.1 and you'll see that **ProcessInput()** also contains a **switch** statement to process the different input keys. If you want to add additional input keys to the program or change the action assigned to a key, this is the place you should turn to. (This assumes that the command to be added uses an extended key code.)

To terminate the browser, press the Esc key. A test for the Esc key is made in the switch statement, but the **do** loop doesn't truly terminate until a test of **Ch** is made at the bottom of the **do** loop.

Working with Buffers

Now that we've seen how the main program operates, let's dig a little deeper to explore the two major components of the program: the file buffer and low-level screen access. The heart of the file browser is the buffer that stores the file's data. To make the browser as efficient as possible, we'll use block read operations to transfer data from the disk file to our internal buffer.

First, we'll define a character pointer to be used to access our internal file buffer:

```
char *BufPtr;
```

After the file is opened, we'll allocate memory for the buffer so we can read the entire file with one call to Turbo C++'s **read()** function:

```
NoBytes = read(fileno(InFile), BufPtr, ffblk.ff_fsize);
```

The **BufPtr** variable can then be used to access the file data as an array of characters. However, this does present one problem since the data is stored as a sequence of bytes and not as lines of text. When one of the scrolling keys is pressed, we want to be able to reference and display sets of lines rapidly so that the screen can be scrolled smoothly. To do this, we'll use the **LinePtr** array that we discussed earlier to store the indexes of the buffer array where new lines begin:

```
int LinePtr[2000];
```

Figure 2.3 illustrates how this line-indexing system works. The array location referenced by **LinePtr[0]** stores the index location of **BufPtr** where the first line is stored, **LinePtr[1]** stores the index location of the second line, and so on. To initialize the **LinePtr** array, the following code is placed in the main program immediately following the **read()** function call:

```
Lc = 0;
LinePtr[Lc++] = 0;        /* Initialize the line index array */
for (I=0; I<NoBytes; I++)
  if (BufPtr[I] == CR)
    LinePtr[Lc++] = I + 1;
```

The **for** loop searches for a carriage return code (value of 10), which indicates the end of a text line. Each time the end-of-line marker is encountered, the next buffer index location (**I+1**) is stored in the **LinePtr** array.

When file data is displayed on the screen with the **ShowScreen()** function, the **LinePtr** array is accessed so that the routine can determine where to start reading from the file buffer referenced by **BufPtr**. The advantage of this technique is that

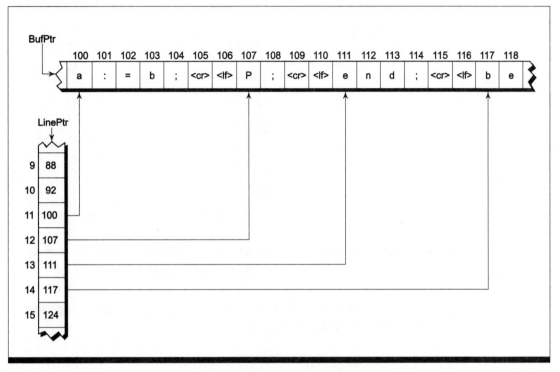

Figure 2.3   The line-indexing system

we don't have to reformat the data in the buffer after it has been read. The only overhead is the initialization code required in the main program to set the **LinePtr** array.

Working with the Screen

It was stated earlier that the file browser writes directly to the PC's screen memory. As Figure 2.4 shows, the PC's screen in text mode consists of 25 rows and 80 columns. The first row and column is addressed as location (0,0) and the last row and column as location (24,79). Each screen location actually consists of two components: a character and an attribute. To support this arrangement, a structure called a **Texel** is used that represents the character and attribute written to a screen location. The definition of a **Texel** is:

```
struct Texel {          /* Record used for direct */
  char Ch;              /* screen access */
  unsigned char Attr;   /* Character attribute */
};
```

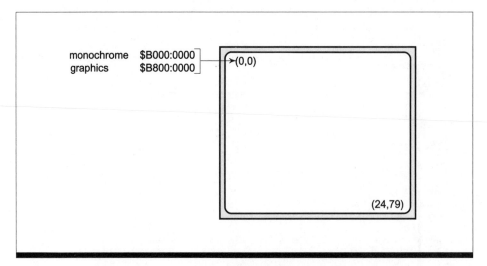

Figure 2.4   The addressing of the text-mode screen

Using this structure we can define a two-dimensional array to correspond to the memory arrangement of the screen:

```
typedef struct Texel ScreenArea[25][80];
```

To write a character and its attribute to a screen location, a screen pointer is used:

```
ScreenArea far *ScreenPtr;
```

As Figure 2.4 indicates, this screen pointer can be set to one of two values: B000:0000h for a monochrome display adapter and B800:0000h for a graphics adapter. To determine which adapter is installed, we've included a function called **SelectMonitor(),** which makes a call to the ROM-BIOS (interrupt 0x10). This function is used as follows to initialize the **ScreenPtr** variable:

```
ScreenPtr = SelectMonitor();
```

Once **ScreenPtr** has been assigned a screen address, a character and an attribute can be written to the screen. But first, to simplify the notation, we've defined the macro constant:

```
#define Screen (*ScreenPtr)
```

Putting all this together, we can easily write the character A with normal video to row 6, column 11 using:

```
Screen[5][10].Ch = 'A';
ScreenPtr[5][10].Attr = 7;
```

We can also use this notation to read a character and its attribute at a specific screen location:

```
Ch = Screen[5][10].Ch;
Attr = Screen[5][10].Attr;
```

The Complete File Browser Program

Now that the main components of the file browser have been covered, it's time to put together the complete program. Listing 2.1 presents the code for the **browse.c** program. Before moving on to the object-oriented version, take a few minutes to review the code in detail and take the program for a test run.

Listing 2.1   browse.c

```
/* browse.c
 * This program allows you to view the contents of an ASCII
 * file. Once a file is displayed, you can scroll through the
 * file using the cursor pad keys (PgUp, PgDn, and so on). To
 * use the program, issue the following command at the DOS
 * prompt:
 *           browse <filename>
 */
#include <stdio.h>
#include <stdlib.h>
#include <string.h>
#include <alloc.h>
#include <dos.h>
#include <dir.h>
#include <conio.h>
#include <sys\stat.h>
#include <io.h>

#define MaxBufSize 65520L /* Roughly 64K maximum file size */
#define ScrSize    23     /* Number of text lines per screen */
#define TabSize    5      /* Five spaces per tab */
#define EscKey     27     /* Extended key codes */
#define PgUp       73
#define PgDn       81
#define Home       71
#define EndKey     79
#define UpKey      72
#define DnKey      80
#define Alt_S      31      /* The search key */
```

```
#define Screen      (*ScreenPtr)
#define TabKey      9
#define CR          10      /* Carriage return */

struct Texel {              /* Record used for direct */
  char Ch;                  /* screen access */
  unsigned char Attr;       /* Character attribute */
};

typedef struct Texel ScreenArea[25][80];

FILE *InFile;
ScreenArea far *ScreenPtr;
long Time, Size;
char *BufPtr, Ch;
int LinePtr[2000]; /* Indexes of beginning lines in BufPtr */
int Attr, NoBytes, I, Lc, Bot, End;

char *GetStr(char *Str);
ScreenArea far *SelectMonitor(void);
void DisplayFStat(char *fname, FILE *InFile, struct ffblk *ffblk);
void DisplayCommands(void);
void ShowScreen(void);
void FileSearch(void);
void ProcessInput(char Ch);

int main(int argc, char *argv[])
{
  struct ffblk ffblk;
  int DosError;

  clrscr();
  if (argc != 2) {
    printf("Incorrect number of arguments\n");
    printf("To browse a file use the command:\n");
    printf("\tbrowse <filename>\n");
    exit(1);
  }
  ScreenPtr = SelectMonitor();
  DosError = findfirst(argv[1], &ffblk, 0);
  if (DosError != 0) {
    printf("Can't find the file %s\n", argv[1]);
    exit(1);
  }
  if ((InFile=fopen(argv[1],"r")) == NULL) {    /* Open file */
    printf("Cannot open file: %s\n", argv[1]);
    exit(1);
  }
  /* Allocate memory for the file buffer */
  if (ffblk.ff_fsize >= MaxBufSize) {
    printf("File too large: %s\n", argv[1]);
    exit(1);
  }
```

```c
    if ((BufPtr=malloc(ffblk.ff_fsize)) == NULL) {
      printf("Not enough memory\n");
      exit(1);
    }

    DisplayFStat(argv[1], InFile, &ffblk);
    DisplayCommands();
    NoBytes = read(fileno(InFile), BufPtr, ffblk.ff_fsize);
    Lc = 0;
    LinePtr[Lc++] = 0;        /* Initialize the line index array */
    for (I=0; I<NoBytes; I++)
      if (BufPtr[I] == CR)
        LinePtr[Lc++] = I + 1;

    fclose(InFile);
    if (Lc > ScrSize)        /* Set the index that can display */
      Bot = Lc - ScrSize;    /* the last screen full of the file */
    else Bot = 0;
    End = Lc - 1;            /* Save line index to end of file */
    Lc = 0;                  /* Set the top line index */
    ShowScreen();
    do {
      Ch = getch();
      switch (Ch) {
        case 0:              /* Extended key pressed */
          Ch = getch();
          ProcessInput(Ch); /* Perform operation */
          break;
        case EscKey: break; /* Do nothing for now */
        default: putch(7);  /* Illegal key; sound the bell */
      }
    } while (Ch != EscKey);
    free(BufPtr);
    textbackground(0);       /* Restore the screen */
    textcolor(7);
    clrscr();
    return 0;
}

char *GetStr(char *Str)
/* Read a string at the current cursor location. Press Esc
   to abort read operation. */
{
  char Ch;
  int Count = 0;

  while ((Ch=getch()) != 13 && Ch != EscKey) {
    printf("%c", Ch);
    Str[Count++] = Ch;
  }
  if (Ch == EscKey) return NULL;
  Str[Count] = '\0';                /* Terminate string */
  return Str;
}
```

```
ScreenArea far *SelectMonitor(void)
/* Determine the type of graphics card installed and return
   the memory address of the video memory */
{
  union REGS Regs;
  unsigned Segment, Offset;

  Regs.h.ah = 15;
  int86(0x10, &Regs, &Regs);
  if (Regs.h.al == 7)
    Segment = 0xB000;                         /* Monochrome */
  else Segment = 0xB800;                      /* Graphics */
  Offset = Regs.h.bh * (unsigned)0x1000;  /* Calculate video page */
  return (ScreenArea *)(((long)Segment << 16) | (long)Offset);
}

void DisplayFStat(char *fname, FILE *InFile, struct ffblk *ffblk)
/* Display the first status line of file information
   including filename, size, date, and time */
{
  int Col;
  struct ftime ft;
  char AtStr[8];

  gotoxy(3,1);                       /* Display filename */
  printf("File: %s",fname);
  gotoxy(26,1);
  getftime(fileno(InFile),&ft);
  printf("Date: %02u-%02u-%04u",ft.ft_month,
          ft.ft_day,ft.ft_year+1980);
  gotoxy(48,1);                      /* Display size */
  printf("Size: %ld",ffblk->ff_fsize);

  if (ffblk->ff_attrib == FA_RDONLY) /* Determine attributes */
    strcpy(AtStr,"R");
  else
    strcpy(AtStr,"R-W");
  if (ffblk->ff_attrib == FA_HIDDEN) strcat(AtStr,"-H");
  if (ffblk->ff_attrib == FA_SYSTEM) strcat(AtStr,"-S");

  gotoxy(63,1);
  printf("Attr: %s",AtStr);          /* Display attributes */

  for (Col=0; Col<80; Col++)    /* Put status bar in reverse video */
    Screen[0][Col].Attr = 112;
}

void DisplayCommands(void)
/* Displays the command bar at the last line of the screen */
{
  int Col;
```

```
    gotoxy(2,25);
    printf("<Home-Top>  <End-Bot>  <PgUp-Prev>  <PgDn-Next> "
           "<Alt-S-Search>  <Esc-Quit>");
     for (Col=0; Col<80; Col++) Screen[24][Col].Attr = 112;
}

void ShowScreen(void)
/* Display a screen image containing 23 lines of the file */
{
    int Row, Col, TLc, I, Tp;

    TLc = Lc;        /* Start with the current line index */
    for (Row=0; Row<ScrSize && Row<=End; Row++) {
      Tp = LinePtr[TLc];
      for (Col=0; Col<80 && Tp<NoBytes && BufPtr[Tp] != CR; Tp++) {
        if (BufPtr[Tp] == TabKey)      /* Look for tab key */
          for (I=0; I<TabSize && Col<80; I++)
            /* Replace tab with spaces */
            Screen[Row+1][Col++].Ch = ' ';
        else Screen[Row+1][Col++].Ch = BufPtr[Tp];
      }
      for (; Col<80; Col++) Screen[Row+1][Col].Ch = ' ';
      TLc++;
    }
    // Fill out the screen if the file has fewer than one
    // screen full of lines
    for (; Row<ScrSize; Row++)
      for (Col=0; Col<80; Col++)
        Screen[Row+1][Col].Ch = ' ';
}

void FileSearch(void)
/* Search the file for a string starting from the current
   top line displayed. If a match is found, the line
   containing the string is highlighted. */
{
    int Col, I, P;
    char *Ptr, SearchStr[81], *S, Line[81];

    for (Col=1; Col<=78; Col++) Screen[24][Col].Ch = ' ';
    gotoxy(2,25); printf("Search for: ");
    /* Get the search string */
    if ((S=GetStr(SearchStr)) == NULL) {
      DisplayCommands();   /* No string entered */
      return;
    }
    I = Lc;
    do {
      P = LinePtr[I];
      for (Col=0; Col<80 && BufPtr[P+Col] != CR; Col++)
        Line[Col] = BufPtr[P+Col];
      Line[Col] = '\0';          /* Terminate line string */
```

```
      Ptr = strstr(Line,S);     /* Look for a match */
      I++;
   } while (Ptr == NULL && I <= End);

   if (Ptr != NULL) {
     if (I > Lc+ScrSize) {
       Lc = I - ScrSize;
       ShowScreen();
     }
     /* Highlight line with match */
     for (Col=0; Col<80; Col++) Screen[I-Lc][Col].Attr = 112;
     /* Wait until a key is pressed */
     if (getch() == 0) (void)getch();
     /* Set line of text back to normal */
     for (Col=0; Col<80; Col++) Screen[I-Lc][Col].Attr = 7;
   }
   DisplayCommands();
}

void ProcessInput(char Ch)
/* Process the input keys */
{
  switch (Ch) {
    case PgUp:
      if (Lc-ScrSize > 0) Lc -= ScrSize;
        else Lc = 0;
      ShowScreen();
      break;
    case PgDn:
      if (Lc+ScrSize < Bot && Bot >= ScrSize) Lc += ScrSize;
        else Lc = Bot;
      ShowScreen();
      break;
    case UpKey:
      if (Lc > 0) {
        Lc--;
        ShowScreen();
      }
      break;
    case DnKey:
      if (Lc < Bot && Bot >= ScrSize) {
        Lc++;
        ShowScreen();
      }
      break;
    case Home:
      Lc = 0;
      ShowScreen();
      break;
    case EndKey:
      if (Bot >= ScrSize) {
        Lc = Bot;
        ShowScreen();
```

```
      }
      break;
    case Alt_S: FileSearch(); break;
  }
}
```

A Second Look at the Browse Program

The file browser provides all the basic features needed to quickly view text files, but the program has one major design flaw—the main components are tightly connected. Think about it. If a change is made, such as recoding the file buffer as a two-dimensional array, many of the procedures as well as the main program must also be changed. The same problems would be encountered if you attempted to change the program so that it could write to the screen in a different manner. The difficult part involves figuring out which routines would need to be modified.

Is there a way around this problem? Yes, it can be avoided by redesigning the code so that the program components, such as the file buffer and the screen array, work as independently of each other as possible. And that's where objects enter the picture.

Thinking with Objects

Before we start rewriting the browser, we need to determine how to partition the program into objects. Three components that are suitable to be objects immediately come to mind: the screen, the file buffer, and the browser itself. You might now be wondering how the object approach can aid our application. Will the program run faster? Not really. Will the program get smaller? No, in fact it will require additional code. However, by packaging these components as objects, we'll combine the code and data needed to represent and process these components. This important step will help restructure the program so that we'll later be able to easily pop open its hood and add useful extensions without having to completely rewrite the program.

For example, if we want to change the input keys used to control the browser, we could go directly to the browser object and make the change rather than wandering through the code looking for the appropriate routine. In a sense, the object-oriented approach allows us to apply a sound principle of good management and design—think globally and act locally.

Figure 2.5 shows how the object-oriented browser is organized. Note that the browser object serves as the main object, so to speak. This object contains references to buffer and screen objects. The objects are designed in this manner so that different buffers can be assigned to the browser or the browser can send its data to

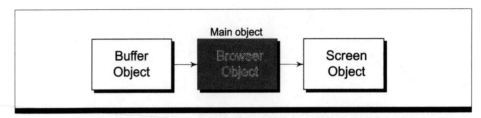

Figure 2.5   Organization of the object-oriented browser

different devices, such as a printer or a graphics monitor configured in graphics mode. Later we'll show you how a hex buffer can be derived from the general buffer and assigned to the browser so that your files can be viewed in both standard ASCII and hex formats. For now, we'll get to work by defining the classes needed to support the three fundamental objects. The complete object-oriented version of the browser program is shown in Listing 2.2.

Browser Objects

Our first task is to determine which functions and variables should be placed in the browser object class. This class is responsible for initializing the browser, displaying text lines, and processing the input keys. The definition for **Browser** is:

```
class Browser {
public:
  ScreenClass *ScrPtr;
  Buffer *MainBuff, *AltBuff;
  int Lc, Bot, End;
  Browser(ScreenClass *Scr, Buffer *Buf1, Buffer *Buf2);
  virtual ~Browser(void) { ; }
  void ProcessInput(char Ch);
  void DisplayFStat(void);
  void DisplayCommands(void);
  void SetLPtr(void);
  void ShowScreen(void);
  void PageUp(void);
  void PageDn(void);
  void LineUp(void);
  void LineDn(void);
  void TopPage(void);
  void BotPage(void);
  void FileSearch(void);
};
```

Note that **Browser** contains three variables that were originally global variables in the **Browse** program: **Lc, Bot**, and **End**. These variables will now be accessed by the browser member functions—such as **ShowScreen(), LineUp(), LineDn(),**

TopPage(), and so on. Essentially, the global data components have been localized so that they are now assigned to the object that needs them.

When you first start to use objects, you'll find that it takes a bit of practice to determine where data members should be placed. In some cases, you'll need to experiment by placing the data members in the different objects that use them until you find the best home for the variables. The best advice we can give is this: Don't be afraid to fine tune your objects.

The **Browser** class also contains some additional variables that are new: **ScrPtr**, **MainBuff**, and **AltBuff**. What do they do? These three data members serve as pointers to the **ScreenClass** and **Buffer** objects we'll be using. We've taken this design approach so that an object created from the **Browser** class can readily access buffer and screen objects. In fact, we'll give the object two file buffers so that we can switch between them.

Some of the member functions in **Browser**, such as **DisplayFStat()**, **Display-Commands()**, and **ShowScreen()**, are similar to the functions used in the original **browse.c** program. These functions house the code we need to display the file. The major change can be seen in the way the main program gets reorganized in the process. We've taken the initialization and display code out of the program body and placed it in the member functions of **Browser**. For example, we now have a routine called **SetLPtr()**, as shown below, which initializes the line pointer variables **Lc**, **End**, and **Bot**.

```
void Browser::SetLPtr(void)
// Set the current and bottom line indexes for the screen
{
  Lc - MainBuff->GetNumLines();
  if (Lc > ScrPtr->ScrSize)   // Set the bottom line index
    Bot - Lc - ScrPtr->ScrSize;
  else Bot - 0;
  End - Lc - 1;
  Lc - 0;                      // Set the top line index
}
```

This function illustrates how the **MainBuff** and **ScrPtr** data members are used to access data and functions in the **ScreenClass** and **Buffer** classes. These pointer variables are assigned to a **Browser** object by **Browser**'s constructor:

```
Browser::Browser(ScreenClass *Scr, Buffer *Buf1, Buffer *Buf2)
// Initialize the browser by setting up pointers to the
// screen and to the two buffers
{
  ScrPtr - Scr;  MainBuff - Buf1;  AltBuff - Buf2;
}
```

The **Browser** class also contains a number of functions that were not used in the original **browse.c** program. These member functions include **PageUp()**, **PageDn()**,

LineUp(), **LineDn()**, **TopPage()**, and **BotPage()**. These are used to process the input keys that control how the file is scrolled and are responsible for resetting the line count variable **Lc** and calling **ShowScreen()** to update the screen. For example, the **TopPage()** member function sets the line index to the first line of the file and then updates the screen:

```
void Browser::TopPage(void)
{
  Lc = 0;  ShowScreen();
}
```

The **Browser** class also contains two additional types of member functions that we haven't encountered before. These two functions, listed immediately after the data members, are called the constructor and destructor for the **Browser** class. The constructor function, which has the same name as the class (**Browser()** in this case), is a routine that gets called whenever a **Browser** object is allocated or a **Browser** object is declared. Using a constructor in a class is optional, but if one exists, it is usually used to initialize the object to a known state and allocate any dynamic memory that the object may need. In the **Browser** class the constructor initializes the screen and buffer pointers.

The **Browser** object's destructor, specified by the line:

```
virtual ~Browser(void) { ; }
```

in the **Browser** class is called whenever the object is deallocated. Destructors are usually used to cleanup and deallocate any dynamic data stored in the object. Here the **Browser** destructor, which has the name of the class along with the ~ character, actually doesn't do anything. In fact, the whole destructor function is listed immediately after the destructor's function header. As you can see, the destructor only contains an empty stub. (You can specify member functions inline like this also, but generally this should be done only if the function body is short.) A destructor has been provided here simply to have a consistent interface with the class since it has a constructor.

The Screen Class

For the most part, the **Browser** class just designed is a natural adaptation of the main program and the **ProcessInput()** function from **browse.c**. That is, the class was created by repackaging the code we already had. To represent the new **ScreenClass** class, however, a new code will have to be introduced. Its definition is:

```
class ScreenClass {
public:
```

```
    ScreenArea far *ScreenPtr;
    int ScrSize;
    ScreenClass(unsigned Segment, unsigned Offset);
    virtual ~ScreenClass(void) { ; }
    char Get(int X, int Y) { return Screen[Y][X].Ch; }
    void Put(int X, int Y, char Ch, unsigned char Atr);
    void MarkLine(int Row, unsigned char Atr);
};
```

The **ScreenPtr** data member is a pointer to the screen area, and **ScrSize** is used to hold the number of text lines that is displayed. We've placed these variables in **ScreenClass** because it is the only program component that needs to access these variables.

As for any well-designed object, a constructor and destructor has been included. The constructor initializes a **ScreenClass** object by setting the **ScreenPtr** variable to the segment and offset address of the physical screen address:

```
ScreenPtr = (ScreenArea far *)(((long)Segment << 16) | (long)Offset);
```

The destructor, however, doesn't do anything. So why was it included? For consistency, and to eventually remind us that, if we expand **ScreenClass**, we might need to do some housekeeping at dispose time. (It pays to plan ahead.)

The member functions **Get()** and **Put()** are used to read and write a character at a specified row and column location. These routines help hide the details involved in reading and writing a character to and from screen memory. For example, to read a character using a screen object called **ScrObj1**, we can use the statement:

```
Ch = ScrObj1.Get(10, 20);
```

In this case, **Get()** returns the character at column 11, row 21 on the screen.

The **MarkLine()** member function performs a useful highlighting function. Our new object-oriented browser program will use it to toggle a line between reverse video and normal video. This feature is used in the search command.

The File Buffer Classes

Next, we'll take a look at defining classes to manipulate the file buffer. Two classes will be defined. The first, **Buffer**, will be used to display the file in ASCII format, which is the normal viewing mode. The second, **HexBuffer**, will allow the file to be viewed in hexadecimal format. We'll show the power of inheritance by deriving **HexBuffer** from **Buffer**, allowing us to share code between the two.

Our basic file buffer class, **Buffer**, introduces a new set of functions. As was the case with the **ScreenClass** and **Browser** classes, the data members for **Buffer** are taken from the global variables used in **browse.c**. Included are things such as the file's size, the file's name and attributes, and a pointer to the text in the buffer.

One other crucial data member has been added: **BuffAlloc**. This variable indicates whether memory has been allocated for the text buffer. We'll soon discuss how to make a copy of a **Buffer** object, and we'll want it to share the text data. The **BuffAlloc** flag tells us whether our object actually allocated that text data, or whether it came from some other object. Let's take a look at the **Buffer** class.

```
class Buffer {
public:
  char *TextPtr, FileName[13];
  unsigned char BuffAlloc;
  int NoBytes, Attr, NumLines, LinePtr[2000];
  long Size;
  ftime Time;
  ffblk ffblk;
  FILE *fp;
  Buffer(void);
  virtual ~Buffer(void) { if (BuffAlloc) free(TextPtr); }
  unsigned char OpenAndRead(char *FName);
  void Dup(Buffer *Buf);
  char GetCh(int Index);
  virtual char *GetLine(char *Str, int Index);
  virtual void SetLines(void);
  int GetNumLines(void) { return NumLines; }
};
```

Note that once again we have a constructor and a destructor. In this case, the constructor **Buffer()** sets the **BuffAlloc** flag to 0, indicating that we haven't allocated the text buffer yet. It doesn't get allocated until we open the file and read its data. This is done by the member function **OpenAndRead()**.

Unlike some of our other destructors in this example, the destructor for **Buffer** actually does something. It deallocates the memory for the text buffer, but only if the object allocated it in the first place. The **BuffAlloc** flag is checked to find this out. This is a good example of encapsulation at work. Only the buffer knows the status of the text buffer. No other object in our program should care.

One new member function has been added to the **Buffer** class: **Dup()**. It allows us to duplicate an existing **Buffer** object. This is done by copying the file attributes and pointing to the source buffer's text data. Since we're not actually copying the text data, we don't allocate a new buffer for it. Thus we must be sure that the **BuffAlloc** is set to 0.

The **Dup()** function is written with derived classes in mind. We'll soon derive the **HexBuffer** class that organizes lines in groups of 16 characters rather than by the natural line breaks in the file. In response, we might need to recompute the line pointer array after the copy, since the source and target buffers may not be of the same type. Let's take a look at **Dup()** to see how this works.

```
void Buffer::Dup(Buffer *Buf)
// Duplicate another file buffer. The file attributes are
// copied, but the file text is not. Instead, we merely point
// to the text. Since we're not allocating the text buffer,
// we make sure BuffAlloc is False (0). We'll change the line
// pointer array, because we might not display lines the same
// way with this new buffer.
{
  TextPtr    = Buf->TextPtr;  // Copy pointers only
  NoBytes    = Buf->NoBytes;  // Copy file attributes
  Size       = Buf->Size;
  Time       = Buf->Time;
  BuffAlloc  = 0;             // Important to do this!
  SetLines();                 // Recompute line pointers
}
```

Recall that polymorphism works by indirection with pointers. Our parameter to **Dup()** is typed as a pointer to a **Buffer**. However, we can really pass in a pointer of any derived class of **Buffer**, as we might do for the **HexBuffer** class we're about to present. Also, this **HexBuffer** class will inherit the **Dup()** member function. Thus the net result is that the source buffer, passed in as a parameter, may not be of the same class as the object through which the **Dup()** member function was called—hence the need for recomputing the line pointers. This is accomplished by calling another new member function: **SetLine()**.

The real workhorse function in **Buffer** is **GetLine()**, which reads a text line from the buffer. This routine uses **GetCh()** to continually read one character at a time, until the line termination character (value of 10) is encountered. The **GetLine()** function allows the browser object to obtain a line of text without having to know how the data is stored in the buffer. Each time the browser needs a new line, it only needs to pass a **GetLine()** message to the active buffer object. For example:

```
strcpy(NewLine, BuffObj->GetLine(Str, P));
```

returns the text line that starts at the buffer position **P**.

The **GetNumLines()** member function returns the number of text lines stored in the file buffer. Although it simply returns the value stored in the **NumLines** variable, it performs a vital role because it allows us to access the line count without having to know how this information is stored.

A Little Bit of Inheritance

Inheritance was introduced in Chapter 1. Here, we can put this OOP property to work to solve an important design issue. Specifically, we would like to add a hex viewing feature to our browser; however, we don't want to perform major surgery on the program. Because we are using objects, there is a simple solution—we can derive a hex buffer class from the **Buffer** class already in place. This will allow us to add member functions to handle hex formats, but we won't have to change the definition of the **Buffer** class. The code needed to create the new class is:

```
class HexBuffer : public Buffer {
public:
  HexBuffer(void): Buffer() { };
  virtual char *GetLine(char *Str, int Index);
  virtual void SetLines(void);
};
```

This object class inherits all of the variables and functions from the **Buffer** class. Note that we're also overriding the definition of the **GetLine()** and **SetLines()** functions. (This is why they are declared as virtual function in the **Buffer** class definition.) By overriding these routines, we'll be able to access file data in a hex format.

To better understand how the **HexBuffer** class works, take a look at how data is displayed in a hex format. Figure 2.6 shows the browser screen in hex mode. Note that each hex line consists of 16 bytes. In addition, the ASCII characters that correspond to the hex codes are displayed to the right of the '|' characters. Recall that the **GetLine()** member function was used with the **Browser()** object to read a line of text from the file browser. To support the new hex format, all we need to do is create a new **GetLine()** member function so that data can be read in the format shown in Figure 2.6.

Using the Objects

Now that you've had a brief tour of the new object classes we've defined, let's take a look at how they are used. The best place to start is with the body of the main program shown in Listing 2.2. Note how the code is now divided into three sections:

1. Initialization section

2. Event loop

3. Cleanup section

The initialization section consists of calls to the **new** operator to allocate memory for the main objects. Note that, at the same time, the constructors for each of the objects is called. The last object initialized is **BrowseObj**:

```
 File: browse.pas        Date: 8-17-1989      Size: 7922      Attr: R-W
70 72 6F 67 72 61 6D 20 42 72 6F 77 73 65 3B 0D │ program Browse;♪
0A 7B 20 54 68 69 73 20 70 72 6F 67 72 61 6D 20 │ ▓{ This program
61 6C 6C 6F 77 73 20 79 6F 75 20 74 6F 20 76 69 │ allows you to vi
65 77 20 74 68 65 20 63 6F 6E 74 65 6E 74 73 20 │ ew the contents
6F 66 20 61 6E 20 41 53 43 49 49 0D 0A 20 20 66 │ of an ASCII♪▓ f
69 6C 65 2E 20 20 4F 6E 63 65 20 61 20 66 69 6C │ ile.  Once a fil
65 20 69 73 20 64 69 73 70 6C 61 79 65 64 2C 20 │ e is displayed,
79 6F 75 20 63 61 6E 20 73 63 72 6F 6C 6C 20 74 │ you can scroll t
68 72 6F 75 67 68 20 74 68 65 0D 0A 20 20 66 69 │ hrough the♪▓ fi
6C 65 20 75 73 69 6E 67 20 74 68 65 20 63 75 72 │ le using the cur
73 6F 72 20 70 61 64 20 6B 65 79 73 20 28 50 67 │ sor pad keys (Pg
55 70 2C 20 50 67 44 6E 2C 20 61 6E 64 20 73 6F │ Up, PgDn, and so
20 6F 6E 29 2E 0D 0A 20 20 54 6F 20 75 73 65 20 │ on).♪▓ To use
74 68 65 20 70 72 6F 67 72 61 6D 2C 20 69 73 73 │ the program, iss
75 65 20 74 68 65 20 66 6F 6C 6C 6F 77 69 6E 67 │ ue the following
20 63 6F 6D 6D 61 6E 64 20 61 74 0D 0A 20 20 74 │  command at♪▓ t
68 65 20 44 4F 53 20 70 72 6F 6D 70 74 3A 0D 0A │ he DOS prompt:♪▓
0D 0A 20 20 20 20 42 72 6F 77 73 65 20 66 69 6C │ ♪▓    Browse fil
65 6E 61 6D 65 0D 0A 7D 0D 0A 0D 0A 75 73 65 73 │ ename♪▓}♪▓♪▓uses
0D 0A 20 20 43 72 74 2C 44 6F 73 3B 0D 0A 0D 0A │ ♪▓  Crt,Dos;♪▓♪▓
63 6F 6E 73 74 0D 0A 20 20 42 75 66 53 69 7A 65 │ const♪▓  BufSize
20 3D 20 36 35 35 32 30 3B 20 20 20 7B 20 36 34 │ = 65520;   { 64
4B 20 6D 61 78 2E 20 66 69 6C 65 20 73 69 7A 65 │ K max. file size
<Home=Top> <End=Bot> <PgUp=Prv> <PgDn=Next> <Alt-S=Search> <Esc=Quit> <F1=Flip>
```

Figure 2.6   Sample screen of the file browser in hex mode

```
if (!(BrowseObj = new Browser(ScreenObj, BufObj, HexBufObj))) {
  printf("Not enough memory\n");
  exit(1);
}
```

Here, we assign a screen object and two buffer objects to the main browser object. We'll be able to flip between these two buffers, which show different views of the file.

We've now isolated the browser from the low-level screen and buffer implementations. If we want to write the file data to a different device or use a different file buffer, we could assign the required objects to the browser. Recall that the browser object doesn't really know how the screen and buffer objects are implemented. This "general" design is what allows us to easily modify our program and add extensions. If we were to recode the buffer as a two-dimensional array, we wouldn't have to change the browser object or the screen object.

After the objects are initialized, the first 23 text lines are displayed by calling **ShowScreen()**:

```
BrowseObj->ShowScreen();
```

Next, the event loop starts and takes control of the program until the user presses the Esc key. Whenever an extended key is pressed, **ProcessInput()** is called:

```
BrowseObj->ProcessInput(Ch);
```

The **ProcessInput()** function handles paging up and down through the file, and also handles flipping between the two different buffers. However, how does this flipping occur? Let's look at **ProcessInput()** to find out. Inside the function, you'll find the following statement block assigned to the F1 key:

```
case F1Key :  // Toggle between the two types of buffers
  TempBuff = MainBuff;
  MainBuff = AltBuff;
  AltBuff  = TempBuff;
  SetLPtr();    // Reset top and bottom line indexes
  ShowScreen(); // Redisplay the screen
  break;
```

The **MainBuff** variable represents the active buffer. By swapping between this main buffer and the alternate one, and then redisplaying the screen, we can, in effect, switch two different views of the program.

The Object-Oriented Browser

Listing 2.2 presents the complete program for the object-oriented browser, **browse2.cpp**. The program operates like the **browse.c** program (Listing 2.1) introduced in the first part of the chapter; however, you can now press the F1 key to switch between an ASCII and hex viewing format.

Listing 2.2   browse2.cpp

```
// browse2.cpp
// This program allows you to view the contents of a file.
// You can display it either in ASCII or hexadecimal format.
// Once a file is displayed, you can scroll through the
// file using the cursor pad keys (PgUp, PgDn, and so on). To
// use the program, issue the following command at the DOS
// prompt:
//                 browse2 <filename>
```

```
#include <stdio.h>
#include <string.h>
#include <stdlib.h>
#include <conio.h>
#include <io.h>
#include <dir.h>
#include <dos.h>

#define Screen (*ScreenPtr)

const long MaxBufSize = 65520L;     // Roughly 64K maximum file size
const int  TabSize    = 5;          // Depends on the file
const unsigned char EscKey = 27;    // Extended key codes
const unsigned char PgUp   = 73;
const unsigned char PgDn   = 81;
const unsigned char Home   = 71;
const unsigned char EndKey = 79;
const unsigned char UpKey  = 72;
const unsigned char DnKey  = 80;
const unsigned char Alt_S  = 31;    // The search key
const unsigned char F1Key  = 59;    // The buffer switching key
const unsigned char TabKey = 9;
const unsigned char CR     = 10;    // Carriage return

struct Texel {                      // Structure used for
  char Ch;                          // direct screen access
  unsigned char Attr;               // Character attribute
};

typedef Texel ScreenArea[25][80];   // The screen

// ———————— The Screen Class ———————— //

class ScreenClass {
public:
  ScreenArea far *ScreenPtr;
  int ScrSize;
  ScreenClass(unsigned Segment, unsigned Offset);
  virtual ~ScreenClass(void) { ; }
  char Get(int X, int Y) { return Screen[Y][X].Ch; }
  void Put(int X, int Y, char Ch, unsigned char Atr);
  void MarkLine(int Row, unsigned char Atr);
};

// ———————— The Buffer Class ———————— //

class Buffer {
public:
  char *TextPtr, FileName[13];
  unsigned char BuffAlloc;
  int NoBytes, Attr, NumLines, LinePtr[2000];
  long Size;
  ftime Time;
```

```
    ffblk ffblk;
    FILE *fp;
    Buffer(void);
    virtual ~Buffer(void) { if (BuffAlloc) free(TextPtr); }
    unsigned char OpenAndRead(char *FName);
    void Dup(Buffer *Buf);
    char GetCh(int Index);
    virtual char *GetLine(char *Str, int Index);
    virtual void SetLines(void);
    int GetNumLines(void) { return NumLines; }
};

// ─────────── The Hex Buffer Class ─────────── //

class HexBuffer : public Buffer {
public:
    HexBuffer(void): Buffer() { };
    virtual char *GetLine(char *Str, int Index);
    virtual void SetLines(void);
};

// ─────────── The Browser Class ─────────── //

class Browser {
public:
    ScreenClass *ScrPtr;
    Buffer *MainBuff, *AltBuff;
    int Lc, Bot, End;
    Browser(ScreenClass *Scr, Buffer *Buf1, Buffer *Buf2);
    virtual ~Browser(void) { ; }
    void ProcessInput(char Ch);
    void DisplayFStat(void);
    void DisplayCommands(void);
    void SetLPtr(void);
    void ShowScreen(void);
    void PageUp(void);
    void PageDn(void);
    void LineUp(void);
    void LineDn(void);
    void TopPage(void);
    void BotPage(void);
    void FileSearch(void);
};

// Miscellaneous support functions
char *GetStr(char *Str);
char *ChToHex(char *Str, char Ch);

// ─────────── The Screen Member Functions ─────────── //

ScreenClass::ScreenClass(unsigned Segment, unsigned Offset)
// Set up the pointer to video memory, and set the size of
// the screen
```

```
{
  ScreenPtr = (ScreenArea far *)(((long)Segment << 16) | (long)Offset);
  ScrSize = 23;
}

void ScreenClass::Put(int X, int Y, char Ch, unsigned char Atr)
// Put a character to the screen at the given location
{
  Screen[Y][X].Ch = Ch;
  Screen[Y][X].Attr = Atr;
}

void ScreenClass::MarkLine(int Row, unsigned char Atr)
// Highlight a line on the screen
{
  int Col;

  for (Col=0; Col<80; Col++) Screen[Row][Col].Attr = Atr;
}

// ————— The Buffer Member Functions ————— //

Buffer::Buffer(void)
// At the beginning, no buffer is allocated
{
  BuffAlloc = 0;
  strcpy(FileName,"");
}

char Buffer::GetCh(int Index)
// Returns the specified character from the file buffer if
// the index is in range. If the index is out of range, a
// Control-Z (0x1A) is returned.
{
  return (Index < NoBytes) ? TextPtr[Index] : 0x1A;
}

unsigned char Buffer::OpenAndRead(char *Fname)
// Return true if the file Fname is opened and the file data
// is read okay
{
  int DosError;

  DosError = findfirst(Fname, &ffblk, 0);
  if (DosError != 0) {
    printf("Can't find file %s\n", Fname);
    return 0;
  }
  else {
    if ((fp=fopen(Fname, "r")) == NULL) {  // Open file
      printf("The file %s cannot be opened\n", Fname);
      return 0;
    }
```

```
      else {
        // Allocate buffer memory
        if ((TextPtr=(char *)malloc(ffblk.ff_fsize)) == NULL) {
          printf("Out of memory\n");
          BuffAlloc = 0;
          return 0;
        }
        else {
          BuffAlloc = 1;              // Set flag noting allocation
          // Read file data into buffer
          getftime(fileno(fp), &Time);
          Size = ffblk.ff_fsize;
          if (Size >= MaxBufSize) {
            printf("File is too large\n");
            fclose(fp);
            return(0);
          }
          else {
            NoBytes = read(fileno(fp), TextPtr, ffblk.ff_fsize);
            strcpy(FileName, Fname); // Record the filename
            fclose(fp);                // Close the file
            return 1;                  // Read operation okay
          }
        }
      }
    }
  }
}

void Buffer::Dup(Buffer *Buf)
// Duplicate another file buffer. The file attributes are
// copied, but the file text is not. Instead, we merely point
// to the text. Since we're not allocating the text buffer,
// ensure that BuffAlloc is False (0). We'll change the line
// pointer array, because we might not display lines the same
// way with this new buffer.
{
  TextPtr   = Buf->TextPtr;  // Copy pointers only
  NoBytes   = Buf->NoBytes;  // Copy file attributes
  Size      = Buf->Size;
  Time      = Buf->Time;
  BuffAlloc = 0;                   // Important to do this!
  SetLines();                      // Recompute line pointers
}

char *Buffer::GetLine(char *Str, int Index)
// Get the specified line from the buffer and return it in a
// string.
{
  char Ch;
  int P=0, I;

  while ((Ch=GetCh(Index)) != CR && Ch != 0x1A) {
    if (Ch == TabKey)          // Look for tab
```

```
        for (I=0; I<TabSize; I++)
          Str[P++] = ' ';
      else Str[P++] = Ch;
      Index++;
    }
  Str[P] = '\0';                   // Terminate string
  return Str;
}

void Buffer::SetLines(void)
// Scan the text for newlines and set the line pointer array
{
  char Ch;
  int L=0, I;

  LinePtr[L++] = 0;               // Initialize the index array
  for (I=0; I<NoBytes; I++)
    if ((Ch=GetCh(I)) == CR) LinePtr[L++] = I + 1;
  NumLines = L;
}

// ———— The Hex Buffer Member Functions ———— //

char *HexBuffer::GetLine(char *Str, int Index)
// Get the specified line from the buffer, returning both hex
// and ASCII representations.
{
  char S[3] = "  ";
  int I;

  strcpy(Str, "");
  for (I=0; I<16; I++) {
    strcat(Str, ChToHex(S, GetCh(Index+I)));
    strcat(Str, " ");
  }
  strcat(Str, "| ");
  for (I=0; I<16; I++) Str[I+50] = GetCh(Index+I);
  Str[66] = '\0';
  return Str;
}

void HexBuffer::SetLines(void)
// Set the line pointer array so that each line
// will point to 16 characters
{
  int L, I;

  NumLines = Size / 16;
  if (Size % 16 != 0) NumLines++;
  for (I=0, L=0; I<NumLines; I++, L+=16)
    LinePtr[I] = L;
}
```

```
// ————— The Browser Member Functions ————— //

Browser::Browser(ScreenClass *Scr, Buffer *Buf1, Buffer *Buf2)
// Initialize the browser by setting up pointers to the
// screen and to the two buffers
{
  ScrPtr = Scr;  MainBuff = Buf1;  AltBuff = Buf2;
}

void Browser::DisplayFStat(void)
// Display the first status line of file information
// including filename, size, date, and time
{
  int Col;
  char AtStr[8];


  gotoxy(3, 1);                    // Display filename
  printf("File: %s", MainBuff->FileName);
  gotoxy(26, 1);
  printf("Date: %02u-%02u-%04u", MainBuff->Time.ft_month,
         MainBuff->Time.ft_day, MainBuff->Time.ft_year+1980);
  gotoxy(48, 1);
  printf("Size: %ld", MainBuff->Size); // Display size
  // Display attributes
  if (MainBuff->ffblk.ff_attrib == FA_RDONLY)
    strcpy(AtStr, "R");
  else strcpy(AtStr, "R-W");
  if (MainBuff->ffblk.ff_attrib == FA_HIDDEN)
    strcat(AtStr, "-H");
  if (MainBuff->ffblk.ff_attrib == FA_SYSTEM)
    strcat(AtStr, "-S");
  gotoxy(63, 1);
  printf("Attr: %s", AtStr);
  // Put status bar in reverse video
  scrPtr->MarkLine(0,112);
}

void Browser::DisplayCommands(void)
// Display the command bar at the last line of the screen
{
  int Col;

  for (Col=0; Col<80; Col++) ScrPtr->Put(Col, 24, ' ', 112);
  gotoxy(1, 25);
  printf("<Home=Top> <End=Bot> <PgUp=Prv> <PgDn=Next> "
    "<Alt-S=Search> <Esc=Quit> <F1=Flip>");
  scrPtr->MarkLine(24,112);
}

void Browser::SetLPtr(void)
// Set the current and bottom line indexes for the screen
```

```
{
  Lc = MainBuff->GetNumLines();
  if (Lc > ScrPtr->ScrSize)   // Set the bottom line index
    Bot = Lc - ScrPtr->ScrSize;
  else Bot = 0;
  End = Lc - 1;
  Lc = 0;                      // Set the top line index
}

void Browser::ShowScreen(void)
// Displays a screen image containing 23 lines of the file
{
  int Row, Col, P, TLc, Length;
  char Str[81];

  TLc = Lc; // Start with the current line index
  for (Row=0; Row<ScrPtr->ScrSize && Row<=End; Row++) {
    P = MainBuff->LinePtr[TLc];
    strcpy(Str, MainBuff->GetLine(Str, P));
    Length = strlen(Str);
    for (Col=0; Col<80 && Col<Length; Col++)
      ScrPtr->Put(Col, Row+1, Str[Col], 7);
    for (; Col<80; Col++)
      ScrPtr->Put(Col, Row+1, ' ', 7);
    TLc++;
  }
  for (; Row<ScrPtr->ScrSize; Row++)
    for (Col=0; Col<80; Col++)
      ScrPtr->Put(Col, Row+1, ' ', 7);
}

void Browser::PageUp(void)
{
  if (Lc-ScrPtr->ScrSize > 0) Lc -= ScrPtr->ScrSize;
    else Lc = 0;
  ShowScreen();
}

void Browser::PageDn(void)
{
  if (Lc+ScrPtr->ScrSize < Bot && Bot >= ScrPtr->ScrSize)
    Lc += ScrPtr->ScrSize;
  else Lc = Bot;
  ShowScreen();
}

void Browser::LineUp(void)
{
  if (Lc > 0) {
    Lc--;  ShowScreen();
  }
}
```

```cpp
void Browser::LineDn(void)
{
  if (Lc < Bot && Bot >= ScrPtr->ScrSize) {
    Lc++;  ShowScreen();
  }
}

void Browser::TopPage(void)
{
  Lc = 0;  ShowScreen();
}

void Browser::BotPage(void)
{
  if (Bot >= ScrPtr->ScrSize) {
    Lc = Bot;  ShowScreen();
  }
}

void Browser::FileSearch(void)
// Searches the buffer for a string. If a match is found, the
// line containing the string is highlighted.
{
  int Col, I, P;
  char SearchStr[81], *S, Line[81], *Ptr;

  for (Col=0; Col<=78; Col++)
    ScrPtr->Put(Col, 24, ' ', 112);
  gotoxy(2, 25);
  printf("Search for: ");
  if ((S=GetStr(SearchStr)) == NULL) {    // Get the search string
    DisplayCommands();
    return;
  }
  I = Lc;
  do {
    P = MainBuff->LinePtr[I];
    Col = 0;
    strcpy(Line, MainBuff->GetLine(Line, P));
    Ptr = strstr(Line, S);     // Look for a match
    I++;
  } while (Ptr == NULL && I <= End);

  if (Ptr != NULL) {                 // Match found
    if (I > Lc + ScrPtr->ScrSize) {
      Lc = I - ScrPtr->ScrSize;
      ShowScreen();
    }
    ScrPtr->MarkLine(I-Lc, 112);  // Highlight line with match
    if (getch() == 0) (void)getch();
    ScrPtr->MarkLine(I-Lc, 7);    // Set line back to normal
  }
  DisplayCommands();
}
```

```
void Browser::ProcessInput(char Ch)
{
  Buffer *TempBuff;

  switch (Ch) {
    case PgUp  : PageUp();  break;
    case PgDn  : PageDn();  break;
    case UpKey : LineUp();  break;
    case DnKey : LineDn();  break;
    case Home  : TopPage(); break;
    case EndKey: BotPage(); break;
    case F1Key :  // Toggle between the two types of buffers
      TempBuff = MainBuff;
      MainBuff = AltBuff;
      AltBuff  = TempBuff;
      SetLPtr();    // Reset top and bottom line indexes
      ShowScreen(); // Redisplay the screen
      break;
    case Alt_S : FileSearch(); break;
  }
}

// ———————— Other Supporting Routines ———— //

long SelectMonitor(void)
// Determine the type of monitor installed and return the
// memory address of the installed monitor
{
  struct REGS Regs;

  Regs.h.ah = 15;
  int86(0x10, &Regs, &Regs);
  if (Regs.h.al == 7) return 0xB000;  // Monochrome
    else return 0xB800;               // Graphics
}

char *GetStr(char *Str)
// Read a string at the current cursor location
{
  char Ch;
  int Count=0;

  while ((Ch=getch()) != 13 && Ch != EscKey) {
    printf("%c", Ch);
    Str[Count++] = Ch;
  }
  if (Ch == EscKey) return NULL;
  Str[Count] = '\0';                 // Terminate string
  return Str;
}

char *ChToHex(char *Str, char Ch)
// A support function for HexBuffer than converts a byte into
// two hex digits
```

```
{
  const char HexDigits[17] = "0123456789ABCDEF";

  strncpy(Str, &HexDigits[Ch >> 4], 1);     // Create a two character
  strncpy(&Str[1], &HexDigits[Ch & 0x0F], 1);  // string
  return Str;
}

// —————————— Main Program ———————— //

main(int argc, char *argv[])
{
  char Ch;
  ScreenClass *ScreenObj;
  Browser *BrowseObj;
  Buffer *BufObj;
  HexBuffer *HexBufObj;

  clrscr();
  if (argc != 2) {
    printf("Incorrect number of arguments.\n");
    printf("To browse a file use the command:\n");
    printf("\tbrowse2 <filename>\n");
    exit(1);
  }

  if (!(ScreenObj = new ScreenClass(SelectMonitor(), 0x00))) {
    printf("Not enough memory\n");
    exit(1);
  }
  // Allocate and initialize buffer, read in data. If error
  // reading data, quit.
  if (!(BufObj = new Buffer())) {
    printf("Not enough memory\n");
    exit(1);
  }
  if (!BufObj->OpenAndRead(argv[1])) exit(1);
  BufObj->SetLines();

  // Make hex buffer that duplicates what's in the other buffer
  if (!(HexBufObj = new HexBuffer())) {
    printf("Not enough memory\n");
    exit(1);
  }
  HexBufObj->Dup(BufObj);

  // Now set up the browser to use the screen and buffer objects
  if (!(BrowseObj = new Browser(ScreenObj, BufObj, HexBufObj))) {
    printf("Not enough memory\n");
    exit(1);
  }

  // Draw browser screen, show initial lines
```

```
BrowseObj->DisplayFStat();
BrowseObj->DisplayCommands();
BrowseObj->SetLPtr();
BrowseObj->ShowScreen();

do {     // Process keys until Esc key pressed
  Ch = getch();
  switch (Ch) {
    case 0:                 // Extended key pressed
      Ch = getch();
      BrowseObj->ProcessInput(Ch);
      break;
    case EscKey: break;
    default: putch(7);    // Illegal key, so sound the bell
  }
} while (Ch != EscKey);

delete BrowseObj;        // Remove objects
delete BufObj;
delete HexBufObj;
delete ScreenObj;

textbackground(0);       // Restore screen back to normal
textcolor(7);
clrscr();
}
```

Code Critique

You've now seen how the object-oriented browser provides a better platform than the first version of the program for adding new features. After we converted the program using Turbo C++'s OOP features, some important advantages were disclosed:

1. The global variables, such as **ScreenPtr**, **Lc**, **Bot**, **End**, and **LinePtr**, were eliminated.

2. The main program works at a much higher level, calling on objects to do all the dirty work.

3. The program was reorganized so that it is now easier to maintain and it is much more flexible. For example, recall how easy it was to add the hex viewing feature.

One important issue that came up as we performed the conversion involved the process of determining which program components should be represented as objects. Although this process might at first seem like magic, there are some basic rules we can apply to help design our object-oriented applications. The bottom line is that you want to design your code to take advantage of the three key properties of OOP: encapsulation, inheritance, and polymorphism. To get started, follow these guidelines:

1. Most traditional data structures—such as linked lists, trees, queues, stacks, buffers, and so on—are typically good candidates for objects. Why? The object structure allows you to encapsulate the operations needed to process the data structure with the data stored in the structure itself. The advantage here is that the program that uses the data structure doesn't really need to know how the data structure is processed.

2. User interface components, such as windows, menus, buttons, dialog boxes, and so on, are also good candidates for objects. Often, these types of screen objects can benefit from the OOP property of inheritance. For example, you can define a window object to work in text mode and then use that object to derive a window that works in graphics mode. The base window object could also be used to derive a menu object or an interactive button object, and so on. In Chapters 3 through 11, these types of interface objects for both text and graphics modes will be covered.

3. Components that are used in your programs that model real-world objects or events such as gauges, graphs, charts, people, countries, planets, and so on should be considered as objects.

4. Hardware components, such as the mouse, keyboard, and screen, also make useful objects. When working with these types of objects, you might want to back up a level and define a general input and output (I/O) device object and then use it to define more specific I/O objects to support the mouse, keyboard, and screen.

5. There are situations where the code that is usually placed in your main program can be represented as an object. The file browser program presented provided an example of this type of approach.

6. In addition, there are situations where algorithms can be represented as objects. For example, you could create a search object to encapsulate different search algorithms or a compression object to encapsulate compression algorithms. You could even represent a general parser as an object and derive different parsers from the general parser object to handle different languages.

Screen and Keyboard Tools

This is the first of several hands-on chapters that focus on object-oriented user-interface tools. In a few chapters you'll have several powerful toolkits that provide such capabilities as pop-up windows, pull-down menus, scroll bars, and more. The most amazing feature of these tools is their ability to work in both text and graphics modes.

Before we begin our tool building, we need to lay some groundwork. This chapter will focus on the low-level support tools for text mode applications. In addition, a few keyboard input routines will be presented. Our goal is to create three packages: **txunit**, **scrnsty**, and **keybrd**—the first two are screen-oriented utilities, while the third is a package of keyboard primitives.

Overview of the Screen Objects

Our first task is to develop a set of routines for accessing the text screen. In the tradition of OOP, we'll combine screen-related operations into a single class. By encapsulating the screen operations into a single package, we'll be starting out on the right track for writing more maintainable code.

The screen tools are designed to operate at a very low level; they won't perform clipping or error handling and they won't support the mouse. These tasks will be left to higher-level objects.

It's also important to realize that the screen tools are optimized to support rectangular-shaped screen objects—windows, menus, and selection buttons. Although the tools described here will only support text screens, in Chapter 10 a similar set of tools will be built to support graphics.

Screen objects provide one important and unique feature, they will support virtual screens—screens larger than the standard 80 columns by 25 rows format. From the outset, the underlying structure for supporting virtual windows will be in place. This feature is explored further in Chapter 9.

Inside the PC's Text Screen

Before building the screen class, we need to review how the PC manages the screen in text mode. All the screen-related details will not be covered, but we'll attempt to present the basics to provide you with a good working knowledge about how the screen is accessed.

What you see on the screen is maintained in a section of memory called a *screen buffer*. The location of the screen buffer depends on whether you are using a monochrome or color video card. For a color system, the memory is located at segment and offset B800:0000h. The buffer for a monochrome system (including a Hercules video adapter) is located at B000:0000h.

The screen buffer is organized into pairs of bytes. The first byte in each pair contains the ASCII code of the character to appear on the screen. The second byte contains the character's attribute, which controls the color and blinking status. This relationship is shown in Figure 3.1. (Valid character attributes are shown in Table 3.1.) We'll call these 2 bytes a texel (*text element*). Therefore, you can ac-

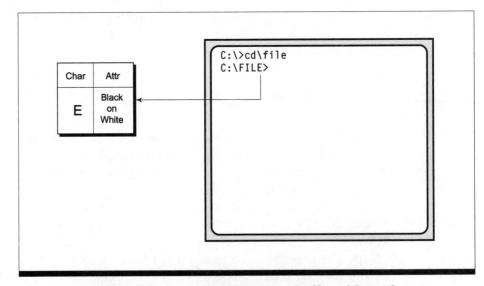

Figure 3.1   Accessing the screen buffer with texels

Table 3.1   Character attributes

Color Codes					
Binary	Hex	Color	Binary	Hex	Color*
0000	0	Black	1000	8	Gray
0001	1	Blue	1001	9	Light Blue
0010	2	Green	1010	a	Light Green
0011	3	Cyan	1011	b	Light Cyan
0100	4	Red	1100	c	Light Red
0101	5	Magenta	1101	d	Light Magenta
0110	6	Brown	1110	e	Light Brown
0111	7	White	1111	f	Bright White

* Only available for foreground colors

tually think of the screen buffer as an array of texels. For example, each texel can be represented as a structure of 2 bytes

```
struct Texel { unsigned char Ch, Attr; };
```

and the typical text mode screen of 80 characters per line by 25 rows can be represented as:

```
Texel ScreenBuffer[25][80];
```

In other words, the first texel in the array corresponds to the first (top-left) character on the screen and the last texel in the screen buffer specifies the last (bottom-right) character on the screen.

An attribute specifies both the foreground and background colors of a character. The upper 4 bits of the attribute specify the background color and the lower 4 bits specify the foreground color. Using Table 3.1, the bit pattern for an attribute needed to set a character to black with a red background would be 01000000. In hex notation, this would be 0x40. Note that the hex notation is a convenient way to specify the background and foreground colors. The left nibble is the background color (4), while the right is the foreground color (0). This fact will be used throughout the book when specifying colors.

For the background, only the colors 0x00 to 0x07 can be used. The values 0x08 to 0x0F will cause the text to blink and set the background to the color computed by stripping off the high bit. For example, setting the background to 0x0C would actually result in a red color (0x04) on a blinking foreground.

Putting all this together, suppose we want to write a black letter z on a red background at the fourth column and third row of the **ScreenBuffer** array defined earlier. This could be done using the statements:

```
ScreenBuffer[3][4].Ch = 'z';
ScreenBuffer[3][4].Attr = 0x0C;
```

A Virtual Screen Class

Now that we've seen how screen memory is managed, let's return to the text mode screen class. The class presented here will provide the following features:

1. Operates on a texel buffer, such as the screen or a section of internal memory

2. Provides support for drawing and writing to rectangular regions of the screen

3. Includes utilities for moving and copying rectangular regions of the screen or a texel buffer

4. Provides support for virtual screen buffers

The class we'll create, **TxBuff**, is included in the files **txunit.h** and **txunit.cpp** (see Listings 3.1 and 3.2) and is shown next. Brief descriptions of the member functions in **TxBuff** are listed in Table 3.2.

```
class TxBuff {
public:
   int Wd, Ht;        // Width and height in texels
   TexelPtr TxRam;    // Pointer to texel buffer
   TexelPtr OrgPtr;   // Pointer to origin
   char Aliased;      // True if buffer is aliased
   TxBuff(TexelPtr T);
   TxBuff(int W, int H, TexelPtr T);
   ~TxBuff(void);
   void SetRamPtr(TexelPtr T);
   TexelPtr TxRamAddr(int X, int Y);
   TexelPtr RelAddr(int X, int Y);
   void SetSize(int W, int H);
   void SetLocn(int X, int Y);
   void Swap(int X, int Y, int W, int H, TxBuff *Other, int Xs, int Ys);
   void Xfr(int X, int Y, int W, int H, TxBuff *Other, int Xs, int Ys);
   void Scroll(int X, int Y, int W, int H, ScrollDir Sd, int Amt);
   void Fill(int X, int Y, int W, int H, char Ch, char Attr);
```

Table 3.2   The member functions in the TxBuff class

Member function	Description
TxBuff()	Initializes a TxBuff object
~TxBuff()	Deallocates memory in TxBuff object
SetRamPtr()	Sets the texel pointer and aliased flag
TxRamAddr()	Computes pointer given a location relative to the beginning of the buffer
RelAddr()	Computes pointer given a location relative to the current origin
SetSize()	Sets the size of a TxBuff and allocates memory for it
SetLocn()	Sets the location of the origin (see RelAddr()
Swap()	Swaps a rectangular region of memory
Xfr()	Copies a rectangular region of memory
Scroll()	Scrolls a rectangular region of memory
Fill()	Fills the character and attributes of a rectangular region
FillB()	Fills either the character or attribute fields of a rectangular region
HzWrt()	Writes a string to TxBuff memory using a particular character attribute
HzWrtB()	Writes a character string to a TxBuff location without changing the attributes
HzFill()	Fills a line using a particular attribute
HzFillB()	Fills a line with either a character or a particular attribute

```
void FillB(int X, int Y, int W, int H, char Ch, char Opt);
void HzWrt(int X, int Y, char *Str, char Attr, unsigned Cnt);
void HzWrt(int X, int Y, char *Str, char Attr) {
  HzWrt(X, Y, Str, Attr, strlen(Str));
}
void HzWrtB(int X, int Y, char *Str, unsigned Cnt);
void HzWrtB(int X, int Y, char *Str) {
  HzWrtB(X, Y, Str, strlen(Str));
}
```

```
    void HzFill(int X, int Y, char Ch, char Attr, unsigned Cnt) {
      Fill(X, Y, Cnt, 1, Ch, Attr);
    }
    void HzFillB(int X, int Y, char Ch, char Opt, unsigned Cnt) {
      FillB(X, Y, Cnt, 1, Ch, Opt);
    }
};
```

The **TxBuff** class contains only five data members. The first two, **Wd** and **Ht**, are the width and height of the texel buffer. The next two variables refer to the start of the texel buffer (**TxRam**) and the top-left location of some object within this buffer (**OrgPtr**). You'll later see that many operations in **TxBuff** are performed relative to the **OrgPtr** location. (See Figure 3.2 for an example of how **TxRam** and **OrgPtr** relate to one another.)

The last data member, **Aliased**, is a boolean character that indicates whether **TxRam** points to some preexisting buffer or to memory that was allocated by the object itself. A **True** condition (value of 1) indicates that **TxRam** points to previously allocated memory, or the video ram; otherwise, it references memory allocated on the heap.

The **TxBuff** class contains three categories of screen operations: buffer initialization, screen swapping, and screen writing.

Buffer Initialization

When allocating a new **TxBuff** object, the **TxBuff()** constructor handles the initialization required. Looking at the **TxBuff** class definition, you'll actually find

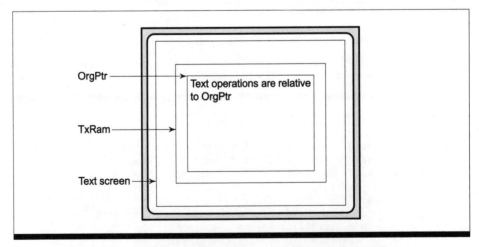

Figure 3.2   Relationship between TxRam and OrgPtr

two declarations for a **TxBuff()** constructor. Is this a mistake? No. In C++ we can overload the name of a function as we have done here. (Note that the parameters to the two constructors are different. Therefore which one gets used depends on which parameters are used to call **TxBuff()**.) We are merely providing two ways that a **TxBuff** object can be initialized. Both functions perform the same basic operations. That is, they initialize the **TxRam** variable and set the **Ht** and **Wd** data members.

Both constructors accept a parameter, **T**, which is a pointer to a texel buffer that is assigned to **TxRam**. If **Ht** and **Wd** variables are passed to **TxBuff()**, they are used to initialize the texel buffer's height and width. If these two values aren't supplied, the height and width of the texel buffer are initialized to zero. In both cases the **OrgPtr** is set to the same value as **TxRam**.

In order to set the **TxRam** pointer, **TxBuff()** calls the **SetRamPtr()** member function and passes the **T** parameter to it. If **T** is not **NULL**, we assume that it references memory that is already allocated, such as the screen memory on a video card. In such a case, **Aliased** is set to **True** and **TxRam** is set to **T**. If **T** is **NULL**, however, **TxRam** will not be aliased and in fact the **TxBuff** object will have to allocate memory for its texel buffer. You'll see how it does this later in this section.

A companion routine to **TxBuff()** is the destructor **~TxBuff()**, which frees memory that has been allocated for **TxRam**. If **TxRam** is aliased, however, the destructor doesn't do anything.

Two other initialization member functions are **SetSize()** and **SetLocn()**. The **SetSize()** function sets the height (**Ht**) and width (**Wd**) dimensions in texel units of the **TxRam** being used and allocates memory for **TxRam** if the memory is not aliased. Since **SetSize()** is responsible for allocating memory, it should always be called before using a **TxBuff** object. If the buffer has already been allocated from a previous call to **SetSize()**, the buffer is reallocated to its new size. However, **SetSize()** does not reallocate the memory if the new size is smaller than the old. This helps prevent heap fragmentation, although sometimes at the cost of using more memory than needed. The statements responsible for allocating the memory for **TxRam are**:

```
if (!Aliased) { // Want buffer on heap
  if (!TxRam) { // Allocate for first time
    TxRam = new Texel[W*H];
  }
  else if (W*H > Wd*Ht)  { // Reallocate?
    delete [Wd*Ht] TxRam;
    TxRam = new Texel[W*H];
  }
  OrgPtr = TxRam;
}
```

The **SetLocn()** routine is used to specify which **X** and **Y** texel location within the buffer the **OrgPtr** is set to. By default, **OrgPtr** points to the beginning of the buffer. In many situations, there will be no need to call **SetLocn()**.

You may have noticed the use of the function **TxRamAddr()** in **SetLocn()**. This routine converts an **X** and **Y** texel coordinate into a pointer. Why do we store a pointer instead of an (X,Y) offset? Mainly for efficiency. We want to avoid having to recompute the offset in the buffer each time we access it. Note that our two-dimensional text buffer is internally represented as a one-dimensional array. The arithmetic for converting our two-dimensional coordinates into one-dimensional coordinates is handled entirely by the **TxBuff** objects—a good example of encapsulation at work.

Now take a look at an example that shows how we must declare and initialize a **TxBuff** object. Suppose we want to initialize a **TxBuff** object called **ScreenBuff**. The statements that would accomplish this are:

```
TxBuff ScreenBuff(VideoPtr());
ScreenBuff.SetSize(80, 25);
```

Note that we have used the function **VideoPtr()** here to retrieve the pointer to the screen memory. Remember from Chapter 2 that the correct video address depends on whether a monochrome or color video card is being used.

Writing to the Screen

One of the more common operations of a window package is to set regions of the screen to a particular color or character. For instance, we'll want to be able to display an entire row of a window border with a single call. We'll also want fill operations that can alter only the attribute fields of a portion of the screen. This can be useful for rapidly highlighting a menu entry, changing the border color of a window, and so on.

Two fill operations in **TxBuff**, **Fill()** and **FillB()** are provided in **TxBuff** to fill a rectangular region of the text screen. The first member function, **Fill()**, is designed to set every character and attribute within a rectangular region of a **TxBuff** object to a specific value (i.e., it fills both bytes of the texels). This operation is useful for such tasks as clearing a window. The **FillB()** function serves a similar purpose, except it only fills one of the bytes in a texel—either the character portion or the attribute.

For example, to fill the screen with red '*' characters, using the **ScreenBuff** object we created earlier, you would write:

```
ScreenBuff.Fill(1, 1, 80, 25, '*', 0x04);
```

The first four parameters specify the column, row, width, and height of the fill region. The next parameter is the character to display followed by the color to use—in this case, red on black.

Alternatively, to set the screen so that it used red on black, without changing any of the characters on the screen, you would use:

```
ScreenBuff.FillB(1, 1, 80, 25, 0x04, 1);
```

Let's dissect this call. The first four parameters are the same as those for **Fill()** and set the location and dimensions of the region to fill. The fifth parameter specifies what character or attribute to fill the texel buffer with. The function determines which field of the texels to fill based on the value of the last parameter. If the value is a zero, then the fifth parameter is assumed to be a character. This character is then assigned to the character fields of the texels in the region to be filled. If, however, the last parameter is a one, as it is in this example, then the value in the fifth parameter is copied into the attribute fields of the region being filled.

The **TxBuff** class also contains the member functions **HzFill()** and **HzFillB()** to write a single row of a texel buffer with a particular character and possibly an attribute. Notice that these functions merely call **Fill()** and **FillB()** with the number of rows set to one. Since these operations are so simple, they are defined within the **TxBuff** class itself. This abbreviated notation is perfect for small member functions such as this.

The **TxBuff** class also contains the member functions **HzWrtB()** and **HzWrt()** to write a string and, in the case of **HzWrt()**, an attribute to a texel buffer. Note that there are actually two sets of declarations for these functions in the **TxBuff** class. As is the case with the **TxBuff()** constructor, two forms of these functions are provided to make later programming tasks a bit easier. Here, we've declared one version of each function that allows us to specify a string and its length and one version that enables us to specify just the string itself.

Moving Screen Memory

Several member functions in **TxBuff** are used to move or swap screen memory. Briefly, **Swap()** exchanges rectangular regions of two **TxBuff** objects and **Xfr()** copies a rectangular portion of one **TxBuff** object to another. They both have the same parameters and very similar code. We'll focus on **Swap()** for a moment. Its function prototype is:

```
void Swap(int X, int Y, int W, int H, TxBuff *Other, int Xs, int Ys);
```

As you can see, **Swap()** takes seven parameters. The first four specify the top-left column and row relative to the **Swap()**'s **OrgPtr**, along with the width and height of the region to exchange. The next parameter, **Other**, points to a **TxBuff** object with which the memory exchange is to take place. The last two parameters specify the location relative to **Other**'s **OrgPtr** at which the swap is to take place. Since **Swap()** only exchanges rectangular regions of the same size, there is no need to specify the height and width of **Other**'s region. The relationship between the two **TxBuff** regions and these parameters is shown in Figure 3.3.

One nice feature about **Swap()** and **Xfr()** is their ability to transfer overlapping regions of screen or texel memory. For example, if a window is to be moved down one row, clearly the old and new positions of the windows overlap. The **Xfr()** routine is designed so that it can move the window correctly with a single call.

This feature requires a little extra effort, however. Basically, we must ensure that the transfer takes place correctly, even if the regions overlap. The relative positions of the regions determine the proper direction of transfer.

To handle possible overlap, **Swap()** and **Xfr()** check the relative positions of the source and destination texel regions by comparing the offset addresses of the source and destination pointers. But what about the segments? If the objects have different segments, they're assumed to be allocated on the heap in separate regions and therefore don't overlap anyway. If the regions are in the same segment, however, we only need to compare their offsets. The relative position of the source

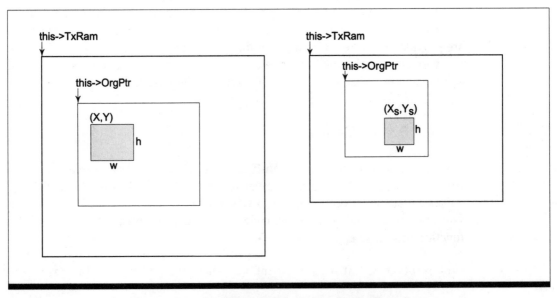

Figure 3.3   Relationship between TxBuff regions

and destination regions determines the order of the swap. Once the direction of the swap is determined, the appropriate **for** loop is executed to swap one row of the memory blocks at a time.

To compare the offset addresses of the two memory blocks, we need a routine that can convert an (X,Y) coordinate location into an address. This is the purpose of the member function **RelAddr()**, which is similar to **TxRamAddr()** mentioned earlier. However, **RelAddr()** bases the (X,Y) coordinate from the **OrgPtr** rather than relative to **TxRam**.

The last member function that moves memory is **Scroll()**, which scrolls rectangular regions up, down, left, or right. The direction of the move is based on the **Sd** (scroll direction) parameter. The settings for this parameter are:

Enumerated Constant	Value
UpScroll	0
DnScroll	1
LeftScroll	2
RightScroll	3

They are defined in **scrnsty.h**. We'll discuss this file in the next section.

The scrolling is performed by the **Xfr()** function. The trick involves transferring one region of the texel buffer to another region in the same buffer. This can be done by calling the object's **Xfr()** function, with the source **TxBuff** being the same object. For example, to scroll up **Amt** number of lines use:

```
Xfr(X, Y, W, H, this, X, Y+Amt);
```

Note that the object passes itself to the **Xfr()** function by using the **this** pointer as the argument to the texel buffer to be copied into.

Miscellaneous Screen Tools

Since we're discussing low-level screen tools, this is a good time to construct a package that contains many of the codes and constants that we'll be using with our interface tools in later chapters. This package will consist of two files: **scrnsty.h** and **scrnsty.cpp**, which are shown in Listings 3.3 and 3.4, respectively.

About half of the **scrnsty** toolkit is dedicated to providing support for managing the colors of text mode screen objects. For instance, **scrnsty.h** defines the **ColorPak** type that we'll be using repeatedly to set the colors of windows, buttons, scroll bars, and so on. **ColorPak** is a structure defined as:

```
struct ColorPak { unsigned char Bc, Wc, Tc, Pc, Fc; };
```

where each of its fields is a color attribute (see Table 3.3). The **ColorPak** structure is useful because it bundles together all the color settings that a typical screen object will have.

In general, you'll want to define these colors so that they complement each other. For instance, you might have a "blue" set of colors that includes a dark blue background, cyan borders, white text, and so on. For convenience, **scrnsty.cpp** defines several **ColorPak** sets. For example, a blue **ColorPak** is given as:

```
ColorPak BlueColors = {0x17, 0x1e, 0x3e, 0x5e, 0x1b};
```

In addition, a variable that holds the default colors for an application, **DefColors**, is declared in **scrnsty.cpp** and is initialized to use monochrome colors. These colors are designed to work equally well for monochrome and color displays.

Finally, the color system is rounded out by the two inline functions **ForeGround()** and **BackGround()**, which return the foreground color of an attribute passed to it and the background color of an attribute. For example, if an attribute has a value of 0x17, then **ForeGround()** would return 0x07 and **BackGround()** would return 0x01. Note that **BackGround()** shifts the 4 bits of the background color into the right nibble so that the color can more easily be checked in a program.

The remaining part of **scrnsty.h** describes the various border and frame styles that we'll be using in later chapters. For instance, the **Dashed** constant, declared with a value of 0x30, will cause the window utilities that we'll be building to draw a window with a dashed border. Note that some of these border styles will be used in text mode and others only in graphics mode.

Similarly, several frame attributes are defined. These attributes describe the characteristics of the frame of a window, such as its border type, border width, type of shadow, and so on. You may have noticed that these frame attributes are

Table 3.3   Descriptions of ColorPak fields

Field	Description
Bc	Border color
Wc	Window interior color
Tc	Title color
Pc	Prompting color
Fc	Field highlighting color

designed so that each sets a different bit in a byte. This is done so we can easily manipulate the different frame styles while keeping their encoding as tight as possible.

As you go through **scrnsty**, you may notice the use of the **LineChars** array, which contains several hexadecimal values. These correspond to the text mode character codes that are required to draw such graphics shapes as lines, T-intersections, and the like. For convenience, **scrnsty** also defines an enumerated data type, **LineChar**, which lists each of the types of characters available in the **LineChars** array. Note that this array supports single, double, and dashed lines.

Finally, **scrnsty.cpp** defines a set of default window styles. For instance, the variables **WindowStyle** and **ButtonStyle** define two typical screen styles that we'll use later. You could also invent your own.

Note that, because the window styles are defined by combinations of unique bit patterns, it is possible to modify a window style by adding or subtracting a particular style from a previously defined one. For instance, **WindowStyle** is defined by adding the following attributes in the statement:

```
WindowStyle = Swappable + Closeable + WithShadow + BorderPrompt +
              OutlineMove;
```

A window style for a window that has all of these features, except shadows, could later be defined as:

```
ShadowlessWindows = WindowStyle - WithShadow;
```

Working with the Keyboard

Thus far we've created several low-level utilities to support the window objects that we'll develop in later chapters. We will also need a few primitives to support the keyboard, which we'll focus on next.

The keyboard tools, which are contained in the source files **keybrd.h** and **keybrd.cpp** (Listings 3.5 and 3.6, respectively) are not object oriented. They are, however, designed to work with the other OOP interface tools that we'll develop.

The **keybrd.h** file provides several constants to represent various key combinations. Its companion file, **keybrd.cpp**, provides two keyboard support routines: **KeyEvent()**, which retrieves a keypress if one exists, and **IsShiftArrow()**, which determines whether a key code is one of the shift-arrow codes.

However, before we look at these functions, we should review how the PC manages keyboard input. Usually when we press a key on the keyboard, we think of it as generating a single character value that corresponds to the ASCII code of the key pressed. Because only a limited number of encodings are possible in a single byte, the PC keyboard actually returns a 2-byte sequence for each key pressed. This is called an extended scan code and is used to support the function, ALT, and cursor keys in addition to the normal ASCII characters. The **keybrd** toolkit contains many of the common extended scan codes conveniently defined as constants.

Many applications never look at the extra byte in the extended scan code, but we're interested in capturing the extended key value so that we can easily represent keyboard events with a single integer—the same representation we'll be using for the other events in our screen tools later in the book. Therefore we'll use the **bioskey()** function to return the complete extended scan code.

The **bioskey()** routine accesses the keyboard through BIOS's interrupt 0x16. The function returns either the extended scan code of the key that has been pressed or the status of the shift keys. Depending on the value of the parameter **Cmd**, one of three actions can occur.

The function **KeyEvent()**, which is also included in our toolkit, illustrates how **bioskey()** is used. This routine is written specifically for the interface tools that we'll soon present, and with events in mind. Basically, **KeyEvent()** checks to see whether a key has been pressed. If one has, it removes the key's code from the keyboard buffer. (This last action is very important; without it, the key's code would remain, and successive calls to **KeyEvent()** would return the same key code.) If no key is pending, **KeyEvent()** does not wait, but instead returns the value zero, which means there's no event. In fact, we have a special event code, called **Idle**, that is defined to be zero. You'll see this defined and used in future chapters.

The other function in our keyboard package, **IsShiftArrow()**, tests a key code to see if it's for one of the Shift-arrow keys. The Shift-arrow keys will be used in the interface tools to move screen objects. We've conveniently included **IsShift-Arrow()** in our keyboard package to check for one of these key combinations.

Testing the Screen and Keyboard

Before we leave this chapter, the tools we've developed should be tested. The following program, **sktest.cpp**, uses many of the routines in **txunit.cpp** and **keybrd.cpp**. Refer to the explanations in the code for detailed descriptions of what you should see on the screen.

```
// sktest.cpp: This program calls most of the functions
// in txunit and keybrd

#include <dos.h>
#include "txunit.h"
#include "keybrd.h"
```

```
main()
{
  int K, X, Y;

  TxBuff Scrn(VideoPtr());
  Scrn.SetSize(80, 25);  // REMEMBER TO ALWAYS CALL SETSIZE

  // Put a white fill pattern on the screen

  Scrn.Fill(0, 0, 80, 25, 176, 0x0f);

  // Alias another txbuff region to start at (30,7)
  // Note that the size must still reflect full scrn!

  TxBuff Win(Scrn.TxRam);
  Win.SetSize(80, 25);
  Win.SetLocn(30, 7);

  // Save a 23 x 7 portion of the screen starting at this region
  // into a save buffer, allocated off the heap.

  TxBuff SaveBuff(0);
  SaveBuff.SetSize(23, 7);
  SaveBuff.Xfr(0, 0, 23, 7, &Win, 0, 0);

  // Draw a white window with a shadow. Note that the shadow only
  // shows up in color mode. Coordinates are relative to Win.

  Win.Fill(0, 0, 21, 6, ' ', 0x70);
  Win.FillB(21, 1, 2, 6, 0x08, 1); // Vertical shadow
  Win.FillB(1, 6, 22, 1, 0x08, 1); // Horizontal shadow

  // Put some lines of text on the window. Note how we must skip
  // over the length byte, and  pass the length of the string.

  Win.HzWrtB(1, 1, "I am a window. Use");
  Win.HzWrtB(1, 2, "shift arrow keys to");
  Win.HzWrtB(1, 3, "move me. Use ENTER");
  Win.HzWrtB(1, 4, "key to quit ...   ");

  // Move the window in an event loop. Look for shift arrow
  // keys, and move the window by swapping to and from
  // the save buffer. Quit when Esc key is pressed and put
  // window back where it came from.

  X = 30; Y = 7;

  do {
    K = bioskey(0);  // Wait for keypress
    if (IsShiftArrow(K)) {
      Scrn.Swap(X, Y, 23, 7, &SaveBuff, 0, 0);  // Hide
      switch (K) {
        case ShiftLeft:  if (X > 0)  X-;        break;
```

```
        case ShiftRight: if (X < (80-23)) X++;  break;
        case ShiftUpKey: if (Y > 0)  Y--;       break;
        case ShiftDnKey: if (Y < (25-7)) Y++;   break;
        default: ;
      }
      Scrn.Swap(X, Y, 23, 7, &SaveBuff, 0, 0);  // Show
      Win.SetLocn(X, Y); // Make sure to set new location too!
  }
} while (K != CrKey);

// Move window back to center

Scrn.Swap(X, Y, 23, 7, &SaveBuff, 0, 0);
Scrn.Swap(30, 7, 23, 7, &SaveBuff, 0, 0);
Win.SetLocn(30,7); // Make sure to set window coordinates

// Put new messages up. Go through loop and move
// a little single character scanner until keypress

Win.Fill(0, 0, 21, 6, ' ', 0x70);
Win.HzWrtB(2, 1, "Now, below is a ");
Win.HzWrtB(2, 2, "scanner. Press  ");
Win.HzWrtB(2, 3, "Enter to stop it");

X = 0;
do {
 Win.Fill(X,4,1,1,' ',0x70);   // Erase scanner
 if (X < 19) X++; else X = 1;
 Win.Fill(X,4,1,1,176,0x70);   // Draw scanner
 delay(10);
 K = KeyEvent();  // Look for, but don't wait for keypress
} while (K == 0);

// Now put up some menu entries. Use up and down arrow to
// select menu entry. Cr Key selects choice, Esc Key quits.

char *MenuChoices[4] = {
  "Do Something",
  "Be Lazy      ",
  "Just Say No ",
  "Go to Miami "
};

Win.Fill(0, 0, 21, 6, ' ', 0x70);
Win.HzWrtB(1, 1, MenuChoices[0]);
Win.HzWrtB(1, 2, MenuChoices[1]);
Win.HzWrtB(1, 3, MenuChoices[2]);
Win.HzWrtB(1, 4, MenuChoices[3]);

Win.HzWrt(0, 8,  "Use arrow keys to move", 0x7f);
Win.HzWrt(0, 9,  "highlight. Use ENTER  ", 0x7f);
Win.HzWrt(0, 10, "to select, ESC to     ", 0x7f);
Win.HzWrt(0, 11, "abort ...             ", 0x7f);
```

```
   X - 1; Y - 1;
   Win.HzFillB(X, Y, 0x07, 1, 19);       // Put up first highlight

   do {
     K - bioskey(0);                      // Wait for key
     Win.HzFillB(X, Y, 0x70, 1, 19);    // Erase old highlight
     switch (K) {
       case UpKey:   if (Y > 1)  Y—; else Y - 4; break;
       case DownKey: if (Y < 4) Y++; else Y - 1;  break;
       default: ;
     }
     Win.HzFillB(X, Y, 0x07, 1, 19);    // Put up new highlight
   } while ((K != CrKey) && (K != EscKey));

   Win.Fill(0, 8, 22, 4, 176, 0x0f);

   // Process the choice

   if (K -- CrKey)  {
      char Saywhat[80];
      strcpy(Saywhat, "Sorry, we won't let you ");
      strcat(Saywhat, MenuChoices[Y-1]);
      Win.HzWrt(0, 8, Saywhat, 0x7f);
   }
   else {
      Win.HzWrt(0, 8, "Can't make up your mind, huh?", 0x7f);
   }

   // Scroll up a line. Put in another menu entry

   Win.HzWrt(0, 9, "But press RETURN and watch the menu scroll!", 0x7f);
   bioskey(0);

   Win.Scroll(1, 1, 19, 4, UpScroll, 1);
   Win.HzWrtB(1, 4, "*** The End ***");
}
```

Listing 3.1   txunit.h

```
// Provides low-level screen support through the TxBuff object

#ifndef H_TXUNIT
#define H_TXUNIT

#include "scrnsty.h"
#include "string.h"

struct Texel { unsigned char Ch, Attr; };
typedef Texel far *TexelPtr;

class TxBuff {
```

```
public:
  int Wd, Ht;       // Width and height in texels
  TexelPtr TxRam;   // Pointer to texel buffer
  TexelPtr OrgPtr;  // Pointer to origin
  char Aliased;     // True if buffer is aliased
  TxBuff(TexelPtr T);
  TxBuff(int W, int H, TexelPtr T);
  ~TxBuff(void);
  void SetRamPtr(TexelPtr T);
  TexelPtr TxRamAddr(int X, int Y);
  TexelPtr RelAddr(int X, int Y);
  void SetSize(int W, int H);
  void SetLocn(int X, int Y);
  void Swap(int X, int Y, int W, int H, TxBuff *Other, int Xs, int Ys);
  void Xfr(int X, int Y, int W, int H, TxBuff *Other, int Xs, int Ys);
  void Scroll(int X, int Y, int W, int H, ScrollDir Sd, int Amt);
  void Fill(int X, int Y, int W, int H, char Ch, char Attr);
  void FillB(int X, int Y, int W, int H, char Ch, char Opt);
  void HzWrt(int X, int Y, char *Str, char Attr, unsigned Cnt);
  void HzWrt(int X, int Y, char *Str, char Attr) {
    HzWrt(X, Y, Str, Attr, strlen(Str));
  }
  void HzWrtB(int X, int Y, char *Str, unsigned Cnt);
  void HzWrtB(int X, int Y, char *Str) {
    HzWrtB(X, Y, Str, strlen(Str));
  }
  void HzFill(int X, int Y, char Ch, char Attr, unsigned Cnt) {
    Fill(X, Y, Cnt, 1, Ch, Attr);
  }
  void HzFillB(int X, int Y, char Ch, char Opt, unsigned Cnt) {
    FillB(X, Y, Cnt, 1, Ch, Opt);
  }
};

TexelPtr VideoPtr(unsigned &Vmode, unsigned &Vpage);
TexelPtr VideoPtr(void);
#endif
```

Listing 3.2   txunit.cpp

```
// Provides low-level screen support through the TxBuff object
#include <dos.h>
#include "txunit.h"

#define True 1
#define False 0

TxBuff::TxBuff(TexelPtr T)
// Initializes a TxBuff object. T is a pointer to the texel buffer
// to use or 0 if TxBuff is supposed to allocate its own texel
// buffer. The height and width are set to 0.
```

```
{
  Wd = 0; Ht = 0;
  SetRamPtr(T);
}


TxBuff::TxBuff(int W, int H, TexelPtr T)
// Initializes a TxBuff object. T is a pointer to the texel buffer
// to use or 0 if TxBuff is supposed to allocate its own texel
// buffer. Then the width and height are set.
{
  SetRamPtr(T);
  SetSize(W, H);
}


void TxBuff::SetRamPtr(TexelPtr T)
// Initializes a TxBuff object. T is a pointer to the texel buffer
// to use or 0 if TxBuff is supposed to allocate its own texel
// buffer.
{
  if (T) {
     Aliased = True;
     TxRam = T;
  }
  else {
     Aliased = False;
     TxRam = 0;
  }
  OrgPtr = TxRam;
}


TxBuff::~TxBuff(void)
// Free texel buffer in TxBuff if object was not aliased
{
  if (!Aliased) delete[Wd*Ht] TxRam;
}


TexelPtr TxBuff::TxRamAddr(int X, int Y)
// Computes pointer for (X,Y) location relative to TxRam
{
  return TxRam + Y*Wd + X;
}


TexelPtr TxBuff::RelAddr(int X, int Y)
// Computes pointer for (X,Y) location relative to OrgPtr
{
  return OrgPtr + Y*Wd + X;
}


void TxBuff::SetSize(int W, int H)
// Set size of texel buffer. If not aliased, and the size
// has been set before, don't reallocate memory unless the
// new size is bigger.
{
```

```
      if (!Aliased) { // Want buffer on heap
         if (!TxRam) { // Allocate for first time
            TxRam = new Texel[W*H];
         }
         else if (W*H > Wd*Ht)  { // Reallocate?
            delete [Wd*Ht] TxRam;
            TxRam = new Texel[W*H];
         }
         OrgPtr = TxRam;
      }
    Wd = W; Ht = H;
}


void TxBuff::SetLocn(int X, int Y)
// Set location of OrgPtr—which is the pointer into TxBuff
// which operations such as Fill, FillB, HzWrt use.
{
   OrgPtr = TxRamAddr(X, Y);
}


void TxBuff::Swap(int X, int Y, int W, int H, TxBuff *Other, int Xs,
                  int Ys)
// Swaps data between the Other Txbuff, starting as (Xs, Ys)
// and this object's OrgPtr, starting at X,Y, and swapping a region
// of width W, height H. The swap takes place row by row.
// Handle possible memory overlap by reversing the directions
// of the swap, assuming that the only way overlap can occur
// is when we're swapping memory within ourselves.
{
   int I, J;
   Texel T;
   TexelPtr Dp, Sp;
   Dp = RelAddr(X, Y);
   Sp = Other->RelAddr(Xs, Ys);
   if (FP_OFF(Sp) < FP_OFF(Dp)) { // Might need to switch directions
      for (I=0; I<H; I++) {
         Dp = RelAddr(X, Y+I);
         Sp = Other->RelAddr(Xs, Ys+I);
         for (J=0; J<W; J++) {
            T = *Dp;
            *Dp++ = *Sp;
            *Sp++ = T;
         }
      }
   }
   else {
      for (I=H-1; I>=0; I--) {
         Dp = RelAddr(X, Y+I) + W;
         Sp = Other->RelAddr(Xs, Ys+I) + W;
         for (J=0; J<W; J++) {
            T = *(--Dp);
            *Dp = *(--Sp);
```

```
                 *Sp - T;
            }
          }
        }
      }


void TxBuff::Xfr(int X, int Y, int W, int H,
                  TxBuff *Other, int Xs, int Ys)
// Transfers data from the Other Txbuff, starting as (Xs, Ys) into
// this object's OrgPtr, starting at X,Y, and transferring a region
// of width W, height H. The transfer takes place row by row.
// Handle possible memory overlap by reversing the directions
// of the transfer, assuming that the only way overlap can occur
// is when we're transferring memory within ourselves.
{
  int I, J;
  TexelPtr Dp, Sp;
  Dp - RelAddr(X, Y);
  Sp - Other->RelAddr(Xs, Ys);
  if (FP_OFF(Dp) < FP_OFF(Sp)) { // Might need to switch directions
     for (I-0; I<H; I++) {
        Dp - RelAddr(X, Y+I);
        Sp - Other->RelAddr(Xs, Ys+I);
        for (J-0; J<W; J++) *Dp++ - *Sp++;
     }
  }
  else {
    for (I-H-1; I>-0; I-) {
      Dp - RelAddr(X, Y+I) + W;
      Sp - Other->RelAddr(Xs, Ys+I) + W;
      for (J-0; J<W; J++) *(-Dp) - *(-Sp);
    }
  }
}


void TxBuff::Scroll(int X, int Y, int W, int H, ScrollDir Sd, int Amt)
// Scroll the text in a specified direction by doing
// overlapping transfers with this
{
  switch(Sd) {
    case UpScroll:    Xfr(X, Y, W, H, this, X, Y+Amt); break;
    case DnScroll:    Xfr(X, Y+Amt, W, H, this, X, Y); break;
    case LeftScroll:  Xfr(X, Y, W, H, this, X+Amt, Y); break;
    case RightScroll: Xfr(X+Amt, Y, W, H, this, X, Y); break;
    default: ;
  }
}


void TxBuff::Fill(int X, int Y, int W, int H, char Ch, char Attr)
// Fill a rectangular region with a particular character and
// attribute. The coordinates are relative to this canvas.
{
  for (int I-0; I<H; I++) {
```

```
        TexelPtr Tp = RelAddr(X, Y+I);
        for (int J=0; J<W; J++) {
            Tp->Ch = Ch;
            Tp->Attr = Attr;
            Tp++;
        }
    }
}

void TxBuff::FillB(int X, int Y, int W, int H, char Ch, char Opt)
// Fill either the character or the attribute fields in a
// rectangular region. The coordinates are relative to this canvas
{
  for (int I=0; I<H; I++) {
     char far *P = (char far *)RelAddr(X,Y+I);
     if (Opt) P++; // Skip over char byte
     for (int J=0; J<W; J++) {
        *P = Ch;
        P += 2;
     }
  }
}

void TxBuff::HzWrt(int X, int Y, char *Str, char Attr, unsigned Cnt)
// Writes to (X,Y) locn (relative to OrgPtr)
{
  TexelPtr Tp = RelAddr(X, Y);
  for (int I=0; I<Cnt; I++, Tp++) {
     Tp->Ch = *Str++;
     Tp->Attr = Attr;
  }
}

void TxBuff::HzWrtB(int X, int Y, char *Str, unsigned Cnt)
// Writes to (X,Y) locn (relative to OrgPtr)
{
  char far *P = (char far *)RelAddr(X, Y);
  for (int J=0; J<Cnt; J++) {
     *P = *Str++;
      P += 2;                    // Skip over attribute
  }
}

TexelPtr VideoPtr(unsigned &Vmode, unsigned &Vpage)
// Discover what text mode we're in, and return video addr
{
  union REGS Regs;
  unsigned Segment, Offset;
  Regs.h.ah = 15;
  int86(0x10, &Regs, &Regs);
  Vmode = Regs.h.al;  Vpage = Regs.h.bh;
  if (Vmode == 7) Segment = 0xb000; else Segment = 0xb800;
  Offset = Vpage * (unsigned)0x1000;
```

```
    return TexelPtr((long(Segment) << 16) | long(Offset));
}

TexelPtr VideoPtr(void)
{
  unsigned Vm, Vp;
  return VideoPtr(Vm, Vp);
}
```

Listing 3.3   scrnsty.h

```
// Screen style definitions

#ifndef H_SCRNSTY
#define H_SCRNSTY

inline unsigned char ForeGround(unsigned char attr)
{
  return attr & 0x0f;
}

inline unsigned char BackGround(unsigned char attr)
{
  return (attr >> 4) & 0x0f;
}

enum LineChar {
  Ulc, Llc, Urc, Lrc, LTee, RTee, UpTee, DnTee, HzBar, VtBar
};

extern char LineChars[4][10];

enum ScrollDir  { UpScroll, DnScroll, LeftScroll, RightScroll };

struct ColorPak { unsigned char Bc, Wc, Tc, Pc, Fc; };

// Border styles

const int NoBorder  = 0x00; // For both text and graphics
const int Single    = 0x10; // For text mode
const int Double    = 0x20; // For text mode
const int Dashed    = 0x30; // For text mode
const int Solid     = 0x10; // For graphics mode
const int Recessed  = 0x20; // For graphics mode
const int Relief    = 0x30; // For graphics mode

// Frame styles

const int Swappable    = 0x01;
const int Closeable    = 0x02;
const int SEShadow     = 0x04;
```

```
const int NEShadow    = 0x08;
const int NWShadow    = 0x10;
const int SWShadow    = 0x20;
const int OutlineMove = 0x40;
const int BorderPrompt = 0x80;
const int Stretchable = 0x100;

// A shadow bit mask

const int AnyShadow = SEShadow + NEShadow + NWShadow + SWShadow;

// A set of predefined color packs and styles

extern ColorPak BlueColors;
extern ColorPak CyanColors;
extern ColorPak RedColors;
extern ColorPak InvColors;
extern ColorPak MonoColors;
extern ColorPak ErrColors;
extern ColorPak MsgColors;
extern ColorPak GrphColors;
extern ColorPak DefColors;

extern ColorPak DefColors;
extern int WithShadow;
extern int WindowStyle;
extern int ButtonStyle;

#endif
```

Listing 3.4   scrnsty.cpp

```
// Style definitions

#include "scrnsty.h"

char LineChars[4][10] = {
    // Blank characters
    {' ', ' ', ' ', ' ', ' ', ' ', ' ', ' ', ' ', ' '},
    // Single line characters
    {0xda, 0xc0, 0xbf, 0xd9, 0xb4, 0xc3, 0xc1, 0xc2, 0xc4, 0xb3},
    // Double line characters
    {0xc9, 0xc8, 0xbb, 0xbc, 0xb4, 0xb9, 0xca, 0xcb, 0xcd, 0xba},
    // Dashed line characters
    {0xda, 0xc0, 0xbf, 0xd9, 0xb4, 0xc3, 0xc1, 0xc2, 0x2d, 0x7c}
};

char barchars[2][6] = {
    //sbar, sbut, upar, dnar, lfar, rtar
    { 0xb0, 0xb2, 0x18, 0x19, 0x1b, 0x1a },
    { 0x20, 0x04, 0x1e, 0x1f, 0x11, 0x10 }
};
```

```
// A set of predefined color packs

ColorPak BlueColors = {0x17, 0x1e, 0x3e, 0x5e, 0x1b};
ColorPak CyanColors = {0x31, 0x30, 0x31, 0x63, 0x70};
ColorPak RedColors  = {0x4c, 0x40, 0x4e, 0x74, 0x4e};
ColorPak InvColors  = {0x70, 0x70, 0x70, 0x0f, 0x70};
ColorPak MonoColors = {0x07, 0x0f, 0x0f, 0x70, 0x70};
ColorPak ErrColors  = {0x4f, 0x4f, 0x40, 0x04, 0x40};
ColorPak MsgColors  = {0x2f, 0x2f, 0x2e, 0x70, 0x2d};
ColorPak GrphColors = {0xb8, 0x30, 0x31, 0x63, 0x70};

ColorPak DefColors = MonoColors;

int WithShadow = SEShadow;
int WindowStyle = Swappable + Closeable + WithShadow +
                  BorderPrompt + OutlineMove;
int ButtonStyle = Swappable + WithShadow + BorderPrompt;
```

Listing 3.5 keybrd.h

```
// keyboard driver: keybrd.h

#ifndef H_KEYBRD
#define H_KEYBRD

#include <bios.h>

// Shift Status Masks

const unsigned InsertOn      = 0x80;
const unsigned CapsLkOn      = 0x40;
const unsigned NumLkOn       = 0x20;
const unsigned ScrollLkOn    = 0x10;
const unsigned AltPressed    = 0x08;
const unsigned CtrlPressed   = 0x04;
const unsigned LShiftPressed = 0x02;
const unsigned RShiftPressed = 0x01;

// Common scan-ascii codes

const unsigned CtrlC         = 0x2e03;
const unsigned CtrlH         = 0x2308;
const unsigned CtrlI         = 0x1709;
const unsigned CtrlL         = 0x260c;
const unsigned CtrlK         = 0x250b;
const unsigned CtrlJ         = 0x240a;
const unsigned CtrlU         = 0x1615;
const unsigned CtrlR         = 0x1312;
const unsigned CrKey         = 0x1c0d;
const unsigned CtrlCrKey     = 0x1c0a;
const unsigned UpKey         = 0x4800;
const unsigned DownKey       = 0x5000;
```

```
const unsigned LeftKey       = 0x4b00;
const unsigned RightKey      = 0x4d00;
const unsigned ShiftLeft     = 0x4b34;
const unsigned ShiftRight    = 0x4d36;
const unsigned DelKey        = 0x5300;
const unsigned InsKey        = 0x5200;
const unsigned BsKey         = 0x0e08;
const unsigned SpaceBar      = 0x3920;
const unsigned PgUpKey       = 0x4900;
const unsigned PgDnKey       = 0x5100;
const unsigned CtrlPgUp      = 0x8400;
const unsigned CtrlPgDn      = 0x7600;
const unsigned ShiftUpKey    = 0x4838;
const unsigned ShiftDnKey    = 0x5032;
const unsigned ShiftPgUpKey  = 0x4939;
const unsigned ShiftPgDnKey  = 0x5133;
const unsigned HomeKey       = 0x4700;
const unsigned EndKey        = 0x4f00;
const unsigned EscKey        = 0x011b;
const unsigned TabKey        = 0x0f09;
const unsigned ShiftTabKey   = 0x0f00;
const unsigned AltD          = 0x2000;
const unsigned AltE          = 0x1200;
const unsigned AltI          = 0x1700;
const unsigned AltN          = 0x3100;
const unsigned AltR          = 0x1300;
const unsigned AltS          = 0x1f00;
const unsigned AltT          = 0x1400;
const unsigned AltX          = 0x2d00;
const unsigned F6Key         = 0x4000;
const unsigned F8Key         = 0x4200;
const unsigned F10Key        = 0x4400;

extern unsigned KeyEvent(void);
extern int IsShiftArrow(unsigned k);

#endif
```

Listing 3.6   keybrd.cpp

```
// keyboard driver: keybrd.cpp

#include "keybrd.h"

unsigned KeyEvent(void)
// Looks for a key pressed. If found, the key
// is removed from the keyboard buffer and returned.
{
  unsigned E;
  E = bioskey(1);
  if (E != 0) E = bioskey(0);
```

```
   return E;
}

int IsShiftArrow(unsigned k)
// Returns true if k is a shift-arrow key combination
{
   return (k == ShiftLeft)  || (k == ShiftRight) ||
          (k == ShiftUpKey) || (k == ShiftDnKey);
}
```

4

An Object-Oriented Mouse Toolkit

 For the rest of this book our goal is to develop powerful text- and graphics-based window and menuing packages; in this chapter we'll create a mouse toolkit that will form the foundation for the user interaction in these applications. Our mouse tools are unique because they are implemented using Turbo C++'s OOP features. The tools consist of a mouse object that encapsulates the operations and state of a mouse. Although we won't be using inheritance in our mouse object, we could use this OOP property to extend the features of the mouse package or to support other input devices using the same mouse interface.

Overview of the Mouse Toolkit

As we construct our mouse toolkit we won't focus on the minute details of using a mouse. Instead, we'll concentrate on commonly used operations, such as determining the position of the mouse, controlling the display of its cursor, and reading the state of its buttons. These utilities are combined into the files **msmouse.h** and **msmouse.cpp** shown in Listings 4.1 and 4.2, respectively.

For simplicity, our mouse package is written to support a Microsoft (MS) compatible mouse. The MS mouse by far is the most popular mouse standard. In fact, many of the non-Microsoft mice, digitizing tablets, and other pointing devices are capable of emulating the MS standard.

Working with the Mouse

Writing a program that works with a mouse is surprisingly straightforward. Why? Most of the low-level details of a mouse's operations are handled by a memory-resident program (often referred to as the mouse driver) called **mouse.com** or **mouse.sys**. This program, usually loaded when the PC starts up, is responsible for the intricate details of controlling the mouse, updating the mouse cursor, and responding to program queries. Our task, therefore, is to provide a mouse package that serves as a wrapper for the low-level mouse driver. Using this approach, we'll be able to create more flexible routines to control and process the mouse.

Table 4.1 lists the low-level mouse driver functions that we'll use to support our object-oriented mouse tools. Keep in mind that these commonly used functions represent only a subset of the routines included with the MS mouse driver. (If you're interested in learning more about the other mouse functions, refer to the *Microsoft Mouse Programmer's Reference Guide*.)

Associated with each mouse function in Table 4.1 is a unique function code and a set of input and output parameters. A mouse function is called by executing a software interrupt and passing parameters to and from the mouse driver through the processor's registers. These parameters include such things as the position of the mouse cursor and the status of the mouse buttons. When we put together the mouse tools you will see how the different parameters are used.

Table 4.1 The mouse driver functions used in msmouse.cpp

Function Code	Description
0	Obtains the mouse status and initializes the mouse
1	Displays the mouse cursor
2	Hides the mouse cursor
3	Gets mouse position and button status
4	Moves the mouse cursor to a specified row and column
5	Gets the button press information
6	Gets the button release information
9	Sets the mouse cursor shape in graphics mode

The Mouse Object

You might now be wondering how OOP can help you tame the mouse. By creating a mouse object, you can package the control logic of the mouse along with the functions most commonly found in mouse-based programs. As you might guess, this approach enables you to hide the details involved in using a mouse. The following is a summary of the main features for the mouse object we'll be developing.

1. Provides a wrapper to access the low-level mouse functions

2. Allows you to process the mouse in both text and graphics modes

3. Includes data members to keep track of the position of the mouse

4. Provides high-level member functions to process mouse events (button presses and releases)

We'll start by creating the main building block of the mouse toolkit—the class **MouseObject**:

```
class MouseObject {
protected:
  int OldX, OldY;    // Used solely by Moved to keep position
  char OK;           // True if mouse initialized
  char MouseOff;     // True if mouse is disabled (Default)
  char LowRes;       // True if in 320 x 200 graphics mode
  char TextMode;     // True if in text mode
public:
  int X, Y, Dx, Dy; // Keeps track of the mouse's movement
  MouseObject(void);
  void Setup(VideoModeType VideoMode);
  int  DriverExists(void);
  int  SetupOK(void);
  void Hide(void);
  void Show(void);
  unsigned Status(int &Mx, int &My);
  unsigned ButtonStatus(void);
  int PressCnt(unsigned ButtonMask);
  int ReleaseCnt(unsigned ButtonMask);
  unsigned Event(int &Mx, int &My);
  unsigned WaitForAnyEvent(int &Mx, int &My);
  void WaitForEvent(unsigned E, int &Mx, int &My);
  int  Moved(void);
  void Move(int Mx, int My);
  void TurnOn(void);
  void TurnOff(void);
```

```
int  Operating(void);
void SetGCursor(const MouseCursor &NewCursor);
};
```

The data members **OK, MouseOff, LowRes**, and so on, store the state of the mouse. They specify whether the mouse is enabled, which screen mode the mouse is being used in, and its location.

Most of the member functions in **MouseObject** perform simple tasks such as hiding and showing the mouse or obtaining its position. These interface functions, including **Hide()**, **Show()**, **Status()**, **PressCnt()**, **ReleaseCnt()**, **Move()**, and **SetGCursor()**, don't have to do much more than make direct calls to the internal mouse driver routines. Of course, by packaging the mouse driver calls as member functions we can add our own error checking and set our own state variables. If the Microsoft mouse driver ever changes, ideally, the interface member functions can easily be updated so that the program that uses the mouse object doesn't have to be changed.

The member functions **Event()**, **WaitForEvent()**, and **WaitForAnyEvent()**, however, serve as higher level routines that are used to process mouse events. After we cover the basics of accessing the mouse driver functions, the member functions included with **MouseObject** will be explored in greater detail.

Communicating with the Mouse Driver

As mentioned earlier, the internal mouse functions are accessed through a software interrupt. In particular, all communication with a mouse is channeled through software interrupt 0x33. In Turbo C++, we use the **int86()** function to invoke interrupt 33h as shown:

```
int86(0x33, &RegisterValues, &RegisterValues);
```

The first parameter is the interrupt number (always 0x33 for the mouse driver) and the second is a structure of type **REGS** predefined in the include file **dos.h**. The structure fields, which correspond to the registers in the processor, are used to communicate with the mouse driver. For instance, the value in the AX register at the time of the interrupt specifies which mouse function is being called. These values correspond to the function numbers shown in Table 4.1. For example, if the AX register is assigned the value 1 and interrupt 33h is called, the mouse function 1 would execute, causing the mouse cursor to be displayed. The other registers, BX, CX, and DX are used to pass parameters back and forth to the mouse driver. The process of invoking a mouse function and using these register values in a program is illustrated in Figure 4.1.

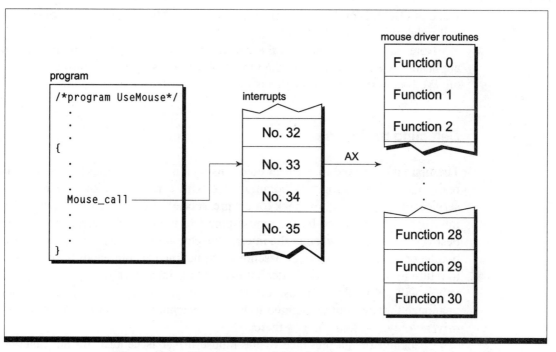

Figure 4.1   The process of invoking a mouse function

Declaring and Using a Mouse Object

To simplify the use of the **msmouse** package, a global variable called **Mouse** will be declared as an instance of the **MouseObject** class. Application programs that use **msmouse**, therefore, won't need to declare a mouse object. The **Mouse** variable is declared and initialized by its constructor:

```
MouseObject Mouse;
```

The constructor is meant to be application independent. In fact, all it does is set the two boolean flags **OK** and **MouseOff** to signal that the mouse is not operating. In other words, **OK** is set to **False** (a value of 0) and **MouseOff** is set to **True** (a value of 1). We'll rely on other member functions to actually configure the mouse to the needs of an application.

The **OK** variable is used internally by the mouse class to indicate whether the mouse is correctly installed and therefore can be used. You can also check the state of this variable in an application to test whether the mouse is present. Actually, the boolean member function **SetupOK()** is included in **MouseObject** to return the value of **OK**. It is probably better programming practice to use this encapsulated call rather than directly access **OK**.

Note that the statements in the constructor do not enable the mouse. In an application we must configure the mouse object to its needs and turn the mouse on. We'll now show you how this is done.

Detecting the Mouse

The first task we need to perform before using a mouse is to make sure that it is really there. Since programs communicate with a mouse through an interrupt service routine, one way to check for the presence of a mouse is to test whether the interrupt vector serviced by the mouse points to the mouse driver. Actually, the best we can do is test whether the interrupt vector at 0x33 does not have a NULL pointer or an **Iret** command (an assembly instruction that commands the computer to return immediately to the code that invoked the interrupt). In either case, these values will tell us that a mouse driver is definitely not installed. This does not guarantee that the routine pointed to by the interrupt vector is indeed the mouse driver—only that *something* is there.

Checking for the presence of the mouse driver is handled by the function **DriverExists()** in **MouseObject** which returns nonzero only if the mouse code passes the test described here. Retrieving the interrupt vector is performed by calling the Turbo C++ function **getvect()** and then testing its returned value:

```
address - getvect(MsCall);
return (address !- NULL) &&
       (*(unsigned char far *)address !- Iret);
```

Here, **MsCall** is a constant defined as 0x33 in the **msmouse.h** header file. We'll be using this constant to access the mouse interrupt vector. The variable **address** is a pointer to the interrupt vector value. The test to check whether the vector points to the mouse driver is performed by the next statement in **DriverExists()** using a simple boolean expression that tests to see whether **address** is not **NULL** and not equal to **Iret**.

We won't call **DriverExists()** directly. Instead, another mouse initialization function, **Setup()**, will be using **DriverExists()**. We'll discuss this routine next.

Configuring the Mouse

The responsibility of calling **DriverExists()** lies with the **MouseObject** function **Setup()**, which sets the data member **OK** to the value returned by **DriverExists()**.

However, checking for the existence of a mouse involves yet another step. We must send a reset message to the mouse driver to make sure that the mouse successfully responds to our message. The following program is how this task is accomplished:

```
if (OK) { // Mouse present, but will it reset?
  regs.x.ax - 0;
  int86(MsCall, &regs, &regs);
  if (regs.x.ax -- 0) OK - False;
}
```

The reset operation is performed by function 0, which returns a value of zero in the AX register only if the mouse responds to the reset command. If the mouse driver responds correctly to the reset command, then the **MouseObject** variable **OK** is set to **True**; otherwise it is set to **False**. As described earlier, an application can check the state of the **OK** flag by calling the member function **SetupOK()**. If **SetupOK()** returns **False**, for instance, you may want to print an appropriate message and terminate the program.

If the mouse does respond to function 0, a few bookkeeping chores are performed: The mouse position is set to the top-left of the screen, and the mouse cursor is turned on. Another task of **Setup()** is to call the member function **TurnOn()** which sets the data member **MouseOff** to **False** and displays the mouse cursor. This flag will always be tested at the beginning of each member function by invoking **Operating()**, to ensure that the mouse is enabled. When **Operating()** returns **False**, the mouse member functions are designed to return with no actions taken. This feature is useful particularly when code is written to support the mouse, but the mouse is not actually being used. Rather than modifying the code, you can simply set the **MouseOff** flag to **True** by calling **TurnOff()** to disable the mouse member functions.

The **Setup()** function performs one other important job—it sets the appropriate flags in the mouse object to indicate which screen mode the mouse is being used with. As we'll see later, we need to know the active screen mode so that the mouse coordinates can be adjusted. The flags **TextMode** and **LowRes** are set based on the parameter **VideoMode** which can take on one of the following **VideoModeType** values defined in **msmouse.h**:

```
enum VideoModeType {TextScrn, LowResGr, HerculesGr, Graphics};
```

As you're looking over **Setup()** presented in Listing 4.2, you might notice the following unusual statement:

```
if (VideoMode -- HerculesGr)
  *(char far *)MK_FP(0x0040,0x0049) - 6;
```

What does it do? This statement is needed to properly set the BIOS video mode so that the mouse can work correctly with the Hercules card in graphics mode. Note: Use the **TextScrn** constant if you are using the Hercules card in text mode.

Controlling the Mouse Cursor

The location of the mouse is indicated on the screen by its cursor. In text mode, the mouse cursor is a highlighted character block. In graphics mode the cursor takes on a different shape—an arrow or a special shape that you define. As you move the mouse, the position of the cursor changes to reflect the mouse's movement. This is all handled automatically by the mouse driver, although we can control the mouse's location by calling one of the internal mouse driver functions as we saw in **Setup()**.

The member functions **Hide()** and **Show()** are two routines in **MouseObject** that control the display of the mouse cursor. Briefly, **Hide()** removes the mouse cursor from the screen and **Show()** displays it. As an example, the **TurnOn()** member function calls **Show()** to display the mouse cursor after everything has been initialized.

Where else are **Hide()** and **Show()** used? It turns out that these two functions house some of the more commonly used mouse calls. To understand why, it's important to realize that the mouse cursor is displayed by directly manipulating the screen. Therefore, whenever one of your programs reads or writes to the screen, it must first remove the mouse cursor by calling **Hide()** so that the mouse cursor does not interfere with the screen operation. After manipulating the screen, your code can restore the mouse cursor by calling **Show()**. If this sequence is not followed, however, the screen may get messed up or the wrong value may be read from the screen.

Because of the way the mouse cursor is drawn and erased by the internal mouse driver, it is important to match every call to **Hide()** with a succeeding call to **Show()**. For instance, if you call **Hide()** twice without an intervening **Show()**, two calls are needed to make the cursor visible again.

Using Mouse Coordinates

The mouse driver provides several functions to determine the current location of the mouse, move the mouse to a particular location, and so on. Since the mouse must be able to work under several different text and graphics modes (each with its own resolution) the mouse uses its own coordinate system which doesn't always correspond to the screen's coordinates.

This system won't work for us because we need to be able to access our mouse object using coordinates that match the screen mode being used. For example, in text mode, the most convenient way to specify the mouse's location is in character coordinates, which are typically 80 columns by 25 rows. How can this be done? The easiest method involves dividing the X and Y coordinates returned from the mouse driver by eight or by multiplying each of the screen coordinates passed to the mouse driver by eight. (In the code we use three shifts to perform the division.) Similarly, in any of the 320 x 200 graphics modes, the mouse coordinates must also be adjusted. However, the high-resolution graphics modes have a one-to-one correspondence with the mouse's coordinates. The class variables **TextMode** and **LowRes**, assigned in **Setup()**, are used to select which of these adjustments must be made to the mouse's coordinates, if any.

If you examine the two member functions **Status()** and **Move()** that process mouse coordinates, you'll see that we've included code to translate internal mouse coordinates to screen coordinates. For example, **Status()** which returns the position of the mouse in the active screen coordinates contains the following conditions:

```
if (TextMode)  {
  Mx >>= 3;  // Adjust for text coordinates
  My >>= 3;
}
if (LowRes)  Mx >>= 1; // Adjust for 320 x 200 coordinates
```

where **Mx** and **My** are the coordinates returned by the mouse driver.

Moving the Mouse

At times it is useful to move the mouse cursor to a particular screen location. This is done, for instance, in **Setup()** by calling **Move()** to set the cursor to the top-left of the screen. The **Move()** routine invokes mouse function 4 to change the mouse's location. Note that **Move()** expects the coordinates passed to it to be in screen coordinates, therefore they are scaled appropriately if the mouse is being used while in text mode or in one of the 320 x 200 graphics modes.

Another movement-oriented function provided with the mouse class, called **Moved()**, returns nonzero if the mouse has been moved since the last time **Moved()** was called. This routine doesn't call an internal mouse function to test for this condition. Instead, it keeps track of the mouse's location, using **X**, **Y**, **OldX**, and **OldY**, and the amount that it has moved, using **Dx** and **Dy**.

After studying **Moved()**, you may be wondering why the variables **OldX**, **OldY**, and so on are not defined as static variables within this member function instead of placing them in the class definition where the other functions can access them.

After all, this would make these variables, which are only used by **Moved()**, retain their values and hide them from the rest of the code. However, this is not done because functions in a class are shared by all instances of that class.

For example, suppose a program has more than one mouse object such as a mouse and a light-pen—both declared as instances of the mouse class. Clearly, we would need to keep track of the movement of each pointing device separately. However, if these movement variables, like **OldX** and **OldY**, are made static within **Moved()**, they would be shared by both objects and would conflict since both objects would use the same **Moved()** function. A better design is to locate the movement variables in the class definition since each instance of the mouse class gets its own copy of the variables. Although from a traditional programming standpoint it seems more sensible to hide these variables within the only routine that uses them, this is not an advisable way to make the class definition flexible from an OOP perspective.

Working with Mouse Buttons

Mouse buttons are typically used to trigger events in a program such as activating a pull-down menu, selecting an option, closing a window, and so on. The MS mouse that our toolkit supports has two buttons. If your mouse has three buttons and is also MS compatible, the middle button is ignored.

The mouse driver supplies three types of button information: the current status of each button, the number of times a button has been pressed since the previous time checked, and the number of times a button has been released since the previous call. This status information is obtained by making calls to the internal mouse functions 3, 5, and 6, respectively. To create programs that make full use of the mouse, we'll need to implement these low-level functions. Let's look at the member functions that do this.

Detecting the current status of the mouse buttons is accomplished by invoking mouse function 3. For convenience, we've built two member functions around function 3 for obtaining button status information. The first is **Status()**, which returns both the button status and the current screen location of the mouse. The other is **ButtonStatus()**, which as its name implies, returns only the button status information. Actually, it makes a call to **Status()** and throws away the mouse location information.

When function 3 is called, the state of the two mouse buttons is returned in the BX register. This information is passed along to the caller of **Status()** without further processing. So how can we use it to determine what the state of each buttons is? First let's look at how the mouse driver encodes button information.

Figure 4.2 shows the format of the button information that function 3 returns in the BX register. As the figure indicates, the lower 2 bits actually contain the button status information. The rightmost bit (bit 0) corresponds to the left button and the second bit corresponds to the right button. Each bit is given a value of one if its corresponding button is currently being pressed. Otherwise, the bit is set to zero.

To check the status of a particular button, we'll use a bit mask. For convenience, **msmouse.h** provides the two **const** values **LeftButton** and **RightButton** that mask out the appropriate bits for their corresponding buttons:

```
const unsigned  LeftButton  -  0x0001;
const unsigned  RightButton -  0x0002;
```

Using one of these constants, the following code is how we test to see if the left button has been pressed:

```
if ((ButtonValue & LeftButton) !- 0) { /*Button pressed*/ }
  else { /*Left button not pressed*/ }
```

Checking the current state of the mouse buttons is useful, but it's difficult to write a complete program that uses the mouse if we have only this information. For instance, what happens if you press and release a button before the program has a chance to detect it? To solve this problem, the mouse driver provides functions 5 and 6 which keep track of the number of button presses and releases, respectively, since the previous time they were called. Therefore, calling these routines guarantees that we'll detect every button state change. The member functions **PressCnt()** and **ReleaseCnt()** are supplied specifically for this reason. Each

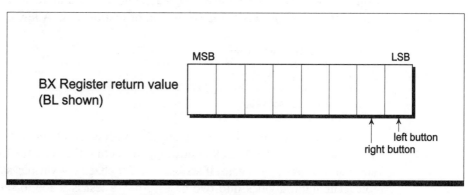

Figure 4.2   The format of the button information in BX

takes a single argument that specifies which button is to be checked (using the appropriate button masks previously discussed) and returns the number of times the button has been pressed or released since the previous time it was called. For example, the statement:

```
TimesPressed = Mouse.PressCnt(LeftButton);
```

will place the number of times the left button has been pressed into the variable **TimesPressed**.

Working with Mouse Events

Determining the status of the mouse buttons or finding out how often they have been pressed or released is valuable, but more often than not, it's useful to view these mouse actions from more abstract vantage points, which we'll call *events*. A mouse event is simply an action that is triggered by the mouse.

To process mouse events, the following member functions are included in **MouseObject**:

Member function	Description
Event()	Returns the last event
WaitForAnyEvent()	Waits until the next event occurs
WaitForEvent()	Waits for a specific event to occur

Events are determined by watching the mouse status and press and release counts. Each event is assigned a logical name as listed in Table 4.2. These labels are defined as constants at the beginning of **msmouse.h**. A few examples are:

```
const unsigned MouseDown        = 0xff01;
const unsigned RMouseDown       = 0xff02;
const unsigned MouseStillDown   = 0xff04;
const unsigned RMouseStillDown  = 0xff08;
const unsigned MouseUp          = 0xff10;
```

The core event handler for the mouse object is the member function **Event()**, which we'll take a close look at now. By inspecting the code for **Event()** you can see that it consists of several **if** statements that check the various states of the buttons. The logic divides into two cases. First, a test is made to see if a button is currently pressed. If one is, then **Event()** checks to see whether that button had

Table 4.2   The mouse event codes

Event name	Description
MouseDown	A mouse button was pressed since previous call
LMouseDown	The left mouse button was pressed since previous call
RMouseDown	The right mouse button was pressed since previous call
MouseStillDown	One of the mouse buttons is still pressed
LMouseStillDown	The left mouse button is still pressed
RMouseStillDown	The right mouse button is still pressed
MouseUp	One of the mouse buttons was just released
LMouseUp	The left mouse button was just released
RMouseUp	The right mouse button was just released
MouseEnter	The mouse cursor has entered a specified region
MouseLeave	The mouse cursor has left a specified region
MouseWithin	The mouse is within a specified region

already been detected by testing to see if its press count equals zero. If so, the corresponding **MouseStillDown** event code is returned. Otherwise, the button must have just been pressed so the appropriate **MouseDown** code is returned. Priority is given to the left mouse button in both cases.

If, however, neither mouse button was down when **Event()** was called, the then part of the **if-else** is executed. In this case, the press and release counts are checked to see if they are greater than zero. If one is, then its corresponding event code is returned. And like before, the left mouse button is given priority. If none of these conditions are met, then a value of 0 (which corresponds to **Idle**) is returned.

Now let's look at the two member function, **WaitForAnyEvent()** and **WaitForEvent()**, which use **Event()**. The first, as the name implies continually loops until some mouse event other than **Idle** occurs. Similarly, **WaitForEvent()** continues until an event passed to it as a parameter occurs. For example, the statement

```
Mouse.WaitForEvent(LMouseDown);
```

will wait for the left mouse button to be pressed.

A Mouse Test Program

Now that we've described how the mouse toolkit is implemented we'll test it out with a small program called **mousetst.cpp**. The output of the program, shown in Figure 4.3, displays the current mouse event and the location of the mouse cursor. This program runs in text mode. We'll be exploring the mouse in graphics mode in the next section.

The **mousetst** program is built around a **do** loop that continues until either mouse button is pressed while the mouse is over the phrase "Press here to quit program" located in the middle of the screen. Within the **do** loop, the **Event()** is continually called to determine the current mouse event. The value of this event is displayed at the bottom-left of the screen along with the mouse's current coordinates which are also returned by **Event()**. In addition, you can click the mouse on the statement "Press here to disable mouse" to temporarily disable the mouse. The program will then prompt you to press any key to reactivate the mouse.

Note that the program configures the mouse to run in text mode by the statements:

```
Press here to disable mouse




                                   Press here to
                                   quit program



                                      ▌



 Current Button Event : No event

 Mouse location (X,Y) :(38,17)
```

Figure 4.3   Output of the mousetst.cpp program

```
Mouse.Setup(TextScrn);     // Initialize the mouse
if (!Mouse.SetupOK()) {    // Mouse intialization failed
  cprintf("Mouse not detected.\r\n");
  exit(0);
}
```

If the initialization fails, the program will terminate with the message "Mouse not detected." You will need a similar call to the member function **Setup()** in your applications. Remember that the object **Mouse** does not have to be declared or allocated in the application. This is handled in **msmouse.cpp**.

```
// mousetst.cpp: This program tests part of the mouse object
// in text mode
#include "stdlib.h"
#include "bios.h"
#include "conio.h"
#include "msmouse.h"

unsigned E;
int Mx, My;
char Ch;

main()
{
  Mouse.Setup(TextScrn);     // Initialize the mouse
  if (!Mouse.SetupOK()) {    // Mouse intialization failed
    cprintf("Mouse not detected.\r\n");
    exit(0);
  }

  clrscr();        // Setup and draw the screen
  gotoxy(35,12); cprintf("Press here to\r\n");
  gotoxy(35,13); cprintf("quit program\r\n");
  gotoxy(1,21);  cprintf("Current Button Event : No event\r\n");
  gotoxy(1,23);  cprintf("Mouse location (X,Y) : \r\n");
  gotoxy(1,1);   cprintf("Press here to disable mouse     \r\n");

  do { // Main interaction loop
    E = Mouse.Event(Mx, My);
    switch(E) {
      case LMouseDown:
        gotoxy(23,21); cprintf("LPressed    \r\n");
        break;
      case RMouseDown:
        gotoxy(23,21); cprintf("RPressed    \r\n");
        break;
      case LMouseStillDown:
        gotoxy(23,21); cprintf("LStill Down\r\n");
        break;
      case RMouseStillDown:
        gotoxy(23,21); cprintf("RStill Down\r\n");
        break;
```

```
    case LMouseUp:
      gotoxy(23,21); cprintf("LMouseUp    \r\n");
      break;
    case RMouseUp:
      gotoxy(23,21); cprintf("RMouseUp    \r\n");
      break;
  }
  gotoxy(23,23); cprintf("(%d,%d)      \r\n", Mx, My);
  if ((E == LMouseDown) && (Mx >= 0) &&
    (Mx <= 26) && (My == 0)) {
    // Disable mouse until a key is pressed
    Mouse.TurnOff();
    gotoxy(1,1); cprintf("Press any key to reenable mouse\r\n");
    bioskey(0);
    gotoxy(1,1); cprintf("Press here to disable mouse     \r\n");
    Mouse.TurnOn();
  }
} while ((E != MouseDown) || (Mx <= 33) || (Mx >= 47) ||
       (My <= 10) || (My >= 13));
Mouse.TurnOff(); // Generally, you should turn off the mouse at end
}
```

The Mouse in Graphics Mode

For the most part we've been focusing on the mouse in text mode. However, as we saw earlier there are special considerations with using the mouse in graphics mode. For instance, we must adjust for the mouse's coordinate system when using a 320 x 200 graphics mode. Another concern is the mouse's cursor. By default the graphics mouse cursor is an arrow where the tip of the arrow points to the pixel considered to be the location of the mouse. In graphics mode the mouse driver enables us to change the mouse cursor by using function 9. We'll explore this in the next sections and then write a small graphics-based test program that displays a few different mouse cursors.

The Two Cursor Masks

We now need to explore how the mouse cursor is placed on the screen in graphics mode. At first glance, it might seem like drawing a cursor on the screen should be trivial. Actually, the procedure is a bit more complicated than you might first think. The main reasons are:

1. To allow the cursor to be moved efficiently

2. To allow portions of the cursor to be transparent

The graphics cursor is constructed by combining two 16 by 16 pixel masks called a *screen mask* and a *cursor mask*. Both masks are represented by 16 by 16 binary patterns. The corresponding bits in each mask are combined using logical operations to create the results shown in Table 4.3. For instance, if the screen mask has a one at the third bit position on the first row and the cursor mask also has a value of one at this bit location, then the pixel on the screen under this mask location is inverted.

Figure 4.4 shows a screen and cursor mask pattern that are combined to create a hand cursor.

Table 4.3   Results of combining the screen and cursor masks

Screen mask value	Cursor mask value	Screen bit value
0	0	Color 0
0	1	Color 15
1	0	Unchanged
1	1	Inverted

```
screen cursor                    mask cursor

1 1 1 1 0 0 1 1 1 1 1 1 1 1 1 1    0 0 0 0 1 1 0 0 0 0 0 0 0 0 0 0
1 1 1 0 0 0 0 1 1 1 1 1 1 1 1 1    0 0 0 1 0 0 1 0 0 0 0 0 0 0 0 0
1 1 1 0 0 0 0 1 1 1 1 1 1 1 1 1    0 0 0 1 0 0 1 0 0 0 0 0 0 0 0 0
1 1 1 0 0 0 0 1 1 1 1 1 1 1 1 1    0 0 0 1 0 0 1 0 0 0 0 0 0 0 0 0
1 1 1 0 0 0 0 0 0 0 0 0 0 0 0 1    0 0 0 1 0 0 1 1 1 1 1 1 1 1 1 0
1 1 1 0 0 0 0 0 0 0 0 0 0 0 0 0    0 0 0 1 0 0 1 0 0 1 0 0 1 0 0 1
1 1 1 0 0 0 0 0 0 0 0 0 0 0 0 0    0 0 0 1 0 0 1 0 0 1 0 0 1 0 0 1
1 1 1 0 0 0 0 0 0 0 0 0 0 0 0 0    0 0 0 1 0 0 1 0 0 1 0 0 1 0 0 1
1 0 0 0 0 0 0 0 0 0 0 0 0 0 0 0    0 1 1 1 0 0 1 0 0 1 0 0 1 0 0 1
0 0 0 0 0 0 0 0 0 0 0 0 0 0 0 0    1 0 0 1 0 0 0 0 0 0 0 0 0 0 0 1
0 0 0 0 0 0 0 0 0 0 0 0 0 0 0 0    1 0 0 1 0 0 0 0 0 0 0 0 0 0 0 1
0 0 0 0 0 0 0 0 0 0 0 0 0 0 0 0    1 0 0 1 0 0 0 0 0 0 0 0 0 0 0 1
0 0 0 0 0 0 0 0 0 0 0 0 0 0 0 0    1 0 0 0 0 0 0 0 0 0 0 0 0 0 0 1
0 0 0 0 0 0 0 0 0 0 0 0 0 0 0 0    1 0 0 0 0 0 0 0 0 0 0 0 0 0 0 1
1 0 0 0 0 0 0 0 0 0 0 0 0 0 0 1    0 1 0 0 0 0 0 0 0 0 0 0 0 0 1 0
1 1 0 0 0 0 0 0 0 0 0 0 0 0 1 1    0 0 1 1 1 1 1 1 1 1 1 1 1 1 0 0
```

Figure 4.4   The two masks that create a hand cursor

Setting the Graphics Cursor

The graphics cursor is set by calling the mouse function 9. The **MouseObject** class provides the function **SetGCursor()** to do this. However, how do we tell the mouse driver what to change the mouse cursor to? Basically this is done by passing function 9, a pointer, to a record containing the screen and cursor masks and the bit within the 16 by 16 cursor grid, which is considered to be the hot spot. (Note: The top location of the cursor grid is location (0,0).) The two following structures have been defined to accommodate the cursor mask.

```
struct HotSpotStruct { int X, Y; };

struct MouseCursor {
  HotSpotStruct HotSpot;
  unsigned ScreenMask[16];
  unsigned CursorMask[16];
};
```

We can declare a particular mouse cursor style in an application by declaring a constant or variable of type **MouseCursor** and setting its values appropriately. We have defined four such cursor styles in the file **mcursor.cpp** (shown in Listing 4.3). This file defines an arrow cursor, hand cursor, and two other arrow cursors. For example, here is a declaration for a hand cursor:

```
const MouseCursor HandCursor = {
  { 4, 0 }, // Hot spot at tip of pointing finger
  { 0xF3FF,0xE1FF,0xE1FF,0xE1FF, // Screen mask
    0xE001,0xE000,0xE000,0xE000,
    0x8000,0x0000,0x0000,0x0000,
    0x0000,0x0000,0x8001,0xC003 },
  { 0x0C00,0x1200,0x1200,0x1200, // Cursor mask
    0x13FE,0x1249,0x1249,0x1249,
    0x7249,0x9001,0x9001,0x9001,
    0x8001,0x8001,0x4002,0x3FFC}
}
```

Now that we can represent the cursor masks, we only need to set up and make the appropriate call to mouse function 9 to set the graphics cursor. The function **SetGCursor()** is used to assign the BX and CX registers to the X and Y coordinates of the hot spot, respectively, and the ES and DX registers to the segment and offset of the address pointing to the screen mask. Mouse function 9 assumes that the cursor mask immediately follows the screen mask in memory. This is the case for our **MouseCursor** type since **CursorMask** is defined immediately after **ScreenMask**. The statements that perform these operations are:

```
regs.x.bx  = NewCursor.HotSpot.X;
regs.x.cx  = NewCursor.HotSpot.Y;
regs.x.dx  = FP_OFF(NewCursor.ScreenMask);
sregs.es   = FP_SEG(NewCursor.ScreenMask);
```

Testing the Graphics Cursor

Now take a look at a small program called **mgrphtst.cpp** (shown next) that tests the mouse cursor in graphics mode. It configures the screen to graphics mode and then lets you switch between the graphics cursor patterns we've placed in **mcursor.cpp**. It does this by dividing the screen into four labeled quadrants as shown in Figure 4.5. As you move the cursor between the quadrants the cursor

Figure 4.5   The output of the mcursor.cpp program

changes to the style of cursor indicated by its label. To exit the program simply press one of the mouse buttons.

```cpp
// mgrphtst.cpp: Tests the mouse in graphics mode using the
// cursor shapes defined in mcursor.cpp
#include <stdlib.h>
#include <conio.h>
#include <graphics.h>
#include "msmouse.h"

int Err, Mx, My, Gd, Gm, Quad, OldQuad;
unsigned E;

main()
{
  Gd = DETECT;
  initgraph(&Gd, &Gm, "c:\\tcpp\\bgi");  // Initialize graphics mode
  if (graphresult() != grOk) { // Graphics initialization failed
    cprintf("A graphics adapter is required for this program.\r\n");
    exit(1);
  }
  // Draw and label quadrants
  moveto(getmaxx() / 2, 0);
  lineto(getmaxx() / 2, getmaxx());
  moveto(0, getmaxy() / 2);
  lineto(getmaxx(), getmaxy() / 2);
  outtextxy(1, 1, "ArrowCursor");
  outtextxy((getmaxx()/2)+4, 1, "HandCursor");
  outtextxy(1, (getmaxy()/2)+4, "LeftRightCursor");
  outtextxy((getmaxx()/2)+4, (getmaxy()/2) + 4, "UpDownCursor");
  Mouse.Setup(Graphics);     // Initialize the mouse
  if (!Mouse.Operating()) {
    closegraph();
    cprintf("Mouse not detected.\n");
    exit(1);
  }
  Mouse.SetGCursor(ArrowCursor);  // Use this as default cursor
  OldQuad = Quad = 1;
  do {
    E = Mouse.Event(Mx,My);
    if (Mx > getmaxx() / 2) {
      if (My > getmaxy() / 2) Quad = 4; else Quad = 2;
    }
    else {
      if (My > getmaxy() / 2) Quad = 3; else Quad = 1;
    }
    if (Quad != OldQuad) {
      switch(Quad) {
        case 1: Mouse.SetGCursor(ArrowCursor); break;
        case 2: Mouse.SetGCursor(HandCursor); break;
        case 3: Mouse.SetGCursor(LeftRightCursor); break;
        case 4: Mouse.SetGCursor(UpDownCursor); break;
      };
```

```
    }
    OldQuad = Quad;
  } while (E != MouseDown);
  Mouse.TurnOff();
  closegraph();
  return 0;
}
```

Code Critique

The **MouseObject** class presented in this chapter shows how objects can be used to interface between application-level programs and low-level drivers. While we've made **MouseObject** fairly flexible, there's more we could have done. Using objects means having more design choices, some of which we'll now discuss.

Abstract Classes

We designed the **MouseObject** class as a standalone object type. In particular, we implemented it specifically for a MS compatible mouse. But suppose we were using a different kind of mouse? No problem. All we have to do is derive a new object type and override those member functions that interface directly with the other mouse driver.

There is, however, one part of our design that could be improved. We could have started with an abstract mouse type—one that didn't talk to any mouse driver at all. Then, we could derive a MS Mouse-specific class, and even derive another mouse class, perhaps one to interface with a digitizing tablet.

Why would using an abstract mouse class be better? Later on we'll be developing a general windowing system. This system will methodically hide and show the mouse cursor when writing to the screen. That means that the code for our window system will contain many calls to a mouse object. But suppose we were writing applications that do not use the mouse? We don't want to take out all calls to the mouse—that would be too error prone. However, we also wouldn't want to pay for the overhead that results if the code for the complete mouse class resides in our program. What can we do? Using an abstract mouse class provides the solution.

All the abstract mouse class would have to do is provide member functions that we can call, but the majority of these routines wouldn't do anything. They just need to give the appearance that the mouse is "off." So, if we didn't want to use the mouse for our application, we could create and use a mouse object from our abstract class. This would cause minimal overhead. Then, if later on we wanted to use a mouse in another application, all we have to do is create a mouse object from a derived class of our abstract mouse class, and use that mouse object instead. In either case, no changes need be made to the windowing system code itself. It wouldn't know if it was talking to a real mouse or an abstract mouse. That's the power of polymorphism.

Event Handling

We've designed the mouse class so that it handles events by polling for changes in the mouse status, rather than by using an interrupt-driven scheme. Polling is much simpler than using interrupts, but does have some drawbacks. In particular, it's hard to detect mouse double clicks (rapidly pressing and releasing the mouse button twice) by using the polling technique. One challenging project would be to create a mouse class that's designed to work with interrupts. (Refer to the *Microsoft Mouse Programmer's Reference Guide* for information on how to obtain the mouse status using an interrupt-driven approach.)

Listing 4.1   msmouse.h

```
// Mouse class: msmouse.h

#ifndef H_MSMOUSE
#define H_MSMOUSE

// Defines graphics mouse cursor styles

struct HotSpotStruct { int X, Y; };

struct MouseCursor {
  HotSpotStruct HotSpot;
  unsigned ScreenMask[16];
  unsigned CursorMask[16];
};

extern const MouseCursor ArrowCursor;
extern const MouseCursor HandCursor;
extern const MouseCursor LeftRightCursor;
extern const MouseCursor UpDownCursor;

// Mouse event codes

const unsigned Idle           - 0x0000;
const unsigned MouseDown      - 0xff01;
const unsigned LMouseDown     - 0xff01;
const unsigned RMouseDown     - 0xff02;
const unsigned MouseStillDown - 0xff04;
```

```
const unsigned LMouseStillDown  = 0xff04;
const unsigned RMouseStillDown  = 0xff08;
const unsigned MouseUp          = 0xff10;
const unsigned LMouseUp         = 0xff10;
const unsigned RMouseUp         = 0xff20;
const unsigned MouseEnter       = 0xff40;
const unsigned MouseLeave       = 0xff80;
const unsigned MouseWithin      = 0xffc0;

// Mouse Button Masks

const unsigned  LeftButton      = 0x0001;
const unsigned  RightButton     = 0x0002;

// The video modes that the mouse is running under

enum VideoModeType {TextScrn, LowResGr, HerculesGr, Graphics};

// The mouse class

class MouseObject {
protected:
  int OldX, OldY;    // Used solely by Moved to keep position
  char OK;           // True if mouse initialized
  char MouseOff;     // True if mouse is disabled (Default)
  char LowRes;       // True if in 320 x 200 graphics mode
  char TextMode;     // True if in text mode
public:
  int X, Y, Dx, Dy; // Keeps track of the mouse's movement
  MouseObject(void);
  void Setup(VideoModeType VideoMode);
  int  DriverExists(void);
  int  SetupOK(void);
  void Hide(void);
  void Show(void);
  unsigned Status(int &Mx, int &My);
  unsigned ButtonStatus(void);
  int PressCnt(unsigned ButtonMask);
  int ReleaseCnt(unsigned ButtonMask);
  unsigned Event(int &Mx, int &My);
  unsigned WaitForAnyEvent(int &Mx, int &My);
  void WaitForEvent(unsigned E, int &Mx, int &My);
  int  Moved(void);
  void Move(int Mx, int My);
  void TurnOn(void);
  void TurnOff(void);
  int  Operating(void);
  void SetGCursor(const MouseCursor &NewCursor);
};

extern MouseObject Mouse;

#endif
```

Listing 4.2   msmouse.cpp

```
// Mouse class: msmouse.cpp

#include "dos.h"
#include "stdlib.h"
#include "msmouse.h"

const int MsCall  = 0x33;
const int Iret    = 0xcf;
const int False   = 0;
const int True    = 1;

MouseObject Mouse;

MouseObject::MouseObject(void)
// Initializes mouse to a known state. Mouse is not turned on yet
{
  OK = False;
  MouseOff = True;
}

int MouseObject::DriverExists(void)
// Returns true if a mouse driver is installed. This function makes
// sure the interrupt vector location serviced by the mouse is
// pointing to something—hopefully the mouse driver.
{
  void far *address;
  // Look for NULL address or IRET instruction
  address = getvect(MsCall);
  return (address != NULL) && (*(unsigned char far *)address != Iret);
}

void MouseObject::Setup(VideoModeType VideoMode)
// Initializes the mouse object by verifying that the mouse driver
// exists, that the mouse responds to its initialization function,
// by moving the mouse to the top left of the screen, and by setting
// various internal variables. Call the function SetupOK after
// calling Init to find out if the mouse initialization was successful.
// The VideoMode parameter specifies which video mode the mouse is
// being used under.
{
  REGS regs;

  OK = DriverExists();
  if (OK) { // Mouse present, but will it reset?
  // Fix up hercules mode for page 0. Use 5 for page 1.
    if (VideoMode == HerculesGr)  *(char far *)MK_FP(0x0040,0x0049) = 6;
    regs.x.ax = 0;
    int86(MsCall, &regs, &regs);
    if (regs.x.ax == 0) OK = False;
  }
```

```
      if (!OK)  {   // Mouse initialization failed. Set
         TurnOff(); // the mouse state off and return.
         return;
      }
      TurnOn();      // Set the mouse state on

      if (VideoMode == TextScrn) TextMode = True; else TextMode = False;
      if (VideoMode == LowResGr) LowRes = True; else LowRes = False;

      OldX = 0;  OldY = 0;   // Initialize various variables
      X = 0;     Y = 0;
      Dx = 0;    Dy = 0;
      Move(0,0); // Set the mouse to top left of screen
   }

   int MouseObject::SetupOK(void)
   // Returns true only if the mouse initialization was successful
   {
      return OK;
   }

   void MouseObject::Hide(void)
   // Hides the mouse cursor. Call this function to remove the mouse
   // cursor from the screen.
   {
      REGS regs;
      if (!Operating()) return;
      regs.x.ax = 2;
      int86(MsCall, &regs, &regs);
   }

   void MouseObject::Show(void)
   // Displays the mouse cursor
   {
      REGS regs;
      if (!Operating()) return;
      regs.x.ax = 1;
      int86(MsCall, &regs, &regs);
   }

   unsigned MouseObject::Status(int &Mx, int &My)
   // This general function returns the location of the mouse in Mx,My
   // and the current status of the buttons in the function name
   {
      REGS regs;

      if (!Operating()) { Mx = 0;  My = 0;  return 0; }
      regs.x.ax = 3;
      int86(MsCall, &regs, &regs);
      Mx = regs.x.cx;    My = regs.x.dx;
      if (TextMode)  {
        Mx >>= 3;  // Adjust for text coordinates
        My >>= 3;
```

```
    }
    if (LowRes)  Mx >>= 1; // Adjust for 320 x 200 coordinates
    return regs.x.bx;
}

unsigned MouseObject::ButtonStatus(void)
// Returns the status of the mouse buttons
{
  int Mx, My;
  if (!Operating()) return 0; else return Status(Mx, My);
}

int MouseObject::PressCnt(unsigned ButtonMask)
// Returns number of times the button has been pressed since
// last time called
{
  REGS regs;
  if (!Operating()) return 0;
  regs.x.ax = 5;
  regs.x.bx = ButtonMask >> 1; // Button selector
  int86(MsCall, &regs, &regs);
  return regs.x.bx;
}

int MouseObject::ReleaseCnt(unsigned ButtonMask)
// Returns number of times the button has been released since
// last time called
{
  REGS regs;
  if (!Operating()) return 0;
  regs.x.ax = 6;
  regs.x.bx = ButtonMask >> 1;   // Button selector
  int86(MsCall, &regs, &regs);
  return regs.x.bx;
}

unsigned MouseObject::Event(int &Mx, int &My)
// Gets the last mouse event. The left mouse button has priority
// over the right button.
{
  unsigned E;

  if (!Operating()) { Mx = 0; My = 0; return Idle; }
  // Get current status of buttons.
  E = Status(Mx,My);
  if (E == 0) {
    // No mouse button down, but maybe there was a button press that
    // was missed. If not, check to see whether a button release was
    // missed. Favor the left mouse button.
    if (PressCnt(LeftButton) > 0) E = LMouseDown;
    else if (PressCnt(RightButton) > 0)  E = RMouseDown;
    // Maybe left one was just released
    else if (ReleaseCnt(LeftButton) > 0) E = LMouseUp;
    // Maybe right one was just released
```

```
        else if (ReleaseCnt(RightButton) > 0) E = RMouseUp;
    }
    else { // A mouse button is down
      // Was the left button already down?
      if (E & LeftButton) {
        // Not already down
        if (PressCnt(LeftButton) > 0)
          E = LMouseDown;              // Must have just been pressed
          else E = LMouseStillDown;  // Already down
      }
      else if (PressCnt(RightButton) > 0)
        E = RMouseDown;              // Must have just been pressed
        else E = RMouseStillDown; // Already down
  }
  return E;      // Return the mouse event code
}

unsigned MouseObject::WaitForAnyEvent(int &Mx, int &My)
// Waits for a mouse event to occur and return its code
{
  unsigned E;

  if (!Operating()) { Mx = 0;  My = 0; return Idle; }
  do {
    E = Event(Mx, My);
  } while (E == Idle);
  return E;
}

void MouseObject::WaitForEvent(unsigned E, int &Mx, int &My)
// Waits for the event E to occur. Return its mouse coordinates.
{
  unsigned Etry;
  if (!Operating()) { Mx = 0; My = 0; return; }
  do {
    Etry = Event(Mx, My);
  } while (Etry != E);
}

int MouseObject::Moved(void)
// Tests to see if the mouse has moved since the last time this
// function was called.
{
  if (!Operating()) return False;
  OldX = X; OldY = Y;
  Status(X, Y);
  Dx = X - OldX; Dy = Y - OldY;
  return (Dx != 0) || (Dy != 0);
}

void MouseObject::Move(int Mx, int My)
// Moves the mouse cursor
{
  REGS regs;
```

```
      if (!Operating()) return;
      regs.x.ax = 4;
      regs.x.cx = Mx;
      regs.x.dx = My;
      if (TextMode) { // Adjust for text coordinates
        regs.x.cx <<= 3;
        regs.x.dx <<= 3;
      }
      if (LowRes) regs.x.cx <<= 1;  // Adjust for 320 x 200 coordinates
      int86(MsCall, &regs, &regs);
    }

void MouseObject::TurnOn(void)
// Enables the mouse code
{
  if (OK && MouseOff) {
      MouseOff = False;
      Show();
  }
}

void MouseObject::TurnOff(void)
// Disables the mouse code. This is useful when you don't want to
// use the mouse, but the code already has mouse calls in it.
{
  if (OK && !MouseOff) {
    Hide();
    MouseOff = True;
  }
}

int MouseObject::Operating(void)
// Returns a boolean flag that is true only if the mouse
// object has been enabled. This is the default state.
{
  return !MouseOff;
}

void MouseObject::SetGCursor(const MouseCursor &NewCursor)
// Sets the graphics mouse cursor to the type specified
{
  REGS regs;
  SREGS sregs;

  if (!Operating()) return;
  regs.x.ax = 9;
  regs.x.bx = NewCursor.HotSpot.X;
  regs.x.cx = NewCursor.HotSpot.Y;
  regs.x.dx = FP_OFF(NewCursor.ScreenMask);
  sregs.es  = FP_SEG(NewCursor.ScreenMask);
  int86x(MsCall, &regs, &regs, &sregs);
}
```

Listing 4.3   mcursor.cpp

```cpp
#include "msmouse.h"

const MouseCursor ArrowCursor = {
    { 0, 0 }, // Set hot spot to tip of arrow
    { 0x3FFF,0x1FFF,0x0FFF,0x07FF,  // Screen mask
      0x03FF,0x01FF,0x00FF,0x007F,
      0x003F,0x00FF,0x01FF,0x10FF,
      0x30FF,0xF87F,0xF87F,0xFC3F },
    { 0x0000,0x4000,0x6000,0x7000,  // Cursor mask
      0x7800,0x7C00,0x7E00,0x7F00,
      0x7F80,0x7E00,0x7C00,0x4600,
      0x0600,0x0300,0x0300,0x0180 }
};

const MouseCursor HandCursor = {
    { 4, 0 }, // Hot spot at tip of pointing finger
    { 0xF3FF,0xE1FF,0xE1FF,0xE1FF, // Screen mask
      0xE001,0xE000,0xE000,0xE000,
      0x8000,0x0000,0x0000,0x0000,
      0x0000,0x0000,0x8001,0xC003 },
    { 0x0C00,0x1200,0x1200,0x1200, // Cursor mask
      0x13FE,0x1249,0x1249,0x1249,
      0x7249,0x9001,0x9001,0x9001,
      0x8001,0x8001,0x4002,0x3FFC}
};

const MouseCursor LeftRightCursor = {
    { 8, 8 }, // Hot spot in middle of arrow
    { 0xffff,0xffff,0xfbdf,0xf3cf, // Screen mask
      0xe3c7,0xc003,0x8001,0x0000,
      0x8001,0xc003,0xe3c7,0xf3cf,
      0xfbdf,0xffff,0xffff,0xffff },
    { 0x0000,0x0000,0x0420,0x0c30, // Cursor mask
      0x1428,0x27e4,0x4002,0x8001,
      0x4002,0x27e4,0x1428,0x0c30,
      0x0420,0x0000,0x0000,0x0000 }
};

const MouseCursor UpDownCursor = {
    { 8, 8 }, // Hot spot in middle of arrow
    { 0xfeff,0xfcff,0xf83f,0xf01f, // Screen mask
      0xe00f,0xc007,0xf83f,0xf83f,
      0xf83f,0xf83f,0xc007,0xe00f,
      0xf01f,0xf83f,0xfc7f,0xfeff },
    { 0x0100,0x0280,0x0440,0x0820, // Cursor mask
      0x1010,0x3c78,0x0440,0x0440,
      0x0440,0x0440,0x3c78,0x1010,
      0x0820,0x0440,0x0280,0x0100 }
};
```

5

Setting the Stage for Windows and Menus

When was the last time a program really caught your attention? Chances are that it made use of interface components such as pop-up windows and menus. Let's face it. The days of command line programs are as ancient as the punch card reader. What programmers need today are tools for use in building modern interfaces that provide screen and mouse support.

A simple window and menu package can be produced in a few hundred lines of code but it wouldn't be useful if it couldn't handle all the interface features that we might need, such as scroll bars, shadows, close boxes, and so on. Most interface code, though, is hard to use and modify. Thus the real challenge is coming up with a truly general purpose set of tools that can be used to create different styles of windows and menus—our goal in this chapter. As a bonus, our interface toolkit will be able to work in both text and graphics modes.

One World, Many Objects

Imagine that you're an architect. You've just been assigned the seemingly impossible task of designing a house that could be built anywhere in the world. The best way to start would be to look for the features that all houses worldwide have in common. Then, the house's foundation and basic structure could be designed using the common elements.

Designing a general purpose interface toolkit is a lot like creating the universal house. For instance, interface objects, such as windows, buttons, and menus, have many attributes in common:

- Their basic shapes consist of simple rectangular regions

- They support interaction (keyboard and the mouse)

- They can be displayed and hidden

- They can be combined to create more complex interface objects such as dialog boxes

- They can be displayed with or without shadows

An important point here is that all interface objects can be created or derived from a basic rectangular shape. And as you'll soon see, our strategy will involve creating a general rectangle class to support a flexible window and menuing system that will work in both text and graphics modes.

What Are Screen Objects?

Figure 5.1 shows some examples of the types of windows and menus that our interface toolkit supports. The object classes range from simple windows to more complex pull-down menuing systems and dialog boxes. Because of the flexible way we've implemented the tools you'll easily be able to modify them and create your own types of interface components.

The interface objects will work with both the mouse and the keyboard. Once they are completed, we'll be able to display and move windows, build pull-down menus whose submenus can be "torn-away" with the click of a mouse, and make graphics selection buttons and slide bars that have a three-dimensional appearance.

The Master Plan

To implement our general purpose interface object toolkit, a number of support routines must be developed. Table 5.1 lists the source files that we'll be creating and using in this chapter and the following chapters. Note that the first four files are from Chapters 3 and 4. The code for the new files **rsounit.h**, **rsounit.cpp**, **trsounit.h**, and **trsounit.cpp** are presented in Listings 5.1 through 5.4. The source files presented in this chapter won't cover all of the tools that we'll eventually need to finish off our interface toolkit. In Chapter 6, the **fsounit** and **tfsounit**

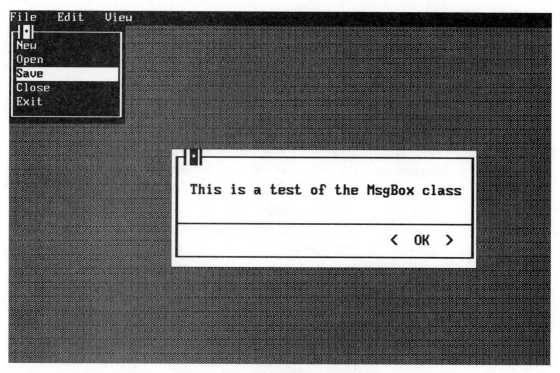

Figure 5.1   Sample screen objects

packages to support framed screen objects will be developed and in Chapter 7, the files **isounit.cpp** and **twsounit.cpp** will be built to manage interactive objects and create windows, respectively. Finally, in Chapter 8, **msounit.cpp** will be created to support and manage menu systems. In a sense, think of this chapter as the first part of a four-part series.

If we attempted to write a general interface toolkit to support text and graphics modes without the aid of OOP features, we'd end up with a lot of complex code that would be difficult to test and maintain. The problem is that we would need a number of dedicated functions to handle the low-level details of displaying screen objects in the two vastly different modes.

To display a window or any other type of interface object in text mode we could write to screen memory the ASCII character codes for an object's border. The coordinate system involved is the standard text coordinates—25 rows by 80 columns. Graphics mode is another story. The only way screen objects could be displayed in graphics mode would be to draw the objects using pixel coordinates.

Considering these incompatibilities, how can we come up with a general set of tools to support both screen types? Using OOP, we can construct a set of

Table 5.1   The interface object packages for text mode

Main file	Description
keybrd.cpp	The keyboard support unit developed in Chapter 3
scrnsty.cpp	The screen color and attribute definitions introduced in Chapter 3
txunit.cpp	The low-level screen support tools developed in Chapter 3
msmouse.cpp	The mouse support class developed in Chapter 4
rsounit.cpp	The unit that contains the Rect (rectangle) and Rso (rectangular screen object) types
trsounit.cpp	The unit that contains the Trso (text rectangular screen object) type
fsounit.cpp	The unit that contains the Fso (framed screen object) developed in Chapter 6
tfsounit.cpp	The unit that contains the Tfso (text-framed screen object) developed in Chapter 6

abstract classes to isolate and represent the common components of *all* interface screen objects. In addition, we'll use separate classes to implement details of manipulating text and graphics modes. The main advantage of the OOP method is that we'll be able to share and reuse a lot of the basic support code—particularly in the abstract classes. And because all of the control logic will be packaged as special purpose objects, we'll be able to easily add and modify interface features.

The Secret Is Inheritance

The encapsulation features that objects provide make them ideal for representing our interactive screen tools. However, the property that really contributes to the flexible design of our interface tools is inheritance. Of course, we've been working with inheritance throughout this book, but now we're about to squeeze as much power as we can out of this property to develop our general interface tools.

Figure 5.2 presents the class hierarchy that will be implemented throughout the remainder of this book. With each level we go through, the classes will become less general in purpose. The general rectangle (**Rect**) class is at the top. This class is then used to derive the rectangular screen object class (**Rso**). Both of these classes are general in nature and are not tied to text or graphics mode.

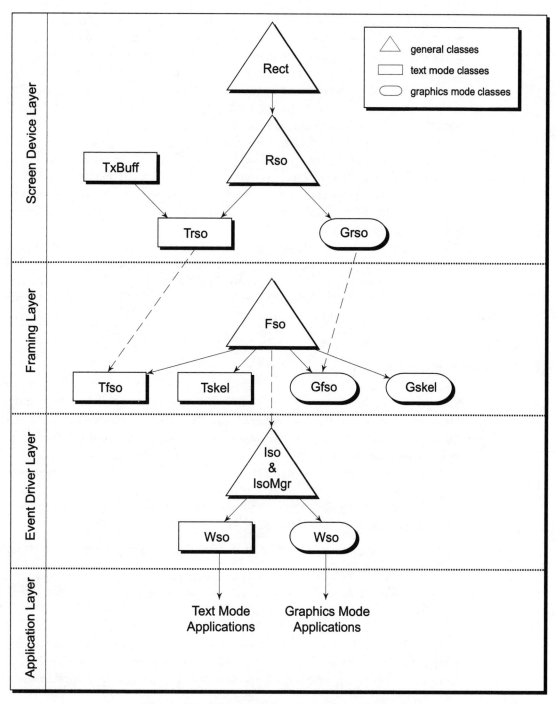

Figure 5.2   The screen object class hierarchy

The first screen-specific classes, **Trso** and **Grso**, are introduced at the third level of the hierarchy. The **Trso** class supports text screens and **Grso**, which is covered in Chapter 10, supports graphics. The **Trso** class provides functions for drawing borders, displaying text, and moving rectangular screen regions. As Figure 5.2 shows, it is implemented by using both **Rso** and **TxBuff**. In this case, **Rso** provides the member functions for managing rectangular regions and **TxBuff** adds the necessary code to support low-level text screen I/O operations.

At the next level of the class hierarchy, we encounter a number of classes to support what we call *framed screen objects*. Essentially, these classes allow us to group three rectangular regions into frames that have borders, interiors, and shadows. Again, note that we are using a general class, **Fso**, and text and graphics modes specific classes, **Tfso**, **Tskel**, **Gfso**, and **Gskel**, to separate the details of working in different video modes.

The penultimate layer is designed to handle the management tasks of our interface screen objects. Because of the importance and complexity of the classes in this layer, Chapter 7 is dedicated to discussing them. The bottom of the hierarchy consists of the menu classes that will be introduced in Chapter 8. As you can see, there's a lot of territory to cover.

Starting with Rectangles

Now that we've seen the road map for the classes we need to build, let's begin the construction of one of the core classes—the **Rect** class. It defines the basic elements of a rectangular object, and handles such tasks as initialization, horizontal and vertical clipping, and testing to see if rectangles overlap.

The major highlights of the **Rect** class are:

1. Sets up rectangular coordinates including the upper left-hand corner, lower right-hand corner, width, and height

2. Defines a clipping region to ensure that data displayed in a rectangular region will fit

3. Provides member functions to test if a coordinate position is within a rectangular region and if two rectangular regions intersect

The **Rect** class, shown next, contains six data members that store the dimensions and coordinates of an object and a variety of functions to manipulate these coordinates. In addition, a constructor is provided to initialize these coordinates:

```
class Rect {
public:
   int Xul, Yul;   // Upper left-hand corner
   int Xlr, Ylr;   // Lower right-hand corner
   int Wd, Ht;     // Overall size
   Rect(int X, int Y, int W, int H);
   virtual ~Rect(void) { ; }
   virtual void SetSize(int W, int H);
   virtual void SetLocn(int Xl, int Yl);
   virtual void ClipSize(int &W, int &H);
   virtual void ClipDim(int &X, int &Y, int &W, int &H);
   virtual int HzClip(int &X, int &Y, int &N);
   virtual int VtClip(int &X, int &Y, int &N);
   virtual int Contains(int X, int Y);
   virtual int Touches(Rect *R);
};
```

The **Rect** class also included a destructor, even though it doesn't contain any code. We've already explained the reason for doing this, but it's worth repeating. We'll be making heavy use of pointers to objects in our screen tools. In particular, generic base type pointers will be used to point to derived objects. If we were to call a destructor with such a pointer, we need to ensure that the proper destructor is called, in order for it to know how much memory to dispose. That's why we've included a destructor here, and why we've made it virtual.

For example, **Trso** objects, which are ultimately derived from **Rect** objects, have additional data members such as a dynamically allocated **texel** buffer. By making the destructor virtual, and overriding it for **Trso**s, we ensure that this extra memory is handled properly by **Trso** objects.

It is important to keep in mind that the **Rect** class is concerned only with the general properties of rectangles. The actual drawing of the rectangle objects is left up to the derived classes—**Rso**, **Trso**, and **Grso**. By using this we're able to separate the processing tasks for rectangular objects into two areas: setting up and testing coordinates, and actually drawing the objects.

Clipping Rectangular Regions

The majority of the code in **Rect** is used to clip rectangular regions. Why is clipping so important? When we later write text inside a rectangle, we must ensure that the text will fit; otherwise, we would end up with a real mess.

Clipping is performed by the member functions **ClipSize()**, **ClipDim()**, **HzClip()**, and **VtClip()**. The **ClipSize()** function adjusts the width and height passed to it to fit within a rectangle, and **ClipDim()** adjusts a rectangle's width and height dimensions and its upper-left and lower-right coordinates to fit within the object that is being used.

The other two routines, **HzClip()** and **VtClip()**, are used to determine whether a horizontal or vertical line will fit within a rectangle. If the coordinates of the line lie entirely outside the rectangle, **False** is returned (a value of 0); otherwise, **True** is returned (a value of 1) and the coordinates are adjusted to ensure the line fits within the rectangle. For example, let's take a closer look at **HzClip()**:

```
int Rect::HzClip(int &X, int &Y, int &N)
// Given a starting coordinate (X,Y) (relative to the rectangle),
// and a length N, this function clips N to fit in the rectangle,
// assuming that the length runs horizontal. If X is negative, it
// is set to zero and the length adjusted accordingly. Y must be in
// range. The function returns true if a nonnull clip is found;
// otherwise, false is returned.
{
  int Rval - False;
  if ((Y >=0) && (Y < Ht)) { // Y must be in range
    if (X < 0) {                // Clip to left
      N += X;
      X - 0;
    }
    if ((N > 0) && (X < Wd)) {
      if ((X + N) > Wd) N - Wd - X; // Clip to right
      Rval - True;
    }
  }
  return Rval;
}
```

The parameters **X,Y** specify a starting coordinate and **N** specifies the length of the line to test. Note that if **X** is negative, it is set to zero and the length **N** is adjusted by reducing it by the value stored in **X**. Why are we doing this? It allows us to perform a left-justified clip. In addition to returning a boolean value and possibly adjusting **X**, **HzClip()** will change the length of the line **N** to ensure that it does not extend past the right boundary of the rectangle.

In discussing this function, we stated that it checks the coordinates of a line of length **N**. This description fits the general nature of **HzClip()**; however, we'll use this member function to clip strings and fill regions in both text and graphics modes. Later you'll see how some of the text writing functions in the **Trso** class use **HzClip()** and **VtClip()** to clip text strings and fill regions.

Intersecting Rectangles

When we start creating interfaces with multiple screen objects we'll need a way to determine if they overlap. We'll also need to be able to test if a specified coordinate position is contained within a screen object. And that's where the **Contains()**

and **Touches()** member functions come in. The **Contains()** routine is quite simple because it tests a coordinate pair with the data members **Xul**, **Xlr**, **Yul**, and **Ylr** that specify the bounds of a rectangle.

The **Touches()** function, however, is slightly more complex. The complete routine is:

```
int Rect::Touches(Rect *R)
// Returns true if R overlaps this object. They overlap if their
// horizontal and vertical extents both cross. Note that as
// defined, a rectangle can't overlap itself.
{
  if (R == this) return False;
  else return
      (Xul <= R->Xlr) && (Xlr >= R->Xul) && // Hz crossing
      (Yul <= R->Ylr) && (Ylr >= R->Yul);   // Vt crossing
}
```

This function returns a value of 1 if the rectangle pointed to by **R**, which is passed as a parameter, overlaps the rectangle region of the object in question. The rectangles overlap if their horizontal and vertical extents both cross. Note that, as defined, a rectangle can't overlap itself. We test this condition with the following trick: by comparing the pointer **R** with **this**. If these two pointers are equal, then **R** and the object that called the function are one and the same. As Figure 5.3 illustrates, we must check eight different conditions in order to determine overlap, and our **if** statement handles them all.

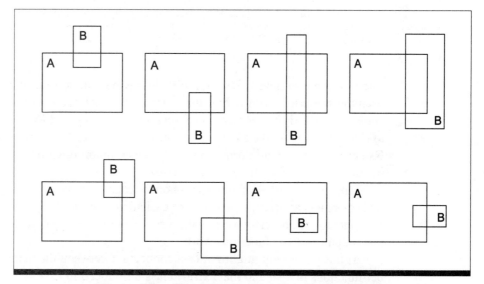

Figure 5.3   Checking for overlapping rectangles

The Rectangular Screen Object Class

The **Rect** class provides everything we need to position, size, and clip rectangular regions. If you take a closer look at **Rect**, you'll notice that it doesn't contain any member functions for displaying text, saving and restoring images, or scrolling. Needless to say, we'll need these operations in order to support windows, buttons, and menus.

By using inheritance, we can easily derive a class from **Rect** to serve as a template for more specific objects—ones that provide functions for performing basic screen operations. We'll call these new objects *rectangular screen objects* (**Rso**). The highlights of the **Rso** class are:

1. **Rso** is a general class such as **Rect**. The **Rso** class will later be used to derive both text and graphics screen object classes.

2. Adds the protocol for performing output (text and borders) to the abstract rectangles.

The class definition for **Rso** is:

```
class Rso : public Rect {
public:
  Rso(int X, int Y, int W, int H) : Rect(X,Y,W,H) { ; }
  virtual void HzWrt(int, int, char *, char) = 0;
  virtual void HzWrtB(int, int, char *) = 0;
  virtual void Fill(int, int, int, int, char, char) = 0;
  virtual void FillB(int, int, int, int, char, char) = 0;
  virtual void Box(int, int, int, int, char, char) = 0;
  virtual void Scroll(ScrollDir, int) { ; }
};
```

The first thing to note is **Rso** doesn't add any data members. In addition, if you examine **rsounit.h**, you'll find that none of the new member functions contain code. In fact, only the constructor **Rso()** does anything and its mission is simple: to chain back and make a call to the constructor of the **Rect** class. Essentially, the **Rso** class is provided in order to specify the common function protocol that is to be used by more specific, derived classes.

Table 5.2 provides a short description for each of the new functions in **Rso**. Our main design goal here is to specify the basic functions we'll need to display text in rectangular regions. As we cover the **Trso** class next, we'll explain how the main text output member functions work.

At this point, you might notice a connection between the names of the member functions in **Rso** and the **TxBuff** class introduced in Chapter 3. This connection is more than a simple coincidence. In fact, the **Rso** class will call the functions

Table 5.2   Member functions included in Rso

Member function	Description
Rso()	Initializes an Rso object
HzWrt()	Displays a horizontal string in a specified attribute
HzWrtB()	Displays a horizontal string without an attribute
Fill()	Fills a rectangular region with a character and an attribute
FillB()	Fills a rectangular region with either a character or an attribute
Box()	Draws a box in a specified attribute and border style
Scroll()	Scrolls the text displayed in a rectangular region

from the **TxBuff** class to write to the screen. If you examine the **Rso** routines, you'll see that they use the same parameters as the **TxBuff** functions.

Moving Toward Text: The Trso Class

You're probably wondering when we're going to stop deriving classes and start displaying some windows or other interactive screen objects. We've created the general classes we'll need for the first layer of our class hierarchy; thus we can now concentrate on building the **Trso** class to implement rectangular screen objects in text mode. A quick rundown of the main features of the **Trso** class is:

1. Derives a text mode implementation of rectangular screen objects

2. Provides clipping support for text output by using the clipping member functions from the **Rect** class

3. Hides and displays the mouse so that the mouse cursor does not interfere with text output

As you study the definition of **Trso**, note the similarities between it and the **Rso** class:

```
class Trso : public Rso {
public:
  TxBuff *Pic;
```

```
   Trso(TxBuff *T);
   virtual ~Trso(void);
   virtual void SetSize(int W, int H);
   virtual void SetLocn(int X1, int Y1);
   virtual void HzWrt(int X, int Y, char *Str, char Attr);
   virtual void HzWrtB(int X, int Y, char *Str);
   virtual void Fill(int X, int Y, int W, int H, char Ch, char Attr);
   virtual void FillB(int X, int Y, int W, int H, char Ch, char Opt);
   virtual void Box(int X, int Y, int W, int H, char Ba, char Attr);
   virtual void Scroll(ScrollDir Sd, int Amt);
   virtual void Swap(int X,int Y,int W,int H, Trso *Other, int Xs,int Ys);
   virtual void Xfr(int X,int Y,int W,int H,  Trso *Src, int Xs,int Ys);
};
```

The single data member, **Pic**, serves as a pointer to a **TxBuff** object. By including a reference to a **TxBuff** object, we'll be able to access the text screen specific data and functions so that we can write directly to text screen memory. In Chapter 11, we'll define a sister class to **Trso** called **Grso** that allows us to access a graphics display.

Following the same format as the other classes we've written thus far, **Trso** contains a constructor. One of the first tasks of **Trso()**, as Figure 5.4 illustrates, is to execute the statement:

```
Trso::Trso(TxBuff *T) : Rso(0, 0, 0, 0)
```

which calls the **Rso** class constructor which in turn calls the constructor from the **Rect** class. In the call to **Rso**'s constructor, note that we've specified a rectangle starting at (0,0) with a zero width and height. The location and size will be initialized by later calling **SetLocn()** and **SetSize()**.

When the **Trso()** constructor is called, a pointer to a screen buffer object defined from the **TxBuff** class is passed as a parameter. This object serves as the interface to the text screen memory and is used to help initialize the **Pic** variable. The member functions, such as **HzWrt()**, **Fill()**, and **Scroll()** will use the object referenced by **Pic** to write text and scroll the rectangular region.

```
       Obj1 -> Trso(NULL);
          └→this -> Rso(0,0,0,0);
                 └→this-> Rect(0,0,0,0);
```

Figure 5.4   The chain of initializer calls

Note that most of the member functions in **Rso** don't do anything, we have to override them in **Trso** in order to do text-based operations. Let's see this overriding process in action by looking at the member function **SetLocn()**:

```
void Trso::SetLocn(int X1, int Y1)
// Sets the rectangle's location and the origin reference
// (OrgPtr) in the texel buffer
{
  Rso::SetLocn(X1, Y1);
  Pic->SetLocn(X1, Y1);
}
```

In this case, we first call the inherited version of **SetLocn()**, the one from **Rso**, to set up the rectangle location, and then we call the texel buffer's **SetLocn()** function to set up **Pic**'s internal texel pointer. Actually, the **SetLocn()** function we are calling for **Rso** is defined in the **Rect** class. (Remember that **Rso** is derived from **Rect**.) Even though **Rso** didn't override **SetLocn()**, we can pretend it does by referring to it by name.

A **Trso** object actually has a lot of power behind it. It can access any of the data and function members in the **Trso**, **Rso**, **Rect**, and **TxBuff** classes. This is where inheritance starts to pay off.

Combining Multiple Objects

An important part of the **Trso** class definition is that it is constructed from two different classes: **Rso** and **TxBuff**. Note, however, that we aren't using Turbo C++'s multiple inheritance capability. Instead we're using single inheritance and a nested pointer to a second object. First, the **Trso** class is defined to inherit the properties of the **Rso** class as a result of the class declaration statement:

```
Trso - object(Rso)
```

Next, the **Trso** data member declaration

```
TxBuff *Pic;
```

provides the link-up we need to incorporate a second class—**Trso**. The **Trso** class gets the best of two worlds: the abstract definition of a rectangle (**Rso**) and the implementation details needed to access a text screen (**TxBuff**). We'll be using this technique in a slightly more powerful form to construct other classes such as **Tfso** and **Gfso** in Chapters 6 and 10.

When inheritance is used to derive a class, we know that the data and member functions of the parent class can be accessed as if they were originally defined in the derived class. We've also seen how we can chain back to access a member function in a base class that has been overridden in a derived class. For example, recall the following statement that was used in **Trso**'s **SetLocn()** function to call the **SetLocn()** function in the **Rso** class.

```
Rso::SetLocn(X1, Y1);
```

Thus, how do we make use of the components of the nested class? Fortunately, this is easy to do. We simply use the nested object directly to access a member function or data member. The following statement illustrates the basic idea:

```
Pic->SetLocn(Xul, Yul);
```

Here, **Pic** points to an object of type **TxBuff** and **SetLocn()** is one of **TxBuff**'s member functions.

As you can see, the only real difference between accessing the inherited class and the nested object is that an extra de-reference is required. We must de-reference the pointer to the nested object ourselves.

Adding Text and Borders

The **Rect** and **Rso** classes don't do anything on the screen. Their primary purpose is to initialize variables and perform behind-the-scenes bookkeeping tasks. By overriding the code for the member functions introduced in **Rso**, we can now support the needed output tasks. Let's take a look at one of the new output routines:

```
void Trso::HzWrt(int X, int Y, char *Str, char Attr)
// Writes a string horizontally in a specified attribute.
// Supports both left- and right-hand clipping.
{
  int Cnt, Offset;
  Cnt = strlen(Str);
  if (X < 0) Offset = -X; else Offset = 0;
  if (HzClip(X,Y,Cnt)) {
    Mouse.Hide();
    Pic->HzWrt(X,Y,Str+Offset,Attr,Cnt);
    Mouse.Show();
  }
}
```

Recall that **HzWrt()**'s job is to output a string horizontally in a rectangular region.

The **Attr** parameter specifies the screen attribute for the string. Before we display the string, there are two tasks we need to perform:

1. Clip the string to the bounds of the object

2. Temporarily hide the mouse cursor (the cursor is redisplayed after the string is written)

If you take a few minutes to review the other output functions in **trsounit.cpp** (Listing 5.4), such as **Fill()** and **HzWrtB()**, you'll see that they all follow this same format. In a similar fashion, the member function **Box()**, which draws a rectangular border, calls **Fill()** to display the border characters. Because of this, the border is automatically clipped if necessary.

The text output functions use a relative coordinate system. As an example, if the upper-left corner of a rectangle were displayed at 10,10 and the following routine were called

```
Tobj.HzWrt(0, 2, "Test String");
```

the string would be written at the screen location 10,12 as shown in Figure 5.5. If a negative coordinate were used such as:

```
Tobj.HzWrt(-1, 20, "Test String");
```

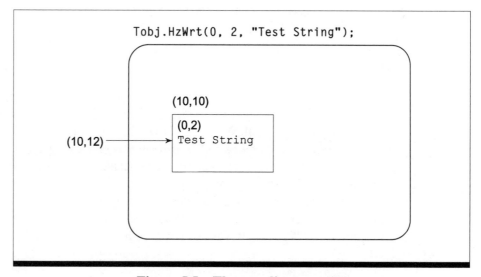

Figure 5.5   The coordinate system

the string would be clipped to the left and would be displayed as:

```
est String
```

Copying and Swapping Images

The **Trso** class also contains two new member functions, **Swap()** and **Xfr()**, to move and copy image data between two **Trso** objects. What role do these functions play? The **Swap()** function exchanges the image of one rectangle with the image from a second rectangle. The **Xfr()** function, however, copies the image from one rectangle to another.

Later, when we attempt to display pop-up windows and menus, we'll use these routines to save and restore screen regions as objects are moved. As shown, **Swap()** takes a **Trso** pointer as a parameter and swaps a specified rectangle region between it and the current object:

```
void Trso::Swap(int X, int Y, int W, int H, Trso *Other, int Xs, int Ys)
// Swaps data between this object's Pic buffer and another Trso's Pic. The
// Other Pic region starts at (Xs, Ys) and this object's Pic region starts
// at X,Y. The swapping region is W by H in size. The coordinates
// are checked to ensure that they are in range and the width and
// height are clipped if necessary.
{
  if (HzClip(X,Y,W) && Other->HzClip(Xs,Ys,W)) {
     if (VtClip(X,Y,H) && Other->VtClip(Xs,Ys,H)) {
        Mouse.Hide();
        Pic->Swap(X, Y, W, H, Other->Pic, Xs, Ys);
        Mouse.Show();
     }
  }
}
```

The locations of the two rectangular regions are defined by the coordinates (**X,Y**) for the current object, and (**Xs,Ys**) for the other object. The size of the swapping region is defined by width **W** and height **H**. The function checks the coordinates to ensure that they are in range and clips them if necessary by calling **HzClip()** and **VtClip()**. The actual image swapping takes place by using the **Swap()** member function from the **TxBuff** class.

The **Xfr()** function works similar to **Swap()** and takes the same parameters. The only difference between the two routines is that **Xfr()** calls the **Xfr()** member function in the **TxBuff** class instead of **Swap()**:

```
Pic->Xfr(X, Y, W, H, Src->Pic, Xs, Ys);
```

In this case, the image stored in the object pointed to by **Src**, starting at (**Xs,Ys**) with width **W** and height **H**, is transferred to the region represented by the pointer **Pic**, starting at X,Y.

The main thing to keep in mind about **Swap()** and **Xfr()** is that they both serve as wrappers for low-level text screen objects created from the **TxBuff** class. In particular, they add clipping and mouse cursor support. This approach further illustrates the building block and data hiding capabilities of OOP. Because of the "loose" connection between the **Trso** and **TxBuff** classes, it would be possible to make changes to one of the classes without requiring major modification to the other. For example, we could change the low-level **Swap()** function in **TxBuff** so that it writes to a different type of text screen and the **Swap()** function in **Trso** could be left alone.

Using the Trso Class

We can't display complex screen objects just yet, but we can create a few **Trso** objects to show how rectangular objects are created and used. The following program puts all of the packages we've introduced in this chapter to work:

```
// trtest.cpp: Test program to demonstrate clipping
// abilities of Trsos

#include <string.h>
#include <stdlib.h>
#include <dos.h>
#include "trsounit.h"
#include "keybrd.h"

main()
{
  // ──────────── Part 1 ────────────
  // Create a screen buffer, clear the screen, and draw a box.
  // ────────────────────────────
  TxBuff ScrnBuff(VideoPtr());
  ScrnBuff.SetSize(80,25);
  Trso Screen(&ScrnBuff);  // Create a Trso, aliased to the screen
  Screen.SetSize(80, 25);  // Default location is (0,0)
  // Clear the screen with a fill pattern
  Screen.Fill(0, 0, Screen.Wd, Screen.Ht, 176, 0x07);
  // Draw a reverse video, single line box in the middle of it
  Screen.Box(30, 8, 15, 5, 0x11, 0x70);
  // ──────────── Part 2 ────────────
  // Create a small window, alias it to the screen. Blank
  // out the window, and clip some text on it.
  // ────────────────────────────
  Trso Window(&ScrnBuff);
  Window.SetLocn(31, 9); // Place and size our window
  Window.SetSize(13, 3); // to be inside our box
  // Blank out the window
```

```
Window.Fill(0, 0, Window.Wd, Window.Ht, ' ', 0x07);
// Here's an example of left- and right-hand clipping
Window.HzWrt(-10, 1, "Hey, you: press any key now", 0x07);
bioskey(0);
// ─────────── Part 3 ───────────
// Now, erase the box and window, and resize and reposition
// the box and window, and show clipping of some boxes
// inside the window.
// ─────────────────────────
Screen.Fill(0, 0, Screen.Wd, Screen.Ht, 176, 0x07);
Screen.Box(20, 4, 42, 17, 0x11, 0x70);
Window.SetLocn(21, 5);
Window.SetSize(40, 15);
Window.Box(35, 5,  15, 4, 0x11, 0x07); // Clip to right
Window.Box(27, -2, 15, 4, 0x11, 0x07); // Clip to top right
Window.Box(-5, -3, 15, 4, 0x11, 0x07); // Clip to top left
Window.Box(-5, 5,  15, 4, 0x11, 0x07); // Clip to left
Window.Box(-2, 13, 15, 4, 0x11, 0x07); // Clip to bottom left
Window.Box(35, 13, 15, 4, 0x11, 0x07); // Clip to bottom right
// All the screen object destructors called automatically
}
```

To run this program, you will need the files listed in Table 5.3. The source files for **rsounit** and **trsounit** are provided in Listings 5.1 through 5.4. The program creates two **Trsos**, **Screen** and **Window**, which are initialized in the first half of the program. The basic steps used to create and initialize a **Trso** object are:

```
Trso Window(&ScrnBuff);
Window.SetLocn(31, 9); // Place and size our window
Window.SetSize(13, 3); // to be inside our box
```

When an object is created, its constructor is called to initialize the data member **Pic** to reference some screen buffer, in this case **ScrnBuff**.

Table 5.3   Files needed to compile trtest.cpp

Main file	Header file	Chapter
scrnsty.cpp	scrnsty.h	3
txunit.cpp	txunit.h	3
msmouse.cpp	msmouse.h	4
rsounit.cpp	rsounit.h	5
trsounit.cpp	trsounit.h	5

The first part of the program sets up a screen buffer, **ScrnBuff**, and a **Trso** object, **Screen**, to access the text video memory. The screen is then cleared and a box is drawn in the center.

In the second part of the program another **Trso** object is created, **Window**, which is aliased and positioned to appear within the box drawn earlier. The window is cleared by calling its **Fill()** member function, and then a string is written and clipped using a negative X coordinate. Note how the message:

```
Hey, you: press any key
```

gets changed to

```
press any key
```

In the third part of the program, we clear the screen, and resize and relocate the window. Then, we demonstrate that boxes can also be clipped by drawing boxes at various positions around the window as illustrated in Figure 5.6. Recall that in C++ the destructors for the objects are called automatically when the program ends.

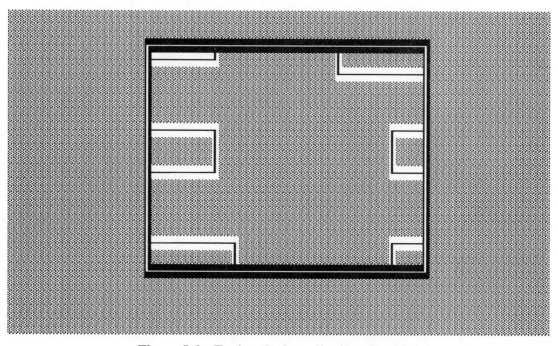

Figure 5.6   Testing the box clipping algorithm

Code Critique

Although the **Rect** and **Rso** classes seem like they are packed with features, a few important routines were omitted because of space limitations. Both of these classes, however, are designed so that it would be easy to add new features. A few of the alterations to **Rect** and **Rso** that you might want to consider follow.

Adding a Clear Function

One feature you might want to add to the **Rso** class is a **Clear()** member function. This function could be coded as:

```
void Rso::Clear(char Ch, char Wa)
{
  Pic->Fill(0, 0, Wd, Ht, Ch, Wa);
}
```

This routine would set a rectangular region to the character specified in **Ch** and the attribute **Wa**.

Supporting Text Cursors

Notice that we have not provided support for a text cursor. To support such a feature, member functions must be provided to save, restore, and move the cursor. This could be accomplished by including two data members for the cursor position, and two member functions to move and obtain the cursor position. The built-in Turbo C++ routines **gotoxy()**, **wherex()**, and **wherey()** could be used to reduce the amount of code you would have to write. If you use this technique, ensure that you translate the absolute screen coordinates to coordinates relative to the rectangle object being used.

Combining Classes

Because **Rso** and **Rect** are small, you might be tempted to combine them into one object class. Is this worthwhile? Not really. In terms of memory usage, you would only save the space required to store a virtual function table. The **Rect** and **Rso** classes each support one important aspect of representing and processing rectangular screen objects. The **Rect** class implements the sizing, clipping, and positioning functions, and the **Rso** class establishes the common protocol for text and graphics mode screen objects. In general, you should try to keep your classes focused as we've done here. Whenever possible, it's a good idea to define smaller classes that are built on top of each other using inheritance instead of creating one large class that's difficult to maintain.

Listing 5.1   rsounit.h

```
// rectangle classes: rsounit.h

#ifndef H_RSOUNIT
#define H_RSOUNIT

#include "scrnsty.h"

enum { False = 0, True = 1 };

// ———— Rectangle Class ————

class Rect {
public:
  int Xul, Yul;  // Upper left-hand corner
  int Xlr, Ylr;  // Lower right-hand corner
  int Wd, Ht;    // Overall size
  Rect(int X, int Y, int W, int H);
  virtual ~Rect(void) { ; }
  virtual void SetSize(int W, int H);
  virtual void SetLocn(int Xl, int Yl);
  virtual void ClipSize(int &W, int &H);
  virtual void ClipDim(int &X, int &Y, int &W, int &H);
  virtual int HzClip(int &X, int &Y, int &N);
  virtual int VtClip(int &X, int &Y, int &N);
  virtual int Contains(int X, int Y);
  virtual int Touches(Rect *R);
};

// ———— Rectangular Screen Object Class ————

class Rso : public Rect {
public:
  Rso(int X, int Y, int W, int H) : Rect(X,Y,W,H) { ; }
  virtual void HzWrt(int, int, char *, char) = 0;
  virtual void HzWrtB(int, int, char *) = 0;
  virtual void Fill(int, int, int, int, char, char) = 0;
  virtual void FillB(int, int, int, int, char, char) = 0;
  virtual void Box(int, int, int, int, char, char) = 0;
  virtual void Scroll(ScrollDir, int) { ; }
};

#endif
```

Listing 5.2   rsounit.cpp

```
#include "rsounit.h"

Rect::Rect(int X, int Y, int W, int H)
// Initializes the dimensions of an Rso
{
  Xul = X;  Yul = Y;   // Upper left-hand corner
  Xlr = X + W - 1;     // Lower right-hand corner
  Ylr = Y + H - 1;
  Wd = W;  Ht = H;  // Overall size
}

void Rect::SetSize(int W, int H)
// Sets the size of a rectangle and adjusts the lower-right
// coordinates
{
  Wd = W;  Ht = H;
  Xlr = Xul + W - 1;     // Adjust lower-right corner
  Ylr = Yul + H - 1;
}

void Rect::SetLocn(int X1, int Y1)
// Sets the top left coordinates and adjust the lower-right
// coordinates also
{
  Xul = X1;  Yul = Y1;
  Xlr = X1 + Wd - 1;
  Ylr = Y1 + Ht - 1;
}

void Rect::ClipSize(int &W, int &H)
// Checks width (W) and height (H) to ensure that they are not
// larger than the rectangle's dimensions. If they are, then
// they are adjusted to fit. Also, the sizes must be greater
// than zero.
{
  if (W > Wd) W = Wd;
  if (W < 1)  W = 1;
  if (H > Ht) H = Ht;
  if (H < 1)  H = 1;
}

void Rect::ClipDim(int &X, int &Y, int &W, int &H)
// Checks the incoming dimensions to ensure they are in range
// of the rectangle. If not, they are adjusted to fit.
{
  int X1, Y1;
  ClipSize(W, H);               // Make sure wd and ht are in range
  if (X < Xul) X = Xul;         // Make sure upper left-hand
  if (Y < Yul) Y = Yul;         // corner is in range
  X1 = X + W - 1;               // Check right-hand coordinate
```

```
   if (X1 > X1r) X -= X1 - X1r;
   Y1 = Y + H - 1;                    // Check lower coordinate
   if (Y1 > Y1r) Y -= Y1 - Y1r;
}


int Rect::HzClip(int &X, int &Y, int &N)
// Given a starting coordinate (X,Y) (relative to the rectangle),
// and a length N, this function clips N to fit in the rectangle,
// assuming that the length runs horizontal. If X is negative, it
// is set to zero and the length adjusted accordingly. Y must be in
// range. The function returns true if a nonnull clip is found;
// otherwise, false is returned.
{
  int Rval = False;
  if ((Y >=0) && (Y < Ht)) { // Y must be in range
     if (X < 0) {                  // Clip to left
        N += X;
        X = 0;
     }
     if ((N > 0) && (X < Wd)) {
        if ((X + N) > Wd) N = Wd - X; // Clip to right
        Rval = True;
     }
  }
  return Rval;
}


int Rect::VtClip(int &X, int &Y, int &N)
// Given a starting coordinate (X,Y) (relative to the rectangle),
// and a length N, this function clips N to fit in the rectangle,
// assuming that the length runs vertical. If Y is negative, it
// is set to zero and the length adjusted accordingly. X must be in
// range. This function returns true if a nonnull clip is found;
// otherwise, false is returned.
{
  int Rval = False;
  if ((X >=0) && (X < Wd)) { // X must be in range
     if (Y < 0)  {                  // Clip above
        N += Y;
        Y = 0;
     }
     if ((N > 0) && (Y < Ht))  {
        if ((Y + N) > Ht)  N = Ht - Y; // Clip below
        Rval = True;
     }
  }
  return Rval;
}


int Rect::Contains(int X, int Y)
// Returns true if (X,Y) are contained in the rectangle
{
  return (X >= Xul) && (X <= X1r) &&
```

```
                (Y >= Yul) && (Y <= Ylr);
}

int Rect::Touches(Rect *R)
// Returns true if R overlaps this object. They overlap if their
// horizontal and vertical extents both cross. Note that as
// defined, a rectangle can't overlap itself.
{
  if (R == this) return False;
  else return
      (Xul <= R->Xlr) && (Xlr >= R->Xul) && // Hz crossing
      (Yul <= R->Ylr) && (Ylr >= R->Yul);   // Vt crossing
}
```

Listing 5.3   trsounit.h

```
// trsounit.h: Text-Based Rectangular Screen Object (Trso) Class

#ifndef H_TRSOUNIT
#define H_TRSOUNIT

#include "msmouse.h"
#include "txunit.h"
#include "rsounit.h"

class Trso : public Rso {
public:
  TxBuff *Pic;
  Trso(TxBuff *T);
  virtual ~Trso(void);
  virtual void SetSize(int W, int H);
  virtual void SetLocn(int Xl, int Yl);
  virtual void HzWrt(int X, int Y, char *Str, char Attr);
  virtual void HzWrtB(int X, int Y, char *Str);
  virtual void Fill(int X, int Y, int W, int H, char Ch, char Attr);
  virtual void FillB(int X, int Y, int W, int H, char Ch, char Opt);
  virtual void Box(int X, int Y, int W, int H, char Ba, char Attr);
  virtual void Scroll(ScrollDir Sd, int Amt);
  virtual void Swap(int X,int Y,int W,int H, Trso *Other, int Xs,int Ys);
  virtual void Xfr(int X,int Y,int W,int H,  Trso *Src, int Xs,int Ys);
};

#endif
```

Listing 5.4   trsounit.cpp

```
// trsounit.cpp: Trso class implementation
// These routines use the built-in rectangle to clip any screen
// transfers. They also take care of the mouse cursor.
```

```
#include <stdlib.h>
#include <string.h>
#include "trsounit.h"

Trso::Trso(TxBuff *T) : Rso(0, 0, 0, 0)
// Initializes a rectangle and sets up the texel buffer
{
  if (T == 0) {
     Pic = new TxBuff(0);
  }
  else {
    Pic = new TxBuff(T->TxRam);
    Rso::SetSize(T->Wd, T->Ht);
    Pic->SetSize(T->Wd, T->Ht);
  }
}


Trso::~Trso(void)
// Deallocates the texel buffer
{
  delete Pic;
}


void Trso::SetSize(int W, int H)
// Sets the size of a rectangle. If the rectangle's buffer
// isn't aliased (which means it was allocated on the heap),
// the buffer is resized as well.
{
  Rso::SetSize(W, H);
  if (!Pic->Aliased) Pic->SetSize(W, H);
}


void Trso::SetLocn(int X1, int Y1)
// Sets the rectangle's location and the origin reference
// (OrgPtr) in the texel buffer
{
  Rso::SetLocn(X1, Y1);
  Pic->SetLocn(X1, Y1);
}


void Trso::HzWrt(int X, int Y, char *Str, char Attr)
// Writes a string horizontally in a specified attribute.
// Supports both left- and right-hand clipping.
{
  int Cnt, Offset;
  Cnt = strlen(Str);
  if (X < 0) Offset = -X; else Offset = 0;
  if (HzClip(X,Y,Cnt)) {
     Mouse.Hide();
     Pic->HzWrt(X,Y,Str+Offset,Attr,Cnt);
     Mouse.Show();
  }
}
```

```
void Trso::HzWrtB(int X, int Y, char *Str)
// Writes a string horizontally without changing the screen
// attribute. Supports both left- and right-hand clipping.
{
  int Cnt, Offset;
  Cnt = strlen(Str);
  if (X < 0)  Offset = -X; else Offset = 0;
  if (HzClip(X,Y,Cnt))  {
    Mouse.Hide();
    Pic->HzWrtB(X,Y,Str+Offset,Cnt);
    Mouse.Show();
  }
}

void Trso::Fill(int X, int Y, int W, int H, char Ch, char Attr)
// Fills a rectangular region with both a character and an
// attribute. Supports clipping on all sides. Note the checks
// for a horizontal (single row) and vertical (single column)
// fills so that the clipping works correctly.
{
  if (((H == 1) && HzClip(X, Y, W)) ||
      ((W == 1) && VtClip(X, Y, H)) ||
      (VtClip(X,Y,H) && HzClip(X,Y,W)))  {
    Mouse.Hide();
    Pic->Fill(X, Y, W, H, Ch, Attr);
    Mouse.Show();
  }
}

void Trso::FillB(int X, int Y, int W, int H, char Ch, char Opt)
// Fills a rectangular region with either a character or an
// attribute, but not both. Clipping is performed on all four sides.
// Here's how the control parameter works:
//
//   Opt == 0 - character fill
//   Opt == 1 - attribute fill
{
  if (((H == 1) && HzClip(X, Y, W)) || // Single row
      ((W == 1) && VtClip(X, Y, H)) || // Single column
      (VtClip(X,Y,H) && HzClip(X,Y,W))) {
    Mouse.Hide();
    Pic->FillB(X, Y, W, H, Ch, Opt);
    Mouse.Show();
  }
}

void Trso::Box(int X, int Y, int W, int H, char Ba, char Attr)
// Draws a text-based box of a specified style and width
{
  unsigned char Bw, Bs, I;
  Bw = (unsigned char)Ba & 0x000f;         // Unpack the border width
  Bs = ((unsigned char)Ba >> 4) & 0x000f;  // Unpack the border style
  Mouse.Hide();
```

```
      if ((Bs < 4))  {
        for (I = 0; I<Bw; I++, X++, Y++, W-=2, H-=2) {
          Fill(X, Y, W, 1, LineChars[Bs][HzBar], Attr);
          Fill(X, Y, 1, H, LineChars[Bs][VtBar], Attr);
          Fill(X, Y, 1, 1, LineChars[Bs][Ulc], Attr);
          Fill(X+W-1, Y, 1, H, LineChars[Bs][VtBar], Attr);
          Fill(X+W-1, Y, 1, 1, LineChars[Bs][Urc], Attr);
          Fill(X, Y+H-1, W, 1, LineChars[Bs][HzBar], Attr);
          Fill(X, Y+H-1, 1, 1, LineChars[Bs][Llc], Attr);
          Fill(X+W-1, Y+H-1, 1, 1, LineChars[Bs][Lrc], Attr);
        }
      }
    Mouse.Show();
}

void Trso::Scroll(ScrollDir Sd, int Amt)
// Scrolls the region defined by the rectangle. The region
// can be scrolled up or down a specified amount.
{
    Mouse.Hide();
    Pic->Scroll(0, 0, Wd, Ht, Sd, Amt);
    Mouse.Show();
}

void Trso::Swap(int X, int Y, int W, int H, Trso *Other, int Xs, int Ys)
// Swaps data between this object's Pic buffer and another Trso's Pic. The
// Other Pic region starts at (Xs, Ys) and this object's Pic region starts
// at X,Y. The swapping region is W by H in size. The coordinates
// are checked to ensure that they are in range and the width and
// height are clipped if necessary.
{
    if (HzClip(X,Y,W) && Other->HzClip(Xs,Ys,W))  {
        if (VtClip(X,Y,H) && Other->VtClip(Xs,Ys,H))  {
            Mouse.Hide();
            Pic->Swap(X, Y, W, H, Other->Pic, Xs, Ys);
            Mouse.Show();
        }
    }
}

void Trso::Xfr(int X, int Y, int W, int H, Trso *Src, int Xs, int Ys)
// Transfers data from the Src Trso Pic region, starting at (Xs, Ys)
// to this object's Pic region, starting at X,Y. The region transfer
// has size W by H. The coordinates are checked to ensure they are in
// range and the width and height are clipped if necessary.
{
    if (HzClip(X,Y,W) && Src->HzClip(Xs,Ys,W)) {
        if (VtClip(X,Y,H) && Src->VtClip(Xs,Ys,H)) {
            Mouse.Hide();
            Pic->Xfr(X, Y, W, H, Src->Pic, Xs, Ys);
            Mouse.Show();
        }
    }
}
```

6

Creating Framed Screen Objects

In Chapter 5 we constructed the first set of classes to serve as the foundation of our interface screen toolkit. The **Rect**, **Rso**, and **Trso** classes that we implemented provide the code needed to support rectangular screen objects. In this chapter we'll build three new classes that combine groups of rectangles into what we call *frames*. We'll start by defining the framed screen object (**Fso**) class and then we'll create a text-specific version called **Tfso**. After we cover these classes, we'll present sample programs that show you how to display pop-up windows. In the last part of the chapter, we'll introduce the **Tskel** class which is used to create rectangular outlines that are useful in moving and resizing screen objects.

Framed Screen Objects

It would be possible to build pop-up windows directly from rectangular screen objects. However, it's convenient to think of a window as being composed of three rectangular regions: the rectangle that bounds the overall extent of the window, including the shadows; the rectangle that bounds the frame or border of the window; and, the rectangle that bounds the interior of the window—the region where textual or graphical figures are drawn. We'll call these rectangles the *overall*, *frame*, and *interior* rectangles, respectively. We'll also call the objects that are composed of three such rectangles *framed screen objects*. Figure 6.1 illustrates the components of a framed screen object.

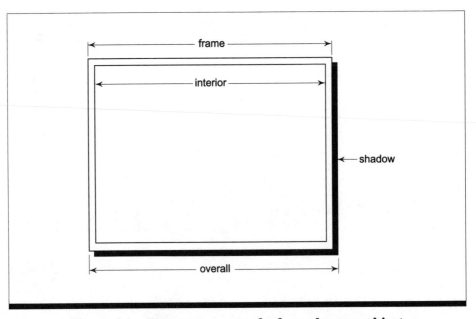

Figure 6.1   The components of a framed screen object

In order to support framed screen objects, we'll be setting up a class hierarchy. As we did with rectangular screen objects, we'll first define a general class, the **Fso** class, and then we'll derive a text-based version, **Tfso**, and a graphics-based version, **Gfso**. The latter will be discussed in Chapter 10.

Essentially, the general class **Fso** plays a role similar to that of the **Rso** class; that is, it helps set up a common protocol to support both the text and graphics worlds. A list of the main features of the **Fso** class is:

1. Uses three rectangular screen objects to construct each framed screen object

2. Manages the colors and styles of frames, including support for both horizontal and vertical shadows

3. Provides member functions for initialization, testing coordinates, writing text, scrolling, and filling

4. Includes data members and high-level functions that serve as the common denominator for text- and graphics-based framed screen objects

The **Fso** class contains more member functions than any of the other classes we've implemented:

```
class Fso {
public:
  Rso *Overall, *Frame, *Interior;
  int Bwd;
  int Bstyle;
  int Fattr;
  ColorPak Colors;
  Fso(int Ba, int Fa, ColorPak &Cp);
  virtual ~Fso(void) { ; }
  virtual int IsSwappable(void);
  virtual int IsCloseable(void);
  virtual int IsStretchable(void);
  virtual int HasShadow(void);
  virtual void SetSize(int W, int H);
  virtual void SetLocn(int X1, int Y1);
  virtual int OnFrame(int X, int Y);
  virtual int OnInterior(int X, int Y);
  virtual int OnBorder(int X, int Y);
  virtual int OnCloseButton(int X, int Y);
  virtual int Touches(Fso *F);
  virtual void Clear(char, char) { ; }
  virtual void DrawFrame(char, char) { ; }
  virtual void GetImage(Rect *) { ; }
  virtual void PutImage(Rect *) { ; }
  virtual void ShadowXfr(Rect *, XfrDirn, int) { ; }
  virtual void DrawShadows(Rect *, XfrDirn, int) { ; }
  virtual void Swap(Rect *, XfrDirn) { ; }
  virtual void Scroll(ScrollDir Sd, int Amt);
  virtual void HzWrt(int X, int Y, char *Str, char Att);
  virtual void HzWrtB(int X, int Y, char *Str);
  virtual void Fill(int X, int Y, int W, int H, char Ch, char Attr);
  virtual void FillB(int X, int Y, int W, int H, char Ch, char Opt);
  virtual void Box(int X, int Y, int W, int H, char Ba, char Attr);
  virtual int TextWidth(char *) { return 0; }
  virtual int TextHeight(int) { return 0; }
};
```

The top-most data members, **Overall**, **Frame**, and **Interior**, support the three different rectangular regions of a framed screen object. Even though these variables are declared as pointers of type **Rso**, you'll later see how they will actually point to either **Trso** (text-based) or **Grso** (graphics-based) objects.

Part of the task of the **Fso** class is to manage the drawing styles of the border and shadow surrounding a screen object, as well as manage the colors of the object. For this purpose, the remaining data members, **Bwd**, **Bstyle**, **Fattr**, and **Colors**, store the attributes used to display a screen object including the border width, border type, frame style, colors, and type of shadow.

Many of the member functions used here, such as **SetSize()**, **Scroll()**, **HzWrt()**, **Fill()**, and **Box()**, might look familiar to you because these same names were used to define member functions in the **Trso** class. The **Fso** functions have similar actions to those of **Trso**; the only difference is that we now have three rectangular screen objects to process instead of one. The main function of the **Fso** class is to manage the three rectangular regions **Overall**, **Frame**, and **Interior**. Because of this, member functions such as **SetSize()** and **SetLocn()** must make calls to each of the underlying **Rso**s. Routines such as **HzWrt()** and **Fill()**, however, are routed to the interior object only. Some examples are:

```
void Fso::SetSize(int W, int H)
{
  Interior->SetSize(W, H);
  Frame->SetSize(W, H);
  Overall->SetSize(W, H);
}

void Fso::SetLocn(int X1, int Y1)
{
  Frame->SetLocn(X1, Y1);
  Overall->SetLocn(X1, Y1);
  Interior->SetLocn(X1, Y1);
}

void Fso::HzWrt(int X, int Y, char *Str, char Attr)
{
  if (Attr == 0) Attr = Colors.Wc;
  Interior->HzWrt(X, Y, Str, Attr);
}
```

As **SetSize()** illustrates, the sizes are passed on to the three **Rso**s: **Interior**, **Frame**, and **Rectangle**. The default framing configuration is to have all three rectangles coincide with one another. Therefore, they all have the same size, as given here, and the same location, as **Fso::SetLocn()** shows. Note, however, that in the derived **Fso** classes (e.g., **Tfso** and **Gfso**) the rectangles will have different sizes and locations.

In general, all the member functions that write text to an **Fso** use the interior rectangle, and they use a default color scheme, as illustrated by the **HzWrt()** member function. Note that in **HzWrt()**, the **Attr** parameter can be passed as a zero value. This value instructs the routine to use the default window color as stored in the **Fso**. Once the color is determined, the string to be written is passed on to **Interior**'s **HzWrt()** function. Note that the location of the string, specified by X and Y is interpreted to be relative to the interior object.

Although data is normally written to the interior rectangle, it's still possible to write to the border or overall rectangle. For instance, if **F** is an **Fso** object, we could use the following statement to write a title on the border of **F**:

```
F.Frame->HzWrt(0, 0, "I am a title", 0x07);
```

Testing Coordinate Status

The **Fso** class also contains a set of new functions to determine whether a point touches one of the main components of a screen object. These routines include **OnInterior()**, **OnFrame()**, **OnBorder()**, **OnCloseButton()**, and **Touches()**. Here are the **OnInterior()** and **OnFrame()** member functions:

```
int Fso::OnInterior(int X, int Y)
{
  return Interior->Contains(X, Y);
}

int Fso:: OnFrame(int X, int Y)
{
  return Frame->Contains(X, Y);
}
```

Both of these routines call the **Contains()** function of the appropriate **Rso**. Note that "On" means that the coordinates are anywhere within the rectangle, including its bounds. Thus, if **OnFrame()** is **True** (a value of 1), it means that the coordinates are either on the border or within it.

The **OnBorder()** function, however, tests to see if the coordinates of a point are somewhere on the border. Since the **Interior** rectangle is usually just within the **Frame** rectangle, you can test for being on the border by testing to see if the **Frame** contains the point, but the **Interior** object doesn't:

```
int Fso::OnBorder(int X, int Y)
{
  return Frame->Contains(X,Y) && !Interior->Contains(X,Y);
}
```

Note that this logic can work with borders of arbitrary shapes. For instance, the frames could have headers where the headers are considered to be part of the border or the frames could be designed not to have a top or bottom at all (which you'll see with scroll bars in Chapter 9). In all these cases, the **OnBorder()** routine will work just fine.

Another member function, **OnCloseButton()**, tests whether a point touches the object's close button. Note that the **Fso** class doesn't dictate where the close button is; this task is left to the derived classes. Thus, the **OnCloseButton()** function of **Fso** simply returns **False** (a value of 0). Once the coordinates of the close button are known, **OnCloseButton()** should be overridden in the derived class in order to do the actual test.

The last member function is the **Touches()** routine. It tests to see if one **Fso** touches another. Note that two **Fsos** are to be considered touching if their **Overall** rectangles touch:

```
int Fso::Touches(Fso *F)
{
  return Overall->Touches(F->Overall);
}
```

Working with Screen Images and Shadows

Another task of the **Fso** class is to manage in a generic way the swapping and transferring of screen images and the drawing of shadows. For this purpose, the member functions **GetImage()**, **PutImage()**, **Swap()**, **ShadowXfr()**, and **DrawShadows()**
are provided. Since **Fso** is a general class, and is not meant to be used directly,
these functions are just stubs, and are meant to be overridden in a derived class.
You'll see how they are used when we present the **Tfso** class later in this chapter.

Working with Attributes and Colors

Each **Fso** stores information regarding the color and style of a frame. This information is initialized by the **Fso()** constructor. For instance, the **Colors** variable,
which stores the set of colors for the **Fso**, is initialized with the parameter **Cp**.
The border and frame attributes are passed using the parameters **Ba** and **Fa**. What is the
difference between the border and frame attributes? The border attribute specifies
the line style and width for the object's border and the frame attribute specifies the
style of frame: whether it has a close button, has shadows, and is swappable (and
thus moveable).

The border attribute is made up of two components: the border's line style and
the border's width. This attribute can be conveniently represented by a two-digit
hex value, where the first digit specifies the line style and the second digit specifies the width. Table 6.1 lists the codes that are supported to define the border's
line style. These constants are defined in **scrnsty.h**, which was presented in

Table 6.1   Border attribute codes for text screen objects

Code	Style	Constant name
0x00	No border	NoBorder
0x10	Single line border	Single
0x20	Double line border	Double
0x30	Dashed line border	Dashed

Chapter 3. Some examples of valid codes for the border attribute are:

0x31   a dashed line with a width of 1 unit

0x12   a single line with a width of 2 units

0x21   a double line with a width of 1 unit

Table 6.2 lists the frame styles that are supported. These constants are also defined in **scrnsty.h**. These attributes are designed so that you can combine them to support different frame styles. For example, the expression

```
Swappable+Closeable+WithShadow
```

creates a screen object that is swappable, has a close button, and has a shadow. The following is a sample declaration of an **Fso** object that illustrates how border and frame attributes are set.

```
Fso F(0x21, Swappable+Closeable+WithShadow, BlueColors);
```

The last argument defines the color set that will be used to display the object. Recall that **scrnsty.cpp** has some pre-defined sets of colors, such as **BlueColors**:

```
ColorPak BlueColors - {0x17, 0x1e, 0x3e, 0x5e, 0x1b};
```

To summarize how the border, frame, and color attributes work, Figure 6.2 shows a window with its attributes and color components labeled.

Table 6.2   Frame attribute codes for text screen objects

Code	Description	Constant name
0x01	Object has a swap buffer	Swappable
0x02	Object can be closed (has close button)	Closeable
0x04	Object has southeast shadow	SEShadow
0x08	Object has northeast shadow	NEShadow
0x10	Object has northwest shadow	NWShadow
0x20	Object has southwest shadow	SWShadow
0x40	Object will be moved as an outline	OutlineMove
0x80	Object's border will change when selected	BorderPrompt
0x0100	Object can be resized	Stretchable

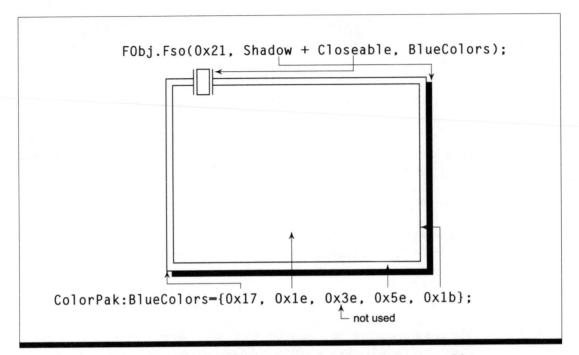

Figure 6.2   The attributes and colors used with a screen object

Because the frame attributes are represented as bits packed into a word, the member functions **IsSwappable()**, **IsCloseable()**, **IsStretchable()**, and **Has-Shadow()** are provided for conveniently testing these attributes. For example, the **IsSwappable()** function is:

```
int Fso::IsSwappable(void) { return (Fattr & Swappable) != 0; }
```

The Tfso Class

Now that we've defined the **Fso** class, it's time to derive a more specific version of it—one that works in text mode. This new class is called **Tfso**, which stands for "text framed screen object." The main features of **Tfso** are:

1. Provides text screen support for the **Fso** class.

2. Includes a **Trso** object called **SaveBuff** to serve as a swap buffer. The buffer allows us to swap screen images while hiding and moving the screen object.

3. Provides support for the horizontal and rectangular shadows. The shadows can be displayed in four different configurations.

4. Supports a close button on the border of the object.

Figure 6.3 shows the type of screen object that can be created with **Tfso**. In this case a window is shown that contains both a close button and a set of shadows. The close button is "hard coded" so that it is drawn on the object's frame at the upper-left corner. The shadows, however, are represented as **Tfso** objects and can be drawn on any side of the screen object.

The complete definition of **Tfso** is:

```
class Tfso : public Fso {
public:
  Trso *SaveBuff;
  Tfso *HzShadow, *VtShadow;
  Tfso(int Ba, int Fa, ColorPak &Cp);
  virtual ~Tfso(void);
  virtual void SetSize(int W, int H);
  virtual void SetLocn(int X1, int Y1);
  virtual int  OnCloseButton(int X, int Y);
```

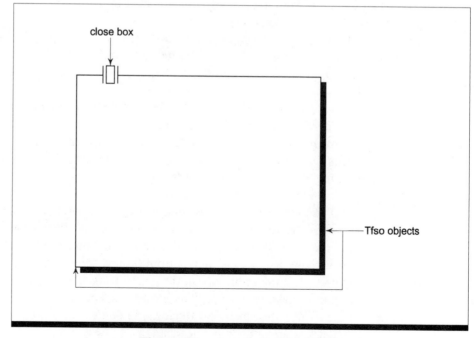

Figure 6.3   A sample Tfso object

```
   virtual void DrawFrame(char Ba, char Attr);
   virtual void Clear(char Ch, char Attr);
   virtual void GetImage(Rect *C);
   virtual void PutImage(Rect *C);
   virtual void ShadowXfr(Rect *C, XfrDirn Xd, int DrawIt);
   virtual void DrawShadows(Rect *C, XfrDirn Xd, int Drawit);
   virtual void Swap(Rect *C, XfrDirn Xd);
   virtual int  TextWidth(char *Str) { return strlen(Str); }
   virtual int  TextHeight(int N)    { return N; }
};
```

The technique that we're using to implement this class is similar to that used to implement the **Trso** class—we are using two classes as parents. In this case, the parents are **Fso** and **Trso**. The **Fso** class provides the components we need to support general framed-screen objects and the **Trso** class provides access to the text screen specific member functions and data members.

There are three data members: **SaveBuff**, **HzShadow**, and **VtShadow**. Note that all three of these variables are pointers to other objects. In particular, **HzShadow** and **VtShadow** are pointers to other **Tfso**s themselves and represent the objects used to the shadow. They are implemented as objects so that they can have their own save buffers and can be located on any side of the frame.

All the member functions in **Tfso** were present in **Fso**. Many of the overridden functions were not actually implemented in **Fso** so the **Tfso** class must provide all of the working code.

To initialize a **Tfso** object, the **Tfso()** constructor is used. This routine initializes the internal objects **Overall**, **Frame**, and **Interior** (inherited from **Fso**) to point to **Trso** objects, and **HzShadow** and **VtShadow** are created if the **Tfso** object uses shadows.

After a **Tfso** is initialized, its size and location can be set by calling **SetSize()** and **SetLocn()**. Unlike the **Fso** class, where the three rectangles **Overall**, **Frame**, and **Interior** coincide, in the **Tfso** class, the three rectangles are actually different regions of the object. The **Interior** region is just inside the **Frame** region, and the **Overall** region covers both the border and any shadows present.

It's important to realize how the coordinates and dimensions to **SetLocn()** and **SetSize()** are interpreted. The location is always set relative to the top left-hand corner of the **Frame** rectangle. The size, however, is always with respect to the **Interior** rectangle. You might wonder about the latter interpretation. Later on, we'll be creating auto-sizing menus from framed screen objects. The size of the menu entries determines the size of the menu. Thus, it's convenient to set the size with respect to the interior, since that's where the menu entries will be drawn. By sizing the **Tfso** with respect to **Interior**, you don't have to know whether or not the menu has a border or frame header.

An example of the steps required to create and initialize a **Tfso** is:

```
Tfso T(0x31, Swappable+WithShadow+CloseAble, CyanColors);
T.SetSize(20, 10);
T.SetLocn(10, 10);
```

In this case we are initializing the object **T** to be displayed at location (10,10) with an interior size of 20 columns and 10 rows. These statements don't actually draw the screen object. In order to do so, we need to call **DrawFrame()**, as shown:

```
T.DrawFrame(0,0);
```

When the two parameters are set to 0, **DrawFrame()** uses the default border attributes and colors assigned to the screen object at initialization time. In this case, the **CyanColors** are used and the border is a single dashed line. The **DrawFrame()** function displays the screen object frame by calling the **Box()** member function from the **Trso** class in the statement:

```
Frame->Box(0, 0, Frame->Wd, Frame->Ht, Ba, Attr);
```

Recall that **Frame** is defined in **Fso** to be a pointer to an **Rso**. However, in the constructor **Tfso()**, we set up **Frame** to actually point to a **Trso**. Thus, the **Box()** member function called above will actually be the function from the **Trso** class, not the **Rso** class—a good example of polymorphism at work.

Swapping Objects and Drawing Shadows

Although we've explained how screen objects are initialized and displayed, we haven't yet told you how objects are moved or how shadows are drawn. The shadowing feature adds the greatest complexity to the **Tfso** class. As Figure 6.4 shows, shadows can be displayed horizontally and vertically in four different configurations.

As you've seen in earlier chapters, the basic technique for moving screen objects around involves swapping images between the screen and an image save buffer. For this purpose, the member functions **GetImage()**, **PutImage()**, and **Swap()** are provided. With **Tfsos**, this swapping is complicated by the fact that we must also handle the shadows as well. For this reason, two other member functions are provided: **ShadowXfr()** and **DrawShadows()**.

The shadows present a unique problem: When should they be clipped, if at all? Later on, you'll see how we can define screen objects that reside in, or are bounded by, other screen objects. The subordinate screen object can move only within the interior of the parent object. While we'll always ensure that the basic frame of the object is never clipped, for esthetic purposes, we will allow the

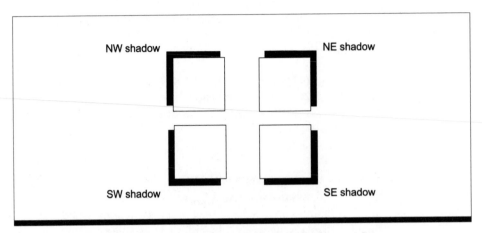

Figure 6.4   The four different shadow styles

shadows to be clipped. For this reason, each of the image transferring functions is passed a pointer to a **Rect** object which serves as a clipping rectangle for the shadows.

Some of the functions take two other parameters for the shadows as well. One parameter determines whether a shadow is to be filled in with gray, or whether we want to transfer to and from the shadow image save buffer. The other parameter determines the direction of image transfer taking place, and is actually an enumerated type:

```
XfrDirn - (GetIm, PutIm);
```

The **GetIm** value means we are transferring an image from the screen to a save buffer. The **PutIm** value means just the opposite.

Let's take a look at the **ShadowXfr()** routine, which is at the heart of all the image transferring functions:

```
void Tfso::ShadowXfr(Rect *C, XfrDirn Xd, int DrawIt)
// Depending on Xd, either put the image in the shadow buffer
// onto the screen, or get the image from the screen into
// the buffer. If getting the image, and if DrawIt is True,
// after saving the screen image, draw the shadow
// by using a gray fill color. It's assumed this is a
// shadow, and it's assumed the buffer is not NULL. C is
// the clipping rectangle for the shadow.
{
  int X, Y, W, H;
  Trso *Tp - (Trso *)Overall;
  X - Tp->Xul - C->Xul;  // Must compute coordinates relative
  Y - Tp->Yul - C->Yul;  // to the clipping rectangle
  W - Tp->Wd; H - Tp->Ht;
  if (C->HzClip(X, Y, W) && C->VtClip(X, Y, H)) {
      X -- Tp->Xul - C->Xul; // Compute coordinates relative
```

```
      Y -= Tp->Yul - C->Yul; // to the shadow
      if (Xd == PutIm) {  // From buffer to screen
        Tp->Xfr(X, Y, W, H, SaveBuff, 0, 0);
      }
      else { // From screen to buffer, then possibly draw
        SaveBuff->Xfr(0, 0, W, H, Tp, X, Y);
        if (DrawIt) Tp->FillB(X, Y, W, H, 8, 1); // Gray fill
      }
    }
  }
}
```

This member function is fairly tricky. First, it assumes that the object in use (i.e., the one defined by **this**) is a shadow, and not just any **Tfso** (recall that shadows are **Tfso**s too). Second, we must convert to coordinates relative to the clipping rectangle, clip those coordinates, convert them back to be relative to the shadow, and then do an image transfer in the appropriate direction. On top of that, if we're doing a **GetIm** transfer, we are saving the region below the shadow, and in some cases, we then actually want to draw the shadow by filling in the region with gray.

The **ShadowXfr()** member function is a low-level routine called by **DrawShadows()**:

```
void Tfso::DrawShadows(Rect *C, XfrDirn Xd, int DrawIt)
{
  if (HasShadow()) {
    HzShadow->ShadowXfr(C, Xd, DrawIt);
    VtShadow->ShadowXfr(C, Xd, DrawIt);
  }
}
```

The **DrawShadows()** function is in turn called by the **GetImage()**, **PutImage()**, and **Swap()** member functions. Let's take a look at the **Swap()** routine (the other two are similar):

```
void Tfso::Swap(Rect *C, XfrDirn Xd)
// Swap the screen image bounded by the frame rectangle and the
// save buffer. The Xfr direction Xd and clipping rectangle C
// are used only for the shadows, which are drawn/erased accordingly.
{
  if (IsSwappable()) {
    Trso *Tf = (Trso *)Frame;
    Tf->Swap(0, 0, Tf->Wd, Tf->Ht, SaveBuff, 0, 0);
    DrawShadows(C, Xd, True);
  }
}
```

The **Swap()** function is actually quite simple. It calls the **Swap()** member function from the inherited **Trso** class to exchange two screen regions. Then, it swaps the shadow images by calling **DrawShadows()**. Note that we keep track of the direction of transfer for those shadows through the parameter **Xd**. Also, in case we are doing a **GetIm** transfer, that is, from the screen to the shadow save buffers—we also set the **DrawIt** parameter of **DrawShadows()** to **True**, so that the shadow regions are actually grayed.

An example of the steps that should be followed if you are processing an object that has a shadow and you want to move the object is:

```
T.Swap(SomeRect, PutIm);   // Hide object-restore screen
T.SetLocn(20, 20);         // Change object's position
T.Swap(SomeRect, GetIm);   // Redisplay the object
```

We've passed in a **Rect** pointer **SomeRect** which serves as the clipping rectangle for the shadows. For instance, if **Rect** is set to the size of the whole screen, then the shadows are clipped to the full screen. Note that the first call to **Swap()** uses the **PutIm** parameter to instruct **DrawShadows()** to erase the window and the shadows by putting the save buffer images back on the screen. The second time around, **GetIm** is specified, which causes the screen image to be saved into the buffers and then the window and shadows to be drawn again.

Determining the Size of Text Strings

There are two member functions in the **Fso** class that we haven't discussed yet: **TextWidth()** and **TextHeight()**. These functions are used to determine the width and height of a string of text. Because **Fso** is a general class, these member functions return zero values only. For the **Tfso** class, we need to return a value that corresponds to the width and height of a text string in text mode. In particular, we want the values to come back in units of texels. In a later chapter, the **Gfso** class will define these member functions to return values in pixels.

The **TextWidth()** function takes a text string for a parameter and simply returns the length of the string. The **TextHeight()** routine takes an integer value, which is meant to represent the number of rows of text to be evaluated, and simply returns that same number. In graphics modes, these routines will be more complicated because they must handle different sizes of fonts.

Displaying Windows

Let's now put the **Tfso** class to work and create a pop-up window. Our first sample program displays a window, writes a few lines of text, scrolls the window, and then moves it to a new location:

```
// tfsotst.cpp - Displays a single window

#include <conio.h>
#include "tfsounit.h"
#include "keybrd.h"

main()
{
  clrscr();
  Tfso T(0x31, Swappable+WithShadow+Closeable, RedColors);
  T.SetSize(40, 15);
  T.SetLocn(10, 5);
  T.GetImage(T.Overall);        // Save image behind window
  T.DrawFrame(0,0);
  T.DrawShadows(T.Overall, GetIm, 1);
  T.Clear(177, 0);
  T.HzWrt(0, 0, "Window 1", 0);
  T.HzWrt(0, 1, "Line 1", 0);
  bioskey(0);
  T.Scroll(UpScroll, 1);        // Scroll up one line
  T.Fill(0,14,40,1,177,0);      // Fill with blank line
  bioskey(0);
  T.Swap(T.Overall, PutIm);     // Hide the window
  bioskey(0);
  T.SetLocn(30, 6);             // Change window's position
  T.Swap(T.Overall, GetIm);     // Redisplay the window
}
```

Figure 6.5 shows the window created by this program. Note that the window has a close box in the upper-left corner. In Chapter 7 we'll be creating a set of classes to manage the windows. One of the management tasks is to detect a mouse click on the close box of a window and to close the window. In this program the close box is drawn but is not used.

To compile the window program, all the source files introduced in this chapter and the files from Chapters 3, 4, and 5 will be needed. One of the first things the program does is to allocate and initialize the screen object **T**:

```
Tfso T(0x31, Swappable+WithShadow+Closeable, RedColors);
```

The parameter **0x31** specifies a single dashed line border, and the frame is made to be swappable and have both shadows and a close button. The last parameter specifies a red color set for this object. Remember that the labels and constants used here are defined **scrnsty.h** and **scrnsty.cpp**.

After setting the size and position for the window, we draw it by calling the member functions **DrawFrame()**, **DrawShadows()**, and **Clear()**. Note that before the window is actually drawn, **GetImage()** is called to save the screen region behind the window. Then, we can move the window to a new location by swapping the image in the buffer with the screen using **Swap()** and **SetLocn()**.

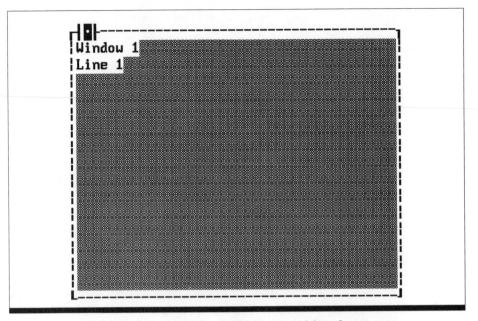

Figure 6.5   A sample window created by tfsotst.cpp

We'll now write a program that displays multiple windows. The program starts by displaying the two windows side-by-side and then it rearranges the windows so that they overlap. As you review the program notice how **Swap()** is used to hide and redisplay the two windows:

```
// tfsotst2.cpp - Displays multiple windows

#include <conio.h>
#include "tfsounit.h"
#include "keybrd.h"

main()
{
  clrscr();
  Tfso T1(0x31, Swappable+Closeable, RedColors);
  T1.SetSize(40, 15);
  T1.SetLocn(5, 5);
  T1.GetImage(T1.Overall);      // Save the image behind the window
  T1.DrawFrame(0,0);            // Draw the window
  T1.Clear(177, 0);
  bioskey(0);
  Tfso T2(0x21, Swappable+Closeable, CyanColors);
  T2.SetSize(30, 10);
  T2.SetLocn(47, 10);
  T2.GetImage(T2.Overall);         // Save the image behind window 2
  T2.DrawFrame(0,0);
  T2.Clear(177, 0);
```

```
T1.HzWrt(0, 1, "Window 1", 0); // Display message in window 1
bioskey(0);
T2.HzWrt(0, 1, "Window 2", 0); // Display message in window 2
bioskey(0);
T1.Swap(T1.Overall, PutIm);    // Hide window 1
bioskey(0);
T2.Swap(T2.Overall, PutIm);    // Hide window 2
T1.SetLocn(30, 6);             // Move window 1 and redisplay
T1.Swap(T1.Overall, GetIm);
bioskey(0);
T2.Swap(T2.Overall, GetIm);    // Put window 2 on top
bioskey(0);
}
```

The windows created by this program are shown in Figure 6.6.

When you run this program, remember that low-level screen interface tools are being used at this point. After the second layer of our object libraries is created in Chapter 7, you'll find that objects such as pop-up windows are much easier to create and manage. Sample programs have been provided in this section so that you can see what is needed to process the rectangular screen objects at a lower level.

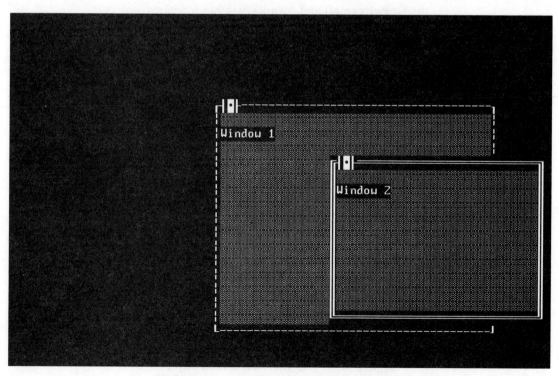

Figure 6.6   Displaying multiple windows

Skeletons in the Closet

We're not quite done with the first two layers of our interface toolkit. We still need an additional class, **Tskel**, which defines "text skeleton" objects that can be used as outlines when moving and resizing a screen object (see Figure 6.7). When a screen object is ready to be moved or resized, a dashed outline is overlaid on top of the screen object border and the outline is manipulated instead. Then, when the move or resize is finished, the outline is erased and the screen object itself is redrawn at the new size or location.

The use of skeletons allows us to move and resize screen objects more efficiently. Recall that screen objects are moved by swapping images between the screen and the swap buffer. With the skeleton objects, only the border, and not the interior is swapped. This makes the swapping much faster, and results in less flicker, especially on slower machines.

Key features of the **Tskel** class are:

1. Contains an array of **Trso** objects to serve as swap buffers for the four sides of the skeleton screen object

2. Draws and moves the rectangular outline shape using derived versions of the **DrawFrame()** and **Swap()** member functions

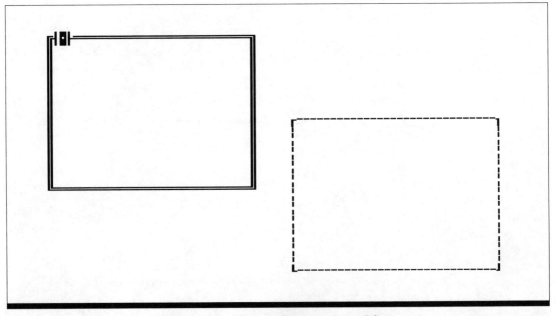

Figure 6.7   The skeleton screen object

3. Provides an example of a different type of frame object than the one produced by the **Tfso** class

The **Tskel** class has only to override those functions used to draw, swap, and transfer images, and to set up the border sizes:

```
class Tskel : public Fso {
public:
  Trso *Sides[4]; // Top, Bottom, Left, Right
  Tskel(ColorPak &Cp);
  virtual ~Tskel(void);
  virtual void SetSize(int W, int H);
  virtual void DrawFrame(char Ba, char Attr);
  virtual void GetImage(Rect *C);
  virtual void PutImage(Rect *C);
  virtual void Swap(Rect *C, XfrDirn Xd);
};
```

The only data member is the array **Sides** which is used to store and retrieve the four sides of the outline as shown in Figure 6.8. When the outline is moved only the screen region under these four objects is saved and restored.

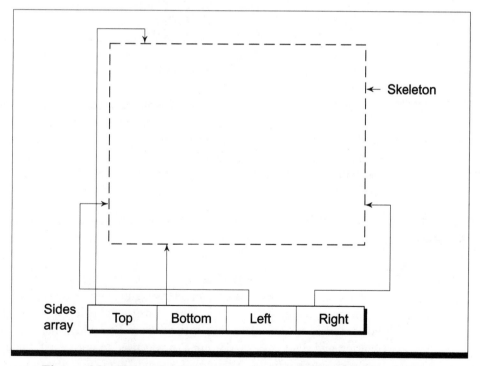

Figure 6.8   Using the Sides array to access the sides of a skeleton

The Tskel Member Functions

Note that the **Tskel()** constructor, which is responsible for initializing a **Tskel** object, takes only a **ColorPak** as a parameter. The border and frame styles are hard-coded to give a swappable, dashed-line frame with no shadows or close box.

The member functions responsible for drawing and moving a skeleton object are **DrawFrame()**, **GetImage()**, **PutImage()**, and **Swap()**. The **DrawFrame()** routine presented here is essentially the same as the **DrawFrame()** function provided with the **Tfso** class except that this overridden version doesn't draw a close box. The **GetImage()**, **PutImage()**, and **Swap()** functions, however, require major modifications so that they transfer only the border image. For example, the new **Swap()** function is:

```
void Tskel::Swap(Rect *, XfrDirn)
// Swap save buffer image and frame buffer image.
// Note: we don't use the parameters.
{
  Trso *Tf = (Trso *)Frame;

  if ((Tf->Ht < 1) || (Tf->Wd < 1)) return;
  Tf->Swap(0, 0, Tf->Wd, 1, Sides[0], 0, 0);          // Top row
  Tf->Swap(0, Tf->Ht-1, Tf->Wd, 1, Sides[1], 0, 0);   // Bottom row
  if (Tf->Ht > 2) {
     Tf->Swap(0, 1, 1, Tf->Ht-2, Sides[2], 0, 0);        // Left side
     Tf->Swap(Tf->Wd-1, 1, 1, Tf->Ht-2, Sides[3], 0, 0); // Right side
  }
}
```

Note that this function calls the **Swap()** member function from the **TxBuff** class four times—once for each side of the outline. Since **Tskel** objects might be used when resizing screen objects, we must be sure to have a rectangle with a width or height greater than one. Also, if the height of the rectangle is one or two rows, then there is no need to handle the left and right sides—the top and bottom will suffice—since the sides won't have any shadows.

Code Critique

The **Fso** class allows us to create flexible screen objects. It represents an abstract screen object that has a border, an interior, and an overall region. As you've seen, the manner in which these regions are constructed is left to more specific classes. For example, a **Tfso** class was derived from **Fso** which has a simple border, an interior, and shadows. In addition **Fso** was used to derive a **Tskel** class which has a border but no interior. Although **Tfso** and **Tskel** share the same parent, they are implemented very differently.

The **Fso** class is powerful because of its general nature. A number of design issues surface when working with this general class. A few of the major issues are discussed in the following sections.

Changing Frames

Although most framed screen objects have a simple border, frames that have a top header can also be created. An example of this is in Chapter 10 when the **Gfso** class is built. Also frames can be created that may not appear to be frames at all. The scroll bar frames presented in Chapter 9 are one such example. These frames have sides that contain scroll arrows, but they do not have a top or bottom border.

Adding Titles

One feature missing from the **Fso** class is support for window titles. This feature could easily be added by changing the **DrawFrame()** member function and passing the title in as a parameter in the **Fso()** constructor.

Restricting Member Function Access

Since the **Tskel** class is derived from the **Fso** class, it has all the member functions of the **Fso** class, including those that write to the interior, such as **HzWrt()** and **Fill()**. However, since a **Tskel** object is supposed to be just an outline, we don't really want to allow the use of these member functions. That is, we want to restrict the access to them. We could use the **public** and **private** keywords in the **Tskel** class to prevent access, but we haven't taken this approach because we want to leave as much flexibility as possible in any classes that you might want to derive from **Tskel**. Alternatively, we could selectively protect some of the inherited member functions from being called by overriding these functions in the **Tskel** class and stubbing them out. Then, if called, they wouldn't do anything useful, which would discourage their use.

Tips on Creating General Classes

When defining a general class such as **Fso**, you won't always know which member functions and data members are needed to serve as the common protocol. Often, you discover what's really needed in the general class only after you have completed the design. You may need to use the class for a while before you find out, so don't be afraid to experiment.

Listing 6.1   fsounit.h

```
// fsounit.h: Framed Screen Object (FSO) General Class

#ifndef H_FSOUNIT
#define H_FSOUNIT

#include <stdlib.h>
#include "rsounit.h"

enum CoordType { Relc, Absc };
enum XfrDirn   { GetIm, PutIm };

class Fso {
public:
  Rso *Overall, *Frame, *Interior;
  int Bwd;
  int Bstyle;
  int Fattr;
  ColorPak Colors;
  Fso(int Ba, int Fa, ColorPak &Cp);
  virtual ~Fso(void) { ; }
  virtual int IsSwappable(void);
  virtual int IsCloseable(void);
  virtual int IsStretchable(void);
  virtual int HasShadow(void);
  virtual void SetSize(int W, int H);
  virtual void SetLocn(int Xl, int Yl);
  virtual int OnFrame(int X, int Y);
  virtual int OnInterior(int X, int Y);
  virtual int OnBorder(int X, int Y);
  virtual int OnCloseButton(int X, int Y);
  virtual int Touches(Fso *F);
  virtual void Clear(char, char) { ; }
  virtual void DrawFrame(char, char) { ; }
  virtual void GetImage(Rect *) { ; }
  virtual void PutImage(Rect *) { ; }
  virtual void ShadowXfr(Rect *, XfrDirn, int) { ; }
  virtual void DrawShadows(Rect *, XfrDirn, int) { ; }
  virtual void Swap(Rect *, XfrDirn) { ; }
  virtual void Scroll(ScrollDir Sd, int Amt);
  virtual void HzWrt(int X, int Y, char *Str, char Att);
  virtual void HzWrtB(int X, int Y, char *Str);
  virtual void Fill(int X, int Y, int W, int H, char Ch, char Attr);
  virtual void FillB(int X, int Y, int W, int H, char Ch, char Opt);
  virtual void Box(int X, int Y, int W, int H, char Ba, char Attr);
  virtual int TextWidth(char *) { return 0; }
```

```
   virtual int TextHeight(int) { return 0; }
};

#endif
```

Listing 6.2   fsounit.cpp

```cpp
// fsounit.cpp: FSO Class Implementation

#include "fsounit.h"

Fso::Fso(int Ba, int Fa, ColorPak &Cp)
// Sets up the frame and border attributes and assigns the three
// Rsos (Frame, Interior, and Overall) to NULL. The Rsos should be
// initialized by a derived class.
{
  Bwd      = Ba & 0x000f;        // Unpack the border width
  Bstyle   = (Ba >> 4) & 0x000f; // and the border type
  Fattr    = Fa;
  Colors   = Cp;
  Frame    = NULL;               // Must be set by derived
  Interior = NULL;               // class
  Overall  = NULL;
}

int Fso::IsSwappable(void) { return (Fattr & Swappable) !- 0; }

int Fso::IsCloseable(void) { return (Fattr & Closeable) !- 0; }

int Fso::IsStretchable(void)
{
  return (Fattr & Stretchable) && IsSwappable();
}

int Fso::HasShadow(void) { return (Fattr & AnyShadow) !- 0; }

int Fso::OnInterior(int X, int Y)
{
  return Interior->Contains(X, Y);
}

int Fso:: OnFrame(int X, int Y)
{
  return Frame->Contains(X, Y);
}

int Fso::OnBorder(int X, int Y)
{
  return Frame->Contains(X,Y) && !Interior->Contains(X,Y);
}
```

```
int Fso::OnCloseButton(int /*X*/, int /*Y*/)
// Checks to see if the location X,Y resides on close button.
// Fsos don't have a close button, but a derived type might.
{
  return False;
}

int Fso::Touches(Fso *F)
{
  return Overall->Touches(F->Overall);
}

// The following screen transfer routines use the interior
// rectangle. Also, the attributes can be defaulted to their
// stored values.

void Fso::Scroll(ScrollDir Sd, int Amt)
{
  Interior->Scroll(Sd, Amt);
}

void Fso::HzWrt(int X, int Y, char *Str, char Attr)
{
  if (Attr == 0) Attr = Colors.Wc;
  Interior->HzWrt(X, Y, Str, Attr);
}

void Fso::HzWrtB(int X, int Y, char *Str)
{
  Interior->HzWrtB(X,Y,Str);
}

void Fso::Fill(int X, int Y, int W, int H, char Ch, char Attr)
{
  if (Attr == 0) Attr = Colors.Wc;
  Interior->Fill(X, Y, W, H, Ch, Attr);
}

void Fso::FillB(int X, int Y, int W, int H, char Ch, char Opt)
{
  Interior->FillB(X, Y, W, H, Ch, Opt);
}

void Fso::Box(int X, int Y, int W, int H,  char Ba, char Attr)
{
  if (Attr == 0) Attr = Colors.Bc;
  if (Ba == 0) Ba = (Bstyle << 4) + Bwd;
  Interior->Box(X, Y, W, H, Ba, Attr);
}

// The default arrangement is for the rectangles to be on
// top of one another as given in these default SetSize and
// SetLocn routines
```

```
void Fso::SetSize(int W, int H)
{
  Interior->SetSize(W, H);
  Frame->SetSize(W, H);
  Overall->SetSize(W, H);
}

void Fso::SetLocn(int X1, int Y1)
{
  Frame->SetLocn(X1, Y1);
  Overall->SetLocn(X1, Y1);
  Interior->SetLocn(X1, Y1);
}
```

Listing 6.3   tfsounit.h

```
// tfsounit.h: Text-Based Framed Screen Object (Tfso) Class

#ifndef H_TFSOUNIT
#define H_TFSOUNIT

#include <string.h>
#include "trsounit.h"
#include "fsounit.h"

class Tfso : public Fso {
public:
  Trso *SaveBuff;
  Tfso *HzShadow, *VtShadow;
  Tfso(int Ba, int Fa, ColorPak &Cp);
  virtual ~Tfso(void);
  virtual void SetSize(int W, int H);
  virtual void SetLocn(int X1, int Y1);
  virtual int  OnCloseButton(int X, int Y);
  virtual void DrawFrame(char Ba, char Attr);
  virtual void Clear(char Ch, char Attr);
  virtual void GetImage(Rect *C);
  virtual void PutImage(Rect *C);
  virtual void ShadowXfr(Rect *C, XfrDirn Xd, int DrawIt);
  virtual void DrawShadows(Rect *C, XfrDirn Xd, int DrawIt);
  virtual void Swap(Rect *C, XfrDirn Xd);
  virtual int  TextWidth(char *Str) { return strlen(Str); }
  virtual int  TextHeight(int N)    { return N; }
};

// — Text based "skeleton" framed screen objects —

class Tskel : public Fso {
public:
  Trso *Sides[4]; // Top, bottom, left, right
  Tskel(ColorPak &Cp);
```

```
    virtual ~Tskel(void);
    virtual void SetSize(int W, int H);
    virtual void DrawFrame(char Ba, char Attr);
    virtual void GetImage(Rect *C);
    virtual void PutImage(Rect *C);
    virtual void Swap(Rect *C, XfrDirn Xd);
};

extern TxBuff ScrnBuff; // The text buffer representing the screen

#endif
```

Listing 6.4   tfsounit.cpp

```
// tfsounit.cpp: Tfso Class Implementation

#include <dos.h>
#include "tfsounit.h"

// Set up a default TxBuff for Tfso and Tskel objects.
// We use the current screen mode, and assume an 80x25 screen.

TxBuff ScrnBuff(80, 25, VideoPtr());

Tfso::Tfso(int Ba, int Fa, ColorPak &Cp)
// Makes a text-based Fso. (We default the Trsos so that they
// use the full-screen texel buffer.) We set up the shadows and
// null out the swap buffer.
: Fso(Ba, Fa, Cp)
{
  Overall  = new Trso(&ScrnBuff);  // Type as Trsos
  Frame    = new Trso(&ScrnBuff);
  Interior = new Trso(&ScrnBuff);
  SaveBuff = NULL;    // To be allocated by SetSize
  if (HasShadow()) { // Shadows are Tfsos themselves
     HzShadow = new Tfso(0x00, Swappable, Cp);
     VtShadow = new Tfso(0x00, Swappable, Cp);
  }
  else { // We don't have any shadows
    HzShadow = NULL;  VtShadow = NULL;
  }
}

Tfso::~Tfso(void)
// Destroy the save buffer and the shadow objects.
// Then destroy the frame rectangles.
{
  if (IsSwappable()) delete SaveBuff;
  if (HasShadow()) { delete HzShadow; delete VtShadow; }
  delete Frame;
  delete Interior;
```

```
      delete Overall;
}

void Tfso::SetSize(int W, int H)
// The size (W,H) is interpreted to be the interior size.
// The other sizes are based off of it. Allocates space
// for the save buffer if swappable.
{
  Interior->SetSize(W, H);
  Frame->SetSize(W+Bwd*2, H+Bwd*2);
  if (HasShadow()) {
     Overall->SetSize(Frame->Wd+2, Frame->Ht+1);
     HzShadow->SetSize(Frame->Wd+1, 1);
     VtShadow->SetSize(2, Frame->Ht-1);
  }
  else {
     Overall->SetSize(Frame->Wd, Frame->Ht);
  }
  if (IsSwappable()) {
     if (SaveBuff == NULL) {
        SaveBuff = new Trso(NULL);
     }
     SaveBuff->SetSize(Frame->Wd, Frame->Ht);
  }
}


void Tfso::SetLocn(int Xl, int Yl)
// Set the upper left-hand corner location of the frames.
// The location is interpreted to be that of the frame
// rectangle. Also, set the shadow locations depending on
// the type of shadow.
{
  Frame->SetLocn(Xl, Yl);
  Interior->SetLocn(Xl+Bwd, Yl+Bwd);
  switch (Fattr & AnyShadow) {
    case SEShadow:
      Overall->SetLocn(Frame->Xul, Frame->Yul);
      HzShadow->SetLocn(Frame->Xul+1, Frame->Ylr+1);
      VtShadow->SetLocn(Frame->Xlr+1, Frame->Yul+1);
      break;
    case NEShadow:
      Overall->SetLocn(Frame->Xul, Frame->Yul-1);
      HzShadow->SetLocn(Frame->Xul+1, Frame->Yul-1);
      VtShadow->SetLocn(Frame->Xlr+1, Frame->Yul);
      break;
    case NWShadow:
      Overall->SetLocn(Frame->Xul-2, Frame->Yul-1);
      HzShadow->SetLocn(Frame->Xul-2, Frame->Yul-1);
      VtShadow->SetLocn(Frame->Xul-2, Frame->Yul);
      break;
    case SWShadow:
      Overall->SetLocn(Frame->Xul-2, Frame->Yul);
      HzShadow->SetLocn(Frame->Xul-2, Frame->Ylr+1);
```

```
            VtShadow->SetLocn(Frame->Xul-2, Frame->Yul+1);
            break;
       default: // No shadow
          Overall->SetLocn(Frame->Xul, Frame->Yul);
    }
}

void Tfso::DrawFrame(char Ba, char Attr)
// Draws the frame by simply drawing a box. A close button
// is added if needed.
{
  if (Bwd > 0) {
     if (Ba == 0) Ba = (Bstyle << 4) + Bwd;
     if (Attr == 0) Attr = Colors.Bc;
     Frame->Box(0, 0, Frame->Wd, Frame->Ht, Ba, Attr);
     if (IsCloseable())
        Frame->HzWrt(1, 0, "\xb4\x08\xc3", Colors.Bc);
  }
}

int Tfso::OnCloseButton(int X, int Y)
// Returns true if location (X,Y) is on the close button.
// The close button is near the upper left-hand corner.
{
  return
    IsCloseable() && (Bwd > 0) &&
    (Y == Frame->Yul) && (X == Frame->Xul + 2);
}

void Tfso::Clear(char Ch, char Attr)
// Clears the interior rectangle using the specified character
// and attribute. The attribute can be defaulted to use the
// value stored with the object.
{
  if (Attr > 0) Colors.Wc = Attr;
  Interior->Fill(0, 0, Interior->Wd, Interior->Ht, Ch, Colors.Wc);
}

void Tfso::GetImage(Rect *C)
// Get the screen image region bounded by the frame rectangle
// and store it in the save buffer (if there is one).
// Get the shadow image too. C is the clipping rectangle
// for the shadow.
{
  if (IsSwappable()) {
     SaveBuff->
       Xfr(0, 0, SaveBuff->Wd, SaveBuff->Ht, (Trso *)Frame, 0, 0);
     DrawShadows(C, GetIm, False);
  }
}

void Tfso::PutImage(Rect *C)
// Put the image stored in the save buffer (if there is
```

```
// one) onto the screen at the region bounded by the frame
// rectangle. Put back the saved shadow buffer too. C is
// the clipping rectangle for the shadow.
{
  if (IsSwappable()) {
    Trso *Tf = (Trso *)Frame;
    Tf->Xfr(0, 0, Tf->Wd, Tf->Ht, SaveBuff, 0, 0);
    DrawShadows(C, PutIm, False);
  }
}

void Tfso::Swap(Rect *C, XfrDirn Xd)
// Swap the screen image bounded by the frame rectangle and the
// save buffer. The Xfr direction Xd and clipping rectangle C
// are used only for the shadows, which are drawn/erased accordingly.
{
  if (IsSwappable()) {
    Trso *Tf = (Trso *)Frame;
    Tf->Swap(0, 0, Tf->Wd, Tf->Ht, SaveBuff, 0, 0);
    DrawShadows(C, Xd, True);
  }
}

void Tfso::DrawShadows(Rect *C, XfrDirn Xd, int DrawIt)
{
  if (HasShadow()) {
    HzShadow->ShadowXfr(C, Xd, DrawIt);
    VtShadow->ShadowXfr(C, Xd, DrawIt);
  }
}

void Tfso::ShadowXfr(Rect *C, XfrDirn Xd, int DrawIt)
// Depending on Xd, either put the image in the shadow buffer
// onto the screen, or get the image from the screen into
// the buffer. If getting the image, and if DrawIt is True,
// after saving the screen image, draw the shadow
// by using a gray fill color. It's assumed this is a
// shadow, and it's assumed the buffer is not NULL. C is
// the clipping rectangle for the shadow.
{
  int X, Y, W, H;
  Trso *Tp = (Trso *)Overall;
  X = Tp->Xul - C->Xul;  // Must compute coordinates relative
  Y = Tp->Yul - C->Yul;  // to the clipping rectangle
  W = Tp->Wd; H = Tp->Ht;
  if (C->HzClip(X, Y, W) && C->VtClip(X, Y, H)) {
    X -= Tp->Xul - C->Xul; // Compute coordinates relative
    Y -= Tp->Yul - C->Yul; // to the shadow
    if (Xd == PutIm) {  // From buffer to screen
      Tp->Xfr(X, Y, W, H, SaveBuff, 0, 0);
    }
    else { // From screen to buffer, then possibly draw
      SaveBuff->Xfr(0, 0, W, H, Tp, X, Y);
```

```
        if (DrawIt) Tp->FillB(X, Y, W, H, 8, 1); // Gray fill
      }
    }
  }


  // ——— Now for the Text Skeleton Methods ———

  Tskel::Tskel(ColorPak &Cp)
  // Much like the Tfso class, except we have swap buffers for
  // the sides, and none for the interior. Sets the size to
  // 80x25. It's assumed the size will be changed during
  // moving/stretching. Setting it to 80x25 here will help
  // alleviate heap fragmentation. Border style has dashed lines,
  // and frame style is swappable and stretchable.
  : Fso(0x31, Swappable+Stretchable, Cp)
  {
    int I;

    Overall  = new Trso(&ScrnBuff); // Type as Trsos
    Frame    = new Trso(&ScrnBuff);
    Interior = new Trso(&ScrnBuff);
    for (I=0; I<4; I++) Sides[I] = NULL;
    SetSize(80, 25); // This allocates the sides
  }


  Tskel::~Tskel(void)
  // Does away with the side swap buffers
  {
    int I;
    for (I=0; I<4; I++) delete Sides[I];
  }

  void Tskel::SetSize(int W, int H)
  // Sets the size of the rectangles and the side swap buffers
  {
    int I;

    Interior->SetSize(W, H);
    Frame->SetSize(Interior->Wd+2, Interior->Ht+2);
    Overall->SetSize(Interior->Wd+2, Interior->Ht+2);

    for (I=0; I<4; I++) {
        if (Sides[I] == NULL) Sides[I] = new Trso(NULL);
        if (I < 2) { // The top and bottom
           Sides[I]->SetSize(Frame->Wd, 1);
        }
        else { // the left and right sides
           Sides[I]->SetSize(1, Frame->Ht);
        }
        Sides[I]->Pic->Fill(0, 0,  // Blank out the sides
          Sides[I]->Pic->Wd, Sides[I]->Pic->Ht, ' ', Colors.Bc);
    }
  }
```

```
void Tskel::DrawFrame(char Ba, char Attr)
// Just like the Tfso version
{
  if (Bwd > 0) {
     if (Ba == 0) Ba = (Bstyle << 4) + Bwd;
     if (Attr == 0) Attr = Colors.Bc;
     Frame->Box(0, 0, Frame->Wd, Frame->Ht, Ba, Attr);
  }
}

void Tskel::GetImage(Rect *)
// Get the sides from screen to buffer.
// Note: We don't use the rectangle parameter.
{
  Trso *Tf = (Trso *)Frame;

  if ((Tf->Ht < 1) || (Tf->Wd < 1)) return;
  Sides[0]->Xfr(0, 0, Tf->Wd, 1, Tf, 0, 0);            // Top row
  Sides[1]->Xfr(0, 0, Tf->Wd, 1, Tf, 0, Tf->Ht-1);     // Bottom row
  if (Tf->Ht > 2) {
     Sides[2]->Xfr(0, 0, 1, Tf->Ht-2, Tf, 0, 1);         // Left side
     Sides[3]->Xfr(0, 0, 1, Tf->Ht-2, Tf, Tf->Wd-1, 1); // Right side
  }
}

void Tskel::PutImage(Rect *)
// Get the sides from buffer to screen.
// Note: we don't use the rectangle parameter.
{
  Trso *Tf = (Trso *)Frame;

  if ((Tf->Ht < 1) || (Tf->Wd < 1)) return;
  Tf->Xfr(0, 0, Tf->Wd, 1, Sides[0], 0, 0);            // Top row
  Tf->Xfr(0, Tf->Ht-1, Tf->Wd, 1, Sides[1], 0, 0);     // Bottom row
  if (Tf->Ht > 2) {
     Tf->Xfr(0, 1, 1, Tf->Ht-2, Sides[2], 0, 0);         // Left side
     Tf->Xfr(Tf->Wd-1, 1, 1, Tf->Ht-2, Sides[3], 0, 0); // Right side
  }
}

void Tskel::Swap(Rect *, XfrDirn)
// Swap save buffer image and frame buffer image.
// Note: we don't use the parameters.
{
  Trso *Tf = (Trso *)Frame;

  if ((Tf->Ht < 1) || (Tf->Wd < 1)) return;
  Tf->Swap(0, 0, Tf->Wd, 1, Sides[0], 0, 0);            // Top row
  Tf->Swap(0, Tf->Ht-1, Tf->Wd, 1, Sides[1], 0, 0);     // Bottom row
  if (Tf->Ht > 2) {
     Tf->Swap(0, 1, 1, Tf->Ht-2, Sides[2], 0, 0);         // Left side
     Tf->Swap(Tf->Wd-1, 1, 1, Tf->Ht-2, Sides[3], 0, 0); // Right side
  }
}
```

![7 chapter marker]

Interactive Screen Objects

In Chapter 6 we created the basic classes that serve as the foundation for our window and menu package. In this chapter, we'll concentrate on two higher-level classes that will manage the interaction between screen objects and handle events from the mouse and keyboard.

We'll start by presenting an overview of the classes that will be created and then we'll take a close look at the interactive screen object (**Iso**) class. This class is responsible for setting up the functions and data structures needed to implement a window and menu class system. Our next stop will be the **IsoMgr** class which provides the management operations for the **Iso** class. After we discuss these general classes, we'll construct a window screen object class (**Wso**) to display and process text windows. At our last stop, we'll derive some classes for processing selection buttons.

Supporting Multiple Screen Objects

The **Rso**, **Trso**, **Fso**, and **Tfso** classes presented in the previous chapters provide the needed support for displaying simple screen objects (text windows). Two important features, however, are missing. First, there is no way of controlling the interaction between windows (e.g., handling overlapping windows). Second, there is no way to control the windows with the keyboard and mouse. We need to add these features to make our screen objects interactive.

Managing interactive objects is not an easy task. There are a number of book-keeping and processing operations that must be performed, such as keeping track of which screen object is active, passing messages to objects, performing an action when an object is selected, moving objects in front of or behind other objects, resizing objects, and processing events such as mouse movements and mouse clicks. As we'll see in this chapter, the **Iso** and **IsoMgr** classes are designed to handle these operations.

An important feature of the **Iso** and **IsoMgr** classes is that they allow screen objects to be grouped together. Figure 7.1 presents an example of one type of interface that can be created with these classes. Note that the screen consists of a large window and a set of smaller selection buttons. Because the buttons are drawn on top of the window and are assigned to the window, they will move and maintain their positions relative to each other when the main window is moved.

The grouping feature of the screen object toolkit is helpful for creating more complex interface objects such as menus and dialog boxes. In Chapters 8 and 9 we'll see how to combine objects such as selection buttons, scrollable windows, and scrollable menus to build interface tools similar to the ones provided with Turbo C++.

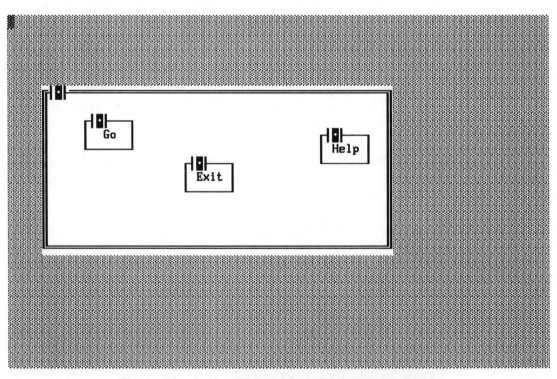

Figure 7.1   An interface with multiple screen objects

The Interactive Screen Object Hierarchy

The **Iso** and **IsoMgr** classes represent the next layer in our interface toolkit. They provide the necessary support to handle the interaction between screen objects. Like the **Rso** and **Fso** classes, the **Iso** and **IsoMgr** classes are general classes, and have no features specific to either text or graphics modes. They provide the essentials to support both of these modes. More specific classes will be derived to create text- or graphics-based windows.

Figure 7.2 shows the hierarchy of the classes used to manage text and graphics screen interface objects. As shown, the **Iso** class sits at the top level and is used to derive window screen object classes for both text and graphics. An **IsoMgr** object is contained in each **Iso** object to help manage and process the events that can occur. It is essentially a stack containing multiple **Iso**s that can be drawn on top of each other, and can be grouped together. From the **Iso** class, the **Wso** class is derived, which is used to define window screen objects. These objects are the first true interactive pop-up window objects. From the **Wso** class, you can then derive different variations of pop-up windows, such as buttons, scroll bars, and so on.

The Iso Class

The **Iso** class is the most complex class that we have written. It contains a number of data members and over 30 member functions. However, don't be put off by its size. As we start to unravel its components, you'll see that it's not at all difficult to understand.

Following in the tradition of the **Rso** and **Fso** classes, **Iso** serves as a general class. This means that it is not used directly to define screen objects, but rather it

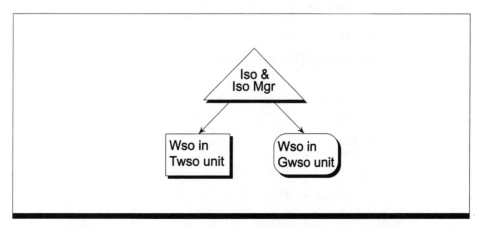

Figure 7.2   The hierarchy of the object manager classes

is used to derive more specific classes that provide such capabilities as text- and graphics-specific windows and selection buttons. Although the **Iso** class is not derived from any of the classes we presented in the previous chapters, it does contain a pointer to an object of type **Fso** so that it can hook into text- and graphics-based framed screen objects.

The following is a summary of the main features of the **Iso** class.

1. Each **Iso** serves as a node on a stack that keeps track of the relationships between screen objects.

2. An **Iso** is essentially an **Fso** with functions to handle user interaction—mouse events and keyboard events. A good way to think of it is that **Iso**s are **Fso**s brought to life.

3. The **Iso** class serves as the backbone for the next layer in the toolkit—the text- or graphics-based windows, menus, dialog boxes, and so on.

Th definition of the **Iso** class is:

```
class Iso {
public:
  Fso *Panel;         // Can be a Tfso or Gfso pointer
  char Active;        // True if Iso is selected
  char Visible;       // True if Iso is showing
  char IsClosed;      // True if Iso is closed
  char TouchFlag;     // True if touching another Iso
  char ClipToFrame;   // Used for scroll bars
  Iso *Base;          // The base for this Iso
  Iso *Under, *Over;  // Iso stack pointers
  IsoMgr *SubMgr;     // The child Iso stack
  Iso(Fso *P);
  virtual ~Iso(void);
  virtual Rso *ClippingRect(void);
  virtual void SetLocn(int X1, int Y1, CoordType Ctype);
  virtual void SetSize(int W, int H);
  virtual void Move(int X, int Y);
  virtual void DeltaMove(int Dx, int Dy);
  virtual void MoveLoop(MsgPkt &M);
  virtual void Stretch(int W, int H);
  virtual void DeltaStretch(int Dw, int Dh);
  virtual void StretchLoop(MsgPkt &M);
  virtual int Obscured(void);
  virtual void Draw(void) { ; }
  virtual void DrawPanel(void);
  virtual void Redraw(void) { DrawPanel(); }
  virtual void Open(Iso *B, int X, int Y);
  virtual void Reopen(int X, int Y);
```

```
    virtual void Swap(void);
    virtual void Hide(void);
    virtual void Show(void);
    virtual void SetVisibleFlag(int F);
    virtual void Select(void);
    virtual void Remove(void);
    virtual void Prompt(void);
    virtual void UnPrompt(void);
    virtual void Enter(MsgPkt &M);
    virtual void Leave(MsgPkt &M);
    virtual void SwitchFocus(MsgPkt &M);
    virtual void Activate(MsgPkt &) { ; }
    virtual void OnMouseEnter(MsgPkt &M);
    virtual void OnMouseLeave(MsgPkt &M);
    virtual void OnMouseWithin(MsgPkt &) { ; }
    virtual void OnClose(MsgPkt &M);
    virtual void OnMouseUp(MsgPkt &M) { Activate(M); }
    virtual void OnMouseDown(MsgPkt &M);
    virtual void BorderHandler(MsgPkt &M);
    virtual void OnMouseStillDown(MsgPkt &) { ; }
    virtual void OnKeyStroke(MsgPkt &M);
    virtual void OnShiftArrow(MsgPkt &M);
    virtual void Dispatch(MsgPkt &M);
};
```

Many of the data members in the **Iso** class are needed to manage the screen object stack, which we'll cover in more detail in the next section. The variables **Active**, **Visible**, **IsClosed**, and **TouchFlag** help to keep track of the status of a screen object. When a screen object's **Active** variable is set to **True** (a value of 1), the object will serve as the active screen object. The system is designed so that only one object can be active at a time.

Table 7.1 lists each member function of the **Iso** class with a short description. While you're examining the **Iso** class, you may want to refer to this table to help you understand the operation of these routines. The member functions provided can be grouped into the following categories:

- Specifying the initial position and size of a screen object

- Hiding and drawing an object

- Opening and closing a screen object

- Moving and resizing a screen object

- Activating and deactivating a screen object

- Mouse and keyboard event handlers for the screen object

Table 7.1 Member functions in the Iso class

Member function	Description
Iso()	Initializes an interactive screen object by linking it to a text or graphics framed screen object
~Iso()	Removes a screen object from the screen object stack
ClippingRect()	Returns the appropriate clipping rectangle
SetLocn()	Sets the location of a screen object
SetSize()	Sets the size of a screen object
Move()	Moves an object to a new absolute position
DeltaMove()	Moves an object by an incremental amount
MoveLoop()	Keeps moving an object while the mouse button is pressed and the object is in a drag state
Stretch()	Stretches or resizes an object
DeltaStretch()	Stretches an object by an incremental amount
StretchLoop()	Keeps stretching an object while the mouse button is pressed and the object is in a drag state
Obscured()	Determines if a screen object is partially hidden
Draw()	Special purpose draw routine to be overridden by derived classes
DrawPanel()	Sets up swap buffers and draws an object's frame, clears the interior, and then calls Draw()
Redraw()	Redraws an object
Open()	Opens an object on the screen by drawing the object and using another object as the base
Reopen()	Reopens an object that was previously closed
Swap()	Swaps images between the saved image buffer and the screen
Hide()	Hides an object
Show()	Displays an object that has been previously hidden
SetVisibleFlag()	Sets the Visible flag to indicate if an object is visible or hidden
Select()	Selects an object to be the active object
Remove()	Removes an object from the stack and hides it
Prompt()	Highlights an object to indicate that it is active
UnPrompt()	Unhighlights an object to indicate it is no longer active

continued

Table 7.1   Member functions in the Iso class (*continued*)

Member function	Description
Enter()	Processes the Enter event which selects an object
Leave()	Processes the Leave event which deactivates an object
SwitchFocus()	Switches the focus from one object to another
Activate()	Executes the action assigned to a screen object
OnMouseEnter()	Processes the event when the mouse enters an object
OnMouseLeave()	Processes the event when the mouse leaves an object
OnMouseWithin()	Processes the event when the mouse is inside an object
OnClose()	Processes the event when an object's close button is activated
OnMouseUp()	Processes the event when the mouse button is released
OnMouseDown()	Processes the event when the mouse button is pressed
OnMouseStillDown()	Processes the event of the mouse button still being pressed
BorderHandler()	Processes a border-related mouse event
OnKeyStroke()	Processes keystroke events
OnShiftArrow()	Processes Shift-arrow key presses
Dispatch()	Dispatches mouse and keyboard events

The Screen Object Stack

Before we get too buried in the code for the **Iso** member functions, we need to explore the heart of the interface toolkit—the internal screen object stack. Recall that, at the start of this chapter it was stated that screen objects can be grouped to become more complex screen objects. How is this feature supported? Each object is associated with a base **Iso**. If a single object is drawn on the screen, its **Base** data member points to the full-screen object. Now if we create and draw more screen objects, the **Base** variable in each object can point to a different object, that is, an object can be drawn on another object. Let's explore an example.

Figure 7.3 shows a screen with three objects. Object A is drawn on the screen and objects B and C are drawn on object A. If object A were moved, objects B and C would also move because they are assigned to A. Note how the **Base** data member is set for each object. If we were to change the arrangement by removing

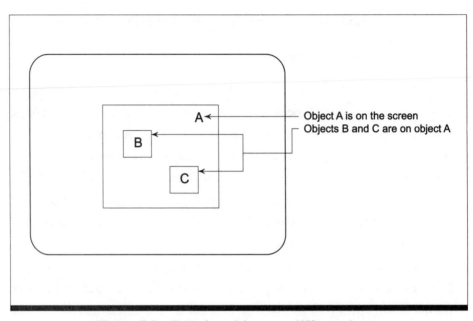

Figure 7.3   Drawing objects on different bases

an object such as object B, object C would also be removed because it is assigned to object B. Such a flexible system can be supported because each screen object has its own stack.

The screen object stacks are slightly complex because each node contains many different pointers to other screen objects. To see what's involved, let's consider another example. Figure 7.4 shows a screen with four objects. Assume that objects A and D use the screen as their base and objects B and C are drawn on object A. Figure 7.5 shows the actual data structure created to represent and process these objects, which is in the form of a threaded stack. Although this structure looks complex, it is actually easy to follow. In the center the **Iso** component for each object is shown. The **Base** pointer references the object which the **Iso** object is drawn on and the **Over** and **Under** pointers reference the objects that are drawn over and under a given object. For example, note that object A's **Over** pointer is set to object D to indicate that D is drawn over A. These pointers are used to determine which objects should be hidden or displayed when another object is selected.

The last object nested in the **Iso** is **SubMgr**. If you review the definition of the **Iso** class you'll see that this data member is declared as type **IsoMgr**. The **IsoMgr** controls how objects are processed by providing the code for an event loop. We won't go into the details of the **IsoMgr** at this point but we will examine the components of this class that are used to help manage the threaded object stack.

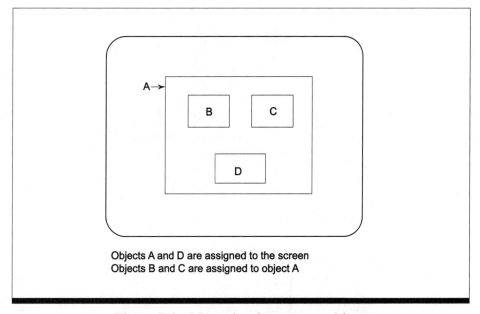

Objects A and D are assigned to the screen
Objects B and C are assigned to object A

Figure 7.4   Managing four screen objects

As Figure 7.5 indicates, each object has its own **IsoMgr** and the **IsoMgr** provides three pointers for accessing the object stack: **Base**, **Top**, and **Bottom**. The **Top** and **Bottom** pointers indicate which objects are on the top and bottom of the object's stack. For example, we know that objects B and C are drawn on object A. If we examine object A's manager, we see that C is on top of the stack and B is on the bottom. The **Base** pointer in the **IsoMgr** tells an object manager which object serves as the base.

After examining Figure 7.5 you'll realize that the object stack we've been discussing actually consists of a set of local stacks, that is, each object manager references and manages its own stack. Whenever an object is moved or removed, the **IsoMgr** is used to determine which objects are assigned to the stack of the object being processed.

Initializing an Iso

When an **Iso** object is initialized, several tasks are performed. First, a framed screen object is assigned to the **Iso**, and some internal flags are set to a known state. Next, the internal stack pointers for the object including **Under**, **Over**, and **Base** are set to **NULL**. Finally, the manager for the object, **SubMgr**, is created and initialized. The code for **Iso**'s constructor is:

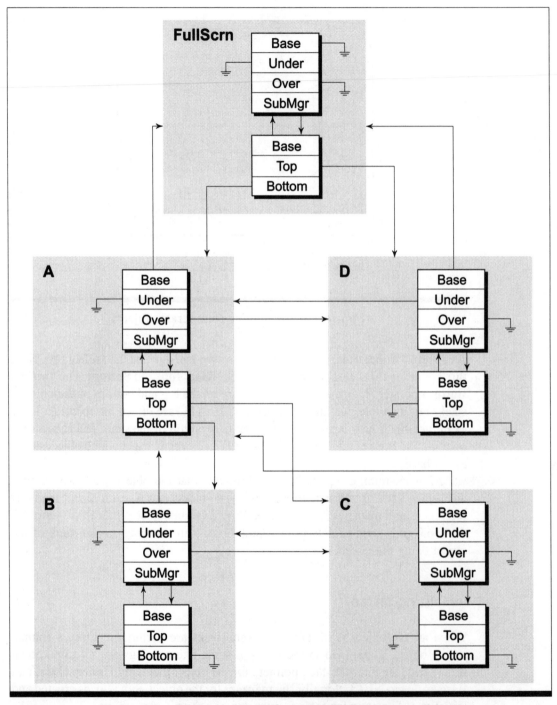

Figure 7.5   Object stack used to process four screen objects

```
Iso::Iso(Fso *P)
// Initializes the Iso by setting all of the data members to
// a default state and sets up an IsoMgr object
{
  Panel - P;                   // P is either a Tfso or Gfso
  Active - False;              // Not selected
  Visible - False;             // Object is not visible
  IsClosed - True;             // Object is not open
  TouchFlag - False;           // Object is not touching another Iso
  ClipToFrame - False;         // Normally, clip to the interior
  Under - NULL; Over - NULL;   // The Iso stack is empty
  Base - NULL;                 // No base to start with
  SubMgr - new IsoMgr(this);   // Make an IsoMgr for this object
}
```

The **Iso()** constructor introduces a subtle trick. Note that the parameter **P**, which is assigned to the **Panel** data member, is typed as a pointer to an **Fso** object. Actually, **P** will be assigned to point to a **Tfso** or **Gfso** object, that is, one of the derived classes of **Fso**. What we are doing here is setting up the **Iso** object so that it can be initialized to work with either text or graphics objects. In effect, the **Iso** object itself won't know if **Panel** is pointing to a **Tfso** or a **Gfso** object. This allows us to use the same code to manage both text and graphics interface objects. (Remember: **Fso** is a general class from which objects are not declared.)

Sizing and Positioning Isos

The two member functions **SetSize()** and **SetLocn()** are used to set the size and position of an **Iso**. Both **SetSize()** and **SetLocn()** use the internal stack. The **SetSize()** function ensures that the size of the object is small enough to fit within the object's base. Note that after initializing an **Iso**, you must also set its size using the **SetSize()** function.

The **SetLocn()** routine allows you to position the size of an object either in terms of absolute coordinates, or in coordinates relative to the object's base. The **SetLocn()** function need not be called directly. It is called by the **Open()** member function (which we're about to discuss) and by the member functions that handle movement of the object. One important feature of **SetLocn()**: It will also reposition any subobjects that happen to reside on the object's own stack. For this reason, the **SetLocn()** function provides a good example of how the stacks are used:

```
void Iso::SetLocn(int X1, int Y1, CoordType Ctype)
// Sets the location of the Iso. If Ctype - Relc, the
// coordinates are relative to the object's base. If the
// object does not have a base (e.g., for FullScrn), then
```

```
// it's assumed the coordinates are always absolute, and
// that SetLocn is only called once.
{
  int Dx, Dy, Dw, Dh;
  Iso *P;
  Rso *Clipper;

  if (Base == NULL) {          // Object does not have a base
     Panel->SetLocn(X1, Y1); // (e.g., FullScrn)
  }
  else { // Object has a base
     Clipper = ClippingRect();
     if (Ctype == Relc) {    // Use relative coordinates
        X1 += Clipper->Xul; // Turn into absolute coordinates
        Y1 += Clipper->Yul; // Turn into absolute coordinates
     }
     // Make sure coordinates are in range. It's assumed that
     // the size is OK at this point.
     Dw = Panel->Frame->Wd; Dh = Panel->Frame->Ht;
     Clipper->ClipDim(X1, Y1, Dw, Dh);
     // Record distance to move for all dependent objects
     Dx = X1 - Panel->Frame->Xul;
     Dy = Y1 - Panel->Frame->Yul;
     // Change location of the object
     Panel->SetLocn(X1, Y1);
     // Change locations of all dependent objects
     P = SubMgr->Top;
     while (P != NULL) {
       P->SetLocn(P->Panel->Frame->Xul+Dx, P->Panel->Frame->Yul+Dy, Absc);
       P = P->Under;  // Get next object on stack
     }
  }
}
```

The location of all objects that are dependent on the object that is being set to a new position must be changed. This is done by starting with the top of the object's stack and changing the location of each object on the stack. Note how **SetLocn()** is called for each of these objects, and they in turn must set the location for the objects on their own stack.

Opening and Closing Isos

After an **Iso** has been initialized and its size set, it can be opened by calling the **Open()** member function.

Opening an object involves three steps. First, the object is given a base and then the object is attached to the base's stack. Second, the size of the object is clipped to ensure that it fits within the base's window. Finally, the object is drawn on the screen by calling **DrawPanel()**. The **Open()** member function is:

```
void Iso::Open(Iso *B, int X, int Y)
// Opens the object by drawing it on a specified base at
// position X,Y relative to the base. Since we now have a
// base, we also clip the size w.r.t to the base. (It's assumed
// that SetSize has already been called at least once.)
{
  Base = B;
  // Push the object onto its base managers' stack
  Base->SubMgr->Push(this);
  IsClosed = False;     // Object now to be open
  // Adjust size if necessary. Can do this by calling SetSize,
  // which will in turn call ClipSize.
  SetSize(Panel->Interior->Wd, Panel->Interior->Ht);
  SetLocn(X, Y, Relc); // Use relative coordinates
  DrawPanel();          // Draw an empty panel
}
```

As an example of how this member function is called, let's look at the statement:

```
Obj1.Open(FullScrn, 10, 2);
```

It will open the screen object **Obj1** on the **FullScrn** object at column 10 and row 2. The **FullScrn** object would then serve as the base for **Obj1**.

In addition to **Open()**, two other member functions are involved with opening and closing an **Iso**. The **OnClose()** member function closes the object by hiding it from view, and setting the **IsClosed** flag. Note that a closed object is not removed from the stack—it is merely hidden. If you want to permanently remove the object, you must use its **Remove()** member function.

The **Reopen()** member function is used to reopen an object that was previously closed. It works by resetting the **IsClosed** flag, positioning the object to a new location that was specified in the parameter list, and then moving the object to the front of the stack and showing it again.

Drawing Isos

Three routines are involved in drawing an **Iso**: **DrawPanel()**, **Draw()**, and **Redraw()**. Drawing an **Iso** actually consists of several steps. Calling **DrawPanel()** initiates the process. This member function draws the panel for the object, and is usually called only by **Open()**. It sets up any swap buffers for the object, draws the frame, including any shadows, clears the interior, and then calls the **Draw()** member function. The code for **DrawPanel()** is:

```
void Iso::DrawPanel(void)
// First, initializes the swap buffer by calling GetImage,
```

```
// draws the frame, draws the shadows, clears the
// interior, and calls the specialized draw routine.
{
  Mouse.Hide();
  Visible = True;   // We'll be visible soon
  if (Panel->IsSwappable()) Panel->GetImage(ClippingRect());
  Panel->DrawFrame(0, 0);
  Panel->DrawShadows(ClippingRect(), GetIm, 1);
  Panel->Clear(' ', 0);
  Draw();
  Mouse.Show();
}
```

The **Draw()** member function, however, serves as the specialized draw routine for an object. It is stubbed out in the **Iso** class, and it is meant to be overridden by classes derived from **Iso**. The **Draw()** function is used to do any additional drawing after the basic panel has been drawn. For instance, a button object's **Draw()** action might be to write the label of the button within the button's interior after the frame has been drawn.

The last member function involved in drawing an **Iso** is **Redraw()**. This function is used to redraw the object after it has been resized. It is called by the **Stretch()** routine that we're about to discuss. The default action of **Redraw()** is to simply call **DrawPanel()**. However, if your object has nested objects drawn on top (e.g., a scroll bar on top of a window), then you might want to override **Redraw()** to handle these nested objects as well. An example of this is presented in Chapter 9 with the **TxScroll** class.

Moving and Stretching Objects

The **Iso** class is powerful in that it allows you to move screen objects as a group, and allows you to resize objects even when they might have nested objects drawn on top of them. To handle these tasks, a series of six member functions are used: **Move()**, **DeltaMove()**, **MoveLoop()**, **Stretch()**, **DeltaStretch()**, and **StretchLoop()**. The first three handle the chores of moving an object, the latter three handle the resizing of an object.

The sequence of actions involved in moving an object are as follows: If the mouse is pressed and dragged on the border of an object, the **MoveLoop()** routine is invoked. This function is essentially a loop that monitors the position of the mouse. If mouse movement is detected, then a call to **DeltaMove()** is made. The **DeltaMove()** function moves the object an incremental amount—the same amount that the mouse is moved. The **DeltaMove()** function in turn calls **Move()**, whose responsibility is to first hide the object, set its new location by calling **SetLocn()**, and then show the object again. Recall that **SetLocn()** will change the location of all subordinate objects of an object. As a result, you can move a whole group of screen objects at once.

The **Stretch()**, **DeltaStretch()**, and **StretchLoop()** member functions work in a similar fashion. If the mouse is pressed on the lower right-hand corner of an object, then **StretchLoop()** is called, which monitors the movement of the mouse. Any such movement is sent to **DeltaStretch()**, which in turn calls **Stretch()**.

The **Stretch()** function is slightly tricky. Before doing the resize, it must hide the object, including all subobjects. The new size must also be limited so that the size of the object is not smaller than the largest subobject. Also, the subobjects may have to be repositioned so that they can still reside within the main object without being clipped. All of the affected objects are then redrawn by calling their **Redraw()** member functions.

The Event Handling System

The **Iso** class is designed around an event handling system. If you have never programmed this type of system, you might be surprised to find that it is relatively easy to set up—especially if you use OOP techniques. Our system is designed to handle both mouse and keyboard events. As Figure 7.6 indicates, the first part of

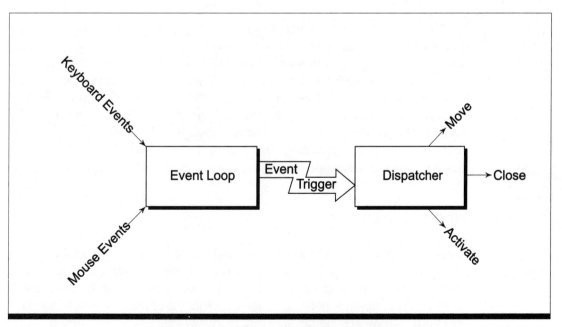

Figure 7.6   The event handling system

the event handler consists of an event loop that monitors incoming events. After an event occurs, a special dispatcher is called to determine which action should be taken (e.g., whether to move, close, or activate a screen object).

To support the event handling system, some member functions will be used to set up an event loop (**EventLoop()** and **EventStep()**), a member function to process events (**Dispatch()**), and member functions to perform actions (**Enter()**, **Leave()**, **Select()**, and so on). All of these routines are found in the **Iso** class except **EventLoop()** and **EventStep()**, which are defined in the **IsoMgr** class.

The Message Passing System

To allow screen objects to communicate with each other, some type of message passing system will be needed. Our system is implemented using a message packet record as shown:

```
struct MsgPkt {        // Message packet
  Iso *Focus;          // Holds current focus
  unsigned Code;       // The event code
  unsigned RtnCode;    // Return event code
  int Mx, My;          // Mouse coordinates
  char Str[80];        // The message
};
```

The event processing member functions, such as **Enter()**, **Leave()**, **Activate()**, **OnMouseEnter()**, and so on, use this message packet for critical status information and to pass back new message codes. When an event occurs, the appropriate event-handling member function is called and the message packet is passed as a parameter so that the function can determine critical status information, such as the coordinates of the mouse cursor or which screen object is active at the time of the event. Note that the message packet also contains a **RtnCode** field so that the object processing the event can cause another event to take place by returning a new code to the event loop.

What's in an Event?

A number of the **Iso** functions are dedicated to processing mouse and keyboard events. Essentially, they serve as the interface to the external world. As stated, when an event occurs such as a mouse button press, a member function is called to carry out the required action. Let's take a look at one of these routines. The code for **OnMouseDown()**, the function that processes a mouse button press, is:

```
void Iso::OnMouseDown(MsgPkt &M)
// If mouse button pressed while inside this object,
// then switch focus to it, handle possibility of
// being on the border
{
  SwitchFocus(M);
  if (Panel->OnBorder(M.Mx, M.My)) BorderHandler(M);
}
```

Note that this message packet is passed as a parameter so that the function can determine the location of the mouse at the time the event occurred. The first task that **OnMouseDown()** performs is to call **SwitchFocus()** which deselects the previously active screen object and then selects the object receiving the **OnMouseDown()** message. The second statement checks to see if the mouse cursor is touching the border of the screen object. If this condition is true, **BorderHandler()** is called to determine if the screen object should be closed, moved, or resized.

The **OnMouseDown()** function should provide you with a good overview of how the different event-handling member functions work. There are six member functions provided for processing mouse events. Table 7.2 lists the mouse-related event codes that are supported by an **Iso** object. Note that the names of the event codes correspond with the names of the functions in **Iso**.

The mouse event codes and mouse processing member functions, such as **OnMouseDown()** and **OnMouseUp()**, tell only half of the story because there are a number of other steps involved in processing a mouse event. When an event occurs, an **Iso** object's **Dispatch()** member function is called to fire the appropriate event handler. The following is how the core of **Dispatch()** appears:

Table 7.2   Mouse events

Event code	Description
MouseDown	A mouse button has been pressed
MouseStillDown	A mouse button is still down
MouseUp	A mouse button has been released
MouseEnter	The mouse cursor has entered a screen object
MouseLeave	The mouse cursor has left a screen object
MouseWithin	The mouse cursor is still within a screen object

```
switch (M.Code) {
  case Idle          :  break;
  case StrMsg        :  break;
  case Close         :  OnClose(M); break;
  case MouseDown     :  OnMouseDown(M); break;
  case MouseStillDown :  OnMouseStillDown(M); break;
  case MouseUp       :  OnMouseUp(M); break;
  case MouseEnter    :  OnMouseEnter(M); break;
  case MouseLeave    :  OnMouseLeave(M); break;
  case MouseWithin   :  OnMouseWithin(M); break;
  default: ;
    OnKeyStroke(M);
}
```

Three categories of events are checked: system level events, mouse events, and keyboard events. For the present, we'll stick to the mouse events. For example, if the mouse button is released, **OnMouseUp()** takes over and then **Activate()** is called to perform the current object's action. If the object is not currently active, **Prompt()** is then called which in turn calls **Select()** to ensure the object is moved to the front of the window stack.

As you start to trace through the event chain for the different mouse events, you'll see that they all follow this basic pattern. The general nature of some of the event-processing member functions, such as **Leave()** and **Activate()**, will allow us to add additional features so that we can later process other types of screen objects including pop-up and pull-down menus.

Keyboard Events

The last member function call, **OnKeyStroke(M)**, in the **switch** statement from **Dispatch()** handles keyboard events. The keyboard is much easier to process than the mouse because only two categories of input keys are processed at this level: the Enter key which selects a screen object, and the Shift-arrow key combinations which are used to move a screen object. If you want to add support for other keyboard actions, **OnKeyStroke()** is the function that must be overridden. (An explanation of how this is done appears later in this chapter.)

Every Screen Object Needs a Manager

We've seen that each screen object has its own manager which is assigned using the **SubMgr** data member. What does this manager actually do? In general, it is responsible for controlling how objects respond to external events. The following is a list of the features that the **IsoMgr** class provides:

1. Moves objects to the top of the stack and handles all other stack-related tasks

2. Dispatches events to the objects

3. Monitors the keyboard and mouse for events

4. Determines which screen objects should be swapped

5. Deallocates all subobjects on the stack

6. Sets up the event loop

The class definition for **IsoMgr** is:

```
class IsoMgr {
public:
  Iso *Top, *Bottom; // Top and bottom of Iso stack
  Iso *Base;         // Who this stack belongs to
  Iso *Hot;          // Who the mouse is currently on
  Iso *Marker;       // A marker used when cycling
  IsoMgr(Iso *B);
  virtual ~IsoMgr(void);
  virtual void Push(Iso *Ip);
  virtual void MoveToFront(Iso *Me, int Keep);
  virtual void ResetTouchFlags(Iso *Me);
  virtual void SetTouchFlags(Iso *Me);
  virtual void OnIso(int Mx, int My, Iso **I);
  virtual Iso *CycleForw(Iso *Curr);
  virtual void ProcessCycle(MsgPkt &M);
  virtual void EventLoop(MsgPkt &M);
  virtual void EventStep(MsgPkt &M);
};
```

Event Loops

The most important job that the **IsoMgr** performs is controlling the event loop for an interface screen object. To implement the event processing system two member functions will be used: **EventLoop()** and **EventStep()**. The **EventLoop()** member function is the main controller for a screen object. It consists of a simple **do-while** loop as shown:

```
do {
  EventStep(M);
  M.Code = M.RtnCode;
  P = Top;
  while ((P != NULL) && (!P->Visible)) P = P->Under;
} while ((M.Code != ShutDown) && (P != NULL));
```

Each iteration of the loop makes a call to **EventStep()** which handles a single event. When **EventStep()** is called it first checks to see if there is a pending event; otherwise, it checks for a new keyboard or mouse event. After **EventStep()** is called, the return code is examined to determine if the event loop should terminate. Note that the loop terminates when there are no screen objects to process or when a shut down event occurs (Alt-X).

Although each object has its own event loop manager, usually only one object's manager is actually invoked. Each manager is capable of handling all subobjects that reside on its stack. For example, later we'll be using a special screen object called **FullScrn** from which all other screen objects are ultimately drawn. The **FullScrn**'s event loop will thus provide complete control for all of our windows. However, in order to provide more flexibility, you may wish to switch event loop managers when entering a new object. This can effectively lock out the processing of all objects that are not children of the new object. An example of this might be for a dialog box, where you might require the user to respond to either the OK or Cancel button in order to continue.

Cycling through Screen Objects

The easiest way to select a screen object is to click on it with the mouse. However, in case you don't have a mouse, a method has been provided where the Tab key is used to cycle through the windows. The member functions **ProcessCycle()**, **Cycle-Forw()**, and **CycleToSibling()** in **IsoMgr** are included for this purpose.

Cycling through the windows is not an easy task. For one thing, we must process the nested stacks by recursively cycling through them. Another problem is that we must be able to skip over screen objects that are not visible. A further complication is that as screen objects are selected, they are moved to the top of the stack they belong to. As a result, the stack order is constantly changing, making it hard to tell when we've actually completed a cycle. To establish a reference point, the variable **Marker** is included in the **IsoMgr** class. This marker is initialized to point to the first screen object to be pushed onto the stack.

The Tab key causes the cycle to work in the forward direction. We've left hooks to provide a backward direction, which would work by pressing the Shift-Tab key.

Creating Text Windows

Now that we've written both of the general classes (**Iso** and **IsoMgr**) for managing interactive screen objects, we need to link these classes to the real world so that we can display and process screen objects. We'll start by creating the **Wso** class to support text window objects:

```
class Wso : public Iso {
public:
  Wso(int Ba, int Fa, ColorPak *Cp);
  virtual void MoveLoop(MsgPkt &M);
  virtual void StretchLoop(MsgPkt &M);
  virtual void Prompt(void);
  virtual void UnPrompt(void);
};
```

The code for the **Wso** class is placed in the **twsounit.h** and **twsounit.cpp** source files provided in Listings 7.3 and 7.4. This class accomplishes three things: it initializes the **Panel** data member of an **Iso** to be a **TfsoPtr** (a pointer to a text-based framed screen object), it handles moving and stretching by using a **Tskel** (skeleton) object, and it supports prompting by changing the border from single line to double line. After you look at **twsounit.cpp** note that very little code is required to implement text screen objects from the general **Iso** class, showing how powerful inheritance can be.

The **Wso()** constructor, shown next, is responsible for initializing a window object. It creates a window by allocating a text framed screen object and using this object to initialize the **Panel** variable of an **Iso** object.

```
Wso::Wso(int Ba, int Fa, ColorPak &Cp)
// Initializes a text window screen object by typing the
// Iso's panel to be a Tfso.
: Iso(new Tfso(Ba,Fa,Cp))
{
  return; // Nothing else to do
}
```

The **MoveLoop()** and **StretchLoop()** member functions incorporate a **Tskel** object so a window can be moved and resized using a dashed-line skeleton rectangle. If you look at these two functions, you'll notice that they are very similar. The main difference is that **MoveLoop()** calls **DeltaMove()** whereas **StretchLoop()** calls **DeltaStretch()**. The other main difference is due to the fact that the location of an **Iso** is relative to the **Frame** rectangle, whereas the size is relative to the **Interior** rectangle. Thus, when moving, we make sure the final movement is with respect to the **Frame** location of the skeleton. In contrast, we make sure the final stretch is with respect to the **Interior** size of the skeleton.

The **Prompt()** and **UnPrompt()** member functions add special features so that we can toggle a window object's border from a single to a double line when the object is selected and from a double to a single line when the object is deselected. The color is also changed back and forth from the border color to the prompt color.

Supporting Text Screens

In order to make the interface tools easier to use with the standard IBM PC text screen, three special-purpose functions have been included in the source file **wsotxscr.cpp** (refer to Listing 7.6). The first function provided, **Setup()**, is used to initialize the mouse and the screen. As an example, the statement

```
Setup(MouseOptional, CyanColors);
```

initializes the **Mouse** object defined in the **msmouse** package for text mode if a mouse is available and initializes the screen using the cyan color set.

The first parameter of **Setup()** specifies how you would like the mouse to be used in your program. The options are described in Table 7.3.

The **wsotxscr.cpp** file declares a global **Wso** object called **FullScrn** to serve as base object for displaying screen objects. The **Setup()** function initializes this object. Note that **FullScrn** is declared in a special way. It's never opened and as such does not have a base of its own.

The second function, **MainEventLoop()**, kicks off the interface screen object manager for the **FullScrn** object by calling the **EventLoop()** member function. (Remember that **EventLoop()** is defined in the **IsoMgr** class.) Once this function is called, it takes over and manages the interactive screen objects that you have previously initialized and opened in your program.

Finally, the **CleanUp()** function deletes **FullScrn** and turns the mouse off. Note that when **FullScrn** is removed, all the other screen objects are removed automatically, so you don't have to close them down individually. Also, note that the

Table 7.3 Setup() mouse parameters

Option	Description
NoMouse	No mouse used.
MouseRequired	Mouse is initialized if possible. Program aborts if error occurs.
MouseOptional	If the mouse can be initialized it is used. Otherwise it's ignored.

mouse object still exists at this point. Since the mouse is a global object, it won't be shut down until the program exits. That's fortunate, since the destructors for the screen objects call the **Hide()** and **Show()** functions of the mouse during their cleanup.

Putting the Wso Class to Work

Let's write a few programs to display and process text windows. Our first program pops up a single text window and allows you to move the window around by moving the mouse cursor to the window's border, pressing the mouse button, and dragging the mouse. If you don't have a mouse, you can move the window using the Shift-arrow keys. You can also resize the window by dragging the mouse on the lower right-hand corner of the window. You can't resize the window with the keyboard, however. To quit the program, either click on the close button, or press Esc or Alt-X.

```
// wsotst1.cpp: This program displays a single pop-up window

#include "wsotxscr.h"

Wso *Window1;

main()
{
  Setup(MouseOptional,MonoColors);     // Setup the environment
  Window1 = new Wso(0x11, WindowStyle+Stretchable, RedColors);
  FullScrn->Panel->Clear(176,0);       // Clear the full screen
  Window1->SetSize(30, 10);
  Window1->Open(FullScrn, 5, 5);       // Open the window on the screen
  MainEventLoop();                     // The event loop takes over
  CleanUp();                           // Remove all the objects
}
```

As shown, the **Wso** class is easy to use. Note that the **Setup()** function just introduced is called at the beginning of the program. After the screen is initialized, the window object is created and then the screen is cleared. The function which actually pops up the window is **Open()**. The window, shown in Figure 7.7, is assigned to the **FullScrn** object and is displayed at row 5 column 5.

After you run the program, experiment with moving the mouse cursor. What happens when the mouse button is pressed while the cursor is within the window's interior? The window is selected and its border is changed from a single line to a double line to indicate that the window is active. If you click on the window's close button the window will be removed and the program will terminate.

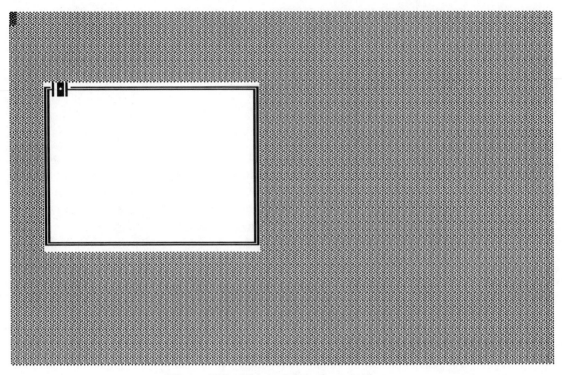

Figure 7.7   The output of wsotst1.cpp

When you drag and move (or resize) the window, note that only an outline of the window is moved. We are able to do this by using an internal **Tskel** object which is created by the **Wso**'s **MoveLoop()** and **StretchLoop()** member functions.

The following program shows how multiple windows are displayed and processed.

```
// wsotst2.cpp: This program displays multiple pop-up windows

#include "wsotxscr.h"

Wso *Window1, *Window2, *Window3;

main()
{
  Setup(MouseOptional,CyanColors);  // Setup the environment
  FullScrn->Panel->Clear('\xb0',0); // Clear the full screen
  // Create the first window
  Window1 = new Wso(0x11, WindowStyle+Stretchable, RedColors);
  Window1->SetSize(50, 15);
  Window1->Open(FullScrn, 2, 2); // Assign the window to the screen
```

```
Window1->Panel->HzWrtB(0,0, "Window 1");
// Create the second window
Window2 = new Wso(0x11, WindowStyle+Stretchable, BlueColors);
Window2->SetSize(20, 8);
Window2->Open(Window1, 2, 3); // Assign the window to window 1
Window2->Panel->HzWrtB(0,0, "Window 2");
Window3 = new Wso(0x11, WindowStyle+Stretchable, InvColors);
Window3->SetSize(20, 10);
Window3->Open(FullScrn, 50, 5);  // Assign the window to the screen
Window3->Panel->HzWrtB(0,0, "Window 3");
MainEventLoop(); // The event loop takes over
CleanUp();       // Remove all the objects
}
```

Figure 7.8 presents the windows that are displayed by this code. This program follows a format that is very similar to the previous example. The only difference is that three windows are defined instead of one. Notice that the first and third windows are opened on the **FullScrn** object. The second window, however, is opened on the first window as shown:

```
Window2->Open(Window1, 2, 3); // Assign the window to window 1
```

This means that whenever the first window is moved, the second window will also be moved. Also, if the first window is resized, its minimum size is limited so that

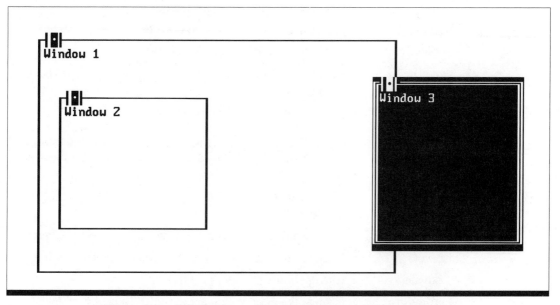

Figure 7.8   Displaying multiple windows with wsotst2.cpp

the second window will always fit within it without being clipped. Note that the second window might be relocated with respect to the first window during resizing. The second window's position is limited to the rectangular region of the first window.

Overriding Member Functions

When we introduced the **Wso** class, we explained how some of the member functions from the **Iso** class such as **MoveLoop()**, **StretchLoop()**, **Prompt()**, and **UnPrompt()** were overridden so that we could add new features. Throughout the rest of this book we'll be using this technique to implement different types of screen objects, such as pop-up and pull-down menus. The trick to applying this technique is knowing which member functions to override. To help you in this process, we've included the most likely candidates in Table 7.4. Some of these functions, such as **Prompt()** and **UnPrompt()**, work together so if you override one of them, make sure that you also override its counterpart.

Table 7.4   Most likely member functions to override

Function	Reason for overriding
~Iso()	Deallocate additionally nested objects
SetLocn()	Position additionally nested objects
SetSize()	Size additionally nested objects
Draw()	Handle specialized drawing after the basic panel has been drawn
Redraw()	Handle specialized redrawing tasks
Open()	Open nested objects
Prompt()	Change how an object is prompted when the object is selected
UnPrompt()	Change how an object is unprompted when the object is deselected
Enter()	Change how an object responds when the object is entered
Leave()	Change how an object responds when the object is left
Activate()	Change how an object is activated
OnKeyStroke()	Change the actions that are assigned to keyboard events

While you can override any of the functions of the **Iso** class, the ones in Table 7.4 should be considered first. Follow this general rule: Try to override as few functions as possible, and override those that give you the most leverage. For instance, we suggest that you override the **Enter()** member function to change the behavior of a screen object when it is first entered. You could override the **MouseEnter()** routine instead. The problem is that this overridden behavior would only work when the object is entered via the mouse, and not by the keyboard. Of course, sometimes that's exactly what you want. In Chapter 11, graphics-based scroll bars will be created that change the mouse cursor as it is passed over the scroll buttons.

There's one other important consideration. Sometimes it's convenient to use nested screen objects. For instance, a scroll bar might contain a scroll button which is included within the object. You'll often open up this subordinate object when the main object is opened. However, for these cases, you don't have to destroy the subordinate object explicitly. That is, you don't need to (and shouldn't) override the destructor to deallocate it. The reason is that the destructor of the **Iso** class will automatically destroy all subordinate objects residing in the main object's stack. The same rule applies to **Iso**'s **SetLocn()** function. It is designed to relocate all subordinate objects automatically.

Making Button Objects

We'll now use the **Wso** class to derive some specialized classes. One class is used to support selection buttons. This class, called **Button**, overrides the **Draw()** and **Activate()** member functions. The **Draw()** function writes the label of the button, and **Activate()** causes a special action routine to be invoked.

The other class, **Count**, serves as an example of overriding the mouse event member functions. It overrides the **OnMouseEnter()**, **OnMouseLeave()**, and **OnMouseWithin()** member functions so that when the mouse enters the object, a counter is activated, and the result of the count is displayed. The counter stops when the mouse leaves the object.

The following program uses both of these new classes.

```
// button1.cpp: Button demo program

#include "string.h"
#include "wsotxscr.h"

typedef void (*ActionProc)(Wso *Src, MsgPkt &M);

class Button : public Wso {
public:
```

```
    ActionProc Action;
    char *Name;
    Button(char *N, ColorPak &Cp, ActionProc A);
    virtual ~Button(void);
    virtual void Draw(void);
    virtual void Activate(MsgPkt &M);
};

class Count : public Wso {
public:
  int C;
  Count(void);
  virtual void OnMouseEnter(MsgPkt &M)  { SwitchFocus(M); }
  virtual void OnMouseLeave(MsgPkt &M)  { Leave(M); }
  virtual void OnMouseWithin(MsgPkt &M);
};

// ————— Button member functions —————

Button::Button(char *N, ColorPak &Cp, ActionProc A)
: Wso(0x11, ButtonStyle, Cp)
{
  Name = strdup(N);
  SetSize(strlen(Name)+2, 1);
  Action = A;
}

Button::~Button(void) { free(Name); }

void Button::Draw(void)
{
  Wso::Draw();
  Panel->HzWrtB(1, 0, Name);
}

void Button::Activate(MsgPkt &M)
{
  if (Active) {
     Wso::Activate(M);
     Action(this, M);
  }
  else {
    Leave(M);
  }
}

// ————— Some common button actions —————

void NoOp(Wso *, MsgPkt &) { ; }

void ExitAction(Wso *, MsgPkt &M)
{
  M.RtnCode = ShutDown;
}
```

```
void Popup(Wso *Src, MsgPkt &M)
{
  Wso *B;
  Src->Leave(M);
  B = new Wso(0x11, WindowStyle, DefColors);
  B->SetSize(30, 3);
  B->Open(FullScrn, 30, 10);
  B->Panel->HzWrt(1, 0, ((Button *)Src)->Name, 0);
  B->SwitchFocus(M);
  M.RtnCode = M.Code;
  do {
    B->SubMgr->EventStep(M);
    M.Code = M.RtnCode;
  } while (M.Code != ShutDown &&
           (!B->Active || M.Code != Close || M.Focus != (Iso *)(B)));
  if (M.Code == Close) {
    B->OnClose(M);
    Mouse.WaitForEvent(MouseUp, M.Mx, M.My);
    M.RtnCode = Idle;
  }
  delete B;
}

// ————— Count object member functions —————

Count::Count(void) : Wso(0x11, WindowStyle, DefColors)
{
  SetSize(6, 1);
  C = 0;
}

void Count::OnMouseWithin(MsgPkt &M)
{
  char Buff[10];
  if (Panel->OnInterior(M.Mx, M.My)) {
    itoa(++C, Buff, 10);
    Panel->HzWrt(0, 0, Buff, 0);
  }
}

Button *MsgBut;
Button *ExitBut;
Wso *S;
Count *CountBut;

main()
{
  Setup(MouseOptional, MonoColors);
  S = new Wso(0x11, WindowStyle, DefColors);
  S->SetSize(60, 20);
  S->Open(FullScrn, 0, 0);
  S->Panel->Clear(177, 7);
  // Create and display the exit and message buttons
  MsgBut = new Button("Message Button", DefColors, Popup);
```

```
   ExitBut - new Button("Exit", DefColors, ExitAction);
   MsgBut->Open(S, 3, 3);
   ExitBut->Open(S, 6, 6);
   // Create and display the counter button
   CountBut - new Count;
   CountBut->Open(S, 22, 12);
   MainEventLoop();
   CleanUp();  // Deletes buttons too
}
```

When you run this program, note that all three buttons are displayed within a window. If you move the window around, the buttons will also move. The program works in this manner because each of the buttons was opened on the window screen object **S**. The **MsgBut** object displays a pop-up window when it is selected, and the **ExitBut** object terminates the program when selected. The **CountBut** object performs a unique action; it starts a counter as soon as the mouse cursor enters the button's region, and stops the counter when the mouse cursor leaves. The secret to how the **Button** class works can be seen in the way objects are initialized:

```
MsgBut - new Button("Message Button", DefColors, Popup);
```

Here we are creating an object called **MsgBut** and assigning the object a name and an action. If the button object is selected by clicking the mouse when the cursor is within the button region, the function **Popup()** will be called.

If you study the definition of the **Button** constructor for buttons, you'll see that a function pointer is passed as the third argument:

```
Button::Button(char *N, ColorPak &Cp, ActionProc A)
```

The type **ActionProc** is defined as:

```
typedef void (*ActionProc)(Wso *Src, MsgPkt &M);
```

Within the body of the constructor, the parameter **A** is assigned to the data member **Action** as shown:

```
Action - A;
```

In conclusion, we have changed the **Activate()** function so that it will call the routine assigned to **Action** when the button object is selected. The important thing to keep in mind is that we didn't have to make any changes to the **Wso** class to support this new feature. We simply used inheritance and overrode the functions we needed to change.

Code Critique

The **Iso** and **IsoMgr** classes are by far the most complex classes in our interface toolkit. Although they were designed to be general purpose, some of the features, such as the Tab key cycling system, are difficult to implement in a general way. The following sections examine some of the important design issues that we encountered in the course of creating the interactive screen objects.

The Cycling System

The Tab key cycling system is tricky to implement for two reasons. First, the order of objects on the stack constantly changes. Each time a screen object is selected, the object is moved to the top of the stack. Trying to select a particular object is like trying to hit a moving target. Since the Tab key cycles through the objects in stack order, the cycling order changes as well. Second, not all screen objects should be selected when the Tab key is pressed to cycle through objects. For example, in Chapter 9 scrollable screen objects will be built that consist of a main window, a scroll bar, and a scroll button. The scroll bar and scroll button aren't really objects that need to be selected, at least not in the way that a full window needs to be. Therefore, it doesn't make sense to select the scroll bar or scroll button when the Tab key is pressed. To get around this problem, we would have to incorporate some special logic so that we could skip over certain types of objects.

The Grouping Feature

The windowing system allows objects to be grouped. This grouping feature makes it easy to build screen objects, such as menus and dialog boxes, which are composed of other screen objects. The grouping is accomplished by letting each screen object have its own child stack. When a screen object moves, all of the children on the stack also move. The child objects are restricted to staying within the interior of the parent window.

Another way to group objects would be to include a group ID in each screen object. Objects assigned the same group ID would belong to the same group. The advantage of this technique is that we would only need one stack instead of the multiple substacks required to process child objects. However, it would be less efficient to move and hide the group of objects because we couldn't assume that a child's window resides on the main window. This means that we couldn't assume a child's image is hidden automatically when the main window's image is swapped out, and we would have to swap the child images individually.

Writing to Windows

Although the windowing system is quite powerful, writing to a window that's partially hidden by another window is not supported. To do this we would need much more complicated output routines. To get around this problem, the system always keeps the currently selected window on top of the stack, so that it's fully visible. This doesn't prevent you from writing to a window underneath, however, because you can call its output functions at any time. It's up to the application to ensure that such an operation can be performed safely.

Message Passing System

The message passing system used by the **Iso** and **IsoMgr** classes is not quite complete. Although it handles keyboard and mouse events, it doesn't handle general messages very well. The event code **StrMsg**, and the **MsgPkt** field **Str** are provided as a starting point. In addition, it would be nice to have a queue for the messages. (The current system effectively has a queue of length one.)

To the message system's credit, however, it wouldn't be too hard to incorporate multitasking. Also, nothing stops you from modifying the event loop to provide for automatic demos. For example, you could store an array of mouse and key event codes, and in a customized event loop, feed these codes individually to the **EventStep()** function of **IsoMgr**. The windowing system would respond as though the keyboard and mouse were actually being used. The power of encapsulation and inheritance is what makes this possible.

Adding Extensions

In the following chapters, the necessary techniques to build on top of the windowing system will be discussed. With the system of classes provided, you'll see that creating screen objects with many different capabilities can easily be accommodated, all by just overriding the appropriate member functions of **Iso** and **IsoMgr**. A word of warning though: The **EventStep()** function, while only a few lines long, is very sensitive to changes. Don't attempt to modify it until you completely understand how it works.

Listing 7.1   isounit.h

```
// isounit.h: interactive screen object (Iso) class

#ifndef H_ISOUNIT
#define H_ISOUNIT

#include <stdlib.h>
#include "fsounit.h"
#include "keybrd.h"

// Some event codes (The msmouse.h and keybrd.h files provide others)
const int Close    = 0x011b;  // Same as the ESC key
const int ShutDown = 0x2d00;  // Same as the ALT-X key
const int Cycle    = 0x0f09;  // Same as the Tab key
const int StrMsg   = 0xffff;  // Indicates there is a string message

class Iso;           // Forward declarations
class IsoMgr;

struct MsgPkt {      // Message packet
  Iso *Focus;        // Holds current focus
  unsigned Code;     // The event code
  unsigned RtnCode;  // Return event code
  int Mx, My;        // Mouse coordinates
  char Str[80];      // The message
};

extern MsgPkt NullMsg; // Defined in isounit.cpp

class Iso {
public:
  Fso *Panel;        // Can be a Tfso or Gfso pointer
  char Active;       // True if Iso is selected
  char Visible;      // True if Iso is showing
  char IsClosed;     // True if Iso is closed
  char TouchFlag;    // True if touching another Iso
  char ClipToFrame;  // Used for scroll bars
  Iso *Base;         // The base for this Iso
  Iso *Under, *Over; // Iso stack pointers
  IsoMgr *SubMgr;    // The child Iso stack
  Iso(Fso *P);
  virtual ~Iso(void);
  virtual Rso *ClippingRect(void);
  virtual void SetLocn(int Xl, int Yl, CoordType Ctype);
  virtual void SetSize(int W, int H);
  virtual void Move(int X, int Y);
  virtual void DeltaMove(int Dx, int Dy);
  virtual void MoveLoop(MsgPkt &M);
  virtual void Stretch(int W, int H);
  virtual void DeltaStretch(int Dw, int Dh);
```

```
    virtual void StretchLoop(MsgPkt &M);
    virtual int Obscured(void);
    virtual void Draw(void) { ; }
    virtual void DrawPanel(void);
    virtual void Redraw(void) { DrawPanel(); }
    virtual void Open(Iso *B, int X, int Y);
    virtual void Reopen(int X, int Y);
    virtual void Swap(void);
    virtual void Hide(void);
    virtual void Show(void);
    virtual void SetVisibleFlag(int F);
    virtual void Select(void);
    virtual void Remove(void);
    virtual void Prompt(void);
    virtual void UnPrompt(void);
    virtual void Enter(MsgPkt &M);
    virtual void Leave(MsgPkt &M);
    virtual void SwitchFocus(MsgPkt &M);
    virtual void Activate(MsgPkt &) { ; }
    virtual void OnMouseEnter(MsgPkt &M);
    virtual void OnMouseLeave(MsgPkt &M);
    virtual void OnMouseWithin(MsgPkt &) { ; }
    virtual void OnClose(MsgPkt &M);
    virtual void OnMouseUp(MsgPkt &M) { Activate(M); }
    virtual void OnMouseDown(MsgPkt &M);
    virtual void BorderHandler(MsgPkt &M);
    virtual void OnMouseStillDown(MsgPkt &) { ; }
    virtual void OnKeyStroke(MsgPkt &M);
    virtual void OnShiftArrow(MsgPkt &M);
    virtual void Dispatch(MsgPkt &M);
};

class IsoMgr {
public:
    Iso *Top, *Bottom; // Top and bottom of Iso stack
    Iso *Base;         // Who this stack belongs to
    Iso *Hot;          // Who the mouse is currently on
    Iso *Marker;       // A marker used when cycling
    IsoMgr(Iso *B);
    virtual ~IsoMgr(void);
    virtual void Push(Iso *Ip);
    virtual void MoveToFront(Iso *Me, int Keep);
    virtual void ResetTouchFlags(Iso *Me);
    virtual void SetTouchFlags(Iso *Me);
    virtual void OnIso(int Mx, int My, Iso **I);
    virtual Iso *CycleForw(Iso *Curr);
    virtual void ProcessCycle(MsgPkt &M);
    virtual void EventLoop(MsgPkt &M);
    virtual void EventStep(MsgPkt &M);
};

#endif
```

Listing 7.2   isounit.cpp

```
// isounit.cpp: Iso class implementation

#include "keybrd.h"
#include "isounit.h"
#include "msmouse.h"

MsgPkt NulMsg = { NULL, Idle, Idle, 0, 0, "" };

Iso::Iso(Fso *P)
// Initializes the Iso by setting all of the data members to
// a default state and sets up an IsoMgr object
{
  Panel = P;                 // P is either a Tfso or Gfso
  Active = False;            // Not selected
  Visible  = False;          // Object is not visible
  IsClosed = True;           // Object is not open
  TouchFlag = False;         // Object is not touching another Iso
  ClipToFrame = False;       // Normally, clip to the interior
  Under = NULL; Over = NULL; // The Iso stack is empty
  Base = NULL;               // No base to start with
  SubMgr = new IsoMgr(this); // Make an IsoMgr for this object
}

Iso::~Iso(void)
// Deallocates memory for an Iso by first removing the object
// from its Base's Iso stack and it destroys its own stack
{
  Remove(); // Hide() & remove from Iso stack
  delete SubMgr;
  delete Panel;
}

Rso *Iso::ClippingRect(void)
// Given the state of the ClipToFrame flag, returns the
// appropriate clipping rectangle
{
  if (ClipToFrame)
     return Base->Panel->Frame;
     else return Base->Panel->Interior;
}

void Iso::SetLocn(int X1, int Y1, CoordType Ctype)
// Sets the location of the Iso. If Ctype == Relc, the
// coordinates are relative to the object's base. If the
// object does not have a base (e.g., FullScrn), then
// it's assumed the coordinates are always absolute, and
// that SetLocn is only called once.
{
  int Dx, Dy, Dw, Dh;
  Iso *P;
```

```
    Rso *Clipper;

    if (Base — NULL) {          // Object does not have a base
       Panel->SetLocn(X1, Y1); // (e.g., FullScrn)
    }
    else { // Object has a base
       Clipper - ClippingRect();
       if (Ctype — Relc) {    // Use relative coordinates
          X1 +- Clipper->Xul; // Turn into absolute coordinates
          Y1 +- Clipper->Yul; // Turn into absolute coordinates
       }
       // Ensure coordinates are in range. It's assumed that
       // the size is OK at this point.
       Dw — Panel->Frame->Wd; Dh — Panel->Frame->Ht;
       Clipper->ClipDim(X1, Y1, Dw, Dh);
       // Record distance to move for all dependent objects
       Dx — X1 - Panel->Frame->Xul;
       Dy — Y1 - Panel->Frame->Yul;
       // Change location of the object
       Panel->SetLocn(X1, Y1);
       // Change locations of all dependent objects
       P — SubMgr->Top;
       while (P !— NULL) {
          P->SetLocn(P->Panel->Frame->Xul+Dx, P->Panel->Frame->Yul+Dy, Absc);
          P — P->Under;  // Get next object on stack
       }
    }
}


void Iso::SetSize(int W, int H)
// The size of an Iso is the size of its panel. W and H are
// the new size of the interior. First, we set the size of
// the panel, which will set the sizes of the interior, frame,
// and overall rectangles. Then, if we have a base, we clip the
// frame size to it. If the frame size changes during clipping,
// we resize the panel w.r.t interior again.
{
  int Dw, Dh, Ow, Oh;
  Rso *Clipper;
  Rso *Pf — Panel->Frame;

  Panel->SetSize(W, H); // First set up panel size
  if (Base !— NULL) {    // Do we have a base to clip to?
     Clipper — ClippingRect();
     Pf — Panel->Frame;
     Ow — Pf->Wd; Oh — Pf->Ht;               // Record old frame size
     Clipper->ClipSize(Pf->Wd, Pf->Ht);  // Adjust frame size
     Dw — Pf->Wd - Ow; Dh — Pf->Ht - Oh; // Compute delta size
     if ((Dw !— 0) || (Dh !— 0)) {
        // Need to set the size of the panel again
        Panel->SetSize(Panel->Interior->Wd+Dw, Panel->Interior->Ht+Dh);
     }
  }
}
```

```
void Iso::DrawPanel(void)
// First, initializes the swap buffer by calling GetImage,
// draws the frame, draws the shadows, clears the
// interior, and calls the specialized draw routine.
{
  Mouse.Hide();
  Visible = True;  // We'll be visible soon
  if (Panel->IsSwappable()) Panel->GetImage(ClippingRect());
  Panel->DrawFrame(0, 0);
  Panel->DrawShadows(ClippingRect(), GetIm, 1);
  Panel->Clear(' ', 0);
  Draw();
  Mouse.Show();
}

void Iso::Open(Iso *B, int X, int Y)
// Opens the object by drawing it on a specified base at
// position X,Y relative to the base. Since we now have a
// base, we also clip the size w.r.t to the base. (It's assumed
// that SetSize has already been called at least once.)
{
  Base = B;
  // Push the object onto its base managers' stack
  Base->SubMgr->Push(this);
  IsClosed = False;     // Object now to be open
  // Adjust size if necessary. Can do this by calling SetSize,
  // which will in turn call ClipSize.
  SetSize(Panel->Interior->Wd, Panel->Interior->Ht);
  SetLocn(X, Y, Relc); // Use relative coordinates
  DrawPanel();          // Draw an empty panel
}

void Iso::Reopen(int X, int Y)
// Reopens an object that was previously closed. The new
// location (X,Y) is relative to the base
{
  IsClosed = False;
  SetLocn(X, Y, Relc);
  Select(); // Move Iso to front and show
}

void Iso::Move(int X, int Y)
// Moves the object to new location. Absolute coordinates
// are used.
{
  if (Panel->IsSwappable()) { // Only swappable objects
    Hide();                   // can be moved
    SetLocn(X, Y, Absc);
    Show();
  }
}

void Iso::DeltaMove(int Dx, int Dy)
// Moves the object by an incremental amount
```

```
{
  // Add in the object's origin
  Move(Panel->Frame->Xul+Dx, Panel->Frame->Yul+Dy);
}

void Iso::MoveLoop(MsgPkt &M)
// Moves an object until mouse button is released
{
  unsigned E;
  Mouse.Moved(); // Resets counters
  do {
    if (Mouse.Moved()) DeltaMove(Mouse.Dx, Mouse.Dy);
    E = Mouse.Event(M.Mx, M.My);
  } while (E != MouseUp);
  M.RtnCode = Idle;
}

void Iso::Stretch(int W, int H)
// Stretch to a new size. First, closes all subwindows and figures
// out the minimum size we can stretch to, hides this object, does
// the resize, and redraws everybody.
{
  Iso *P;
  int Mw, Mh;

  if (Panel->IsStretchable()) {
    // Hide the sub-Isos. While we're at it, find maximum
    // size of sub-Isos, which serves as our minimum.
    Mw = 8; Mh = 3;  // Absolute minimums
    P = SubMgr->Top;
    while (P != NULL) { // Hide all subwindows
      if (P->Panel->Frame->Wd > Mw) Mw = P->Panel->Frame->Wd;
      if (P->Panel->Frame->Ht > Mh) Mh = P->Panel->Frame->Ht;
      P->Hide();
      P = P->Under;
    }
    if (W < Mw) W = Mw; // Adjust sizes to lower bound
    if (H < Mh) H = Mh;
    Hide(); // Hide image
    SetSize(W, H);
    // This next call is to relocate the shadows
    SetLocn(Panel->Frame->Xul, Panel->Frame->Yul, Absc);
    Redraw();
    P = SubMgr->Bottom;
    while (P != NULL) { // Reshow the subwindows
      P->SetLocn(P->Panel->Frame->Xul, P->Panel->Frame->Yul, Absc);
      if (!P->IsClosed) P->Show();
      P = P->Over;
    }
  }
}

void Iso::DeltaStretch(int Dw, int Dh)
// Do an incremental stretch
```

```
{
  Stretch(Panel->Interior->Wd+Dw, Panel->Interior->Ht+Dh);
}

void Iso::StretchLoop(MsgPkt &M)
// Stretches the window until a MouseUp event
{
   unsigned E;
   Mouse.Moved(); // Resets counters
   do {
     if (Mouse.Moved()) DeltaStretch(Mouse.Dx, Mouse.Dy);
     E = Mouse.Event(M.Mx, M.My);
   } while (E != MouseUp);
   M.RtnCode = Idle;
}

void Iso::Swap(void)
// Swap between the object's save buffer and the screen. The
// shadow clipping region is set to the base's interior, unless
// the Iso has no base, it's set to the Iso's overall rectangle.
{
  XfrDirn Xd;
  if (Visible) Xd = PutIm; else Xd = GetIm;
  if (Base != NULL)
     Panel->Swap(Base->Panel->Interior, Xd);
     else Panel->Swap(Panel->Overall, Xd);
}

void Iso::Hide(void)
// Hides the object by swapping images
{
  if (IsClosed) return;      // Don't hide if already closed
  if (Visible) {             // or already hidden
     Swap();                 // Swap out the object
     SetVisibleFlag(False);  // Recursively reset visible flags
  }
}

void Iso::Show(void)
// Shows the object by swapping images
{
  if (IsClosed) return;      // Don't show if closed
  if (!Visible) {            // or already visible
     Swap();
     SetVisibleFlag(True);   // Recursively set visible flags
  }
}

void Iso::SetVisibleFlag(int F)
// Recursively set/reset the visible flags of this
// object and all of its children
{
  Iso *P;
  if (IsClosed) return;
```

```
    P - SubMgr->Top;  // Start at the top of the stack
    while (P !- NULL) {
      P->SetVisibleFlag(F);
      P - P->Under;
    }
    Visible - F;
}

void Iso::Select(void)
// Selects an object to be the active screen object. When
// the object is selected it is brought to the front.
{
  if (Base !- NULL) {
    Base->Select();  // Ensure parent is selected first
    // Then, select yourself
    Base->SubMgr->MoveToFront(this, True);
  }
  Show(); // Ensure it's showing
}

void Iso::Remove(void)
// Removes the Iso by moving it to the front of the stack, and
// detaching it from the stack. Set base to NULL to indicate
// it no longer belongs to a stack.
{
  if (Base !- NULL) Base->SubMgr->MoveToFront(this, False);
  Base - NULL;
}

void Iso::Prompt(void)
// Default prompt action is to select the object, and
// set the Active flag
{
  Select(); Active - True;
}

void Iso::UnPrompt(void)
// Default unprompt action is to merely set the Active
// flag to false
{
  Active - False;
}

void Iso::SwitchFocus(MsgPkt &M)
// Switch the focus to this object by first leaving the old focus
// (if there was one), and entering the object. Don't need to
// do anything if this object is already the focus
{
  if (M.Focus !- this) {     // Nothing to do
    if (M.Focus !- NULL) {
      M.Focus->Leave(M);   // Leave old focus
    }
    M.Focus - this;          // Enter this object
```

```
      Enter(M);
  }
  M.RtnCode - Idle;
}


void Iso::Enter(MsgPkt &)
// Default Enter action is to prompt the object if
// not already active
{
  if (!Active) Prompt();
}


void Iso::Leave(MsgPkt &M)
// Unprompts the object if it is active. If you are the
// current focus, you MUST set the focus to NULL
{
  if (Active) UnPrompt();
  if (M.Focus — this) M.Focus - NULL;
}


// ——————— Mouse event member functions ———————

void Iso::OnMouseEnter(MsgPkt &M)
// If mouse button is down when the mouse enters this
// object, switch focus to this object
{
  if (Mouse.ButtonStatus() !- 0) SwitchFocus(M);
}


void Iso::OnMouseLeave(MsgPkt &M)
// If mouse button is down when the mouse leaves this
// object, then leave this object
{
  if (Mouse.ButtonStatus() !- 0) Leave(M);
}


void Iso::OnClose(MsgPkt &M)
// On a Close event, hide this object and set its closed flag
{
  Leave(M);
  // If if statement below traps the fullscrn case too
  if (Panel->IsCloseable()) {
     Hide();
     IsClosed - True;
  }
}



void Iso::OnMouseDown(MsgPkt &M)
// If mouse button pressed while inside this object,
// then switch focus to it, handle possibility of being on the border
{
  SwitchFocus(M);
```

```
    if (Panel->OnBorder(M.Mx, M.My)) BorderHandler(M);
}

void Iso::BorderHandler(MsgPkt &M)
// Handle border conditions: either activate close button,
// stretch, or move the object. Stretching occurs if on
// lower right-hand corner, UNLESS the window is only
// 1x1 in size (e.g., scroll buttons.)
{
  if (Panel->OnCloseButton(M.Mx, M.My)) {
    M.RtnCode - Close;
    M.Focus- this;
  }
  else if ((M.Mx -- Panel->Frame->Xlr) &&
           (M.My -- Panel->Frame->Ylr) &&
           // These tests are so we don't cause Move() to
           // to fail on Isos like scroll buttons
           (Panel->Frame->Wd > 1) &&
           (Panel->Frame->Ht > 1))
           {
      StretchLoop(M);
  }
  else {
    MoveLoop(M);
  }
}

// ---- Member functions to process keyboard events ----

void Iso::OnKeyStroke(MsgPkt &M)
// Process all key press events. Default is to handle only
// the return key, and the shift arrow keys
{
  switch (M.Code) {
    case CrKey:
      Activate(M);
      M.Code - Idle;
    break;
    default :
    if (IsShiftArrow(M.Code)) {
      OnShiftArrow(M);
      M.Code - Idle;
    }
  }
}

void Iso::OnShiftArrow(MsgPkt &M)
// The shift arrow key events cause the window to move
{
  switch (M.Code) {
    case ShiftLeft  : DeltaMove(-1, 0); break;
    case ShiftRight : DeltaMove(1, 0);  break;
    case ShiftUpKey : DeltaMove(0, -1); break;
```

```
      case ShiftDnKey :  DeltaMove(0, 1);  break;
      default: ;
   }
}

void Iso::Dispatch(MsgPkt &M)
// Dispatches the events to the appropriate function
{
   M.RtnCode - Idle;  // Default new message is to "idle"
   switch (M.Code) {
      case Idle          :  break;
      case StrMsg        :  break;
      case Close         :  OnClose(M); break;
      case MouseDown     :  OnMouseDown(M); break;
      case MouseStillDown :  OnMouseStillDown(M); break;
      case MouseUp       :  OnMouseUp(M); break;
      case MouseEnter    :  OnMouseEnter(M); break;
      case MouseLeave    :  OnMouseLeave(M); break;
      case MouseWithin   :  OnMouseWithin(M); break;
      default:
        OnKeyStroke(M);
   }
}

int Iso::Obscured(void)
// Returns true if this object is partially hidden by object from above
{
   Iso *Ip - Over;
   while (Ip !- NULL) {
     if (Panel->Touches(Ip->Panel)) {
        return True;
     }
     Ip - Ip->Over;
   }
   return False;
}

// ——————— IsoMgr Member Functions ———————

IsoMgr::IsoMgr(Iso *B)
// Initializes the IsoMgr object by setting the top and bottom
// stack pointers to NULL, and recording who is the base.
{
   Top   - NULL;  Bottom - NULL;
   Base - B;
   Hot - NULL;
   Marker - NULL;
}

IsoMgr::~IsoMgr(void)
// Destroys all Isos on the stack
{
   Iso *P, *Q;
```

```
      P - Top;
      while (P !- NULL) {
        Q - P->Under;
        delete P;
        P - Q;
      }
    }

void IsoMgr::Push(Iso *Ip)
// Attachs the Iso by pushing onto the Iso stack
{
  if (Top !- NULL) {
    Top->Over - Ip;    // Link top of stack to new node
    Ip->Under - Top;   // Link new node to top of stack
  }
  else {               // First one on the stack
    Ip->Over  - NULL;
    Ip->Under - NULL;
    Bottom    - Ip;    // Make it the bottom too
    Marker    - Ip;    // Set the marker on it
  }
  Top - Ip;            // Set top of stack to new node
}

void IsoMgr::MoveToFront(Iso *Me, int Keep)
// If Keep -- 1, MoveToFront moves Me to the top of the stack
// and makes it the active Iso.
// If Keep -- 0, Me is removed from the stack and hidden. Note
// that nothing happens if Me is already at the top and we wish
// to keep it there. Also, if not keeping Me, it is simply detached
// from the stack, it is not destroyed!
{
  Iso *Ip;

  if (Keep && (Me -- Top)) return; // Short circuit
  Mouse.Hide();
  // If Me is an overlapping Iso, move its image to the top
  if (Me->Panel->IsSwappable()) {  // Must erase image at old position
    ResetTouchFlags(Me);
    SetTouchFlags(Me);
    if (!Me->TouchFlag) {      // Nobody overlaps from above
      if (!Keep) Me->Hide(); // Erase image if deleting
    }
    else { // Somebody overlaps from above, so ...
      // Swap isos in descending order, downto me
      Ip - Top;
      while (Ip !- Me->Under) {
        if (Ip->TouchFlag) Ip->Hide();
        Ip - Ip->Under;
      }
      // Put Iso images (only those above me) back
      Ip - Me->Over;
      while (Ip !- NULL) {
```

```
              if (Ip->TouchFlag) Ip->Show();
              Ip - Ip->Over;
           }
        }
     }
     // Through processing overlapping windows so
     // link up window underneath Me with the Iso above it
     // Note: if Me -- Top, it is also true that we're
     // deleting Me

   if (Me -- Top) {          // We know we're deleting
      if (Me -- Bottom) { // Stack will be empty
         Bottom - NULL;
         Top - NULL;
      }
      else {                    // Iso underneath to become new top
         Me->Under->Over - NULL;
         Top - Me->Under;
      }
      Me->Under - NULL;    // Reset under/over pointers
      Me->Over  - NULL;
   }
   else {
      // Me is not top, and we may or may not be deleting
      // at this point, we know we have at least two Isos on stack
      if (Me -- Bottom) { // We're getting a new bottom
         Me->Over->Under - NULL;
         Bottom - Me->Over;
      }
      else { // We're somewhere in the middle
         Me->Under->Over - Me->Over;
         Me->Over->Under - Me->Under;
      }
      if (Keep) {  // Want to make Me the new top iso
         Top->Over - Me;
         Me->Under - Top;
         Me->Over  - NULL;
         Top - Me;
         if (Me->TouchFlag) Me->Show(); // Put back image
      }
      else { // Reset under/over pointers
         Me->Under - NULL; Me->Over - NULL;
      }
   }
   Mouse.Show();
}


Iso *CycleToSibling(Iso *Curr)
// An auxiliary recursive function of CycleForw that finds
// a sibling to cycle to. Note: This is not a member function!
{
   Iso *I;
```

```
    I = Curr->Base;  // Is there a base ?
    if (I == NULL) { // No, so we don't belong to a stack
      I = Curr;      // so about all we can do is stay put
    }
    else { // We belong to a stack
      I = Curr->Base->SubMgr->Bottom;    // Possibly our sibling
      // Scan for first visible sibling, but stop if you hit marker
      while ((I != NULL) && (!I->Visible) &&
        (I != Curr->Base->SubMgr->Marker)) I = I->Over;
      // If no sibling, or we've already been there ...
      if ((I == NULL) || (I == Curr->Base->SubMgr->Marker)) {
        I = CycleToSibling(Curr->Base); // Try going forward from base
      } // Else we'll take i
    }
    return I;
}

Iso *IsoMgr::CycleForw(Iso *Curr)
// Cycle forward through the stacks looking for someone
// to become the new focus
{
  Iso *I;

  if (Curr == NULL) return NULL;
  I = Curr->SubMgr->Bottom;      // I == first child
  // Scan for a visible child
  while ((I != NULL) && (!I->Visible)) I = I->Over;
  // If no child, try to go to sibling
  if (I == NULL) I = CycleToSibling(Curr);
  return I;
}

void IsoMgr::ProcessCycle(MsgPkt &M)
// A TabKey event means to cycle forward. A ShiftTabKey means
// to cycle backward (currently not implemented).
{
  Iso *NewIso;
  if ((M.Code == TabKey) || (M.Code == ShiftTabKey)) {
    if (M.Focus == NULL) {
      if ((Bottom != NULL) && Bottom->Visible) {
        Bottom->SwitchFocus(M);
      }
    }
    else {
      switch(M.Code) {
        case TabKey :
          NewIso = CycleForw(M.Focus);
          if (NewIso != NULL) NewIso->SwitchFocus(M);
          break;
        case ShiftTabKey :
          // Cycle backward ... not currently implemented
          break;
        default: ;
```

```
          }
        }
      }
}

void IsoMgr::ResetTouchFlags(Iso *Me)
{
  while (Me != NULL) {
     Me->TouchFlag = False;
     Me = Me->Over;
  }
}

void IsoMgr::SetTouchFlags(Iso *Me)
// Sets touch flags for all Isos above Me that touch
// Me. Must do this recursively for all touching Isos.
// Note that hidden Isos are not included!
{
  Iso *Ip;

  Ip = Me->Over;
  while (Ip != NULL) {
    if (Ip->Visible) { // Must be visible to be touching
      // The swappable check prevents flickering
      if ((Ip->Panel->IsSwappable()) &&
          Me->Panel->Touches(Ip->Panel)) {
        Me->TouchFlag = True;
        Ip->TouchFlag = True;
        SetTouchFlags(Ip); // Must do this!!
      }
    }
    Ip = Ip->Over;
  }
}

void IsoMgr::OnIso(int Mx, int My, Iso **I)
// Recursive routine that finds the highest Iso which contains
// the coordinates Mx, and My. It looks through the substack
// first. If it can't find anyone there, it tries the
// Base Iso. Note that hidden Isos are not included!
{
  Iso *P, *Q;
  int Found;

  P = Top;  Found = False;
  while ((P != NULL) && (!Found)) {
    // Iso has to be visible to be elgible
    if (P->Visible && P->Panel->OnFrame(Mx, My)) {
      Found = True;
      P->SubMgr->OnIso(Mx, My, &Q);
      if (Q != NULL) P = Q;
    }
    else {
```

```
            P = P->Under;
        }
    }
    if ((P == NULL) && (Base != NULL)) {
        if (Base->Visible && Base->Panel->OnFrame(Mx, My))
        P = Base;
    }
    *I = P;
}


void IsoMgr::EventLoop(MsgPkt &M)
// Loop through the event handler until either a Shutdown
// event (Alt-X) occurs, or there are no Isos on the stack
{
    Iso *P;

    do {
        EventStep(M);
        M.Code = M.RtnCode;
        P = Top;
        while ((P != NULL) && (!P->Visible)) P = P->Under;
    } while ((M.Code != ShutDown) && (P != NULL));
}


void IsoMgr::EventStep(MsgPkt &M)
// First, handle any p}ing events, look for new ones.
// Also, monitor the mouse movement between Isos.
{
    Iso *HotIso;
    unsigned E;

    // Handle any pending messages
    HotIso = NULL; // Very important to do this!
    if ((M.Code != Idle) && (M.Focus != NULL)) {
        M.Focus->Dispatch(M); // Note: the focus might change here
    }
    else { // Handle any key strokes
        E = KeyEvent();
        if (E != Idle) {
            M.Code = E;
            ProcessCycle(M);  // Process possible cycle keys
        }
        else { // Handle any mouse activity
            E = Mouse.Event(M.Mx, M.My);
            OnIso(M.Mx, M.My, &HotIso);
            if (HotIso != Hot) {
                if (Hot != NULL) Hot->OnMouseLeave(M);
                if (HotIso != NULL) HotIso->OnMouseEnter(M);
            }
            Hot = HotIso;
        }
        if (E != Idle) {
            if (HotIso != M.Focus) {
```

```
            if (M.Focus !- NULL) M.Focus->OnMouseLeave(M);
            if (HotIso !- NULL)  HotIso->OnMouseEnter(M);
        }
    }
    else if (M.Focus !- NULL) E - MouseWithin;
    M.RtnCode - E; // Key/mouse event becomes new message for Focus
  }
}
```

Listing 7.3   twsounit.h

```
// twsounit.h: text window object (Twso) class

#ifndef H_TWSOUNIT
#define H_TWSOUNIT

#include "isounit.h"
#include "tfsounit.h"

class Wso : public Iso {
public:
  Wso(int Ba, int Fa, ColorPak &Cp);
  virtual void MoveLoop(MsgPkt &M);
  virtual void StretchLoop(MsgPkt &M);
  virtual void Prompt(void);
  virtual void UnPrompt(void);
};

#endif
```

Listing 7.4   twsounit.cpp

```
// twsounit.cpp: Twso class implementation
#include "twsounit.h"

Wso::Wso(int Ba, int Fa, ColorPak &Cp)
// Initializes a text window screen object by typing the
// Iso's panel to be a Tfso.
: Iso(new Tfso(Ba,Fa,Cp))
{
  return; // Nothing else to do
}

void Wso::MoveLoop(MsgPkt &M)
// The move loop drags a skeleton outline around, and
// when the mouse button is released, the Wso is moved to the
// same location as the skeleton. If the Wso does not have the
// "outline move" attribute, the Wso is dragged directly.
{
```

```
      Tskel *Red;
      Iso   *Skeleton;

      if (Panel->IsSwappable()) {
        if ((Panel->Fattr & OutlineMove) !- 0) {
           Red - new Tskel(Panel->Colors);
           Red->SetSize(Panel->Interior->Wd, Panel->Interior->Ht);
           Skeleton - new Iso(Red);
           Skeleton->Open(Base,
                        Panel->Frame->Xul-Base->Panel->Interior->Xul,
                        Panel->Frame->Yul-Base->Panel->Interior->Yul);
           Skeleton->MoveLoop(M);
           Skeleton->Remove();
           if ((Panel->Frame->Xul !- Skeleton->Panel->Frame->Xul) ||
               (Panel->Frame->Yul !- Skeleton->Panel->Frame->Yul))
           Move(Skeleton->Panel->Frame->Xul,
                Skeleton->Panel->Frame->Yul);
           delete Skeleton;
        }
        else { // Call inherited version that moves the whole window
          Iso::MoveLoop(M);
        }
      }
    }

void Wso::StretchLoop(MsgPkt &M)
// Very similar to MoveLoop
{
      Tskel *Red;
      Iso   *Skeleton;

      if (Panel->IsStretchable()) {
        if ((Panel->Fattr & OutlineMove) !- 0) {
           Red - new Tskel(Panel->Colors);
           Red->SetSize(Panel->Interior->Wd, Panel->Interior->Ht);
           Skeleton - new Iso(Red);
           Skeleton->Open(Base,
                        Panel->Frame->Xul-Base->Panel->Interior->Xul,
                        Panel->Frame->Yul-Base->Panel->Interior->Yul);
           Skeleton->StretchLoop(M);
           Skeleton->Remove();
           if ((Panel->Frame->Wd !- Skeleton->Panel->Frame->Wd) ||
               (Panel->Frame->Ht !- Skeleton->Panel->Frame->Ht))
           // Need to subtract borders from size
           Stretch(Skeleton->Panel->Frame->Wd-2,
                   Skeleton->Panel->Frame->Ht-2);
           delete Skeleton;
        }
        else { // Call inherited version that stretches the whole window
          Iso::StretchLoop(M);
        }
      }
    }
```

```
void Wso::Prompt(void)
// Prompts by drawing a double border (if there is a border)
{
  Iso::Prompt(); // Do inherited prompting
  if ((Panel->Bstyle > 0) &&
      ((Panel->Fattr & BorderPrompt) != 0))
    Panel->DrawFrame(Double + Panel->Bwd, 0);
}

void Wso::UnPrompt(void)
// Unprompts by restoring the border to its original attributes
{
  if (Active) {
    if ((Panel->Bstyle > 0) &&
        ((Panel->Fattr & BorderPrompt) != 0))
      Panel->DrawFrame(0, 0); // 0, 0 means use default
    Iso::UnPrompt(); // Do inherited unprompting
  }
}
```

Listing 7.5   wsotxscr.h

```
// wsotxscr.h: Header file for text based window setup

#ifndef H_WSOTXSCR
#define H_WSOTXSCR

#include "twsounit.h"

enum MouseOpt { NoMouse, MouseRequired, MouseOptional };

extern Wso *FullScrn;
extern MsgPkt StartMsg;

extern void Setup(MouseOpt Mo, ColorPak &Cp);
extern void MainEventLoop(void);
extern void CleanUp(void);

#endif
```

Listing 7.6   wsotxscr.cpp

```
// wsotxscr.cpp: text based windows startup code

#include "wsotxscr.h"

Wso *FullScrn;
MsgPkt StartMsg;
```

```
void Setup(MouseOpt Mo, ColorPak &Cp)
// Sets up the text screen environment by initializing the mouse
// and creating a the FullScrn object to reference the text
// screen.  The FullScrn object can serve as the base for other
// window objects.
{
  FullScrn = new Wso(0x00, 0x00, Cp); // Initialize without a border
  StartMsg = NullMsg;
  if (Mo != NoMouse) {
    Mouse.Setup(TextScrn);
    if ((!Mouse.SetupOK()) && (Mo == MouseRequired)) {
      FullScrn->Panel->Clear(' ', 0);
      FullScrn->Panel->HzWrtB(0, 0, "Unable to initialize mouse.");
      exit(1);
    }
  }
}

void MainEventLoop(void)
// Starts up the main event loop by calling the FullScrn object's
//  EventLoop member function. But first, set the focus to the top Iso.
{
  if (FullScrn->SubMgr->Top != NULL)
    FullScrn->SubMgr->Top->SwitchFocus(StartMsg);
  FullScrn->SubMgr->EventLoop(StartMsg);
}

void CleanUp(void)
// Shuts down the text screen environment by deallocating the
// FullScrn and turning off the mouse
{
  delete FullScrn;
  Mouse.TurnOff();
}
```

![8](box with number 8)

Building Pull-Down Menus

What do you get when rectangular screen objects, an interactive screen object manager, and objects to display and process lists are combined? If pop-up and pull-down menus is the answer, then you already know what we're going to do in this chapter. We're now ready to put together the last basic component of our screen interface toolkit—**msounit**.

We'll start by taking a quick look at the types of menus that the interface tools will support. Then we'll create the menu classes we'll need. These object classes are different from the ones we've been building because they function at a much higher level. In fact, you'll now be able to see how some of the member functions in the lower-level objects, such as the **Iso** object, can be overridden to create additional interface tools.

An Overview of Menus

The screen interface tools that we've constructed in Chapters 5, 6, and 7, along with the screen and mouse classes from Chapters 3 and 4, will serve as the foundation for the text and graphics menu tools that we're about to build. Essentially, our tools support two types of menus: pop-up and pull-down. Figure 8.1 shows an example of a pop-up menu. Note that the menu can have a shadow and a close box—similar to the window objects created in Chapter 7. To select menu items you can use the mouse or the cursor keys.

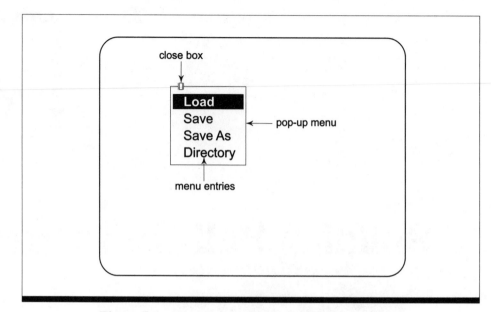

Figure 8.1   A sample menu created with msounit

The pull-down menu system as shown in Figure 8.2 is much more complex than most pop-up menus. This menu system requires multiple components: a pull-down menu bar and drop menus that are assigned to each menu bar entry. Our pull-down menu system works like the menu system used in Turbo C++. The mouse is used to select the drop menus and select a menu option by releasing the mouse button.

The unique feature of the menu system is that each entry in a menu is represented as an object. This design approach allows us to easily assign actions to menu entries.

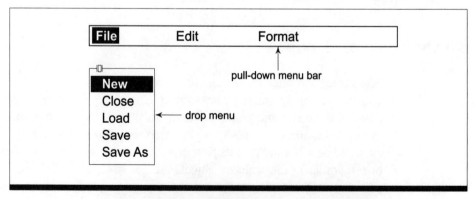

Figure 8.2   Components of a pop-up menu

Overview of the Menu Classes

Figure 8.3 shows the class hierarchy that we'll be using to support pop-up and pull-down menus in both text and graphics modes. The **Wso** class developed in Chapter 7 is at the top of the hierarchy, with the second level composed of the general menu classes including the menu entry screen object (**Meso**), the menu screen object (**Mso**), and the pull-down menu screen object (**Pmso**). The third level consists of the pull-down menu entry screen object (**Pmeso**), the drop menu screen object (**Dmso**), and the pull-down menu bar object (**PulldnBar**). Only the **Meso** and **Mso** classes are required to display and process simple pop-up menus. The other classes are needed to support pull-down menu systems.

Before we start building the menu classes, the components required by a menu system will be reviewed. Figure 8.4 shows a menu system with its components labeled. The simplest components are the menu entries that refer to the names of the selections that are inside a menu. Each menu has a fixed number of rows and columns. The width of the menu is called the *horizontal extent* and the height is determined by the number of menu entry rows. The distance between menu items in a horizontal menu is called the *menu entry spacing*. Note that a highlighted menu selection bar is used to indicate which menu entry has been selected. When an entry is highlighted, click the mouse button or press the return key to activate the entry.

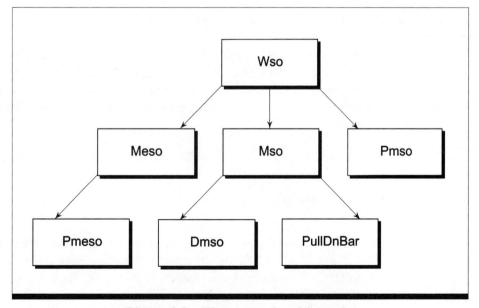

Figure 8.3   The menu class hierarchy

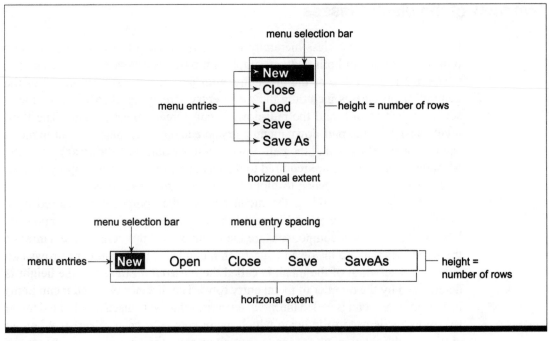

Figure 8.4   Components of a menu system

Working with msounit: Text or Graphics?

The menu support classes just introduced are included in the source files **msounit.h** and **msounit.cpp** (see Listings 8.1 and 8.2). Although it might seem difficult to believe, these classes will work for both text and graphics modes. How do we pull this off? If you take a quick look at **msounit.h**, you'll find the following compiler directive:

```
#ifdef GRAPHICS
#include "gwsounit.h"
#else
#include "twsounit.h"
#endif
```

The **#ifdef** statement selects which header file, and as a result which display mode classes are used, based on whether **GRAPHICS** is defined. By default, **GRAPHICS** is not defined, therefore the text-specific file, **twsounit.h** is used. The graphics-specific routines can be selected in one of three ways: using a **#define GRAPHICS** statement, defining **GRAPHICS** in Turbo C++'s environment, or defining **GRAPHICS** on the command-line using **tcc**. The code in the menu classes is at a high enough level that it can hook into the lower-level text or graphics screen interface classes. Note that you'll also need to change your project file to select which file is linked with the menu toolkit.

Starting with Menu Entries

To support both pop-up and pull-down menus, we'll need a way to represent and process menu entries. You can think of a menu as a rectangular screen object with items that can be highlighted and selected by using the cursor keys and the mouse. Our next goal is to come up with a way of adding menu entries without having to change the interface objects that we have already created. Fortunately, this is much easier than you might first think.

Because menu entries make good objects we'll start by building a class called the menu entry screen object (**Meso**) to represent menu entries. Here's a quick overview of the features that **Meso** provides:

1. Associates a name and action with a menu entry.

2. Provides member functions to initialize, display, highlight, and select a menu entry.

3. Used by the **MesoList** class to implement a list of menu entries.

As shown, **Meso** is derived from the window class **Wso**:

```
class Meso : public Wso {
public:
 char Name[40];        // Menu entry label
 ActionProc Action;    // The action assigned to the entry
 Meso *Next;           // References the next menu entry
 Meso(char *N, ActionProc A);
 virtual void Draw(void);
 virtual void Prompt(void);
 virtual void UnPrompt(void);
 virtual void OnKeyStroke(MsgPkt &M);
 virtual void OnClose(MsgPkt &M);
 virtual void Activate(MsgPkt &M);
};
```

This new class has two important jobs to perform: display a menu entry and associate an action with an entry. Let's take a closer look at each of these activities.

Because of inheritance and virtual functions, it's easy to create a menu entry using code that already exists. The member function responsible for drawing a screen object, **Draw()**, has been overridden so that the name of the menu entry can be displayed:

```
void Meso::Draw(void)
// Displays a menu entry
{
  Wso::Draw();  // Draw the window object
  Panel->HzWrt(0, 0, Name, Panel->Colors.Wc);
}
```

This function shows the real power of inheritance. We are able to create a new type of screen object by reusing code from the **Wso** class. The first statement is responsible for drawing a window screen object; the second statement displays the name of the entry.

Take a moment to explore the other member functions, such as **Prompt()**, **UnPrompt()**, **OnKeyStroke()**, and **OnClose()**; note that we are using inheritance to its full potential. These overridden functions allow us to select and unselect menu entries, override keystrokes by sending them to the menu itself, and close a menu by sending the close command to the active menu. When we override a member function, we alter the flow of control in the program so that we can perform only those operations needed to process new interface objects.

Assigning Menu Actions

The tricky part of the **Meso** class is the way that menu entry actions are added and activated. The two routines for setting up this system are the constructor **Meso()** and the function **Activate()**. Note how the constructor is defined in the **Meso** class:

```
Meso(char *N, ActionProc A);
```

What's unusual here is the second argument. If you dig a little deeper, you'll find that the type **ActionProc** is defined as:

```
typedef void (*ActionProc)(Wso *Src, MsgPkt &M);
```

The **ActionProc** argument, then, serves as a pointer to a function that will be executed when the menu entry is selected. The function name, which we call the menu entry action, is assigned to the data member **Action** by the constructor:

```
Action = A;
```

As an example, if we executed the following statement to initialize a menu entry:

```
Meso MEntry("Open", MenuAction);
```

the entry would be assigned the name "Open" and the function **MenuAction()**. How does this function get called later? When the menu entry is selected by a mouse button click or by pressing the Enter key, the **Activate()** member function is called, which in turn executes the statement:

```
Action(this, M);
```

The menu entry object itself along with the message packet is passed to the **Action** function. When you define a function to be used as an action routine, make sure that you use the following format:

```
void MenuAction(Wso *Src, MsgPkt &M)
{
    // Place code here to process menu action
}
```

The Menu List Class

The **Mso** class contains a nested object called **MesoList** which we use to group menu entries into a list. As can be seen by its definition, **MesoList** accesses a **Meso** object with the data member **Last**:

```
class MesoList { // A circular list for storing menu entries
public:
  Meso *Last;      // References last menu entry on list
  MesoList(void);
  virtual ~MesoList(void);
  virtual void Append(Meso *Me);
};
```

A menu entry is added to the list with the **Append()** member function. The process for creating a list object and adding new entries is:

1. Allocate a new **MesoList** object and call its constructor

2. Allocate a set of **Meso** objects and call their constructors

3. Add each **Meso** to the **MesoList** by calling the **Append()** member function

The menu entry list is actually maintained as a circular list. Because the pointer **Last** references the last entry in the list, the following format is used to retrieve the first node in the list:

```
P = MList->Last->Next;
```

In this case, **MList** is the name of a **MesoList** pointer and **Next** is the pointer from the **Meso** class which is used to link menu entry objects. Essentially, we are retrieving the entry that is linked to the last entry in the list (see Figure 8.5). A close look at the **Append()** member function shows how easy it is to support circular lists:

```
void MesoList::Append(Meso *Me)
// Appends a menu entry to the menu list
{
  if (Last != NULL) {     // List has entries
      Me->Next = Last->Next;
      Last->Next = Me;    // Add new element
      Last = Last->Next;  // Update end of list pointer
  }
  else {                  // List is empty
      Last = Me;          // Place at top of list
      Last->Next = Me;
  }
}
```

The Mso Class

We're now ready to build the main menu screen object class—**Mso**. This class is used to create working pop-up menus. A summary of the features provided is:

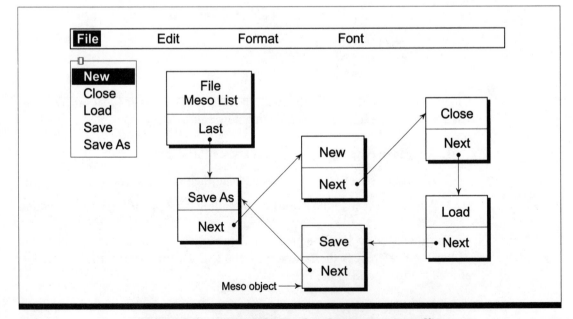

Figure 8.5   Accessing the circular menu entry list

1. Stores a list of the menu entries assigned to a menu

2. Supports both horizontal and vertical menus

3. Performs menu auto-sizing

4. Works in both text and graphics modes

5. Keeps track of the current highlighted menu item

6. Provides methods for initializing, drawing, moving, and activating menus

The full definition of **Mso** is:

```
class Mso : public Wso {      // The menu screen object type
public:
  MesoList *Entries;          // The list of menu entries
  Meso *CurrSeln;             // The selected menu entry
  int EntriesDrawn;           // "Entries have been drawn" flag
  int Nrows, Ncols, Spacing;  // Menu dimensions
  Mso(MesoList *El, int Nc, int Nr, int Sp, int W, int H,
      int Bd, int Fa, ColorPak &Cp);
  virtual void SetupDim(int &Nc, int &Nr, int &W, int &H);
  virtual int EntryWidth(Meso *Me);
  virtual void SetupEntries(void);
  virtual int  IsHz(void) { return Nrows == 1; }
  virtual int  IsVt(void) { return Ncols == 1; }
  virtual void Open(Iso *B, int X, int Y);
  virtual void MoveLoop(MsgPkt &M);
  virtual void Activate(MsgPkt &M);
  virtual void Leave(MsgPkt &M);
  virtual void OnKeyStroke(MsgPkt &M);
  virtual void Forw(MsgPkt &M);
  virtual void Back(MsgPkt &M);
};
```

Let's start with the data members. Note that **Mso** provides two components for accessing menu entry screen objects: **Entries** and **CurrSeln**. The **Entries** pointer is used to reference the list of menu entries assigned to a menu object. With this pointer, a **Mso** object can easily access the member functions needed to process menu entries such as **Prompt()**, **UnPrompt()**, and **Activate()**. The **CurrSeln** pointer references the most recently selected menu entry. If a menu is temporarily removed and then redisplayed, this pointer is used to highlight the menu entry that was selected before the menu was removed.

The **EntriesDrawn** variable serves as a flag to indicate if the menu entries have been drawn or not. The last three variables—**Nrows**, **Ncols**, and **Spacing**— keep track of the number of rows, number of columns, and distance between horizontal menu entries, respectively.

The member functions are described in Table 8.1. The first four functions are responsible for initializing and sizing menu objects. Note that these routines are new. The next set of new member functions, **IsHz()** and **IsVt()**, are used to determine the style of menu—horizontal or vertical—that the object represents.

The **Mso** class also contains some inherited functions that have been overridden. Although menus are similar to windows (**Wso** objects) in the sense that they have borders, shadows, and interior regions, special-purpose member functions are necessary for handling tasks such as displaying menu entries, activating a menu entry, and processing the keys right arrow, left arrow, up arrow, and down arrow.

One thing that's missing from the **Mso** class is a destructor. Is one necessary to dispose of the menu entries in the menu? Yes, it is, but we can use the one inherited from the **Iso** class. Remember that **Mso** is ultimately derived from **Iso**, and the **Iso** destructor handles all the children of an **Iso** automatically. The menu entries, being drawn with an **Mso** as a base, are children of that **Mso**.

Setting Up Menus

The trickiest part about setting up a menu is determining the menu's size and how the menu entries should be displayed. To automate the sizing process, **Mso** provides capabilities for auto-sizing through its constructor:

```
Mso::Mso(MesoList *El, int Nc, int Nr, int Sp, int W, int H,
         int Bd, int Fa, ColorPak &Cp)
// Initializes the menu object by creating a window
// and setting up the menu entries
: Wso(Bd, Fa, Cp) // Initialize the menu's window
{
  Entries  = El;
  CurrSeln = Entries->Last->Next;
  EntriesDrawn = 0;
  Spacing = Sp;
  SetupDim(Nc, Nr, W, H);  // Sets up the menu dimensions
  Ncols = Nc; Nrows = Nr;  // Store number of columns and rows
  SetSize(W, H);  // Sets the menu width and height
  SetupEntries(); // Sets the size and attribute for each entry
}
```

The constructor is responsible for initializing the menu object by creating a window and setting up the menu entries. The **SetupDim()** member function performs the sizing calculations. (The **SetSize()** member function stores the width and height dimensions after they have been calculated by **SetupDim()**.)

Table 8.1   The member functions in the Mso class

Member function	Description
Mso()	Initializes a menu screen object
SetupDim()	Sets up a menu's dimensions
EntryWidth()	Determines the width of a menu entry
SetupEntries()	Sets up the size and colors for each menu entry
IsHz()	Determines if a menu is a horizontal menu
IsVt()	Determines if a menu is a vertical menu
Open()	Opens a menu with its entries
MoveLoop()	Moves a menu
Activate()	Executes the action assigned to a menu entry
Leave()	Leaves a menu
OnKeyStroke()	Processes an input key
Forw()	Moves to and highlights the next menu entry
Back()	Moves to and highlights the previous menu entry

Before we get into **SetupDim()**, let's take a look at how the constructor can be used:

```
Mso Menu1(MList, 1, 10, 1, 15, 10, 0x11,
          WithShadow+Swappable, DefColors);
```

This statement would produce a vertical menu with five rows (assuming that **MList** is a pointer to a **MesoList** object that contains five menu entries). Since it is a vertical menu, the menu entry spacing parameter **Sp**, which is set to 1, doesn't have any effect. The actual interior size of the menu is 15 characters (width) and 10 rows (height). These relationships are illustrated in Figure 8.6. By changing the parameters around, we could easily create a horizontal menu. This statement:

```
Mso Menu1(MList, 5, 1, 3, 60, 1, 0x11,
          WithShadow+Swappable, DefColors);
```

would produce the menu shown in Figure 8.7. In this case, the **Sp** parameter, which is set to 3, specifies the character spacing for each menu entry.

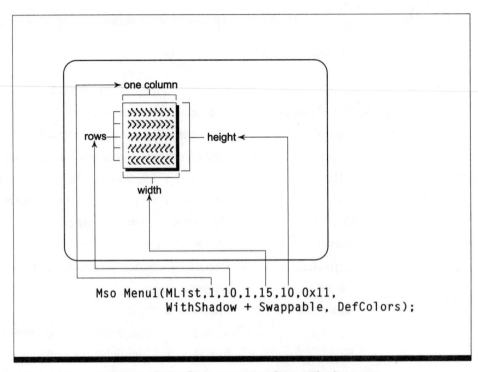

Figure 8.6   Components of a vertical menu

The portion of **SetupDim()** that determines the dimensions for a vertical menu is:

```
do {
  // We use Absc below so coords will not be translated just yet
  P->SetLocn(0, Panel->TextHeight(NumEntries), Absc);
  TxtLen - Panel->TextWidth(P->Name);
  if (TxtLen > MaxEntryLen) MaxEntryLen - TxtLen;
  NumEntries++;
  P - P->Next;
} while (P !- Entries->Last->Next);
if (MaxEntryLen > W) W - MaxEntryLen;
H - Panel->TextHeight(NumEntries);
Nr - NumEntries; Nc - 1;
```

Before the **do** loop starts, the variable **P** is set to the first menu entry in the list. The loop then continues to process each menu entry by calculating each entry length. Note that the variable **MaxEntryLen** keeps track of the longest menu entry. After the loop terminates, the code checks to see if the length of the longest entry is greater than the width of the menu specified when the object was initial-

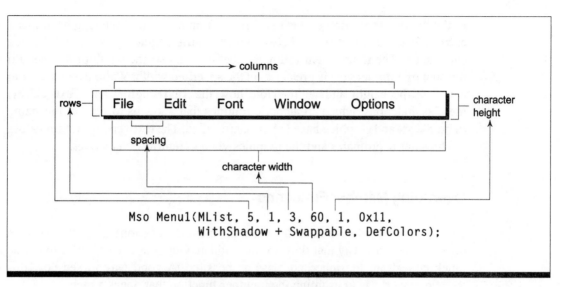

Figure 8.7   Horizontal menu

ized. This feature makes it unnecessary to specify the correct menu width when you create a menu that is the same width as the longest menu entry. For example, we'll change the call to the constructor used in the vertical menu example, so that it creates a "perfect fit" menu:

```
Mso Menu1(MList, 1, 10, 1, 0, 10, 0x11,
          WithShadow+Swappable, DefColors);
```

In this case, note that the width parameter is set to 0.

The auto-sizing code for horizontal menus is similar to the code just looked at for vertical menus. The main difference is that we need to calculate the width of a menu by summing the lengths of all the menu entries. Its code is:

```
do {
  // Absc is used so coordinates will not be translated yet
  P->SetLocn(SumLen, 0, Absc);
  SumLen += Panel->TextWidth(P->Name) + Spacing;
  NumEntries++;
  P = P->Next;
} while (P != Entries->Last->Next);
SumLen -= Spacing;
if (SumLen > W) W = SumLen;
H = Panel->TextHeight(1);
Nc = NumEntries;
Nr = 1;
```

In the **do** loop the variable **SumLen** keeps a running total of the lengths of menu entries. Note that the distance between menu entries, **Spacing**, is also used in the calculation. The **if** statement following the loop adjusts the width of the menu if the sum of entry lengths is greater than the specified width. We're using a trick to calculate the height and width. Note how the **TextHeight()** and **TextWidth()** member functions, which are generic routines that allow us to support the sizing of both text- and graphics-based menus, are called. The text versions return values in character coordinates and the graphics version returns pixel values.

Overriding Member Functions

One of the more interesting things about the member functions in the menu screen object class is the way that they are overridden. Our goal once again is to use as much code from the inherited class as possible. A good way to see how this technique works is to examine the member function that opens a menu:

```
void Mso::Open(Iso *B, int X, int Y)
// Open up the menu, open up the menu entries too
{
  Meso *P;

  Wso::Open(B, X, Y);
  P = Entries->Last->Next; // Get the first menu entry
  do {
    // Display the menu item
    P->Open(this, P->Panel->Overall->Xul, P->Panel->Overall->Yul);
    P = P->Next;   // Get the next menu entry
  } while(P != Entries->Last->Next);
  EntriesDrawn = True; // Indicates menu entries are displayed
}
```

Note the call to **Open()** of the inherited **Wso** class. This function handles most of the initial drawing operations of the menu for us. All we have to do is add some new code to display the menu entries. Because each entry is a screen object itself, it is displayed by opening it on the menu object:

```
P->Open(this, P->Panel->Overall->Xul,
        P->Panel->Overall->Yul);
```

Note how we use the coordinates calculated by **SetupDim()**. If you take a few minutes to examine the other overridden member functions including **MoveLoop()**, **Activate()**, **Leave()**, and **OnKeyStroke()**, you'll see that we're using a similar code-sharing technique to process menu objects.

A Menu Example

Let's now put the **Meso**, **MesoList**, and **Mso** classes to work and write a program that displays and processes a simple pop-up menu. After the menu is displayed, you can use the mouse or arrow keys to select a menu entry. Each menu entry is assigned an action that executes when the entry is selected. To quit the program type Alt-X or select the Exit option from the File menu. The program is:

```
// tmenu1.cpp: menu test program

#include "wsotxscr.h"
#include "msounit.h"

void ExitAction(Wso *, MsgPkt &M)
// Quits the pull-down menu program
{
  M.RtnCode = ShutDown;
}

void PopupAction(Wso *Src, MsgPkt &M)
// Displays a pop-up menu for the menu entry selected
{
  Wso *B;
  char Buff[80];
  ((Meso *)Src)->OnClose(M);      // Close the submenu
  M.Code = M.RtnCode;             // Use the return code
  FullScrn->SubMgr->EventStep(M);
  // Create the pop-up window
  B = new Wso(0x11, WindowStyle, DefColors);
  strcpy(Buff, ((Meso *)Src)->Name);
  strcat(Buff, " Action");
  B->SetSize(B->Panel->TextWidth(Buff), B->Panel->TextHeight(2));
  B->Open(FullScrn, 30, 10);
  B->Panel->HzWrt(0, 0, Buff, 0);
  B->SwitchFocus(M);
  M.RtnCode = Idle; M.Code = Idle;
  do {
    B->SubMgr->EventStep(M);
    M.Code = M.RtnCode;
  } while (M.Code != ShutDown &&
          (!B->Active || M.Code != Close || M.Focus != (Iso *)(B)));
  if (M.Code == Close) {
    B->OnClose(M);
    Mouse.WaitForEvent(MouseUp, M.Mx, M.My);
    M.RtnCode = Idle;
  }
  delete B; // Remove the window
  // Control is now returned to the menu
}
```

```
MesoList *MList;
Meso *Entry1, *Entry2, *Entry3, *Entry4, *Entry5;
Mso *Menu1;

main()
{
  // —————————Part 1—————————
  DefColors = CyanColors;                // Set up the display colors
  Setup(MouseOptional, DefColors);  // Set up the environment
  MList = new MesoList;                   // Create the menu list
  // Add each menu entry to the list
  Entry1 = new Meso("New", PopupAction);
  MList->Append(Entry1);
  Entry2 = new Meso("Open", PopupAction);
  MList->Append(Entry2);
  Entry3 = new Meso("Save", PopupAction);
  MList->Append(Entry3);
  Entry4 = new Meso("Close", PopupAction);
  MList->Append(Entry4);
  Entry5 = new Meso("Exit", ExitAction);
  MList->Append(Entry5);
  // —————————Part 2: Create the menu object—————————
  Menu1 = new Mso(MList, 1, 5, 1, 15, 5, 0x11,
                  WithShadow+Swappable, DefColors);
  FullScrn->Panel->Clear(177,4);
  Menu1->Open(FullScrn, 10, 5);
  MainEventLoop();
  CleanUp();
}
```

Figure 8.8 shows the menu created by **tmenu1**. To run the program, you'll need to have available **msounit.cpp**, which is provided in Listing 8.1. You'll also need the other unit files we have presented in Chapters 3 through 7.

The main body of the program is quite simple. In the first part, we set up the environment by calling the **Setup()** function defined in **wsotxscr.cpp** and then we create a pointer to a menu list object, **MList**, and add each menu entry to the list. In the second part, we create the menu object pointer, **Menu1**, and display the menu by opening it on the **FullScrn** object. Note that menus are opened like other screen objects such as windows.

You might now be wondering how the program knows what to do when a menu item is selected. That's where the **PopupAction()** and **ExitAction()** functions enter. When each menu item is created, the constructor is called to assign the entry to one of these actions. For example, the statement

```
Entry1 = new Meso("New", PopupAction);
```

assigns **PopupAction()** to the "New" entry.

Figure 8.8   Ouput of the program tmenu1.cpp

The **PopupAction()** function displays a pop-up window with the name of the menu entry and **ExitAction()** quits the program. Notice that both of these functions require two parameters: a pointer to the window object that was active when the menu item was selected (**Src**) and the message packet (**M**).

Because menus are derived from windows they can be moved by dragging them with the mouse, thereby creating *tear-away* menus. To set up a tear-away menu, use the **Swappable** setting for the frame attribute parameter.

Creating Pull-Down Menus

The pop-up menus that have been introduced are easy to set up because only two steps are required: construct a list of menu entry objects and assign the list to a menu object. Pull-down menus, however, are much more complex to set up because two types of menus must be used: a horizontal menu bar and a set of drop menus assigned to the entries in the pull-down bar. Figure 8.9 shows a pull-down menu system with its components labeled. Note that four new classes are introduced: **Pmso**, **PullDnBar**, **Pmeso**, and **Dmso**.

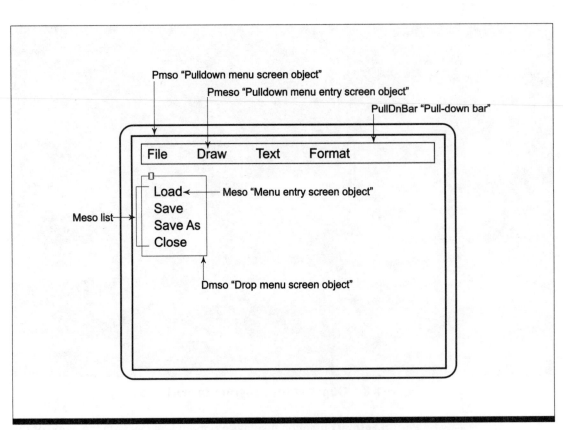

Figure 8.9   The components of the pull-down menu system

The main class, pull-down menu screen object (**Pmso**), defines the full-screen region for the pull-down menu system. It is responsible for setting up the pull-down menu bar object (**PullDnBar**) and initializing the screen. The **PullDnBar** object contains a set of menu entries that are called **Pmeso** objects. Finally, the drop menu screen object class (**Dmso**) is used to create the drop menu objects that are assigned to the pull-down menu bar entries.

To create a pull-down menu system, three steps must be followed:

1. Build the drop menus by creating **Dmso** objects. The **Dmso** objects are constructed like **Mso** objects, that is, a list of menu entries is assigned to the menu object.

2. Create the menu entries for the pull-down menu bar object—**PullDnBar**.

3. Create the main pull-down menu screen object—a **Pmso**—for the pull-down system.

The Pmso Class

As stated, the **Pmso** class is the top-level class that implements the pull-down menu system. Note that this class requires only a few new data members and member functions:

```
class Pmso : public Wso {
public:
  PullDnBar *Bar;        // The pull-down menu bar
  Wso *Inner;            // The window region for the menu system
  Pmso(MesoList *Items, int W, int H, int Sp,
       int Ba, int Fa, ColorPak &Cp);
  virtual void Open(Iso *B, int X, int Y);
};
```

Note that the parent of the **Pmso** class is the **Wso** class. In terms of its data members, the **Bar** pointer is used to access the pull-down menu bar object and **Inner** references the screen region assigned to the pull-down menu screen object.

The **Pmso()** constructor is responsible for initializing the pull-down menu object. It also uses **Bar** to initialize the pull-down menu bar. The **MesoList** parameter specifies the list of menu entries assigned to the pull-down bar. These entries are created using the technique we introduced when we discussed pop-up menus. The parameters **W** and **H** specify the screen width and height of the pull-down menu system. Normally, the values 80 and 25 are used in text mode to create a pull-down menu object that covers the full screen. (When pull-down menu objects are created in graphics mode, pixel coordinates should be used.)

Working our way through the construtor's parameter list, **Sp** is used to define the spacing between menu entries in the pull-down menu bar. The last three parameters, **Ba**, **Fa**, and **Cp**, specify the menu border attribute, frame attribute, and colors, respectively.

Open() is used to display the pull-down menu object. Note that this member function has been overridden from the base class (**Wso**) version. The new member function is:

```
void Pmso::Open(Iso *B, int X, int Y)
// Displays the pull-down menu system by opening the main
// pull-down object on an Iso
{
  Wso::Open(B, X, Y);
  Bar->Open(this, 0, 0);
  Inner->Open(this, 0, Panel->TextHeight(1));
}
```

In this case, three objects must be opened: the **Pmso**'s window, the menu bar, and the **Inner** object.

Building the Pull-Down Menu Bar

We'll need two classes to support the pull-down menu bar—**PullDnBar** and **Pmeso**. The **PullDnBar** object is managed internally by the **Pmso** object. The **Pmeso** object, however, must be explicitly created and initialized by the program that uses a pull-down menu system. Let's take a look at **PullDnBar** first:

```
class PullDnBar : public Mso {
public:
  Mso *SubMso;
  PullDnBar(MesoList *Items, int W, int Sp, ColorPak &Cp);
  virtual void OnKeyStroke(MsgPkt &M);
};
```

The **SubMso** pointer is used to reference the drop menu that is currently active (displayed). We need to keep track of this information so that we can erase the current drop menu before displaying a new one.

As you might guess, the **PullDnBar()** constructor initializes the pull-down menu bar object. Remember, the **Pmso** object is responsible for initializing the pull-down bar.

To complete the construction of the pull-down bar, we'll need a way to represent the horizontal menu entries—and that's where **Pmeso** comes in:

```
class Pmeso : public Meso {
public:
  Dmso *Vm; // The drop menu assigned to the menu entry
  Pmeso(char *N, Dmso *D);
  virtual void SwitchFocus(MsgPkt &M);
  virtual void OnKeyStroke(MsgPkt &M);
};
```

Here **Vm** serves as the link between a menu-bar entry and its drop menu. At initialization, the menu entry name along with its associated drop menu object are passed as parameters. For example:

```
Pmeso EditBut("Edit", EditSubM);
```

In this case, **Vm** would point to the **Dmso** object pointed to by **EditSubM**. The name "Edit" would be displayed in the pull-down menu bar.

Representing Drop Menus

We need to discuss another component of the pull-down menu system—drop menus. For each entry in the pull-down menu bar, a drop menu must be provided.

The drop menu is assigned to a menu bar entry and is displayed whenever the menu bar entry is selected. A drop menu object is very similar to a pop-up menu object (**Mso**); however, we'll need to add a few features so that the drop menu can be linked to a menu bar entry. The class definition we'll use to create drop menu objects is:

```
class Dmso : public Mso {
public:
  Pmeso *Parent; // The top-level menu that the drop menu
                 // is assigned to
  Dmso(MesoList *Items, int W, int Ba, int Fa, ColorPak &Cp);
  virtual void OnClose(MsgPkt &M);
  virtual void OnKeyStroke(MsgPkt &M);
};
```

The only new data member to the **Mso** class is **Parent**, which is used to determine which pull-down menu entry a drop menu is assigned.

Note that the **Dmso** class contains two overridden functions: **OnClose()** and **OnKeyStroke()**. Because drop menus work a little differently from standard pop-up menus, new versions of these member functions are needed to control how drop menus are closed and activated. For an example, let's take a look at **OnClose()**:

```
void Dmso::OnClose(MsgPkt &M)
// Closes a drop menu screen object. Note how we must
// set the PullDnBar's SubMso field to NULL, and how we
// must do a typecast.
{
  ((PullDnBar *)(Parent->Base))->SubMso = NULL;
  Mso::OnClose(M);
}
```

The first statement is responsible for setting the pull-down menu bar pointer assigned to the drop menu to **NULL** so that the pull-down menu will know that the drop menu is closed. The menu itself is then closed by calling the inherited **OnClose()** function.

To process input keys, a drop menu object must check to see if the left or right arrow key has been pressed. This action instructs the **OnKeyStroke()** member function to call the **OnKeyStroke()** function from the drop menu's **Parent** object so that a different drop menu can be displayed. This process is illustrated in Figure 8.10.

A Pull-Down Menu System Example

Our last sample program illustrates how a pull-down menu system is created. This program creates the menu system shown in Figure 8.11. Note that the menu bar

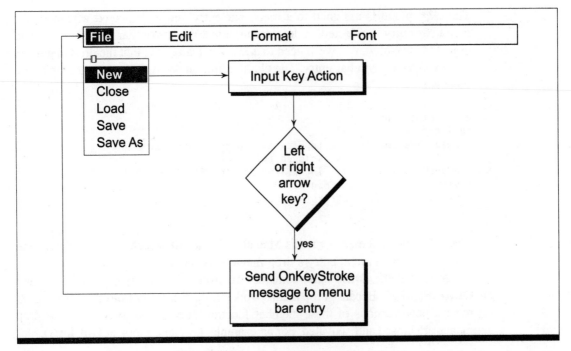

Figure 8.10   Processing an input key

contains three entries: File, Edit, and View. Each of these entries is assigned a drop
menu.

```
// tmenutst.cpp: Menu test program

#include "wsotxscr.h"
#include "msounit.h"

void ExitAction(Wso *, MsgPkt &M)
// Quits the pull-down menu program
{
  M.RtnCode - ShutDown;
}

void NoAction(Wso *, MsgPkt &)
// No action here
{
  return;
}

void PopupAction(Wso *Src, MsgPkt &M)
// Displays a pop-up menu for the menu entry selected
{
  Wso *B;
  char Buff[80];
```

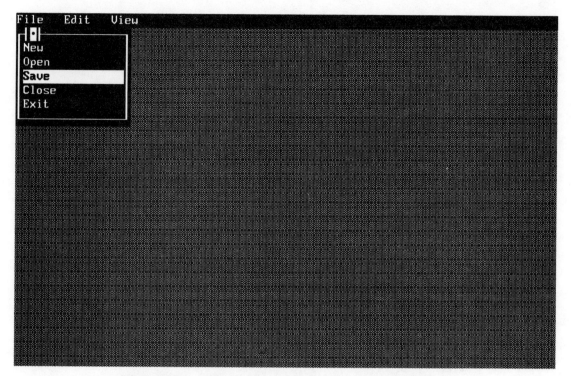

Figure 8.11   The output of the program tmenutst.cpp

```
((Meso *)Src)->OnClose(M);      // Close the submenu
M.Code - M.RtnCode;
FullScrn->SubMgr->EventStep(M);
// Create the pop-up window
B - new Wso(0x11, WindowStyle, DefColors);
strcpy(Buff, ((Meso *)Src)->Name);
strcat(Buff, " Action");
B->SetSize(B->Panel->TextWidth(Buff), B->Panel->TextHeight(2));
B->Open(FullScrn, 30, 10);
B->Panel->HzWrt(0, 0, Buff, 0);
B->SwitchFocus(M);
M.RtnCode - Idle; M.Code - Idle;
do {
  B->SubMgr->EventStep(M);
  M.Code - M.RtnCode;
} while (M.Code !- ShutDown &&
      (!B->Active || M.Code !- Close || M.Focus !- (Iso *)(B)));
if (M.Code -- Close) {
  B->OnClose(M);
  Mouse.WaitForEvent(MouseUp, M.Mx, M.My);
  M.RtnCode - Idle;
}
delete B;
}
```

```
Pmeso *FileBut;        // The File button
Dmso *FileMenu;        // The File drop menu
MesoList *FileMList;   // The list of entries for File
Meso *NewBut;
Meso *OpenBut;
Meso *SaveBut;
Meso *CloseBut;
Meso *VtExitBut;

Pmeso *EditBut;        // The Edit button
Dmso *EditMenu;        // The Edit drop menu
MesoList *EditMList;   // The list of entries for Edit
Meso *CutBut;
Meso *CopyBut;
Meso *PasteBut;

Pmeso *ViewBut;        // The View button
Dmso *ViewMenu;        // The View drop menu
MesoList *ViewMList;   // The list of entries for View
Meso *AsciiBut;
Meso *HexBut;

Pmso *Hm;              // The horizontal pull-down menu
MesoList *HzMenuList;  // The list of entries for the pull-down
                       // menu bar

main()
{
  DefColors = CyanColors;
  Setup(MouseOptional, DefColors);
  // ———————Part 1: Set up the File drop menu———————
  FileMList = new MesoList;
  NewBut = new Meso("New", PopupAction);
  FileMList->Append(NewBut);
  OpenBut = new Meso("Open", PopupAction);
  FileMList->Append(OpenBut);
  SaveBut = new Meso("Save", PopupAction);
  FileMList->Append(SaveBut);
  CloseBut = new Meso("Close", PopupAction);
  FileMList->Append(CloseBut);
  VtExitBut = new Meso("Exit", ExitAction);
  FileMList->Append(VtExitBut);
  FileMenu = new Dmso(FileMList, 15, 0x11, WindowStyle, DefColors);
  // ———————Part 2: Set up the Edit drop menu———————
  EditMList = new MesoList;
  CutBut = new Meso("Cut", PopupAction);
  EditMList->Append(CutBut);
  CopyBut = new Meso("Copy", PopupAction);
  EditMList->Append(CopyBut);
  PasteBut = new Meso("Paste", PopupAction);
  EditMList->Append(PasteBut);
  EditMenu = new Dmso(EditMList, 15, 0x11, WindowStyle, DefColors);
```

```
// ——Part 3: Set up the View drop menu——
ViewMList = new MesoList;
AsciiBut = new Meso("Ascii", PopupAction);
ViewMList->Append(AsciiBut);
HexBut = new Meso("Hex", PopupAction);
ViewMList->Append(HexBut);
ViewMenu = new Dmso(ViewMList, 15, 0x11, WindowStyle, DefColors);
// ——Part 4: Set up the main menu bar——
HzMenuList = new MesoList;
FileBut = new Pmeso("File", FileMenu);
HzMenuList->Append(FileBut);
EditBut = new Pmeso("Edit", EditMenu);
HzMenuList->Append(EditBut);
ViewBut = new Pmeso("View", ViewMenu);
HzMenuList->Append(ViewBut);
Hm = new Pmso(HzMenuList, 80, 25, 3, 0x00, 0x00, CyanColors);
Hm->Open(FullScrn, 0, 0);
Hm->Inner->Panel->Clear(177, 4);
MainEventLoop();                        // Start the event loop
CleanUp();
}
```

Code Critique

We've now completed our design and coding of the interface screen object toolkit. Using the files developed in Chapters 3 through 8, you now have everything you need to display and process windows, selection buttons, pop-up menus, and pull-down menus. In the chapters to follow new classes will be created to add more features to our basic interface toolkit. Before we get started, however, we need to discuss a few design issues that concern the menu tools developed in this chapter.

Graphics Menus

Because of polymorphism and encapsulation, our menuing system is generic enough to work in both text and graphics modes. The only change you need to make is to link up to the **Wso** class provided in **gwsounit.cpp** (discussed in Chapter 11). Remember that either **twsounit.h** or **gwsounit.h** is selected using the compiler directive at the top of the **msounit.h** file.

Classes with Multiple Parents

One situation encountered several times in our windowing system was the need for classes with two parents. Multiple inheritance might have been used, especially because we were trying to develop tools to support both text- and graphics-based objects; however, we've taken a different approach.

In order to build a derived class so that it can access a second object type, we have used what we call dynamic inheritance. The derived class includes a pointer to an object that is assigned at runtime. Take for instance, the **Iso** class. When we initialize an **Iso** object, we pass it the type of frame (**Fso**) we're going to use: either a **Tfso** (text-based) or a **Gfso** (graphics-based) frame. In a sense, what we're really doing is "inheriting" both the properties of an **Fso** class, and a screen driver (text or graphics).

Recall that our two base-menu objects, **Meso** and **Mso**, were derived from **Wso**. As with **Iso**, there is another way. Instead of deriving **Meso** and **Mso** from **Wso**, we could have included a **Wso** object within **Meso** and **Mso**. Then, we could have derived two classes from **Wso**, **Twso** and **Gwso**, which would be text- and graphics-based versions, respectively. Our last step would involve initializing a **Wso** object to be either a **Twso** or a **Gwso** object, and pass it to the initialization routines for **Meso** and **Mso**.

Note that the compiler directive method only allows us to support either text- or graphics-based menus in an application, but not both. With the dynamic inheritance approach, we could conceivably support both. For instance, we could switch between text and graphics mode while running the program, and by reinitializing the menu to use the appropriate **Twso** or **Gwso** object, the menus would still work.

Would this be worthwhile? Probably not. The reason is that, for most applications, it's unlikely that you would be using both text- *and* graphics-based menus. You would probably use one or the other.

Typecasts

You'll notice in our menu package that there are places where we have to do explicit typecasts. This problem occurs because the window and menu screen objects are based on stacks of generic **Iso** objects. Thus the underlying routines don't know that they may actually be using more specific menu objects.

We had to use typecasts partly because we were directly using data members from the underlying classes. For instance, the **Pmeso::OnSwitchFocus()** member function accesses the **Base** variable of the **Iso** class. In the **Iso** class, **Base** is typed as an **Iso** object. However, in the **Pmeso** class, we know that **Base** is really a pointer to a **PullDnBar** object and we had to typecast it as such. As an alternative, we could include another data member in **Pmeso**, called **Bar**, and typecast it to be a pointer to a **PullDnBar** object. We would then initialize it to **Base** when the **Pmeso** object was opened. An example of this technique is:

```
class Pmeso : public Meso {
public:
 PullDnBar *Bar;
 Dmso *Vm; // The drop menu assigned to the menu entry
 virtual void Open(Iso *B, int X, int Y);
 // The rest of the Pmeso class goes here
};

...

void Pmeso::Open(Iso *B, int X, int Y)
{
  Meso.Open(B, X, Y);
  Bar = (PullDnBar *)Base;
}
```

Note that the **Open()** member function sets up **Bar** to be a pointer to the **PullDnBar** class. Unfortunately, we still had to use a typecast. We can't entirely eliminate them. However, at least we wouldn't have to use the typecasts later in **OnSwitchFocus()**, or in any of the other member functions.

Using Arrow Keys

As you experiment with the menu system, you'll discover you can also use the arrow keys to navigate the menus. You can select an entry with the arrow keys, and then press Enter to activate it. You can also move around the entries by using the Tab key. Recall that this key allows you to cycle between screen objects. Since menu entries *are* screen objects, you can cycle through them using the Tab key. However, this cycling uses the order of the stacks, which changes constantly. Thus the movement may seem random. That's the reason our menus keep separate lists of entries, and the arrow keys use these lists for navigation. It is not recommended that you rely on the Tab key to move around. In fact, like all of the screen objects you're about to see in later chapters, the menus work best with the mouse.

Rectangular Menus

The menu system currently supports only vertical (single column) and horizontal (single row) menus. You may want to support rectangular menus, and add scrolling as well. In Chapter 9, you'll see how you can add scrolling to a window. The techniques presented there could conceivably be applied to support scrolling menus.

Listing 8.1 msounit.h

```
// msounit.h: menu screen object (mso) class definitions

#ifndef H_MSOUNIT
#define H_MSOUNIT

// Conditional directives used to determine which files
// should be included

#ifdef GRAPHICS
#include "gwsounit.h"
#else
#include "twsounit.h"
#endif

typedef void (*ActionProc)(Wso *Src, MsgPkt &M);

// ─── Generic menu entry screen object type ───

class Meso : public Wso {
public:
 char Name[40];        // Menu entry label
 ActionProc Action;   // The action assigned to the entry
 Meso *Next;          // References the next menu entry
 Meso(char *N, ActionProc A);
 virtual void Draw(void);
 virtual void Prompt(void);
 virtual void UnPrompt(void);
 virtual void OnKeyStroke(MsgPkt &M);
 virtual void OnClose(MsgPkt &M);
 virtual void Activate(MsgPkt &M);
};

class MesoList { // A circular list for storing menu entries
public:
  Meso *Last;       // References last menu entry on list
  MesoList(void);
  virtual ~MesoList(void);
  virtual void Append(Meso *Me);
};

class Mso : public Wso {      // The menu screen object type
public:
  MesoList *Entries;          // The list of menu entries
  Meso *CurrSeln;             // The selected menu entry
  int EntriesDrawn;           // "Entries have been drawn" flag
  int Nrows, Ncols, Spacing;  // Menu dimensions
  Mso(MesoList *El, int Nc, int Nr, int Sp, int W, int H,
      int Bd, int Fa, ColorPak &Cp);
  virtual void SetupDim(int &Nc, int &Nr, int &W, int &H);
  virtual int EntryWidth(Meso *Me);
  virtual void SetupEntries(void);
```

```
    virtual int  IsHz(void) { return Nrows - 1; }
    virtual int  IsVt(void) { return Ncols - 1; }
    virtual void Open(Iso *B, int X, int Y);
    virtual void MoveLoop(MsgPkt &M);
    virtual void Activate(MsgPkt &M);
    virtual void Leave(MsgPkt &M);
    virtual void OnKeyStroke(MsgPkt &M);
    virtual void Forw(MsgPkt &M);
    virtual void Back(MsgPkt &M);
};

// —— Types used to support pull-down menu systems ——

// This type is used to create a pull-down menu bar

class PullDnBar : public Mso {
public:
  Mso *SubMso;
  PullDnBar(MesoList *Items, int W, int Sp, ColorPak &Cp);
  virtual void OnKeyStroke(MsgPkt &M);
};

// This type is used to create a pull-down menu system

class Pmso : public Wso {
public:
  PullDnBar *Bar;         // The pull-down menu bar
  Wso *Inner;             // The window region for the menu system
  Pmso(MesoList *Items, int W, int H, int Sp,
       int Ba, int Fa, ColorPak &Cp);
  virtual void Open(Iso *B, int X, int Y);
};

// This type is used to create an entry for the pull-down menu bar

class Dmso; // Forward reference

class Pmeso : public Meso {
public:
 Dmso *Vm; // The drop menu assigned to the menu entry
 Pmeso(char *N, Dmso *D);
 virtual void SwitchFocus(MsgPkt &M);
 virtual void OnKeyStroke(MsgPkt &M);
};

// This type is used to create a drop menu

class Dmso : public Mso {
public:
  Pmeso *Parent; // The top-level menu that the drop menu
                 // is assigned to
  Dmso(MesoList *Items, int W, int Ba, int Fa, ColorPak &Cp);
  virtual void OnClose(MsgPkt &M);
```

```
     virtual void OnKeyStroke(MsgPkt &M);
};

#endif
```

Listing 8.2   msounit.cpp

```
// msounit.cpp: menu screen object (mso) class implementation

#include "stdio.h"
#include "process.h"
#include "stdlib.h"
#include "string.h"
#include "msounit.h"

// —————————— Meso methods ——————————
Meso::Meso(char *N, ActionProc A)
// Initializes a menu entry object by assigning it a name and
// action. The object will have no border and will have
// default colors.
: Wso(0x00, 0x00, DefColors)
{
  strncpy(Name, N, 39);  Name[39] = 0; // Ensure null termination
  Action = A;
  SetSize(Panel->TextWidth(N), Panel->TextHeight(1));
}

void Meso::Draw(void)
// Displays a menu entry
{
  Wso::Draw();  // Draw the window object
  Panel->HzWrt(0, 0, Name, Panel->Colors.Wc);
}

void Meso::Prompt(void)
// Prompts a menu entry by highlighting it
{
  Wso::Prompt();  // Select the window
  Panel->Fill(0, 0, Panel->Interior->Wd, Panel->TextHeight(1),
              ' ', Panel->Colors.Fc);
  Panel->HzWrt(0, 0, Name, Panel->Colors.Fc);
}

void Meso::UnPrompt(void)
// Unprompts the menu entry by redisplaying it
// with its standard attribute
{
  Panel->Fill(0, 0, Panel->Interior->Wd, Panel->TextHeight(1),
              ' ', Panel->Colors.Wc);
  Panel->HzWrt(0, 0, Name, Panel->Colors.Wc);
  Wso::UnPrompt(); // Deselect window
}
```

```
void Meso::OnKeyStroke(MsgPkt &M)
// Processes an input key.  The Enter key selects the entry. If
// any other key is pressed the entry's Base (which is the
// menu itself) handles it
{
  if (M.Code == CrKey)
     Activate(M);
     else Base->OnKeyStroke(M); // Send key to base
}

void Meso::OnClose(MsgPkt &M)
// Closing a menu entry means to close the menu as well
{
  Base->SwitchFocus(M);
  M.RtnCode = Close; // Effectively tells the base to close
}

void Meso::Activate(MsgPkt &M)
// Call the menu entry's action. Otherwise, leave the menu
// entry. (Thus, if a MouseUp event occurs outside the menu,
// the entry is deselected.)
{
  if (Active) { // The entry must be selected
     Wso::Activate(M);
     Action(this, M); // Execute the assigned action
  }
  else {
     Leave(M);          // Leave the menu entry
  }
}


// ——————— Meso list methods ———————
MesoList::MesoList(void)
// Initializes the list of menu entry objects. The list is
// implemented as a circular list.
{
  Last = NULL;   // Indicates the list is empty
}

MesoList::~MesoList(void)
// This method does nothing because the entries on the list
// also appear on the Iso stack, and will be destroyed when
// the stack is destroyed.
{
  return;
}

void MesoList::Append(Meso *Me)
// Appends a menu entry to the menu list
{
  if (Last != NULL) {     // List has entries
     Me->Next = Last->Next;
     Last->Next = Me;    // Add new element
     Last = Last->Next;  // Update end of list pointer
```

```
   }
   else {                    // List is empty
      Last - Me;             // Place at top of list
      Last->Next - Me;
   }
}

// ———— Menu screen object methods ————
Mso::Mso(MesoList *El, int Nc, int Nr, int Sp, int W, int H,
         int Bd, int Fa, ColorPak &Cp)
// Initializes the menu object by creating a window
// and setting up the menu entries
: Wso(Bd, Fa, Cp) // Initialize the menu's window
{
   Entries   - El;
   CurrSeln - Entries->Last->Next;
   EntriesDrawn - 0;
   Spacing - Sp;
   SetupDim(Nc, Nr, W, H);   // Sets up the menu dimensions
   Ncols - Nc; Nrows - Nr;   // Store number of columns and rows
   SetSize(W, H);   // Sets the menu width and height
   SetupEntries(); // Sets the size and attribute for each entry
}

void Mso::SetupDim(int &Nc, int &Nr, int &W, int &H)
// Sets up the menu's dimensions
{
   int SumLen, NumEntries, MaxEntryLen, TxtLen;
   Meso *P;

   NumEntries - 0; MaxEntryLen - 0; SumLen - 0;
   P - Entries->Last->Next;
   if (Nr -- 1)  { // Horizontal menu
      do {
         // Absc is used so coordinates will not be translated yet
         P->SetLocn(SumLen, 0, Absc);
         SumLen += Panel->TextWidth(P->Name) + Spacing;
         NumEntries++;
         P - P->Next;
      } while (P !- Entries->Last->Next);
      SumLen -- Spacing;
      if (SumLen > W) W - SumLen;
      H - Panel->TextHeight(1);
      Nc - NumEntries;
      Nr - 1;
   }
   else if (Nc -- 1) { // Vertical menu
      do {
         // Absc is used so coordinates will not be translated yet
         P->SetLocn(0, Panel->TextHeight(NumEntries), Absc);
         TxtLen - Panel->TextWidth(P->Name);
         if (TxtLen > MaxEntryLen) MaxEntryLen - TxtLen;
         NumEntries++;
```

```
         P = P->Next;
       } while (P != Entries->Last->Next);
       if (MaxEntryLen > W) W = MaxEntryLen;
       H = Panel->TextHeight(NumEntries);
       Nr = NumEntries; Nc = 1;
  }
  else {   // Rectangular menu:
    printf("Rectangular menus not supported\n");
    exit(1);
  }
}

int Mso::EntryWidth(Meso *Me)
// Calculates the width of a menu entry
{
  if (IsHz())
      return Panel->TextWidth(Me->Name);
      else return Panel->Interior->Wd;
}

void Mso::SetupEntries(void)
// Sizes the menu entries and initializes their colors
{
  Meso *P;
  P = Entries->Last->Next;  // Get the first menu entry
  do {
    P->Panel->SetSize(EntryWidth(P), Panel->TextHeight(1));
    P->Panel->Colors = Panel->Colors;
    P = P->Next;
  } while (P != Entries->Last->Next);
}

void Mso::Open(Iso *B, int X, int Y)
// Open up the menu, open up the menu entries too
{
  Meso *P;

  Wso::Open(B, X, Y);
  P = Entries->Last->Next; // Get the first menu entry
  do {
    // Display the menu item
    P->Open(this, P->Panel->Overall->Xul, P->Panel->Overall->Yul);
    P = P->Next;  // Get the next menu entry
  } while(P != Entries->Last->Next);
  EntriesDrawn = True; // Indicates menu entries are displayed
}


void Mso::MoveLoop(MsgPkt &M)
// Calls the MoveLoop from the parent class to move the menu.
// This feature supports tear-away menus. We return a MouseUp
// event to cause the current menu entry to be selected.
{
```

```
      Wso::MoveLoop(M);
      M.RtnCode = MouseUp;
    }

    void Mso::Activate(MsgPkt &M)
    // This method handles the case when a MouseUp occurs on
    // the menu's border (see MoveLoop). We wish to switch focus
    // to the current menu entry so that it is highlighted.
    {
      CurrSeln = (Meso *)(SubMgr->Top);
      CurrSeln->SwitchFocus(M);
    }

    void Mso::Leave(MsgPkt &M)
    // Leaves a menu. Before leaving, we must record the
    // current menu entry selection.
    {
      CurrSeln = (Meso *)(SubMgr->Top);  // Save current entry
      Wso::Leave(M);                     // Leave the menu
    }

    void Mso::OnKeyStroke(MsgPkt &M)
    // Trap and process the arrow keys, otherwise pass the
    // key press event to the inherited method.
    {
      switch(M.Code) { // Check for arrow keys
        case UpKey    : if (IsVt()) Back(M); break; // To previous entry
        case DownKey  : if (IsVt()) Forw(M); break; // To next entry
        case LeftKey  : if (IsHz()) Back(M); break;
        case RightKey : if (IsHz()) Forw(M); break;
        default:
          Wso::OnKeyStroke(M); // Send other keys to base class
      }
    }

    void Mso::Forw(MsgPkt &M)
    // Advances to the next menu entry in the menu object
    {
      CurrSeln = (Meso *)(SubMgr->Top); // Find current selection
      CurrSeln->Next->SwitchFocus(M);   // Go to next entry
    }

    void Mso::Back(MsgPkt &M)
    // Backs up to the previous menu entry
    {
      Meso *P;
      CurrSeln = (Meso *)(SubMgr->Top); // Find current selection
      P = CurrSeln;
      while (P->Next != CurrSeln) P = P->Next;
      CurrSeln = P;                 // Go to previous entry
      CurrSeln->SwitchFocus(M); // Select the new entry
    }
```

```
// ——— Pull-down menu bar methods ———
PullDnBar::PullDnBar(MesoList *Items, int W, int Sp, ColorPak &Cp)
// Initializea a pull-down menu bar object
: Mso(Items, 0, 1, Sp, W,
      Items->Last->Next->Panel->Overall->Ht, 0x00, 0x00, Cp)
{
  SubMso — NULL;
}


void PullDnBar::OnKeyStroke(MsgPkt &M)
// First, let the inherited Mso::OnKeyStroke handle the
// keystroke. If the keystroke is a left or right arrow key,
// a new entry will be selected by Mso::OnKeyStroke, so
// activate the new menu entry, causing the drop menu to
// drop down.
{
  Mso::OnKeyStroke(M);
  if ((M.Code — LeftKey) || (M.Code — RightKey))
    M.Focus->Activate(M);
}


// ————— Pull-down menu —————

Pmso::Pmso(MesoList *Items, int W, int H, int Sp,
           int Ba, int Fa, ColorPak &Cp)
// Initializes the main pull-down menu screen object
: Wso(Ba, Fa, Cp)
{
  Bar — new PullDnBar(Items, W, Sp, Cp);
  SetSize(Bar->Panel->Frame->Wd, H);
  Inner — new Wso(0x00, 0x00, Cp);
  Inner->SetSize(Panel->Interior->Wd,
                      Panel->Interior->Ht -
                      Panel->TextHeight(1));
}


void Pmso::Open(Iso *B, int X, int Y)
// Displays the pull-down menu system by opening the main
// pull-down object on an Iso
{
  Wso::Open(B, X, Y);
  Bar->Open(this, 0, 0);
  Inner->Open(this, 0, Panel->TextHeight(1));
}


// ——————————————————————
Dmso::Dmso(MesoList *Items, int W, int Ba, int Fa, ColorPak &Cp)
// Initializes a drop-menu screen object
: Mso(Items, 1, 0, 2, W, 0, Ba, Fa, Cp)
{
  Parent — NULL;
}
```

```
void Dmso::OnClose(MsgPkt &M)
// Closes a drop-menu screen object. Note how we must
// set the PullDnBar's SubMso field to NULL, and how we
// must do a typecast.
{
  ((PullDnBar *)(Parent->Base))->SubMso = NULL;
  Mso::OnClose(M);
}

void Dmso::OnKeyStroke(MsgPkt &M)
// Sends all LeftKey and RightKey events to the pull-down
// menu, else, let the inherited method (Mso::OnKeyStroke)
// handle the event.
{
  if (M.Code == LeftKey || M.Code == RightKey) {
      Parent->Base->OnKeyStroke(M);
  }
  else {
    Mso::OnKeyStroke(M);
  }
}

// ─────────────────────────────────

void PmesoAction(Wso *Src, MsgPkt &M)
// The action for a pull-down menu entry screen object is
// to switch focus to the last menu entry selected in the
// drop menu.
{
  ((Pmeso *)(Src))->Vm->CurrSeln->SwitchFocus(M);
}

Pmeso::Pmeso(char *N, Dmso *D)
// Initializes a pull-down menu entry screen object
: Meso(N, PmesoAction)
{
  Vm = D;
}

void Pmeso::OnKeyStroke(MsgPkt &M)
// Traps DownKey events so that they cause the submenu to drop
{
  if (M.Code == DownKey)
      Activate(M); else Meso::OnKeyStroke(M);
}

void Pmeso::SwitchFocus(MsgPkt &M)
// Switches focus to this object, erases any drop menu
// currently displayed, and draws this object's drop menu
{
  int Xcoord;
  if (!Active) {
    Meso::SwitchFocus(M); // Must do this first
```

```
        if (((PullDnBar *)(Base))->SubMso != NULL) {
            ((PullDnBar *)(Base))->SubMso->Leave(M);
            ((PullDnBar *)(Base))->SubMso->OnClose(M);
            ((PullDnBar *)(Base))->SubMso = NULL;
        }
        if (Vm != NULL) {       // If there is a drop menu
            Xcoord = Panel->Overall->Xul - Base->Panel->Overall->Xul;
            if (!Vm->EntriesDrawn) {
                Vm->Open(((Pmso *)(Base->Base))->Inner, Xcoord, 0);
            }
            else Vm->Reopen(Xcoord, 0);
            ((PullDnBar *)Base)->SubMso = Vm;
            Vm->Parent = this;
        }
    }
}
```

9

Putting Text Screen Objects to Work

You've now made it to the end of the road, at least as far as the basic interface screen object toolkit is concerned. We've created some useful and powerful screen, window, and menu management tools. Where do we go from here? It's time to put the interface tools to work and add some useful extensions. Because we've implemented the tools with OOP techniques, we'll be able to add useful extensions without having to rewrite any of the existing code. In particular, we're going to add three new types of screen objects to our toolkit: scrollable windows, scroll bars, and dialog boxes.

Our first project is scrollable windows. To implement these objects, we'll need to develop a new object—scroll bars. Then, we'll integrate these scroll bars with a window object, and as a result, create a scrollable window. As a side benefit we'll see how objects can communicate with one another through the message packet we developed in Chapter 8.

We'll end the chapter by developing a few different styles of dialog boxes. Although only the basics will be covered, the examples provided will show you how multiple screen objects can be grouped to create more complex interface objects.

Scrollable Windows

In the first part of this chapter we'll develop a new class that supports scrollable windows (see Figure 9.1). A scrollable window is a window that provides scrolling features so that data buffers larger than the size of the window can be viewed.

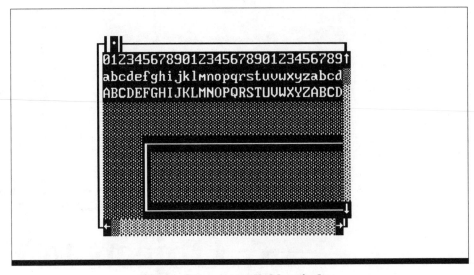

Figure 9.1   A scrollable window

The windows we'll create can be scrolled along both rows and columns. The scrolling action is controlled by slide bars which are activated by the arrow keys or the mouse.

The nuts and bolts of our scrollable window objects consist of a handful of new classes. Table 9.1 provides a summary of the new classes and Figure 9.2 illustrates how these classes are used to represent the different components of a scrollable window.

Table 9.1   New classes used in scrollable windows

Class	Description
ScrollFrame	New window frame style required for scroll bars
Slider	The slider component of the slide bar
ScrollBar	A complete slide bar object built from a ScrollFrame and Slider
Swso	An abstract window class with scroll bars
Vwso	A specific scroll window class that implements scrollable windows with a virtual buffer

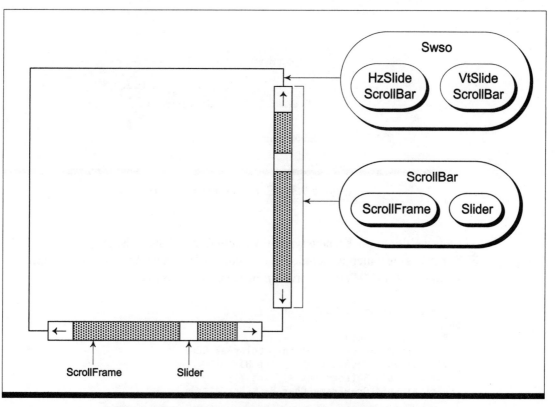

Figure 9.2   The components of a scrollable window

Scroll Bars

There are two issues that must be addressed before creating scroll bars. First, is it possible to construct the scroll bars from the tools we have? Second, how will we integrate the user-interaction of a scroll bar into an application?

Let's explore the first issue—creating the scroll bars. As Figure 9.3 shows, we can think of a scroll bar in terms of its components. It has an object that slides back and forth within a frame. This suggests that we need two objects: one for the base of the scroll bar and one for the slider.

We'll begin with the scroll bar itself. You might think we can use a **Wso** object as the scroll bar, but we need a special type of frame—one that is a single row of characters with two arrow symbols on each end. We also need to allow the slider to move between these arrow symbols, but nowhere else. To provide these fea-

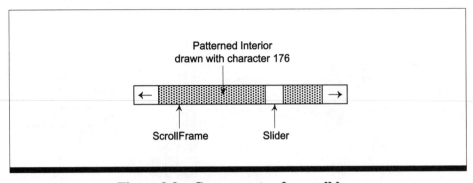

Figure 9.3   Components of a scroll bar

tures we'll introduce a new type of window frame. This is the purpose of the class **ScrollFrame** which is included in the source files **txscroll.h** and **txscroll.cpp** (see Listings 9.1 and 9.2, respectively). Its class definition is:

```
class ScrollFrame : public Tfso {
public:
  BarOrient Orientation;
  ScrollFrame(BarOrient Orient, ColorPak &Cp);
  virtual void SetSize(int W, int H);
  virtual void SetLocn(int X1, int Y);
  virtual void DrawFrame(char Ba, char Attr);
};
```

Note that **ScrollFrame** is derived from our text mode frame class **Tfso**. Because **ScrollFrame**'s main purpose is to provide a new frame style, it only overrides a few of **Tfso**'s member functions. As you might guess, **ScrollFrame** replaces **Tfso**'s **DrawFrame()** with its own version. In addition, **SetSize()** and **SetLocn()** are overridden to set the coordinates correctly for the new frame style. They are also overridden so that we can support either horizontal or vertical orientations for the scroll bars.

Recall that a **Tfso** object is built from three objects: an interior object, a frame object, and an overall object. Our new **ScrollFrame** objects will have these same components, but their orientation will be different. Figure 9.4 illustrates how the new frame style in the **ScrollFrame** class uses these three nested objects. The **SetSize()** and **SetLocn()** functions are overridden to configure things correctly. As you examine these routines, note that they can handle both horizontal and vertical scroll bars.

The frame's orientation is set when the **ScrollFrame()** constructor is called. In particular, the constructor assigns the parameter **Orient**, which can either be **HzOrient** or **VtOrient**, to the **ScrollFrame** data member **Orientation**. This

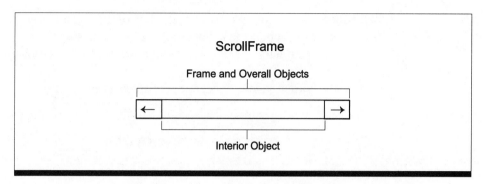

Figure 9.4   Frame style for a scroll bar

variable is later used by the member functions in **ScrollFrame** to determine a scroll bar's orientation. Note also that the frame and border styles are not passed as parameters to the constructor because we'll be hard coding these to create the specific scroll bar style we need.

The **DrawFrame()** member function really demonstrates the fact that we are introducing a new frame style. In fact, it is overridden in order to completely replace **Tfso**'s **DrawFrame()** function. It simply draws two arrow symbols on both ends of the scroll bar. For example, if the scroll bar is horizontal the following statements are executed:

```
if (Orientation — HzOrient) {
  Frame->HzWrt(0, 0, "\x1b", 0x70);          // Left arrow
  Frame->HzWrt(Frame->Wd-1, 0, "\x1a", 0x70); // Right arrow
}
else {
  Frame->HzWrt(0, 0, "\x18", 0x70);          // Up arrow
  Frame->HzWrt(0, Frame->Ht-1, "\x19", 0x70); // Down arrow
}
```

These statements display a left and right black-and-white arrow at each end of the **Frame** object.

A Slider Class

Now that we've constructed the scroll frame style, let's create another component of the scroll bar class we'll be needing—the **Slider** class. This class will become the moving component of a scroll bar.

A **Slider** object is a one-character-wide **Wso** object that does not have a border. Although it is only one character in size, it will have all of the properties of a **Wso** object. For instance, it will be a swappable window. We'll use this feature to put the **Slider** in motion. We'll override a few of the member functions in the **Wso** class in order to support the keyboard and to send messages.

Here is a summary of the features supplied by the **Slider** class:

1. Calls border handler whenever the slider is selected

2. Sends messages to the base scroll bar object whenever the slider is moved

3. Passes key strokes on to the base scroll bar

Its class definition is:

```
class Slider : public Wso {
public:
  Slider(ColorPak &Cp) : Wso(0x00, Swappable, Cp) { ; }
  virtual void Draw(void);
  virtual void OnMouseDown(MsgPkt &M);
  virtual void Move(int X, int Y);
  virtual void OnKeyStroke(MsgPkt &M);
};
```

We'll begin with the **Slider()** constructor, which calls the constructor from the inherited **Wso** type and passes the appropriate style parameters in order to make a **Slider** object moveable and without a border.

Because a **Slider** object does not have a border, we wouldn't normally be able to select and move the object with the mouse. The **BorderHandler()** member function, which provides the logic for moving an object, is only called when we have clicked the mouse while on an object's border. Since a **Slider** doesn't have a border, **BorderHandler()** will never be called. How can we fix this? The easiest way is to override **OnMouseDown()** (which is invoked each time the mouse is pressed while on a **Slider**) and force it to call **BorderHandler()**:

```
void Slider::OnMouseDown(MsgPkt &M)
// Call BorderHandler to move slider object whenever mouse is
// pressed while on the slider
{
  SwitchFocus(M);
  BorderHandler(M);
}
```

The **Slider** class also overrides the **OnKeyStroke()** and **Move()** member functions. Briefly, **OnKeyStroke()** is overridden so that it can process any keypresses detected while the **Slider** is active. Similarly, **Move()** is overridden so that each time the **Slider** is moved it will send a message to its base window signaling this event. We'll see how these actions fit into the bigger picture in the following sections.

Creating a Scroll Bar

Thus far, we've created the frame for a scroll bar and an object that represents its slider. What's next? We'll now fill in the details of a scroll bar by developing the **ScrollBar** class used to create a scroll bar. The **ScrollBar** class will:

1. Set the dimensions of the scroll bar frame

2. Draw the interior of the scroll bar

3. Display the scroll bar's slider

4. Pass position messages between its base window and the slider

The **ScrollBar** class is also in the files **txscroll.h** and **txscroll.cpp**. Its definition is:

```
class ScrollBar : public Iso {
public:
  Slider *Slide;
  int DelayCntr, DelayLimit;
  int InhibitMessage;
  ScrollBar(BarOrient Orient, ColorPak &Cp);
  virtual void Draw(void);
  virtual void Redraw(void);
  virtual void Open(Iso *B, int X, int Y);
  virtual void BorderHandler(MsgPkt &M);
  virtual void OnMouseDown(MsgPkt &M);
  virtual void OnMouseStillDown(MsgPkt &M);
  virtual void SendScrollPosn(void);
  virtual void RcvScrollPosn(float P, BarOrient Which);
  virtual void OnKeyStroke(MsgPkt &M);
};
```

Note that the **ScrollBar** class is derived from the **Iso** class. We didn't use the **Wso** class this time because we need to pass **Iso** the new frame style, **ScrollFrame**, rather than the more general **Tfso** style. This is done in the **ScrollBar()** constructor by the statement following the function header:

```
: Iso(new ScrollFrame(Orient, Cp))
```

The constructor is also responsible for allocating memory and initializing a **Slide** object. Similarly, **Open()** is overridden so that it opens both the **ScrollBar** object and the nested **Slide** object.

The constructor also sets the new data members **DelayCntr** and **DelayLimit** which are used by **OnMouseStillDown()** to determine how often the **MouseStillDown()** event is processed. You may need to adjust **DelayLimit** so that a single mouse click will only move the scroll bar one step. Currently, the code sets **DelayLimit** to 50, which is good for many computers.

The **Draw()** member function is overridden so we can draw a patterned interior in the scroll bar. This is accomplished by the call to **Clear()** using the graphics character 176:

```
Panel->Clear(176, 0); // A patterned interior
```

The **Redraw()** member function is overridden to ensure that the Slider is redrawn in conjunction with the bar. The **BorderHandler()** member function is also an overridden function and is called whenever a mouse button is pressed while on the scroll bar's border. This event indicates that the mouse is on one of the scroll bar's arrows.

Whenever **BorderHandler()** is called, we want the slider to start moving in the direction indicated by the arrow selected. We'll accomplish this by sending a fake keypress to the base window. You'll later see that the base window is responsible for processing these keystrokes and telling the **ScrollBar** what its new position should be. This may seem like a roundabout way of moving the slider, but it is necessary. Why? If we made each click on the **ScrollFrame** arrow move the slider by one position, we wouldn't be able to scroll a window smoothly, because of the coarse resolution of the positions on the scroll bar.

The simulated keypress sent to the base window depends on which arrow the mouse is on. For instance, if the mouse is pressed while on the left arrow of a horizontal scroll bar, a **LeftKey** event code is passed to the base window of the scroll bar. This is accomplished by the statements:

```
FakeMsg.Code = LeftKey;    // Act like key was pressed
Base->Dispatch(FakeMsg);
```

While we are discussing key presses, note that **OnKeyStroke()** is overridden so that it sends any key presses that the scroll bar detects to its base window.

The Mouse in Action

We must also change two of the mouse event member functions in order to support the scroll bar interaction we need. Therefore, we have overridden the functions **OnMouseDown()** and **OnMouseStillDown()**. The **OnMouseDown()** routine is overridden so that we can click anywhere within the interior of a scroll bar and have the slider jump to the location of the mouse cursor. The move operation is performed by calling **Slide**'s **Move()** member function. Immediately after **Move()**

is called, **OnMouseDown()** is invoked which enables the mouse to take control of the slides.

The **OnMouseStillDown()** member function is responsible for filtering out some of the scrolling action. Only with a sufficiently long enough **DelayLimit** value will you be able to incrementally move the scroll bar by clicking on its arrow characters.

Communicating with Other Objects

Now that we have a scroll bar, let's discuss how we can use it with other objects. Usually, we'll connect a scroll bar to another object and the scroll bar will report its position to the other object. For instance, in a scrollable window, the window will scroll through its virtual buffer as the slider is moved in the scroll bar.

The **ScrollBar** object presented here is designed to communicate with other objects through its base window. In particular, a scroll bar sends messages to its base window whenever the slider position has changed. This process is illustrated in Figure 9.5. It is up to the base window to grab this message and perform an appropriate action. As an example, a file browser might respond to a scroll bar message by updating the portion of a file that is being viewed.

The **ScrollBar** class provides two member functions, **SendScrollPosn()** and **RcvScrollPosn()**, to send and receive messages to and from its base window. Usually **SendScrollPosn()** is called when the mouse has moved the scroll bar's slider and its new position must be passed to other objects. **RcvScrollPosn()** is used to respond to messages sent from the base window, which sends these messages whenever the window is scrolled by the arrow keys or by other events of which the scroll bar has no knowledge.

The message passing is accomplished by using a **MsgPkt** with position information. For instance, in **SendScrollPosn()**, the position of the slider is encoded as a real number between zero and one where zero represents the leftmost position of a horizontal scroll bar and the topmost location of a vertical scroll bar and one represents the other end. Thus how do we calculate this value? Basically, it is determined by dividing the slider's relative position in the scroll bar by its full-scale position.

For example, if the scroll bar in question is a horizontal scroll bar, its encoded location is calculated by the statements:

```
// Compute relative position of slider to sliderbar
Ip = Slide->Panel->Frame->Xul - Pint->Xul;
if (Pint->Wd == 1)
  Rp = 0.0;
  else Rp = float(Ip) / float(Panel->Interior->Wd-1);
```

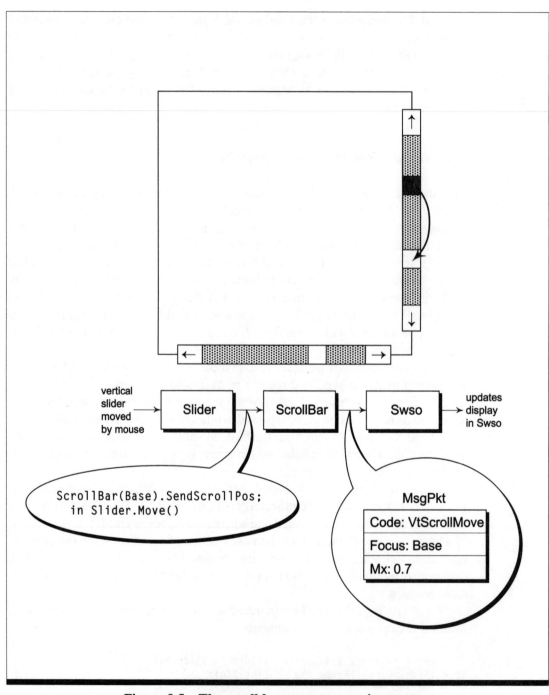

Figure 9.5 The scroll bar message-passing system

The value **Ip** is the relative position of the slider on the scroll bar and **Rp** translates this value into a real number between zero and one by dividing **Ip** by the maximum possible position of the slider.

Now that we can represent the slider's position, how do we tell other objects what it is? We've already decided to use a **MsgPkt** protocol, but we have a few more details to resolve. First, we need to introduce a new event code. By doing this, we'll be able to have the base window trap for this unique code.

One such event code, **HzScrollMove**, is defined at the top of **txscroll.h** as:

```
const int HzScrollMove = 0xfe00;
```

Later we'll write the routines for the base window so that it will trap for this event code. Therefore, we'll assign this event code to the **Code** field of a **MsgPkt**. We also must pass along the **Rp** value we calculated earlier. Unfortunately, we don't have a real number field in **MsgPkt** that we can use. Therefore, we'll multiply **Rp** by 10,000, truncate its result to an integer, and assign this value to the **Mx** or **My** field of **MsgPkt**, depending on whether it is a vertical or horizontal scroll bar, respectively. Here is the conversion needed for a horizontal scroll bar:

```
M.Mx = floor(Rp * 10000.0); M.My = 0;
```

Finally, we'll send the message to the base window by calling its **Dispatch()** member function. When we present the scrollable window class, you'll see how the message is actually captured and used.

Receiving Messages

The **ScrollBar** class includes a member function called **RcvScrollPosn()** which receives messages from other objects and tells the scroll bar what position it should be at. The **RcvScrollPosn()** function is simpler than its cousin **Send-ScrollPosn()** because it doesn't use the message packet.

We will expect that other screen objects will invoke the **RcvScrollPosn()** directly. In fact, **RcvScrollPosn()** is passed a parameter **P**, which is a real value that indicates where the scroll bar's slider should be moved. This value has the same meaning as it did in **SendScrollPosn()**, and goes from zero to one. The **RcvScrollPosn()** function is also passed the flag **Orient**, which indicates the orientation of the scroll bar that is supposed to be updated. We must know the orientation so that we can correctly compute the slider's new location. For example, if **Orient** is **HzOrient** then the new relative location of the slider on the scroll bar is calculated by the statement:

```
NewPos = ceil(P * ((float)(Panel->Interior->Wd-1));
```

Next, the corresponding slider button's **Move()** member function is called to move the slider to the new location. This is performed by the three statements:

```
InhibitMessage = True;
Slide->Move(Panel->Interior->Xul+NewPos,
            Panel->Interior->Yul);
InhibitMessage = False;
```

The call to **Move()** is straightforward, but what does **InhibitMessage** do? It prevents the scroll bar object from sending a message back to the screen object that is tied to the scroll bar. There are two sources that can cause the slider to move. First, the mouse could move it. We saw earlier, that when this happens, the slider's **Move()** member function is called. In fact, we overrode **Move()** so that when it was called it would send a message to **SendScrollPosn()** to report its new location. It passes the new location to the base window. However, the slider may also be moved in response to a message passed with **RcvScrollPosn()** from some other object—presumably the base window. If this occurs, **Move()** is called again and it will update the location of the slider. No problem so far. However, **Move()**'s next step is to call **SendScrollPosn()** which sends a message to the base window to update its position. This isn't needed because the base window was the object that initiated the scroll message. To prevent **Move()**'s **SendScrollPosn()** from generating this unwanted message, the **InhibitMessage** flag is set to **True**.

A Generic Scrollable Window Class

Now that we have a working scroll bar class in hand, we'll integrate it with the window class. This will give us the essentials for a scrollable window class. Rather than develop a full-functioning scrollable window here, we'll develop only a generic version of this class. You'll see that many implementation details must still be resolved and are left to more specific derived classes.

Our general scrollable window class, called **Swso**, is derived from the **Wso** window class. In fact, it is simply a **Wso** window with two scroll bars attached to it—one scroll bar on its right border and the other on its bottom border. The purpose of the **Swso** class is to define how the scrollable window is to be constructed. The exact nature of what needs to be done when a key is pressed or when the scroll bars are moved is left up to a derived class.

The **Swso** class definition defined in **txscroll.h** is:

```
class Swso : public Wso {
public:
```

```
ScrollBar *HzSlide, *VtSlide;
Swso(int Fa, ColorPak &Cp);
virtual void SetSize(int W, int H);
virtual void Stretch(int W, int H);
virtual void Open(Iso *B, int X, int Y);
virtual void Redraw(void);
virtual void Prompt(void);
virtual void UnPrompt(void);
virtual void SendScrollPosn(void) { ; }
virtual void RcvScrollPosn(float, BarOrient) { ; }
virtual void Dispatch(MsgPkt &M);
};
```

As you can see from this type definition, a **Swso** object contains pointers to two nested objects of type **ScrollBar**. These pointers, **HzSlide** and **VtSlide**, correspond to the scroll bars at the bottom and right edges of the window, respectively. This implies that a **Swso** object serves as the base window for these two scroll bars. Now you may understand why the **ScrollBar** objects are designed to send messages to their bases. By doing this, they are effectively sending the messages to a scrollable window object. Table 9.2 lists each of the new or overridden member functions in **Swso**.

We'll begin with its constructor, which initializes a **Swso** object by assigning it a single character border that, in turn, uses the frame and color attributes passed to the constructor. Next, **Swso** allocates memory for the two scroll bars and initializes them. Note that the member variable **ClipToFrame** is set to **True** for both the horizontal and vertical scroll bar objects. This is done so that the base window

Table 9.2   New and overridden member functions in Swso

Member function	Description
Swso()	Initializes a Swso object
SetSize()	Sets the dimensions of the window and its scroll bars
Open()	Opens a Swso window and its nested scroll bars
Redraw()	Redraws a Swso window and its nested scroll bars
Prompt()	Displays prompt for an object
UnPrompt()	Removes prompt from an object
SendScrollPosn()	Stub for sending messages
RcvScrollPosn()	Stub for receiving messages
Dispatch()	Traps event codes used by scroll bars

will permit these scroll bars to be positioned on its border. Recall that objects normally can only be placed in the interior of a window.

The member functions **SetSize()** and **Open()** are straightforward. Basically, they are overridden so that the same calls can be made to the nested scroll bar objects. For instance, **Open()** also calls **Open()** for the horizontal and vertical scroll bars.

The **Prompt()** and **UnPrompt()** member functions are overridden for a different reason. They are used here to prevent the system from displaying a border prompt, because this could conflict with the scroll bars. We can accomplish this by skipping over the **Wso** version of these member functions, and instead call the **Iso** version, which does not draw a border prompt.

The remaining three member functions in **Swso** are used for passing messages to and from the scroll bars. These functions are **SendScrollPosn()**, **RcvScrollPosn()**, and **Dispatch()**. The first two are code stubs because the details of these member functions will be handled in the derived classes. The **Dispatch()** function, however, is not implementation specific so it is included here. Its purpose is to trap all occurrences of the **ScrollMove** event code and take an appropriate action. Recall that **Dispatch()** was invoked in **ScrollBar** to send messages to the base window—where the messages are being received. For instance, if the horizontal scroll bar sent the message, the **Swso**'s **RcvScrollPosn()** member function is called with the new position of the scroll bar. Of course, the **RcvScrollPosn()** function has not been implemented, but presumably it will cause the **Swso** window to update whatever it is displaying:

```
if (M.Code — HzScrollMove) {
  RcvScrollPosn(float(M.Mx) / 10000.0, HzOrient);
  M.RtnCode = M.Code - Idle;
}
else if (M.Code — VtScrollMove) {
  RcvScrollPosn(float(M.My) / 10000.0, VtOrient);
  M.RtnCode = M.Code - Idle;
}
else Wso::Dispatch(M);
```

A Scrollable Window Class

Now that we've developed a general scrollable window class, let's derive a specific implementation that displays a virtual buffer. This class, **Vwso**, is included in the program **vw.cpp** (its listing follows this discussion). The major responsibilities of the **Vwso** class are:

1. Maintains a virtual buffer

2. Handles keyboard input

3. Displays the virtual buffer

4. Implements the message protocol to the scroll bars

Its class definition is:

```
class Vwso : public Swso {
public:
  Trso *VirtBuff;
  int Vx, Vy;
  Vwso(int Fa, ColorPak &Cp);
  virtual ~Vwso(void);
  virtual void Draw(void);
  virtual void Open(Iso *B, int X, int Y);
  virtual void OnKeyStroke(MsgPkt &M);
  virtual void SendScrollPosn(void);
  virtual void RcvScrollPosn(float P, BarOrient Which);
};
```

The virtual buffer in **Vwso** is implemented as a **Trso** of size 100 by 100 texels. You can easily change its size by altering the call to **VirtBuff->SetSize()** in the **Vwso()** constructor. By making the virtual buffer a **Trso** object, we'll be able to easily write to it and display its contents in **Vwso**'s window.

In fact, **Draw()** is overridden so that a section of the virtual buffer's memory is copied to **Vwso**'s window. This is accomplished by the following statement in **Draw()**:

```
Tp->Xfr(0, 0, Tp->Wd, Tp->Ht, VirtBuff, Vx, Vy);
```

The variables **Vx** and **Vy** are introduced in **Vwso** to point to the location in the virtual buffer that should become the top-left character in **Vwso**'s window. These variables are modified when we press an arrow key or **Vwso** receives a message to scroll through the data it is displaying. We'll discuss each of these cases.

If a key is pressed, our window management system calls the **OnKeyStroke()** member function. We've overridden this function so that we can capture any arrow keys. If an arrow key is pressed, we'll move one line or column up or down in the virtual buffer. This is a simple matter of modifying **Vx** or **Vy**, redrawing the virtual display, and then sending a message to the appropriate scroll bar to update its location. For instance, if the left arrow key is pressed the statements

```
case LeftKey:
  if (Vx > 0) Vx-;
  Draw();
  SendScrollPosn();
break;
```

will cause the virtual buffer to scroll one character to the left.

The **SendScrollPosn()** and **RcvScrollPosn()** member functions also use the **Vx** and **Vy** variables. The **SendScrollPosn()** function uses these variables to position the scroll bars. For instance, the horizontal scroll bar's position is updated by the statements:

```
W = VirtBuff->Wd-Panel->Interior->Wd;
if (W == 0) P = 0.0; else P = float(Vx) / float(W);
HzSlide->RcvScrollPosn(P, HzOrient);
```

The **RcvScrollPosn()** function, however, calculates **Vx** and **Vy** based on the encoded scroll position, **P**. Recall that **P** is a real value between zero and one that specifies the location in the virtual buffer that we want to display. If **RcvScrollPosn()** is called from the horizontal scroll bar, its parameter **Which** will be equal to **HzOrient** and the **Vx** will be updated by the statements:

```
if (Which == HzOrient) {
  W = VirtBuff->Wd - Panel->Interior->Wd;
  Vx = ceil(P*W);
}
```

Now that we've described how the **Vwso** class operates, take a look at the program that uses it. Basically, the program draws a scrollable window. To demonstrate the scrolling features of **Vwso**, we've provided several statements in the main function that initialize the virtual buffer with several text strings and figures. Try using the scroll bars and arrow keys to scan through the buffer. The **vw** program is:

```
// vw.cpp: implements a scrollable window with a virtual buffer

#include <math.h>
#include "txscroll.h"

// A specific type of Swso scroll window: a virtual window

class Vwso : public Swso {
public:
  Trso *VirtBuff;
  int Vx, Vy;
  Vwso(int Fa, ColorPak &Cp);
  virtual ~Vwso(void);
  virtual void Draw(void);
  virtual void Open(Iso *B, int X, int Y);
  virtual void OnKeyStroke(MsgPkt &M);
  virtual void SendScrollPosn(void);
  virtual void RcvScrollPosn(float P, BarOrient Which);
};
```

```
// ——————— Vwso Member Functions ———————

Vwso::Vwso(int Fa, ColorPak &Cp)
// Initialize Vwso object and its virtual buffer
: Swso(Fa, Cp)
{
  Vx = 0;  Vy = 0;
  VirtBuff = new Trso(NULL);
  VirtBuff->SetSize(100, 100); // Hard coded as 100 x 100 characters
}

Vwso::~Vwso(void)
// Free virtual buffer
{
  delete VirtBuff;
}

void Vwso::Draw(void)
// Put a portion of the virtual buffer up on the screen
{
  Trso *Tp;

  Swso::Draw();
  Tp = (Trso *)(Panel->Interior);
  // Copy from virtual buffer at (Vx, Vy) to the interior
  Tp->Xfr(0, 0, Tp->Wd, Tp->Ht, VirtBuff, Vx, Vy);
}


char Line1[] = "01234567890123456789012345678901234567890123456789";
char Line2[] = "abcdefghijklmnopqrstuvwxyzabcdefghijklmnopqrstuvwxyz";
char Line3[] = "ABCDEFGHIJKLMNOPQRSTUVWXYZABCDEFGHIJKLMNOPQRSTUVWXYZ";
char Last[]  = "Bottom-Right of virtual buffer";

void Vwso::Open(Iso *B, int X, int Y)
// First, fill virtual buffer with some stuff, open up
{
  // Clear virtual buffer with a red graphics fill character
  VirtBuff->Fill(0, 0, VirtBuff->Wd, VirtBuff->Ht, 176, 0x04);
  // Then draw some lines
  VirtBuff->HzWrt(0, 0, Line1, 0x70);
  VirtBuff->HzWrt(0, 1, Line2, 0x70);
  VirtBuff->HzWrt(0, 2, Line3, 0x70);
  VirtBuff->HzWrt(70, 99, Last, 0x70);
  // And some boxes
  VirtBuff->Box(5, 5, 50, 5, 0x11, 0x70);
  VirtBuff->Box(70, 50, 25, 3, 0x11, 0x73);
  VirtBuff->Box(10, 30, 20, 5, 0x11, 0x74);
  // Now open up the virtual window
  Swso::Open(B, X, Y);
}
```

```
void Vwso::OnKeyStroke(MsgPkt &M)
// Keypresses are passed to the Vwso object. Handle them here. Depending
// on which arrow key is pressed, update the offsets, Vx and Vy, into
// the virtual buffer which determines what will be displayed in the
// scrollable window. Call Draw to update the window and finally
// SendScrollPosn to send a message to scroll bars indicating the
// new location in the virtual buffer.
{
  switch(M.Code) {
    case UpKey:
      if (Vy > 0) Vy-;
      Draw();
      SendScrollPosn();    // Update bar position
      break;
    case DownKey:
      if (Vy < (VirtBuff->Ht - Panel->Interior->Ht)) Vy++;
      Draw();
      SendScrollPosn();
      break;
    case LeftKey:
      if (Vx > 0) Vx-;
      Draw();
      SendScrollPosn();
      break;
    case RightKey:
      if (Vx < (VirtBuff->Wd - Panel->Interior->Wd)) Vx++;
      Draw();
      SendScrollPosn();
      break;
    default:
      Swso::OnKeyStroke(M);  // Let parent class handle it
  }
}

void Vwso::SendScrollPosn(void)
// Send messages to both scroll bars indicating current offset into
// virtual buffer
{
  float P;
  int W;

  W = VirtBuff->Wd-Panel->Interior->Wd;
  if (W == 0) P = 0.0; else P = float(Vx) / float(W);
  HzSlide->RcvScrollPosn(P, HzOrient);

  W = VirtBuff->Ht-Panel->Interior->Ht;
  if (W == 0) P = 0.0; else P = float(Vy) / float(W);
  VtSlide->RcvScrollPosn(P, VtOrient);
}

void Vwso::RcvScrollPosn(float P, BarOrient Which)
// Update the current offset into the virtual buffer, based on the
// value P. Redraw the display window with this new setting.
```

```
{
  int W;
  if (Which == HzOrient) {
    W = VirtBuff->Wd - Panel->Interior->Wd;
    Vx = ceil(P*W);
  }
  else {
    W = VirtBuff->Ht - Panel->Interior->Ht;
    Vy = ceil(P*W);
  }
  Draw();
}

Wso *W;

main()
{
  Setup(MouseOptional, DefColors);
  FullScrn->Panel->Clear(176, 0x07);
  W = new Vwso(WindowStyle+Stretchable, CyanColors);
  W->SetSize(30, 10);
  W->Open(FullScrn, 5, 5);
  MainEventLoop();
  CleanUp();
}
```

Dialog Boxes

Let's now shift gears and develop a different type of screen object—a dialog box. Actually, we'll experiment with two types of dialog boxes: a message box and a dialog box that displays a handful of options. The message box object will be useful for displaying error messages and status information in a program. We'll develop this class so that it handles the tasks required to automatically display a message. The option dialog box, however, will be fairly hard coded. Nonetheless, we're providing this example to illustrate how the tools we've been developing can be overridden to create objects unlike any you've seen thus far.

To implement both types of dialog boxes we'll create a new generic dialog box class which is designed to display the dialog box shell. We'll derive the message and option boxes from this class to develop specific implementations.

In addition, we'll create two types of interactive buttons that we'll use in the dialog boxes. One class provides buttons that are used to select an action, such as < **OK** > or <**Cancel**>. The other type will implement option items that can be toggled on and off by clicking on a set of square brackets.

These dialog box tools are provided in the source files **dialogue.h** and **dialogue.cpp**, which are shown in Listings 9.3 and 9.4, respectively.

A General Dialog Box Class

Before we can develop any specific dialog boxes we need to lay some ground-work. In particular, we need to develop a generic dialog box class that will provide us with the basic form of the dialog boxes we'll use later.

The new dialog box class, called **DlgBox**, is defined in **dialogue.h** as:

```
class DlgBox : public Wso { // A dialog box class
public:
  DlgBox(int Ba, int Fa, ColorPak &Cp) : Wso(Ba, Fa, Cp) { ; }
  virtual void SetSize(int W, int H);
  virtual void Draw(void);
};
```

As the class definition illustrates, **DlgBox** is derived from the **Wso** class. Therefore, it can take advantage of all of the features of a window. For example, it can be moveable, have shadows, and so on. Note that its class definition does little more than provide a constructor, modify how **SetSize()** works, and override **Draw()**.

The main thing to notice in the constructor is that it allocates the dialog box to be a **Wso** window that does not have a border prompt. Alternatively, we could have overridden the member functions **Prompt()** and **UnPrompt()** to prevent the border prompt from occurring.

Because the style of a dialog box is different than that of the windows we've been using so far, one of the responsibilities of **DlgBox** is to override the **Draw()** member function. Its new implementation displays a window by calling the inherited function and then adds a horizontal line two rows from the bottom of the window. This is accomplished by the statements:

```
Wso::Draw();
// Draw rule two lines from the bottom
Y = Panel->Frame->Ht - 3;
Panel->Frame->Fill(0, Y, 1, 1, 0xC3, Panel->Colors.Bc);
Panel->Frame->Fill(1, Y, Panel->Frame->Wd-2, 1,
                   0xC4, Panel->Colors.Bc);
Panel->Frame->Fill(Panel->Frame->Wd-1, Y, 1, 1,
                   0xB4, Panel->Colors.Bc);
```

We'll place command buttons, such as < **OK** >, within this lower region of the dialog box. Since this region of the window will be dedicated to these command buttons, we've also overridden **SetSize()** so that it extends the window's height by two so that this lower region is not considered part of the interior of the window.

A Message Box

A useful type of dialog box is one that displays a message. We'll now create a message box class that displays a string. Note that the message box class has an OK button that you can select to close the dialog box. Optionally, you can press on its close box near the top-left corner of its border.

The message box class, **MsgBox**, is defined in the file **dialogue.h** and has the following definition:

```
class MsgBox : public DlgBox { // A message box class
public:
  char Text[40];
  CmndButton *OKButton;
  MsgBox(char *T, int Ba, int Fa, ColorPak &Cp);
  virtual void Open(Iso *B, int X, int Y);
  virtual void Draw(void);
};
```

As its definition indicates, **MsgBox** is a special case of a **DlgBox** and contains an OK button. The **MsgBox()** constructor sets up the dialog box and **Open()** and **Draw()** are overridden to display it. For example, the following statements will display a message box with the text "MsgBox Test:"

```
MsgBox Mb("MsgBox Test", 0x11, WindowStyle, InvColors);
Mb.Open(FullScrn, 30, 30);
```

The program **msgtst.cpp**, listed next, tests the **MsgBox** object contained in **dialogue**. Its output is shown in Figure 9.6.

```
// msgtst.cpp: This program demonstrates how you can create a simple
// dialog box—like those in Turbo C++—that displays help messages

#include "dialogue.h"

void PopupMsg(char *Str, MsgPkt &M)
// Popup a dialog box
{
  MsgBox *MB;

  MB = new MsgBox(Str, 0x11, WindowStyle-BorderPrompt, InvColors);
  MB->Open(FullScrn, (80-MB->Panel->Overall->Wd) / 2,
                     (25-MB->Panel->Overall->Ht) / 2);
  MB->SwitchFocus(M);
  M.RtnCode = Idle; M.Code = Idle;
  do {
```

```
      MB->SubMgr->EventStep(M);
      M.Code - M.RtnCode;
   } while (M.Code !- ShutDown &&
            (!MB->Active || M.Code !- Close || M.Focus !- (Iso *)MB));
   if (M.Code -- Close) {
      MB->OnClose(M);
      M.RtnCode - Idle;
   }
   delete MB;
}

Wso *W;

main()
{
   Setup(MouseOptional, CyanColors);
   FullScrn->Panel->Clear(177, 0x07);
   W - new Wso(0x11, WindowStyle, CyanColors);
   W->SetSize(70,18);
   W->Open(FullScrn,2,2);
   PopupMsg("This is a test of the MsgBox type",StartMsg);
   CleanUp();
}
```

Figure 9.6   Sample output of the msgtst program

Dialog Boxes with Options

Now we'll develop a slightly different type of dialog box. The program **optexmpl.cpp** illustrates how such a dialog box can be constructed and is listed after this section. Figure 9.7 displays the dialog box that it creates.

Since most of the code in **optexmpl** is similar to code we've seen before, we won't go into the details of how the prompts are overridden, the text is displayed, and so on. Instead, let's explore the new features that **optexmpl** introduces.

The style of dialog box it creates is shown in Figure 9.7. Ideally, we'd like to have a general purpose dialog box tool from which we could create dialog boxes of various shapes, sizes, and with different contents. For space reasons we've elected to hard code many of the components of this dialog box. In fact, we haven't created a new class at all; we've simply written a function that handles the details.

The **optexmpl** program introduces a new button class—**OptButton**. These buttons represent options that can be toggled on or off by clicking on a set of square brackets. These options should be fairly easy to understand. Basically, they are derived from **Wso** objects and have overridden member functions to display a text

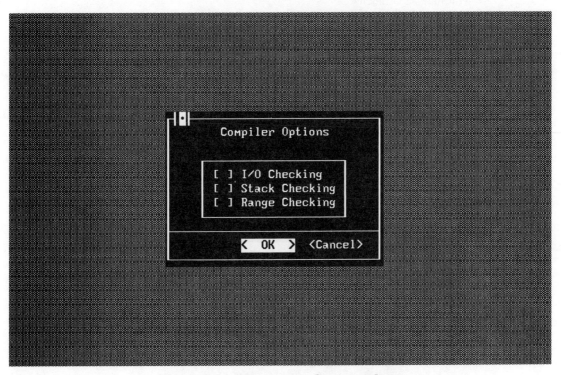

Figure 9.7   The output of optexmpl.cpp

string proceeded by the option box. In addition, we've overridden the **Activate()** member function so that it toggles the boolean status flag **SelectStat** and displays an X or a blank to indicate the current status.

The real challenge in using a dialog box such as the one shown here is integrating it with an application. Essentially we want to derive the **Activate()** function for the OK command button so that it saves the state of the various option buttons in the dialog box to the application. Of course, if the Cancel command is selected, these options should be ignored. Similarly, the initial state of the option buttons should be set according to the values in the application. Note that the example shown here doesn't do this. Since most of these details are application dependent, we haven't implemented them. If you follow the same type of communication pattern we used in the scroll bars, however, you should not have too much difficulty in getting something working.

The complete **optexmpl.cpp** program is:

```
// optexmpl.cpp: This simple program demonstrates how you can create
// a simple dialog box-like those in Turbo C++'s environment-that
// displays a list of options

#include <string.h>
#include "dialogue.h"

// Event says a list of options is being passed

const int PassedOpts - 0xfd00;

class OptButton : public Wso {
public:
  char Text[40];
  int SelectStat;
  OptButton(char *T, ColorPak &Cp);
  virtual void Draw(void);
  virtual void Activate(MsgPkt &M);
  virtual void Prompt(void);
  virtual void UnPrompt(void);
};

// ———————— Option Type ————————

OptButton::OptButton(char *T, ColorPak &Cp)
: Wso(0x00, 0x00, Cp)
{
  strcpy(Text, "[ ] ");
  strncat(Text,T,35); Text[39] - 0; // Ensure null termination
  SetSize(strlen(Text), 1);
  SelectStat - False;
}

void OptButton::Draw(void)
{
```

```
      Wso::Draw();
      Panel->HzWrtB(0, 0, Text);
}

void OptButton::Prompt(void)
{
   if (!Active) {
      Wso::Prompt();
      Panel->FillB(0, 0, 3, 1, Panel->Colors.Pc, 1);
   }
}

void OptButton::UnPrompt(void)
{
   if (Active) {
      Panel->FillB(0, 0, 3, 1, Panel->Colors.Wc, 1);
      Wso::UnPrompt();
   }
}

void OptButton::Activate(MsgPkt &)
{
   if (SelectStat) {
      Panel->HzWrtB(1, 0, " ");
      SelectStat = False;
   }
   else {
      Panel->HzWrtB(1, 0, "X");
      SelectStat = True;
   }
}

void PopupOpt(Wso *W, MsgPkt &M)
// Pop-up a dialogue box containing several options
{
   DlgBox     *DB;
   OptButton  *IoOpt;
   OptButton  *StackOpt;
   OptButton  *RangeOpt;
   CmndButton *OK;
   CmndButton *Cancel;

   DB = new DlgBox(0x11, WindowStyle-BorderPrompt, InvColors);
   DB->SetSize(30,5);
   DB->Open(W, (W->Panel->Interior->Wd-DB->Panel->Overall->Wd) / 2,
               (W->Panel->Interior->Ht-DB->Panel->Overall->Ht) / 2);
   DB->Panel->Interior->Box(4,2,22,5,0x11,DB->Panel->Colors.Wc);
   DB->Panel->Interior->HzWrtB(7,0,"Compiler Options");

   IoOpt = new OptButton("I/O Checking", InvColors);
   IoOpt->Open(DB, 6, 3);
   StackOpt = new OptButton("Stack Checking", InvColors);
   StackOpt->Open(DB, 6, 4);
   RangeOpt = new OptButton("Range Checking", InvColors);
```

```
      RangeOpt->Open(DB, 6, 5);

      OK = new CmndButton("OK", InvColors);
      Cancel = new CmndButton("Cancel", InvColors);

      OK->Open(DB,
               DB->Panel->Frame->Wd - OK->Panel->Frame->Wd -
               Cancel->Panel->Frame->Wd-6,
               DB->Panel->Frame->Ht-2);
      Cancel->Open(DB,
                   DB->Panel->Frame->Wd - Cancel->Panel->Frame->Wd-4,
                   DB->Panel->Frame->Ht-2);

      M.RtnCode = Idle; M.Code = Idle;
      OK->SwitchFocus(M);
      do {
        DB->SubMgr->EventStep(M);
        M.Code = M.RtnCode;
      } while (M.Code != ShutDown &&
               (!DB->Active || M.Code != Close || M.Focus != (Iso *)DB));
      if (M.Code == Close) {
        DB->OnClose(M);
        M.RtnCode = Idle;
      }
      delete DB;
    }

main()
{
  Setup(MouseOptional, CyanColors);
  FullScrn->Panel->Clear(177, 0x07);
  PopupOpt(FullScrn, StartMsg);
  CleanUp();
}
```

Code Critique

The different classes derived in this chapter probably could have been implemented in a dozen ways. In fact, the real advantage of OOP is that it provides us with a number of options for designing programs and tools. As you work with the interface toolkit, you may come up with extensions of your own. We'll discuss some key design issues here to help you expand the tools.

Flexible Scroll Windows

We've designed each scroll window so that it always has two scroll bars. You might want to modify the scroll window class so that a scroll window object can accept a parameter which directs it to use only one scroll bar. Such a configuration might be useful for a vertical scrollable menu with only the vertical scroll bar appearing.

Scrollable Window Objects

The scrollable window object example presented provides a virtual buffer that we filled with some test data. You might want to incorporate some of the features from the file browser program presented in Chapter 2 to create a useful scrollable browser.

Grouping Objects

Our scrollable windows were created by grouping different types of screen objects— including window, scroll bar, and slider objects. As an alternative, we could take the brute-force approach and merge the window, scroll bar, and sliders into one object. The scroll bars and sliders could be drawn directly on a window using routines such as **HzWrt()** and **Fill()**. Then, we could write custom border routines to manage the scroll bar. (Recall that we used a similar technique to implement close buttons.)

Therefore, is it better to hard code the scroll bars and sliders or use separate objects to represent them? The first technique is more direct, and probably more efficient. However, it's more natural to think of the scroll bars, sliders, and the underlying windows as separate entities that communicate with each other. Another related design issue to keep in mind: We could easily hard code the scroll bars and sliders in text mode; however, graphics mode presents a problem due to the complex drawing features required. Therefore, to make a generic scrolling window system— one that works in both text and graphics mode or at least shares code used to implement windows in the two modes—it would be easier if we used OOP techniques.

Communicating between Objects

Because we formed scroll windows from a group of objects, we encounter two design issues: How do we link the objects together, and what form of communication do we use?

In our scrollable window, we linked the sliders, scroll bars, and windows together by either passing messages or calling an object's member function directly. For example, in the scroll bar class we accessed the slider as a data member **Slide**, because it was part of the **ScrollBar** object. To access the underlying window, however, we used the **Base** pointer. In the latter case, we were taking advantage of the fact that we knew that the scroll window we wished to communicate with just happened to be our base window.

The technique used in linking up the objects affected the form of communication we used. For instance, when we wanted the scroll bar to send a message to instruct the slider to move, we called the **Slider::Move()** member function. However, when we sent the slider's position to the scroll window, we used the message dispatcher.

Recall that **ScrollBar** uses the **Base** pointer to find the underlying scroll window. If we had tried to call the **RcvScrollPosn()** function of **Base** we would have received a compiler error, because **Base** is an **Iso**, and **Iso**s don't have a **RcvScrollPosn()** member function. Although *we* know that **Base** is a pointer to an object of type **Swso**, the *compiler* doesn't.

We could use a typecast to get around the problem but instead we chose to use the message dispatcher. You'll note that this typecasting problem is the same one we encountered with our generic lists and menus.

Listing 9.1   txscroll.h

```
// txscroll.h: implements scrollable windows in text mode

#ifndef H_TXSCROLL
#define H_TXSCROLL

#include "wsotxscr.h"

// Scroll bar event code
const int HzScrollMove = 0xfe00;
const int VtScrollMove = 0xfe01;

enum BarOrient { HzOrient, VtOrient };

// The slider frame type sets up a "frame" that's simply
// a character bar with two arrows at the end. The bar
// can be either horizontal or vertical.

class ScrollFrame : public Tfso {
public:
  BarOrient Orientation;
  ScrollFrame(BarOrient Orient, ColorPak &Cp);
  virtual void SetSize(int W, int H);
  virtual void SetLocn(int X1, int Y1);
  virtual void DrawFrame(char Ba, char Attr);
};

// The Slider Button Type

class Slider : public Wso {
public:
```

```
    Slider(ColorPak &Cp) : Wso(0x00, Swappable, Cp) { ; }
    virtual void Draw(void);
    virtual void OnMouseDown(MsgPkt &M);
    virtual void Move(int X, int Y);
    virtual void OnKeyStroke(MsgPkt &M);
};

// The slider bar type. We inherit from Iso and set the panel
//  of the Iso to be a slider frame.

class ScrollBar : public Iso {
public:
  Slider *Slide;
  int DelayCntr, DelayLimit;
  int InhibitMessage;
  ScrollBar(BarOrient Orient, ColorPak &Cp);
  virtual void Draw(void);
  virtual void Redraw(void);
  virtual void Open(Iso *B, int X, int Y);
  virtual void BorderHandler(MsgPkt &M);
  virtual void OnMouseDown(MsgPkt &M);
  virtual void OnMouseStillDown(MsgPkt &M);
  virtual void SendScrollPosn(void);
  virtual void RcvScrollPosn(float P, BarOrient Which);
  virtual void OnKeyStroke(MsgPkt &M);
};

// A Generic Scroll Window Screen Object Type

class Swso : public Wso {
public:
  ScrollBar *HzSlide, *VtSlide;
  Swso(int Fa, ColorPak &Cp);
  virtual void SetSize(int W, int H);
  virtual void Stretch(int W, int H);
  virtual void Open(Iso *B, int X, int Y);
  virtual void Redraw(void);
  virtual void Prompt(void);
  virtual void UnPrompt(void);
  virtual void SendScrollPosn(void) { ; }
  virtual void RcvScrollPosn(float, BarOrient) { ; }
  virtual void Dispatch(MsgPkt &M);
};

#endif
```

Listing 9.2 txscroll.cpp

```
// txscroll.cpp: scrollable window class member functions

#include <math.h>
#include "txscroll.h"
```

```
// ———— ScrollFrame Member Functions ————

ScrollFrame::ScrollFrame(BarOrient Orient, ColorPak &Cp)
// Initializes a scroll bar's frame object.
: Tfso(0x00, 0x00, Cp)
{
  Orientation = Orient;
}

void ScrollFrame::SetSize(int W, int H)
// The size (W,H) is interpreted to be the interior size. The
// other sizes are based off of it. Depending on the orientation,
// one of the sizes is ignored.
{
  if (Orientation == HzOrient) {
    Interior->SetSize(W, 1);  // Height ignored
    Frame->SetSize(W+2, 1);
    Overall->SetSize(W+2, 1);
  }
  else {
    Interior->SetSize(1, H);   // Width ignored
    Frame->SetSize(1, H+2);
    Overall->SetSize(1, H+2);
  }
}

void ScrollFrame::SetLocn(int X1, int Y1)
// Set the upper left-hand corner location of the frame.
// The location is interpreted to be that of the frame
// rectangle.
{
  Frame->SetLocn(X1, Y1);
  Overall->SetLocn(Frame->Xul, Frame->Yul);
  if (Orientation == HzOrient)
    Interior->SetLocn(Frame->Xul+1, Frame->Yul);
    else Interior->SetLocn(Frame->Xul, Frame->Yul+1);
}

void ScrollFrame::DrawFrame(char, char)
// The frame is just two arrows
{
  if (Orientation == HzOrient) {
    Frame->HzWrt(0, 0, "\x1b", 0x70);              // Left arrow
    Frame->HzWrt(Frame->Wd-1, 0, "\x1a", 0x70); // Right arrow
  }
  else {
    Frame->HzWrt(0, 0, "\x18", 0x70);              // Up arrow
    Frame->HzWrt(0, Frame->Ht-1, "\x19", 0x70); // Down arrow
  }
}

// ———— Slider Member Functions ————

void Slider::Draw(void)
```

```
// Draws a single character for the slider button
{
  Panel->Interior->HzWrtB(0, 0, "\xb1");
}

void Slider::OnMouseDown(MsgPkt &M)
// Call BorderHandler to move slider object whenever mouse is
// pressed while on the slider
{
  SwitchFocus(M);
  BorderHandler(M);
}

void Slider::Move(int X, int Y)
// Move to new absolute coordinates. Send a message to the
// scroll bar indicating its new position.
{
  Wso::Move(X, Y);
  ((ScrollBar *)Base)->SendScrollPosn();
}

void Slider::OnKeyStroke(MsgPkt &M)
// Send keystrokes detected while Slider is active to the scroll bar
{
  Base->OnKeyStroke(M);
}


// ———— ScrollBar Member Functions ————

ScrollBar::ScrollBar(BarOrient Orient, ColorPak &Cp)
// Initialize ScrollBar to use a ScrollFrame frame. Allocate
// Slider object.
: Iso(new ScrollFrame(Orient, Cp))
{
  Slide = new Slider(Cp);
  Slide->SetSize(1, 1); // Always one texel big
  DelayCntr = 0;  DelayLimit = 50; // Default delay
  InhibitMessage = False;
}

void ScrollBar::Draw()
// Draw the patterned interior of the scroll bar
{
  Iso::Draw();
  Panel->Clear(176, 0); // A patterned interior
}

void ScrollBar::Redraw()
// Call default redraw action, then redraw the slider
{
  Iso::Redraw();
  Slide->Redraw();
}
```

```
void ScrollBar::Open(Iso *B, int X, int Y)
// Open the scrollbar, and then open the slider on top of it
{
  Iso::Open(B, X, Y);
  Slide->Open(this, 0, 0);
}


void ScrollBar::BorderHandler(MsgPkt &M)
// Mouse is on one of the arrows. Send a simulated keypress to the
// scroll bar's base corresponding to which arrow is selected.
{
  ScrollFrame *Sf = (ScrollFrame *)Panel;
  MsgPkt FakeMsg = NullMsg;

  FakeMsg.Focus = Base;
  if (Sf->Orientation == HzOrient) {
    if (M.Mx == Sf->Frame->Xul) { // Mouse on left arrow
      FakeMsg.Code = LeftKey;     // Act like key was pressed
      Base->Dispatch(FakeMsg);
    }
    else if (M.Mx == Sf->Frame->Xlr) { // On right arrow
      FakeMsg.Code = RightKey;
      Base->Dispatch(FakeMsg);
    }
  }
  else {
    if (M.My == Sf->Frame->Yul) {       // On up arrow
      FakeMsg.Code = UpKey;
      Base->Dispatch(FakeMsg);
    }
    else if (M.My == Sf->Frame->Ylr) { // On Down arrow
      FakeMsg.Code = DownKey;
      Base->Dispatch(FakeMsg);
    }
  }
}


void ScrollBar::OnMouseDown(MsgPkt &M)
// Mouse is pressed when it is within the scroll bar.
// Move the slider to that location.
{
  if (Panel->OnInterior(M.Mx, M.My))  {
    Slide->Move(M.Mx, M.My);
    // Need to do this so you can leave the mouse button down
    // and still move.
    Slide->OnMouseDown(M);
  }
  else if (Panel->OnBorder(M.Mx, M.My)) BorderHandler(M);
  DelayCntr = 0;  // Start count over
}


void ScrollBar::OnMouseStillDown(MsgPkt &M)
// Mouse is still pressed on one of the scroll bar arrows.
// If the DelayCntr has reached DelayLimit, then update
```

```
    // the slider position.
    {
      DelayCntr++;
      if (DelayCntr > DelayLimit) {
         if (Panel->OnBorder(M.Mx, M.My)) {
            BorderHandler(M);
         }
         DelayCntr = 0;
      }
    }

void ScrollBar::OnKeyStroke(MsgPkt &M)
// Send keystrokes to base window.
{
      Base->OnKeyStroke(M);
}

void ScrollBar::SendScrollPosn(void)
// Send a message to the base window of the scroll bar indicating its
// position. The location of the slider in the scroll bar is encoded
// to be a number between 0 and 10000 where a value of 10000
// indicates that the slider is at full scale.
{
      int Ip;
      float Rp;
      MsgPkt M;
      Rso *Pint = Panel->Interior;

      if (InhibitMessage) return;
      M.Focus = Base;

      if (((ScrollFrame *)Panel)->Orientation == HzOrient) {
         // Compute relative position of slider to sliderbar
         Ip = Slide->Panel->Frame->Xul - Pint->Xul;
         if (Pint->Wd == 1)
            Rp = 0.0;
            else Rp = float(Ip) / float(Panel->Interior->Wd-1);
         M.Code = HzScrollMove; // M.RtnCode = Idle assumed
         M.Mx = floor(Rp * 10000.0); M.My = 0;
      }
      else {  // Object is a vertical scroll bar
        Ip = Slide->Panel->Frame->Yul - Pint->Yul;
        if (Pint->Ht == 1)
           Rp = 0.0;
           else Rp = float(Ip) / float(Panel->Interior->Ht-1);
        M.Code = VtScrollMove; // M.RtnCode = Idle assumed
        M.Mx = 0; M.My = floor(Rp * 10000.0);
      }
      Base->Dispatch(M);
}


void ScrollBar::RcvScrollPosn(float P, BarOrient Which)
// This function takes the number P, between 0.0 and 1.0, and
```

```
// causes the Slider to move to the appropriate position.
{
  int NewPos;

  if (Which == HzOrient) {
    // Compute relative position to move slider within slidebar
    NewPos = ceil(P * ((float)Panel->Interior->Wd-1));
    InhibitMessage = True;
    // Prevent Move from sending message back
    Slide->Move(Panel->Interior->Xul+NewPos,Panel->Interior->Yul);
    InhibitMessage = False;
  }
  else {
    // Compute relative position to move slider within slidebar
    NewPos = ceil(P * (float)(Panel->Interior->Ht-1));
    InhibitMessage = True;
    Slide->Move(Panel->Interior->Xul,NewPos+Panel->Interior->Yul);
    InhibitMessage = False;
  }
}


// ———————— Generic Scroll Window Functions ————————

Swso::Swso(int Fa, ColorPak &Cp)
// Initialize Swso object by setting its border and allocating
// the nested scroll bar objects.
: Wso(0x11, Fa, Cp)
{
  HzSlide = new ScrollBar(HzOrient, Cp);
  // Set True so it can draw slider bars on border of window
  HzSlide->ClipToFrame = True;
  VtSlide = new ScrollBar(VtOrient, Cp);
  VtSlide->ClipToFrame = True;
}

void Swso::SetSize(int W, int H)
// Set the size of the Swso object and the nested scroll bars.
// Note: We have to relocate the scroll bars too. SetLocn has
// no way of knowing they need to be relocated if the window
// is resized.
{
  Wso::SetSize(W, H);
  HzSlide->SetSize(W-2, 1);
  HzSlide->SetLocn(1, Panel->Frame->Ht-1, Relc);
  VtSlide->SetSize(1, H-2);
  VtSlide->SetLocn(Panel->Frame->Wd-1, 1, Relc);
}

void Swso::Stretch(int W, int H)
// Stretch a scroll window. We must fake out the stretch
// algorithm by setting the scroll bars to a minimum size
// temporarily, otherwise, we can't make the window smaller.
```

```
{
  HzSlide->SetSize(1,1);
  VtSlide->SetSize(1,1);
  Wso::Stretch(W,H);
}

void Swso::Open(Iso *B, int X, int Y)
// Open Swso object and the two nested scroll bars
{
  Wso::Open(B, X, Y);
  HzSlide->Open(this, 1, Panel->Frame->Ht-1);
  VtSlide->Open(this, Panel->Frame->Wd-1, 1);
}

void Swso::Redraw(void)
// Redraw the window plus scroll bars
{
  Wso::Redraw();
  HzSlide->Redraw();
  VtSlide->Redraw();
}

void Swso::Prompt(void)
// We don't want to prompt Swso object because this would
// overwrite the scroll bars, so we'll skip back two levels
// in the hierarchy and call Iso's prompter
{
  Iso::Prompt();
}

void Swso::UnPrompt(void)
// We don't want to call Wso's prompter, since it would
// overwrite the scroll bars, so we'll skip back two
// levels in the hierarchy and call Iso's prompter
{
  Iso::UnPrompt();
}

void Swso::Dispatch(MsgPkt &M)
// Trap for ScrollMove event codes passed to the Swso object. These
// events cause the scroll window to update what it displays.
{
  if (M.Code == HzScrollMove) {
    RcvScrollPosn(float(M.Mx) / 10000.0, HzOrient);
    M.RtnCode = M.Code = Idle;
  }
  else if (M.Code == VtScrollMove) {
    RcvScrollPosn(float(M.My) / 10000.0, VtOrient);
    M.RtnCode = M.Code = Idle;
  }
  else Wso::Dispatch(M);
}
```

Listing 9.3   dialogue.h

```cpp
// Dialogue box class definitions: dialogue.h

#ifndef H_DIALOGUE
#define H_DIALOGUE

#include "wsotxscr.h"

class CmndButton : public Wso { // A command button for dialog boxes
public:
  char Text[7];
  int SelectStat;
  CmndButton(char *T, ColorPak &Cp);
  virtual void Draw(void);
  virtual void Activate(MsgPkt &M);
  virtual void Prompt(void);
  virtual void UnPrompt(void);
};

class DlgBox : public Wso { // A dialog box class
public:
  DlgBox(int Ba, int Fa, ColorPak &Cp) : Wso(Ba, Fa, Cp) { ; }
  virtual void SetSize(int W, int H);
  virtual void Draw(void);
};

class MsgBox : public DlgBox { // A message box class
public:
  char Text[40];
  CmndButton *OKButton;
  MsgBox(char *T, int Ba, int Fa, ColorPak &Cp);
  virtual void Open(Iso *B, int X, int Y);
  virtual void Draw(void);
};

#endif
```

Listing 9.4   dialogue.cpp

```cpp
// dialogue.cpp: Dialog box member functions

#include <string.h>
#include "dialogue.h"

// ———— CmndButton Member Functions ————

CmndButton::CmndButton(char *T, ColorPak &Cp)
: Wso(0x00, 0x00, Cp)
{
  strncpy(Text, T, 6);
```

```
  Text[6] = 0;  // Ensure null termination
  SetSize(8,1); // Command buttons are always 8 characters long
  SelectStat = False;
}

void CmndButton::Draw(void)
{
  Wso::Draw();
  Panel->HzWrtB(0, 0, "<      >");
  Panel->HzWrtB((7-strlen(Text)) / 2 + 1, 0, Text);
}

void CmndButton::Prompt(void)
{
  Wso::Prompt();
  Panel->FillB(0,0,Panel->Interior->Wd,1,Panel->Colors.Pc,1);
}

void CmndButton::UnPrompt(void)
{
  if (Active) {
    Panel->FillB(0,0,Panel->Interior->Wd,1,Panel->Colors.Wc,1);
    Wso::UnPrompt();
  }
}

void CmndButton::Activate(MsgPkt &M)
{
  Base->SwitchFocus(M);
  M.RtnCode = Close; // Effectively tells base to close
}

// ————— DlgBox Member Functions —————

void DlgBox::SetSize(int W, int H)
{
  Wso::SetSize(W, H+2);
}

void DlgBox::Draw(void)
{
  int Y;

  Mouse.Hide();
  Wso::Draw();
  // Draw rule two lines from the bottom
  Y = Panel->Frame->Ht - 3;
  Panel->Frame->Fill(0, Y, 1, 1, 0xC3, Panel->Colors.Bc);
  Panel->Frame->Fill(1, Y, Panel->Frame->Wd-2, 1,
                     0xC4, Panel->Colors.Bc);
  Panel->Frame->Fill(Panel->Frame->Wd-1, Y, 1, 1,
                     0xB4, Panel->Colors.Bc);
  Mouse.Show();
}
```

```
// ————— MsgBox Member Functions —————

MsgBox::MsgBox(char *T, int Ba, int Fa, ColorPak &Cp)
: DlgBox(Ba, Fa, Cp)
{
  strncpy(Text, T, 39); Text[39] = 0; // Ensure null termination
  SetSize(Panel->TextWidth(T)+2, Panel->TextHeight(3));
  OKButton = new CmndButton("OK", Cp);
}

void MsgBox::Open(Iso *B, int X, int Y)
{
  DlgBox::Open(B, X, Y);
  OKButton->Open(this,
                 Panel->Frame->Wd - OKButton->Panel->Frame->Wd-4,
                 Panel->Frame->Ht-2);
}

void MsgBox::Draw(void)
{
  DlgBox::Draw();
  // Write message to dialog box
  Panel->HzWrt(1, 1, Text, 0);
}
```

10

Graphics Screen Objects

Have you ever developed a program that runs in text mode, only to decide later that you'd like it to run in graphics mode? If you're like most programmers who have encountered this situation, you're well aware of the extensive amount of recoding often required to produce a graphics version of a program.

In this chapter we'll explore how inheritance can be used in a well-designed object-oriented program to partially avoid this pitfall. In particular, we'll derive several classes from the window tools developed in Chapters 6 through 8 so that they can be used in graphics mode. In fact, by the time we're done, we'll have a full-fledged pull-down graphics menu system that functions much like the text mode menu system discussed in Chapter 8.

From Text to Graphics

In earlier chapters we built a powerful windowing system that runs in text mode. Unfortunately, the tools, as they now stand, won't work in graphics mode. If we had written the tools without using OOP techniques we would probably have to change a lot of the code in order for the system to support graphics.

When we created the interface tools in the previous chapters, we anticipated the need to eventually extend the code to work in graphics mode. Therefore, some design decisions were made along the way to ease the transition. For example, the menu package from Chapter 8 is written at a high enough level so that it won't have to be modified at all. It exploits polymorphism to create a transparent screen interface. We will, however, need to derive several lower-level graphics tools from our text screen toolkit. Figure 10.1 shows, with shaded regions, the new classes we'll be creating in this chapter. Table 10.1 lists each of the new classes, along with a brief description.

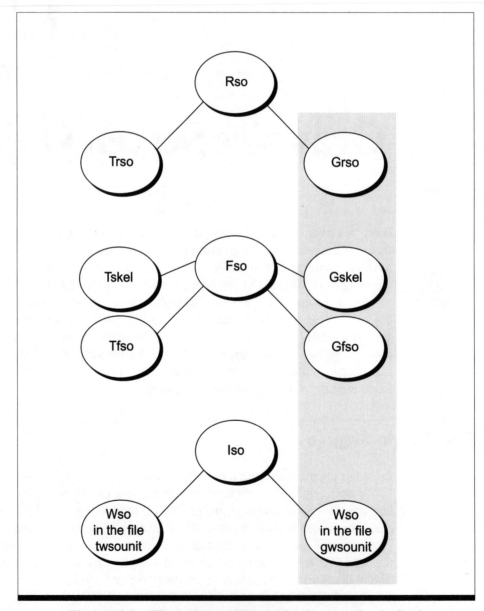

Figure 10.1   The new graphics mode classes to be derived

Table 10.1 Derived classes that support graphics objects

Class	Description
Grso	Low-level graphics support for rectangular screen objects
Gfso	Graphics support for framed screen objects
Gskel	Skeleton object used when moving objects
Wso	Interactive graphics window objects

As Figure 10.1 indicates, the new classes we'll develop are derived from the generic screen interface classes created earlier. We could have derived the classes directly from the text mode tools we built earlier, but we would have needed to override most of the member functions. By using the generic classes, such as **Rso**, **Fso**, and **Iso**, we are able to share the code that is common to both text and graphics screen objects.

An Overview of the Graphics Classes

The graphics screen objects we'll present are not carbon copies of our text screen objects. They'll support several new window styles as shown in Figure 10.2. Note that four styles of graphics windows are provided: windows with borders, windows without borders, windows with close buttons and headers, and three-deminsional-like windows. We'll also be relying more on the mouse, although the

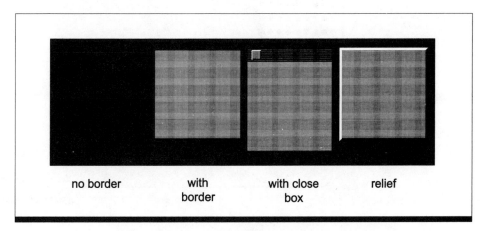

Figure 10.2 New graphics window styles

code presented also inherits the keyboard processing routines provided with the underlying classes.

Working with Graphics

Before we start building graphics screen objects, we'll review how a graphics program manipulates the screen. First, the screen is viewed as a two-dimensional array of small dots called pixels. The top-left coordinate is (0,0) and the bottom-right coordinate is the maximum row and column of the screen, which is dependent on the graphics adapter and mode being used. Figure 10.3 shows how the graphics screen is represented with pixels.

At the lowest level, every screen operation we perform is done at the pixel level. For instance, we can set the color of a pixel, draw a series of pixels to create a rectangle, write text as a sequence of pixels, and so on.

One difficulty with graphics programming is that there are several graphics boards on the market—each with its own resolution, color range, addressing scheme, and so on. To make it easier for you to write programs that will work with these different graphics boards, Turbo C++ provides the Borland Graphics Interface (BGI) library that supplies a comprehensive set of low-level graphics primitives.

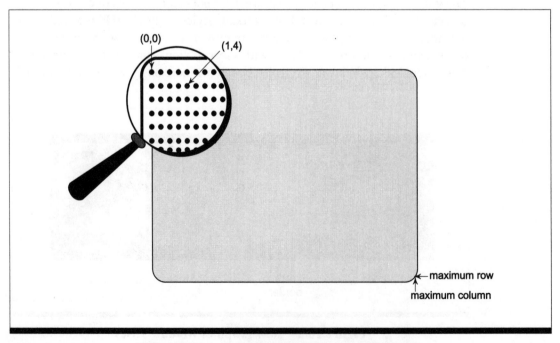

Figure 10.3   Accessing pixels in graphics mode

Even with the BGI, it is still a challenge to write graphics programs that work equally well in all the different graphics modes. Therefore, we'll concentrate primarily on the EGA and VGA standards. Note, however, that the tools developed here may work with other graphics standards, although modifications may be necessary.

Rectangles in Graphics

Like our text mode screen objects, the core of the graphics objects will be constructed from a set of rectangular objects. In text mode the **Trso** class was used, which was derived from **Rso**, to support rectangles. In this section, we'll build a comparable class to support rectangles in graphics mode. It will be derived from the **Rso** class which is defined in the file **rsounit.h** (see Chapter 5). We'll be taking advantage of the BGI to simplify this low-level class.

The **Grso** class, contained in **grsounit.h** and **grsounit.cpp** (see Listings 10.1 and 10.2, respectively), is defined as:

```
class Grso : public Rso {
public:
 int TxtHt;
 Grso(void);
 virtual void HzWrt(int X, int Y, char *Str, char Attr);
 virtual void HzWrtB(int X, int Y, char *Str);
 virtual void Fill(int X, int Y, int W, int H, char Ch, char Attr);
 virtual void FillB(int X, int Y, int W, int H, char Ch, char Opt);
 virtual void Box(int X, int Y, int W, int H, char Ba, char Attr);
 virtual int  TextWidth(char *Str);
 virtual int  TextHeight(int N);
};
```

We'll now discuss the individual components of **Grso**.

Initializing Grso Objects

The **Grso** constructor initializes a **Grso** object by performing two tasks. First, it inherits the base constructor from the **Rso** class and calls it with the statement

```
: Rso(0, 0, 0, 0)
```

which sets the dimensions of the rectangular object to a known state—in this case, all zeros.

Second, the vertical size of the current font is saved in the data member **TxtHt** so that the **Grso** object will be able to size windows with respect to the current font style in use. The text height is retrieved by a call to the BGI function **textheight()**. You might be wondering about the strange arithmetic used to compute **TxtHt**:

```
TxtHt = ::textheight("H") * 4 / 3;
```

We take the height in pixels returned by **textheight()** and increase it by one third. The BGI function **textheight()** doesn't compensate for characters such as the letter **g** that have tails extending below the text line, so we must do the compensation ourselves. Note that we passed in the letter **H** to **textheight()**. It doesn't matter what character you pass in. The same height is returned for all characters of a particular font style.

Why does **Grso**'s constructor save the text height? It's done for the sake of efficiency. Rather than continually calling BGI's **textheight()** function throughout the code, the call is made once in the constructor and the height is saved for later use. This means, however, that the font style can't be changed after an object has been created. This limitation could be removed by saving the font style with each object and switching to the appropriate font whenever a window is accessed.

Working with Pixels

The **Grso** class, like its **Trso** text mode companion, contains routines to write horizontal strings of characters, fill regions, and draw boxes. Each of these member functions is overridden from **Rso** so that they can support the intricacies of graphics mode. A major difference between these member functions and their **Trso** counterparts is that they are all based on pixel coordinates rather than character coordinates. This will also be true for our other graphics tools.

Because our graphics objects use pixel coordinates, **Grso** overrides the member functions **TextWidth()** and **TextHeight()**, and adds the new data member **TxtHt**. With these, the pixel dimensions of text strings written to the screen can be determined.

In text mode, a character always has the same size. In graphics mode, however, text can be scaled to various sizes. Since we knew that we'd be supporting graphics objects when we created the text screen objects, we added **TextWidth()** and **TextHeight()** even though they weren't really needed at the time.

The **TextWidth()** member function determines the pixel length of a string by calling the BGI function of the same name. The **TextHeight()** function performs a different calculation. It returns the pixel height for **N** rows of text where **N** is a parameter to **TextHeight()**. That is, **TextHeight()** returns a value calculated by multiplying **N** by the text height of a typical character. This latter value is stored in the data member **TxtHt**, which is computed once in **Init** as we explained earlier.

We didn't use a variable similar to **TxtHt** for the text width because stroked font characters of a particular scale can vary greatly in width. Using an average size isn't precise enough in this case.

Working with Window Styles

Now take a look at the parameters we'll use to control the styles of the graphics objects. As in text mode, three parameters define the style of a window. They are the border, frame, and color attributes specified with the parameters **Ba**, **Fa**, and **Cp**, respectively.

The border and frame attributes are interpreted slightly differently in graphics mode than in text mode. For example, windows with shadows are not supported in graphics mode. In addition, a few new window styles are provided as was seen in Figure 10.2. The border and frame styles that are supported in graphics mode are defined in the file **scrnsty.h** assembled in Chapter 3. Table 10.2 lists the border styles supported and Table 10.3 lists the graphics mode frame styles.

Table 10.2   Graphics mode border styles

Constant	Value	Description
NoBorder	0x00	Window without a border
Solid	0x10	Window with a solid border one or more pixels thick
Recessed	0x20	Three-dimensional window that appears as if it is recessed
Relief	0x30	Three-dimensional window that appears to be sticking out of the screen

Table 10.3   Frame styles supported in graphics objects

Constant	Value	Description
Swappable	0x01	Object can be moved on the screen
Closeable	0x02	Object has a close button
OutlineMove	0x40	Object is moved using its outline
BorderPrompt	0x80	Border changes if the object is selected

Note that **ColorPak** used with text screen objects is used to define the color attributes for graphics objects. The graphics tools were carefully written so that the colors would work as they do in text mode. Colors operate differently in graphics mode because the background and foreground colors are not set at the same time, yet each color attribute has both components packed into a single byte. As a result, we must unpack the colors for graphics mode. That's why the functions **ForeGround()** and **BackGround()**, which are included in **scrnsty.h**, are needed.

Writing Strings

The **Grso** class is designed to provide an interface for writing to the screen. In Chapters 3 and 5 the **HzWrt()** and **HzWrtB()** member functions were introduced to write to a text mode screen. Now it is necessary to derive comparable functions to support graphics mode.

Deriving **HzWrt()** is straightforward. First, the clip coordinates are saved and then set to the bounds of a rectangle by calling the BGI routine **setviewport()**. Then, we clear the region where the text is to be written by a call to **FillB()** using the background color specified by the parameter **Attr**. Next, the drawing color is set to the foreground color of **Attr**, and the text is displayed by calling the BGI function **outtextxy()**. The statements that perform this task are:

```
setcolor(ForeGround(Attr));
outtextxy(X, Y, Str);
```

The clip coordinates are then set to their original value.

The **HzWrtB()** member function works a little differently. Recall that it was used in text mode to write strings using the current foreground color specified in each texel. That is, the color is not changed. Because we are now using pixels instead of texels, we must apply a different technique. Therefore, **HzWrtB()** is designed to use the current drawing color when writing its text. This difference between text and graphics mode may cause problems in some applications that are written to work in both text and graphics.

Fill Operations

Another important part of supporting rectangular screen objects is the fill operation. Recall that the **Rso** class provides the two member functions **Fill()** and **FillB()** to fill the interior of a region. Unfortunately, both of these functions are somewhat biased toward text mode.

For instance, **Fill()** fills a region with a particular character **Ch** and attribute, and **FillB()** fills the region with either a character or attribute, but not both. It's difficult to implement all the options supported by these routines in graphics mode, so instead, both **Fill()** and **FillB()** draw a solid bar with the specified attribute. In fact, we've implemented **FillB()** so that it simply calls **Fill()**.

Since we're forced to use the same parameters in the text and graphics versions of the **Fill()** and **FillB()** member functions (recall that they are virtual functions originating from the **Rso** class), both the **Ch** parameter of **Fill** and the **Opt** parameter of **FillB** are ignored.

Drawing a Rectangle

The **Box()** member function is used to draw the borders of windows, buttons, and menus. Once again our implementation of **Box()** is different from its text mode counterpart. The **Box()** function supports the four border styles provided in graphics mode. The choice of which border is drawn is specified by the border attribute parameter **Ba** which is a byte value that contains a border style in its upper four bits and a border width specified in its lower four bits. The possible settings are listed in Table 10.3. The color used to draw the border is specified by the parameter **Attr**. The foreground-background color setting has the same encoding as used in text mode.

The first task for **Box()** is to determine which border style to use and how wide to make it. This is accomplished by unpacking the border attribute variable **Ba** by the statements:

```
Bw = Ba & 0x000f;        // Unpack border width
Bs = (Ba >> 4) & 0x000f; // and the border style
```

A border is drawn only if **Bs** is not zero. For example, if the border style is a one, then a set of rectangles that fit within one another are drawn on the screen using the foreground color of **Attr**. This is performed by the **for** loop which draws a number of rectangles equal to the border width:

```
for (I = 0; i < Bw; I++) {
  setcolor(ForeGround(Attr));
  rectangle(Xul+X, Yul+Y, Xul+X+W-1, Yul+Y+H-1);
  X++; Y++; W -= 2; H -= 2;
}
```

Otherwise, the border style should have a value of two or three. In these cases a three-dimensional border is used like the one shown in Figure 10.4. By using

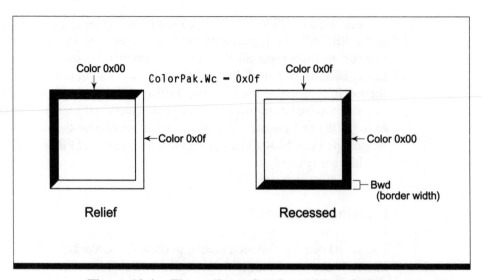

Figure 10.4   Three-dimensional graphics windows

shades of light and dark on the borders of the window, it is possible to produce the illusion that the screen object is three dimensional. In fact, by reversing the lighting colors used it is possible to make one screen object look recessed while the other is in relief. This is achieved by swapping the colors in **Attr** by the operations:

```
B - ForeGround(Attr);
Attr - BackGround(Attr) + (B << 4);
```

The borders of a three-dimensional screen object are drawn using a series of lines much like the rectangles used earlier. The **for** loop that performs this task is:

```
Xs - X+Xul; Xf - Xs + W - 1;
Ys - Y+Yul; Yf - Ys + H - 1;
for (I - 0; I < Bw; I++) {
  setcolor(BackGround(Attr));
  moveto(Xs+I, Yf-I);
  lineto(Xs+I, Ys+I);
  lineto(Xf-I, Ys+I);
  setcolor(ForeGround(Attr));
  moveto(Xf-I, Ys+I+1);
  lineto(Xf-I, Yf-I);
  lineto(Xs+I+1, Yf-I);
}
```

As mentioned earlier, the new three-dimensional window styles are set using the **Relief** and **Recessed** frame attribute constants defined in the unit **scrnsty.h**.

The Gfso Class

The next two classes we need to develop are used to draw and move rectangular graphics objects. These classes, **Gfso** and **Gskel**, are both derived from the **Fso** (Frame Screen Object) class that we wrote in Chapter 6. They are both included in the files **gfsounit.h** and **gfsounit.cpp** (see Listings 10.3 and 10.4, respectively). We'll start with **Gfso**. As Figure 10.1 indicates, **Gfso** is comparable to the **Tfso** class described in Chapter 6 and contains the member functions listed in Table 10.4. The **Gfso** class creates the first true semblance of graphics-based windows. Now they have borders, interiors, mouse interaction, and more.

The complete definition for **Gfso** is:

```
class Gfso : public Fso { // A graphics frame screen object
public:
  char *SaveBuff, *SwapBuff;
  unsigned SaveSize;
  Grso *CloseBox;
  int HeaderHt;
  Gfso(int Ba, int Fa, ColorPak &Cp);
```

Table 10.4   The member functions in Gfso

Member function	Description
Gfso()	Initializes a Gfso object
~Gfso()	Frees nested rectangle objects contained in a Gfso object
SetSize()	Sets the dimensions of the object and allocates space for its swap buffers
SetLocn()	Specifies the location of the object
DrawFrame()	Draws the object's border
OnCloseButton()	Executes when the close button is selected
Clear()	Erases the interior of the object
GetImage()	Moves an image of the screen to the save buffer
PutImage()	Moves an image from the save buffer to the screen
Swap()	Swaps between the save buffer and the screen
TextWidth()	Gets the pixel width of a string
TextHeight()	Gets the pixel height of some number of text rows

```
    virtual ~Gfso(void);
    virtual void SetSize(int W, int H);
    virtual void SetLocn(int X1, int Y1);
    virtual void DrawFrame(char Ba, char Attr);
    virtual void Clear(char Ch, char Attr);
    virtual void GetImage(Rect *C);
    virtual void PutImage(Rect *C);
    virtual void Swap(Rect *C, XfrDirn Xd);
    virtual int  OnCloseButton(int X, int Y);
    virtual int  TextWidth(char *Str);
    virtual int  Textheight()(int N);
};
```

Initializing a Gfso Object

The purpose of **Gfso** is to provide a graphics-based version of the general class **Fso**. This is accomplished in its constructor by assigning the three rectangles of a **Gfso** object to be of type **Grso**.

Another part of the constructor initializes the save buffers that we will describe later in this chapter. These buffers are used to move the object if it is **Swappable**.

The last few lines of the **Gfso** constructor set up a close box and header if the **IsCloseable** flag is set. Figure 10.5 shows an example of a window with this style. The close boxes are hard coded to 11 pixels in size and are placed on a 16-pixel header. This header is used in closeable windows no matter what border style has been selected.

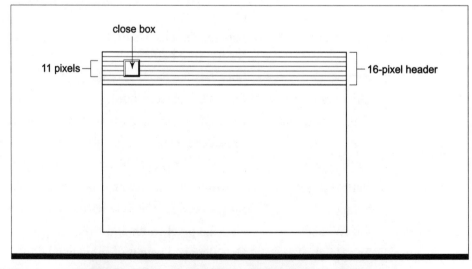

Figure 10.5   A graphics window with a close box

The **Gfso** destructor deallocates the three **Grso** objects in a **Gfso** object as well as the close button object if one exists. It also frees any memory that might have been allocated for swapping images of the object.

Two other member functions involved in the initialization of a **Gfso** window are **SetSize()** and **SetLocn()**. **SetSize()** is responsible for allocating memory if the object is swappable. Because it allocates memory, you must always call **SetSize()** before using the object. Note that it expands the height of the frame to include the frame header if the window is closeable. As is the case for all frame objects (**Fso**s), **SetSize()** works with respect to the interior, whereas **SetLocn()** works with respect to the frame.

One issue that arises with graphics mode, and that wasn't critical before, involves the amount of memory required to move objects on the screen. In graphics mode, the high-resolution modes will force an application to dedicate an extensive amount of memory for saving the images of objects that are to be moved on the screen. In fact, in the higher resolution EGA and VGA modes, more than 64K is required to save a full-screen image. Because the BGI functions can save large graphics regions directly, the screen objects will have to be less than 64K in size when they are saved. Although we could subdivide the screen and save it in pieces less than 64K each, we won't take this approach since large graphic objects would consume a great portion of memory. Note that the code does not trap for windows being too large. You may want to handle this potential error.

Finally, the **SetLocn()** function defines the upper-left-hand pixel coordinate of the three **Grso** objects contained in **Gfso** and its close button, if one exists.

Drawing Gfso Objects

Let's take a look at **DrawFrame()**, which is responsible for drawing the frame of a **Gfso** object. This is accomplished by calling the **Frame**'s **Box()** member function. The **DrawFrame()** member function has several parts. First, you'll note that it begins by ensuring that a border actually exists, that is, the border width, **Bwd**, is greater than zero. In addition, the function is designed so that the border and color attribute parameters, if passed as zeroes, instruct the function to use the values specified by the object itself in the **ColorPak** defined by the **Colors** data member.

In addition, if there is a close box, it is also drawn by **DrawFrame()**. The task is broken up into two steps. First, a header is drawn across the top of the frame object by drawing alternating lines of black and the window's background color:

```
for (I = 0; I < HeaderHt; I++) {
  if ((I % 2) == 0)
    setcolor(0);
  else setcolor(BackGround(Colors.Wc));
```

```
    moveto(Frame->Xul+Bwd, Frame->Yul+Bwd+I);
    lineto(Frame->Xlr-Bwd, Frame->Yul+Bwd+I);
}
```

Finally, the region where the close box is to appear in the header is cleared and then a box around it is drawn by the two operations:

```
CloseBox->Fill(0, 0, CloseBox->Wd, CloseBox->Ht, ' ', Colors.Wc);
CloseBox->Box(0, 0, CloseBox->Wd, CloseBox->Ht, Relief+1, Attr);
```

Note that the style used to draw a close box is hard coded so that it is in relief and has a border width of one pixel. In addition, it uses the same colors as the frame's.

Moving Gfso Objects

If a **Gfso** screen object is configured so that it is moveable—the **Swappable** bit is set in the frame attribute parameter to its constructor—then the internal data member **IsSwappable** is set to 1. The **Gfso** class provides for the movement of an object across the graphics screen by overriding the member functions **Swap()**, **GetImage()**, and **PutImage()**.

The **GetImage()** and **PutImage()** member functions of **Gfso** simply call the BGI primitives **getimage()** and **putimage()**, respectively, to copy or place an image on the screen. The **Swap()** member function calls these two functions to copy the screen where an image is to appear and then places a saved image on the screen by the statements:

```
::getimage(Frame->Xul, Frame->Yul, Frame->Xlr, Frame->Ylr, SwapBuff);
::putimage(Frame->Xul, Frame->Yul, SaveBuff, COPY_PUT);
```

Then, it exchanges the **SaveBuff** and **SwapBuff** pointers so that the next time **Swap()** is called it will display the image just retrieved by the call to **getimage()**.

Note the use of the C++ file scoping operator (::) in the calls to **getimage()** and **putimage()** here. Although they are not strictly necessary, since there aren't any conflicts with these two function names, we're using the scoping operator here to emphasize that these are not the same functions as the **GetImage()** and **PutImage()** functions in the **Gfso** class.

Revisiting Skeletons

The **Gskel** class is also derived from **Fso** and it is included in **gfsounit.h** and **gfsounit.cpp**. Its purpose is to provide an outline of a screen object that can be used when the object is dragged across the screen. In this way, the object image does not have to be repainted as the object is moved. Without this feature, large windows and screen objects would move too slowly. Let's take a closer look at **Gskel**:

```
class Gskel : public Fso { // Graphics skeleton
public:
  Gskel(ColorPak &Cp);
  virtual void DrawFrame(char Ba, char Attr);
  virtual void Swap(Rect *C, XfrDirn Xd);
};
```

The **Gskel** class has only three member functions as listed in Table 10.5. The outlining feature of **Gskel** exploits Turbo C++'s ability to exclusive-OR lines to the screen. This feature can be used to draw and erase the skeleton on the screen without disturbing what is underneath it. Generally, the idea is to draw a dashed outline on the screen using the BGI's exclusive-OR feature and then to remove it; the line is drawn again at the same location.

In particular, the skeleton is drawn using exclusive-OR dashed lines in the member function **DrawFrame()**:

```
setlinestyle(DASHED_LINE,0,NORM_WIDTH);
setwritemode(XOR_PUT);
```

The **DrawFrame()** member function calls **Box()** to draw a single rectangle to represent the outline of the screen object.

Once the **Gskel** frame is drawn, the write mode is restored to its normal mode and the line style to solid lines by:

```
setwritemode(COPY_PUT);
setlinestyle(SOLID_LINE,0,NORM_WIDTH);
```

To move the skeleton across the screen, **Swap()** simply calls **DrawFrame()** repeatedly. Note that even though **Swap()** doesn't use the parameters passed to it,

Table 10.5   Gskel member functions

Member function	Description
Gskel()	Initializes a skeleton object
DrawFrame()	Draws the outline used to move an object
Swap()	Moves the outline across the screen

the parameters still must be provided. Because **Swap()** is a virtual function, the parameter passed to it must be the same for all versions of the member function.

The Wso Class

The last class we'll create to support graphics windows, **Wso**, is derived from **Iso**. You'll find the graphics mode version of the **Wso** class in **gwsounit.h** and **gwsounit.cpp** (see Listing 10.5 and Listing 10.6, respectively). The key reasons for having the **Wso** class are:

1. To set up an **Iso** object to be graphics based

2. To provide support for skeletons used when moving objects

3. To provide prompting for graphics objects

You may recall that we had a class called **Wso** in text mode. Why are we using the same name here? The reason is to make the menu code in **msounit.cpp** generic. Remember that the menus are derived from the **Wso** class. But which **Wso** class does the system use—the text-based version from **twsounit**, or the graphics-based version we're discussing here in **gwsounit**? This depends on a compiler switch in **msounit**.

The class definition for **Wso** is:

```
class Wso : public Iso {
public:
  Wso(int Ba, int Fa, ColorPak &Cp);
  virtual void MoveLoop(MsgPkt &M);
  virtual void Prompt(void);
  virtual void UnPrompt(void);
};
```

The Wso Member Functions

As you examine the **Wso** member functions, notice that they're virtually identical to their text mode cousins in Chapter 7. The same routines are included: a constructor, **Prompt()**, **UnPrompt()**, and **MoveLoop()**. The most critical member function in the **Wso** class is its constructor, which makes our screen object graphics based. This is done by passing a pointer to a **Gfso** panel to the base constructor in the **Iso** class.

Note how the **Prompt()** and **UnPrompt()** member functions work. In their text-based versions, these routines switched the border styles between single- and double-line borders. Since these styles aren't used in graphics modes, we need a different prompting technique. We've chosen to simply alter the border colors instead.

Graphics Mode Tools

Before we build our first graphics mode menu application, we should write a package of graphics utilities that will be common to many of the graphics programs we write. These routines, shown in Table 10.6, are included in the file **grphscrn.cpp** (see Listing 10.8).

The **Setup()** function is designed to be called at the beginning of an application to initialize various components of a graphics system. One responsibility of **Setup()** is to configure the graphics mode. This is done through the parameters **GDriver**, **GMode**, and **DriverPath**. These parameters are used in a call to the BGI function **initgraph()** to determine the video mode to be used by the program. See the Turbo C++ documentation on **initgraph()** for details on these parameters.

Another parameter passed to **Setup()** is **Font**, which determines the type of text font to use in the program. The **Font** parameter is passed to the BGI function **settextstyle()**. You should read the Turbo C++ documentation on **settextstyle()** for the valid values for **Font**.

If the graphics and font initialization succeed, the mouse is then initialized. Here, one of three actions can occur, depending on the value of the **MouseOpt** parameter passed to **Setup()**. The value can be one of the three values listed in Table 10.7. These values are defined at the top of **grphscrn.h**.

After intializing the mouse, **Setup()** then initializes the global **FullScrn** object so that it uses the full screen. It is the base window on which all other objects will be referenced.

Finally, **Setup()** configures the first message, specified by the **StartMsg** message packet, to **NullMsg**, which means no message has yet been sent.

As an example, suppose we want an application to use the mouse, configure itself to the highest resolution graphics mode, and load the Sans Serif font located

Table 10.6   Graphics-support routines in grphscrn.cpp

Function	Description
Setup()	Initializes the mouse and graphics system
CleanUp()	Restores the default video mode
MainEventLoop()	An encapsulated call to the EventLoop() handler

Table 10.7   Predefined mouse configurations

Constant	Value	Description
NoMouse	0x00	Mouse is not initialized
MouseRequired	0x01	Mouse must be successfully initialized or program terminates
MouseOptional	0x02	Mouse is initialized if possible

in the directory \tc\bgi. This would be accomplished by the following call to **Setup()**:

```
int Gd=DETECT, Gm;

Setup(MouseRequired, Gd, Gm, "\\tc\\bgi", SANS_SERIF_FONT);
```

Another function in **grphscrn.cpp**, **MainEventLoop()**, is provided to encapsulate the call to the primary event loop that the window manager uses. In addition, **MainEventLoop()** passes it the first message, **StartMsg**. This is the routine you want to typically call in your application to initiate the user interaction.

Finally, the **CleanUp()** routine in **grphscrn.cpp** is provided to deallocate the **FullScrn** object, turn the mouse off, and restore the screen to its default mode—typically text mode. Remember, by destroying **FullScrn**, *all* windows are destroyed.

A Simple Example

Now a small program will be built to test the tools we've just discussed. This application, **gtest.cpp**, is listed next. It generates the screen shown in Figure 10.6.

```
// gtest.cpp: Tests the Grso, Gfso, and Wso types by displaying
// two objects and writing to them. Try moving the objects around
// by dragging them by their borders using the mouse or use the
// shift arrow keys. Press ALT-X to quit the program.

#include "grphscrn.h"
#include <conio.h>

Wso *W1, *W2;
int I, J;
int Gd, Gm;
```

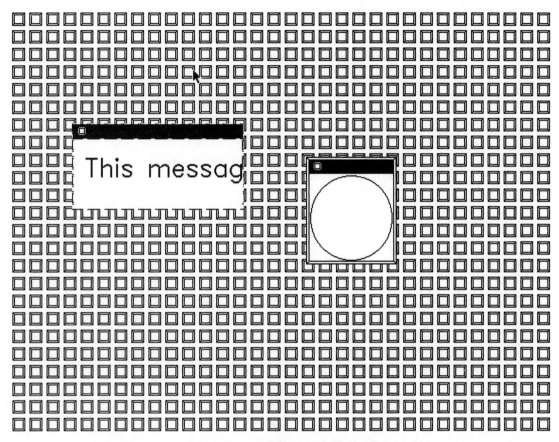

Figure 10.6   Output of gtest.cpp

```
main()
{
  Rso *Ip;

  Gd = DETECT;
  Setup(MouseOptional, Gd, Gm, "\\tcpp\\bgi", SANS_SERIF_FONT);
  FullScrn->Panel->Clear(' ', 0x70);   // Clear the screen using gray
  // Draw a series of boxes on the screen
  Mouse.Hide();
  for (J = 0; J <= getmaxy() / 20; J++) {
     for (I = 0; I <= getmaxx() / 20; I++) {
    FullScrn->Panel->Interior->Box(
      I*20+3, J*20+2, 15, 15, Relief+1, GrphColors.Bc);
     }
  }
  Mouse.Show();
  // Create a window and display a message to it that will be clipped
```

```
    W2 - new Wso(0x11, WindowStyle, ErrColors);
    W2->SetSize(200, 80);
    W2->Open(FullScrn, 5, 5);
    W2->Panel->HzWrt(15, 15, "This message is clipped", 0);
    // Display another window and write a circle in it
    W1 - new Wso(Relief+3, WindowStyle-BorderPrompt, GrphColors);
    W1->SetSize(101, 100);
    W1->Open(FullScrn, 210, 70);
    setcolor(0);
    Mouse.Hide();
    Ip - W1->Panel->Interior;
      circle(Ip->Xul+Ip->Wd/2, Ip->Yul+Ip->Ht/2, Ip->Wd/2);
    Mouse.Show();
    MainEventLoop();
    CleanUp();
}
```

A Menu Example

With all the tools now in order, we are ready to write a graphics-based menu application. This test program, **gmenutst.cpp**, is very much like the text mode **tmenutst.cpp** program in Chapter 8. A screen print of the program is shown in Figure 10.7. Since **gmenutst** is similar to its text mode counterpart, we won't go into great detail here to explain how the menu structure is created. However, we'll explore some of the graphics-specific details.

First, note that all the dimensions of the windows are specified in terms of pixels. Second, the use of the **Swappable** flag is more important than it was in text mode. Although the **Swappable** flag still causes a graphics object to be moveable, in graphics mode it may be very slow to do so. This is because a lot of memory has to be shuffled around to move the object. As a compromise, if an object is swappable, it should also have the **OutlineMove** bit set, which will force the system to use an outline when the object is being moved. This is a particularly good idea, especially when the object size gets larger.

Note that the **Setup()** routine is currently set to load fonts from the \tcpp\bgi directory. It also demands that a mouse be present, by use of the **MouseRequired** parameter. This is a good idea for any graphics program using the tools created here because the keyboard interaction is so limited.

Finally, when you are compiling **gmenutst**, remember to provide a **#define** value equal to the word **GRAPHICS**. This will force **msounit** to use the graphics version of the **Wso** class.

```
// gmenutst.cpp: Implements pull-down, tear-away menus in graphics
// mode. This program is very similar to the text mode program
// in Chapter 8.
```

Figure 10.7   Output of gmenutst.cpp

```
#include "string.h"
#include "grphscrn.h"
#include "msounit.h"

void ExitAction(Wso *, MsgPkt &M)
{
  M.RtnCode - ShutDown;
}

void NoAction(Wso *, MsgPkt &) { ; }

void PopupAction(Wso *Src, MsgPkt &M)
// Pop-up a window with the name of the object written in it
{
  Wso *B;
  char Label[80];

  strcpy(Label, ((Meso *)(Src))->Name);
```

```
        strcat(Label, " Action");

        ((Meso *)Src)->OnClose(M);              // Close pull-down window
        M.Code = M.RtnCode;
        FullScrn->SubMgr->EventStep(M);
        // Open pop-up window
        B = new Wso(Relief+3, WindowStyle-BorderPrompt, GrphColors);
        B->SetSize(B->Panel->TextWidth(Label), B->Panel->TextHeight(2));
        B->Open(FullScrn, 300, 100); // Hard coded location of pop-up window
        B->Panel->HzWrt(0, 0, Label, 0);
        B->SwitchFocus(M);
        M.RtnCode = Idle; M.Code = Idle;
        do {                                    // Wait until a person closes window
          B->SubMgr->EventStep(M);      // or pressed ALT-X.
          M.Code = M.RtnCode;
        } while (!((M.Code == ShutDown) ||
                  (B->Active && M.Code == Close &&
                  M.Focus == ((Iso *)(B))))));
        if (M.Code == Close) {
          B->OnClose(M);
          Mouse.WaitForEvent(MouseUp, M.Mx, M.My);
          M.RtnCode = Idle;
        }
        delete B;
}

// Horizontal pulldown menu
Pmeso *FileBut;
Dmso *FileMenu;
MesoList *FileMList;
Meso *NewBut;
Meso *OpenBut;
Meso *SaveBut;
Meso *CloseBut;
Meso *VtExitBut;
// Edit menu
Pmeso *EditBut;
Dmso *EditMenu;
MesoList *EditMList;
Meso *CutBut;
Meso *CopyBut;
Meso *PasteBut;
// Action menu
Pmeso *ActionBut;
Dmso *PanicMenu;
MesoList *PanicMList;
Meso *PanicBut;
Meso *CalmBut;
// Main header menu
Pmso *Hm;
MesoList *HzMenuList;

int Gd, Gm;
```

```
int GmenuStyle;
main()
{
  Gd = DETECT;
  Setup(MouseRequired, Gd, Gm, "\\tcpp\\bgi", SANS_SERIF_FONT);
  GmenuStyle = WindowStyle - BorderPrompt;

  // Allocate and set up the menu system
  FileMList = new MesoList();
  NewBut = new Meso("New", PopupAction);
  FileMList->Append(NewBut);
  OpenBut = new Meso("Open", PopupAction);
  FileMList->Append(OpenBut);
  SaveBut = new Meso("Save", PopupAction);
  FileMList->Append(SaveBut);
  CloseBut = new Meso("Close", PopupAction);
  FileMList->Append(CloseBut);
  VtExitBut = new Meso("Exit", ExitAction);
  FileMList->Append(VtExitBut);
  FileMenu = new Dmso(FileMList, 90, Relief+3, GmenuStyle, GrphColors);

  EditMList = new MesoList();
  CutBut = new Meso("Cut", PopupAction);
  EditMList->Append(CutBut);
  CopyBut = new Meso("Copy", PopupAction);
  EditMList->Append(CopyBut);
  PasteBut = new Meso("Paste", PopupAction);
  EditMList->Append(PasteBut);
  EditMenu = new Dmso(EditMList, 90, Relief+3, GmenuStyle, GrphColors);

  PanicMList = new MesoList();
  PanicBut = new Meso("Panic", PopupAction);
  PanicMList->Append(PanicBut);
  CalmBut = new Meso("Don't Panic", PopupAction);
  PanicMList->Append(CalmBut);
  PanicMenu = new Dmso(PanicMList, 90, Relief+3, GmenuStyle, GrphColors);

  HzMenuList = new MesoList;
  FileBut = new Pmeso("File", FileMenu);
  HzMenuList->Append(FileBut);
  EditBut = new Pmeso("Edit", EditMenu);
  HzMenuList->Append(EditBut);
  ActionBut = new Pmeso("Panic", PanicMenu);
  HzMenuList->Append(ActionBut);
  Hm = new Pmso(HzMenuList, 300, 200, 20, 0x33, GmenuStyle, GrphColors);

  // Draw a background to the screen
  Hm->Open(FullScrn, 0, 0);
  Hm->Inner->Panel->Clear(' ', 0x70);
  MainEventLoop();
  CleanUp();
}
```

Code Critique

This chapter started by extending the generic screen tools to make them work in graphics mode. This was done without changing any of the underlying classes such as **Rso**, **Fso**, and **Iso**. Although we implemented most of the basic features of a graphics-based system, such as 3D windows and pull-down menus, many more features could be added.

Faster Swap Routines

Probably the greatest drawback to our graphics-based windowing system is that graphics images aren't swapped very efficiently. The slow swapping is particularly noticeable when windows are being moved. The main culprits are the BGI routines **getimage()** and **putimage()**, which are called by **Gfso**'s **GetImage()** and **PutImage()** member functions. To improve the performance of screen image transfers, you may want to override these member functions and provide your own custom versions.

Providing Larger Swap Buffers

One problem with graphics-based windows is that their swap buffers can easily become larger than 64K—especially in the high-resolution modes. If this occurs, **getimage()** and **putimage()** won't work correctly. You'll need to devise some way to manage these larger buffers.

Using Multiple Fonts

Currently it is assumed that the font style is the same for every window on the screen. We could improve this, however, by having each window keep track of its own font information. You could add the code to support this feature in the **Grso** class.

Adding Fill Patterns

The **Grso** member functions **Fill()** and **FillB()** currently fill regions with a solid fill pattern. A better implementation would allow them to fill regions using one of several fill patterns. This could be encoded with the unused **Ch** parameter in these functions.

Other Features

You might want to add shadows as we did in text mode. Another interesting feature would be to have scalable windows.

Listing 10.1   grsounit.h

```
// grsounit.h: graphics-based rectangular screen object (Grso) class

#ifndef H_GRSOUNIT
#define H_GRSOUNIT

#include <graphics.h>
#include "msmouse.h"
#include "scrnsty.h"
#include "rsounit.h"

class Grso : public Rso {
public:
 int TxtHt;
 Grso(void);
 virtual void HzWrt(int X, int Y, char *Str, char Attr);
 virtual void HzWrtB(int X, int Y, char *Str);
 virtual void Fill(int X, int Y, int W, int H, char Ch, char Attr);
 virtual void FillB(int X, int Y, int W, int H, char Ch, char Opt);
 virtual void Box(int X, int Y, int W, int H, char Ba, char Attr);
 virtual int  TextWidth(char *Str);
 virtual int  Textheight(int N);
};

#endif
```

Listing 10.2   grsounit.cpp

```
#include "grsounit.h"

// grsounit.cpp: graphics-based rectangular screen object definitions
// These routines use the built-in rectangle to clip the
// transfers. They take care of the mouse cursor as well.

Grso::Grso(void)
// Initializes a Grso object. Note: It saves the height of the current
// font being used. This font style is assumed to be the currently
// registered font while this Grso object is being used.
: Rso(0, 0, 0, 0)
{
   TxtHt = ::TextHeight("H") * 4 / 3;
}
```

```
void Grso::HzWrt(int X, int Y, char *Str, char Attr)
// Writes a string to a Grso object. The string is clipped to
// the boundaries of the object. The text is displayed using
// the foreground color of the Attr parameter. The region below
// the text is cleared using the background color of Attr.
{
  int W, H;
  viewporttype Vp;

  getviewsettings(&Vp);
  W - TextWidth(Str);
  setviewport(Xul,Yul,Xlr,Ylr,1);
  H - Textheight()(1);
  FillB(X, Y, W, H, Attr, 1);
  Mouse.Hide();
  setcolor(ForeGround(Attr));
  outtextxy(X, Y, Str);
  setviewport(Vp.left, Vp.top, Vp.right, Vp.bottom, Vp.clip);
  Mouse.Show();
}

void Grso::HzWrtB(int X, int Y, char *Str)
// Writes a string to this object. The string is clipped. Note that
// this routine does not clear the space where the text is displayed
// and that it uses the current drawing color—whatever it may be.
{
  viewporttype Vp;
  getviewsettings(&Vp);
  setviewport(Xul,Yul,Xlr,Ylr,1);
  Mouse.Hide();
  outtextxy(X, Y, Str);
  Mouse.Show();
  setviewport(Vp.left, Vp.top, Vp.right, Vp.bottom, Vp.clip);
}

void Grso::Fill(int X, int Y, int W, int H,  char, char Attr)
// Fills a region with a particular color. Note: The unnamed
// parameter, which should be the fill character, is ignored.
{
  if (((H - 1) && HzClip(X, Y, W)) ||
      ((W - 1) && VtClip(X, Y, H)) ||
      (VtClip(X,Y,H) && HzClip(X,Y,W)))  {
    Mouse.Hide();
    setfillstyle(SOLID_FILL,BackGround(Attr));
    bar(Xul+X, Yul+Y, Xul+X+W-1, Yul+Y+H-1);
    Mouse.Show();
  }
}

void Grso::FillB(int X, int Y, int W, int H, char Ch, char)
// Fills a region. Note: This interpretation is different from
// its text-mode counterpart in trsounit.cpp. The last parameter,
// which is the Opt parameter, is ignored.
```

```
{
  Fill(X, Y, W, H, ' ', Ch);
}


void Grso::Box(int X, int Y, int W, int H, char Ba, char Attr)
// Draws a box
{
  unsigned char Bw, Bs, B;
  int I, Xs, Ys, Xf, Yf;

  Bw = Ba & 0x000f;            // Unpack the border width
  Bs = (Ba >> 4) & 0x000f;     // and the border style
  if ((Bs > 0) && (Bs < 4)) {
      Mouse.Hide();
      if (Bs == 1) {
        for (I = 0; I < Bw; I++) {
            setcolor(ForeGround(Attr));
            rectangle(Xul+X, Yul+Y, Xul+X+W-1, Yul+Y+H-1);
            X++; Y++; W -= 2; H -= 2;
        }
      }
      else { // Use a 3D style
        if ((Bs << 4) == Recessed) {
          B = ForeGround(Attr);
          Attr = BackGround(Attr) + (B << 4);
        }
        Xs = X+Xul; Xf = Xs + W - 1;
        Ys = Y+Yul; Yf = Ys + H - 1;
        for (I = 0; I < Bw; I++) {
            setcolor(BackGround(Attr));
            moveto(Xs+I, Yf-I);
            lineto(Xs+I, Ys+I);
            lineto(Xf-I, Ys+I);
            setcolor(ForeGround(Attr));
            moveto(Xf-I, Ys+I+1);
            lineto(Xf-I, Yf-I);
            lineto(Xs+I+1, Yf-I);
        }
      }
      Mouse.Show();
  }
}


int Grso::TextWidth(char *Str)
// Returns the pixel width of a string
{
  return ::TextWidth(Str);
}


int Grso::Textheight()(int N)
// Returns the pixel height of N rows of text
{
  return TxtHt*N;
}
```

Listing 10.3   gfsounit.h

```
// gfsounit.h: Provides graphics mode "frames" that are used in
// the Iso screen objects. A frame consists of an interior, panel,
// and overall object.

#ifndef H_GFSOUNIT
#define H_GFSOUNIT

#include "fsounit.h"
#include "grsounit.h"

class Gfso : public Fso { // A graphics frame screen object
public:
  char *SaveBuff, *SwapBuff;
  unsigned SaveSize;
  Grso *CloseBox;
  int HeaderHt;
  Gfso(int Ba, int Fa, ColorPak &Cp);
  virtual ~Gfso(void);
  virtual void SetSize(int W, int H);
  virtual void SetLocn(int X1, int Y1);
  virtual void DrawFrame(char Ba, char Attr);
  virtual void Clear(char Ch, char Attr);
  virtual void GetImage(Rect *C);
  virtual void PutImage(Rect *C);
  virtual void Swap(Rect *C, XfrDirn Xd);
  virtual int  OnCloseButton(int X, int Y);
  virtual int  TextWidth(char *Str);
  virtual int  Textheight()(int N);
};

class Gskel : public Fso { // Graphics skeleton
public:
  Gskel(ColorPak &Cp);
  virtual void DrawFrame(char Ba, char Attr);
  virtual void Swap(Rect *C, XfrDirn Xd);
};

#endif
```

Listing 10.4   gfsounit.cpp

```
#include <stdlib.h>
#include "gfsounit.h"

Gfso::Gfso(int Ba, int Fa, ColorPak &Cp)
// Initializes the three components of a Gfso: the interior, frame,
// and overall objects. Gfso also supports a new type of frame
// style: windows with CloseBoxes. The dimensions of the close box
```

```
  // is hard coded, but looks good in most cases.
  : Fso(Ba, Fa, Cp)
  {
    Overall - new Grso;
    Frame   - new Grso;
    Interior - new Grso;
    SaveBuff - NULL;  SwapBuff - NULL;
    SaveSize - 0;
    if (IsCloseable()) {
       // Create a close box and place it within a 16-pixel header
       // at the top of the window
       CloseBox - new Grso;
       CloseBox->SetSize(11, 11);   // Hard coded
       HeaderHt - 16; // Frame header height is hard coded
    }
    else CloseBox - NULL;
  }

  Gfso::~Gfso(void)
  // Frees the swap buffers and the four nested Grso objects
  {
    if (IsSwappable()) {
       delete[SaveSize] SaveBuff;
       delete[SaveSize] SwapBuff;
    }
    if (IsCloseable()) delete CloseBox;
    delete Frame;
    delete Interior;
    delete Overall;
  }

  void Gfso::SetSize(int W, int H)
  // Sets the size of the three components of a Gfso object and
  // its CloseBox if it has one. The size (W,H) is interpreted
  // to be the interior size. Memory for the swap buffers is also
  // allocated if the object is swappable, but only for the first
  // time, or if the new size is bigger than the old.
  {
    unsigned OldSaveSize;

    Interior->SetSize(W, H);
    if (IsCloseable())
       Frame->SetSize(W+Bwd*2, H+HeaderHt+Bwd*2);
       else Frame->SetSize(W+Bwd*2, H+Bwd*2);
    Overall->SetSize(Frame->Wd, Frame->Ht);
    if (IsSwappable()) {
       OldSaveSize - SaveSize;
       SaveSize - imagesize(Frame->Xul,Frame->Yul,Frame->Xlr,Frame->Ylr);
       if (SaveSize > OldSaveSize) { // Allocate
          if (SaveBuff !- NULL) {    // Reallocate
             delete[OldSaveSize] SaveBuff;
             delete[OldSaveSize] SwapBuff;
          }
```

```
          SaveBuff - new char[SaveSize];
          SwapBuff - new char[SaveSize];
      }
    }
}

void Gfso::SetLocn(int X1, int Y1)
// Sets the upper-left location of the three Grsos and the
// CloseBox if this object has one
{
  Frame->SetLocn(X1, Y1);
  if (IsCloseable()) {
    Interior->SetLocn(X1+Bwd, Y1+Bwd+HeaderHt);
    CloseBox->SetLocn(X1+Bwd+5, Y1+Bwd+2);
  }
  else Interior->SetLocn(X1+Bwd, Y1+Bwd);
  Overall->SetLocn(X1, Y1);
}

void Gfso::DrawFrame(char Ba, char Attr)
// Draws this object's frame and its CloseBox if it has one
{
  int I;

  if (Bwd > 0) {
      if (Ba - 0) Ba - (Bstyle << 4) | Bwd;
      if (Attr - 0) Attr - Colors.Bc;
      Frame->Box(0, 0, Frame->Wd, Frame->Ht, Ba, Attr);
      if (IsCloseable()) {
          // This object has a CloseBox. Display it now
          Mouse.Hide();
          for (I - 0; I < HeaderHt; I++) {
            if ((I % 2) - 0)
                setcolor(0);
                else setcolor(BackGround(Colors.Wc));
              moveto(Frame->Xul+Bwd, Frame->Yul+Bwd+I);
              lineto(Frame->Xlr-Bwd, Frame->Yul+Bwd+I);
      }
      CloseBox->Fill(0, 0, CloseBox->Wd, CloseBox->Ht, ' ', Colors.Wc);
      CloseBox->Box(0, 0, CloseBox->Wd, CloseBox->Ht, Relief+1, Attr);
      Mouse.Show();
       }
   }
}

int Gfso::OnCloseButton(int X, int Y)
// Returns True if the coordinate is within the object's CloseBox.
// This function returns False if the object does not have a CloseBox.
{
  return (IsCloseable() && CloseBox->Contains(X, Y));
}
```

```
void Gfso::Clear(char Ch, char Attr)
// Clears the interior of this object using the colors in Attr. If
// Attr is zero, then the window color field of this object is used.
{
    if (Attr > 0) Colors.Wc = Attr;
    Interior->Fill(0, 0, Interior->Wd, Interior->Ht, Ch, Colors.Wc);
}

void Gfso::GetImage(Rect *)
// Gets image from frame buffer and stores it in the save buffer if
// the object is swappable. The clipping rectangle for the
// shadows is not currently used.
{
  Mouse.Hide();
  if (IsSwappable())
     ::getimage(Frame->Xul, Frame->Yul, Frame->Xlr, Frame->Ylr, SaveBuff);
  Mouse.Show();
}

void Gfso::PutImage(Rect *)
// Puts save buffer image onto Frame buffer if the object
// is swappable. The clipping rectangle for the shadows
// is not currently used.
{
  Mouse.Hide();
  if (IsSwappable())
     ::putimage(Frame->Xul, Frame->Yul, SaveBuff, COPY_PUT);
  Mouse.Show();
}

void Gfso::Swap(Rect *, XfrDirn)
// Swaps the image on the screen.
// Note: The parameters aren't used here.
{
  char *Tmp;

  if (IsSwappable()) {
     Mouse.Hide();
     ::getimage(Frame->Xul, Frame->Yul, Frame->Xlr, Frame->Ylr, SwapBuff);
     ::putimage(Frame->Xul, Frame->Yul, SaveBuff, COPY_PUT);
     Mouse.Show();
     // Just swap pointers between SwapBuff and SaveBuff
     Tmp = SaveBuff; SaveBuff = SwapBuff;  SwapBuff = Tmp;
  }
}

int Gfso::TextWidth(char *Str)
// Returns the pixel width of the string.
// Note the typecast, so that the right width is returned.
{
  return ((Grso *)Interior)->TextWidth(Str);
}
```

```
int Gfso::Textheight()(int N)
// Returns the pixel height of N rows of text
// Note the typecast, so that the right height is returned.
{
  return ((Grso *)Interior)->Textheight()(N);
}


// ─────── Graphics Skeleton Methods ───────

Gskel::Gskel(ColorPak &Cp)
// Initializes a graphics skeleton object so that it has a
// single pixel border and is swappable
: Fso(0x11, Swappable, Cp)
{
  Overall  = new Grso;
  Frame    = new Grso;
  Interior = new Grso;
}

void Gskel::DrawFrame(char Ba, char Attr)
// Draws the frame of a skeleton object using dashed,
// exclusive-OR lines
{
  setlinestyle(DASHED_LINE,0,NORM_WIDTH);
  setwritemode(XOR_PUT);
  if (Ba == 0) Ba = (Bstyle << 4) + Bwd;
  if (Attr == 0) Attr = Colors.Bc;
  Box(0, 0, Frame->Wd, Frame->Ht, Ba, Attr);
  setwritemode(COPY_PUT);
  setlinestyle(SOLID_LINE,0,NORM_WIDTH);
}


void Gskel::Swap(Rect *, XfrDirn)
// Swapping graphics skeleton objects is simply accomplished by
// calling DrawFrame again. This works because DrawFrame uses
// exclusive-OR lines. Note: This version doesn't use the parameters.
{
  DrawFrame(0,0);
}
```

Listing 10.5   gwsounit.h

```
// gwsounit.h: graphics-based window screen object class

#ifndef H_GWSOUNIT
#define H_GWSOUNIT

#include "isounit.h"
#include "gfsounit.h"
```

```
class Wso : public Iso {
public:
  Wso(int Ba, int Fa, ColorPak &Cp);
  virtual void MoveLoop(MsgPkt &M);
  virtual void Prompt(void);
  virtual void UnPrompt(void);
};

#endif
```

Listing 10.6   gwsounit.cpp

```
// gwsounit.cpp:
// Provides graphics screen objects based on the Iso type. In particular,
// this type overrides the prompting and moving functions in order to
// implement them according to the specifics of graphics mode.

#include "gwsounit.h"

Wso::Wso(int Ba, int Fa, ColorPak &Cp)
// Initializes a Wso object as a Gfso object passed to Iso
: Iso(new Gfso(Ba, Fa, Cp))
{
  return;
}

void Wso::MoveLoop(MsgPkt &M)
// Moves a Swappable object by using a skeleton if the OutlineMove
// bit is set. Otherwise the object is moved by swapping the image
// in and out of screen memory.
{
  Gskel *Red;
  Iso   *Skeleton;
  ColorPak C;

  if (Panel->IsSwappable()) {
    if ((Panel->Fattr & OutlineMove) != 0) {
      C = MonoColors;
      C.Bc = 0xff;  // Use white for border color for XOR lines
      Red = new Gskel(C);
      Red->SetSize(Panel->Frame->Wd, Panel->Frame->Ht);
      Skeleton = new Iso(Red); // Make a skeleton Iso
      Skeleton->Open(Base,
                    Panel->Frame->Xul-Base->Panel->Interior->Xul,
                    Panel->Frame->Yul-Base->Panel->Interior->Yul);
      Skeleton->MoveLoop(M);
      Skeleton->Remove();
      if ((Panel->Frame->Xul != Skeleton->Panel->Frame->Xul) ||
          (Panel->Frame->Yul != Skeleton->Panel->Frame->Yul))
```

```
                Move(Skeleton->Panel->Frame->Xul,
                    Skeleton->Panel->Frame->Yul);
          delete Skeleton;
        }
      else Iso::MoveLoop(M); // Just move whole window around
  }
}

void Wso::Prompt()
// Graphics mode prompting is accomplished by redrawing the frame of
// the object using the prompt color, Pc.
{
  Iso::Prompt();
  if ((Panel->Bstyle > 0) &&
      ((Panel->Fattr & BorderPrompt) != 0))
      Panel->DrawFrame(0, Panel->Colors.Pc);
}

void Wso::UnPrompt(void)
// Restores the object's border by redrawing it using its default colors
{
  if (Active) {
    if ((Panel->Bstyle > 0) && ((Panel->Fattr & BorderPrompt) != 0))
        Panel->DrawFrame(0, 0);  // 0, 0 means use default
    Iso::UnPrompt();
  }
}
```

Listing 10.7   grphscrn.h

```
// grphscrn.h:  A set of utilities used in the graphics
// applications in Chapters 10 and 11

#ifndef H_GRPHSCRN
#define H_GRPHSCRN

#include "gwsounit.h"

enum MouseOpt { NoMouse, MouseRequired, MouseOptional };

extern Wso *FullScrn;
extern MsgPkt StartMsg;

void Setup(int MouseOpt, int &GDriver, int &GMode,
           char *DriverPath, unsigned Font);
void MainEventLoop(void);
void CleanUp(void);

#endif
```

Listing 10.8   grphscrn.cpp

```
// grphscrn.cpp: a set of utilities used in the graphics
// applications in Chapters 10 and 11

#include <stdio.h>
#include "grphscrn.h"

Wso *FullScrn;
MsgPkt StartMsg;

void Setup(int MouseOpt, int &GDriver, int &GMode,
           char *DriverPath, unsigned Font)
// Configures the graphics screen and mouse. Gmode is the graphics
// mode to use. It should be one of Turbo C++'s constants defined in
// graphics.h. MouseOpt can be one of the options listed at the
// beginning of this file. FontPath and FontStyle specify the font
// to be used in the application. It also sets up the FullScrn object
// which will be the root window for all windows on the screen.
{
  int ErrCode;

  initgraph(&GDriver,&GMode,DriverPath);
  ErrCode = graphresult();
  if (ErrCode != grOk) {
    printf("Graphics error: %s",grapherrormsg(ErrCode));
    exit(1);
  }
  if (MouseOpt != NoMouse) {
     // Setup mouse according to graphics mode used
     if (getmaxx() == 320) Mouse.Setup(LowResGr);
     else if (GDriver == HERCMONOHI) Mouse.Setup(HerculesGr);
     else Mouse.Setup(Graphics);
     if ((!Mouse.SetupOK()) && (MouseOpt == MouseRequired)) {
        closegraph();
        printf("Unable to initialize mouse.");
        exit(1);
     }
  }
  settextstyle(Font,HORIZ_DIR,4);
  FullScrn = new Wso(0x00, 0x00, MonoColors);
  FullScrn->SetSize(getmaxx(),getmaxy());
  StartMsg = NullMsg;
}

void MainEventLoop(void)
// Starts up the main event loop by calling the FullScrn object's
// EventLoop function. But first, set the focus to the top Iso.
{
  if (FullScrn->SubMgr->Top != NULL)
```

```
        FullScrn->SubMgr->Top->SwitchFocus(StartMsg);
    FullScrn->SubMgr->EventLoop(StartMsg);
}

void CleanUp(void)
// Restore screen to its default mode and turn off the mouse
{
    delete FullScrn;
    Mouse.TurnOff();
    closegraph();
}
```

Interactive Graphics Objects

In this chapter we'll continue to demonstrate the power of inheritance as we derive several new types of graphics objects from the general purpose screen tools we've been creating. In particular, we'll develop graphics objects that support selection buttons, icons, slidebars, and scrollable windows. Despite the fact that these objects are new, they will be able to inherit, and thereby share, a major portion of the interface screen tools that have already been developed.

Making Graphics Objects

The new graphics screen objects we'll present are built from the **Wso** class contained in **gwsounit.h** and **gwsounit.cpp**. Recall that the **Wso** class presented in Chapter 10 provides most of the screen management and user-interaction code that are needed to support pop-up windows. Our goal now is to derive classes from **Wso** to implement different types of screen objects. Thus we can enhance our toolkit of screen objects by using the code we already have as the foundation.

Deriving Selection Buttons

We'll begin by developing a class that allows us to display and process selection buttons. Like the text mode buttons presented in Chapter 8, these objects consist of a string of text surrounded by a box as shown in Figure 11.1. When a button is

Figure 11.1   Sample selection buttons

activated by clicking on it with the mouse or by pressing Enter while the button is selected, the button performs an action. The graphics mode buttons, however, are slightly different from their text mode counterparts, as we'll soon see.

In the text mode version, a button's size was adjusted to fit its text string. Our graphics buttons take the opposite approach; the text is scaled to fit within the button's region. This is what we really wanted to do in text mode, but we had no control over the size of characters in that mode. In graphics mode, we can scale the text to virtually any size we want.

The button class presented next, **TextButton**, is included in the **gbutton.h** and **gbutton.cpp** (Listings 11.1 and 11.2, respectively). The complete definition for **TextButton** is:

```
class TextButton : public Wso {
public:
  ActionProc Action;
  char Str[80];
  char Font[80];
  TextButton(char *S, char *F, int Ba, int Fa,
             ColorPak &Cp, ActionProc A);
  virtual void Draw(void);
  virtual void Activate(MsgPkt &M);
  virtual void ChangeText(char *S, char *F);
};
```

This class contains three data members that are initialized in its constructor. The variables **Str** and **Font** store the button's string and font style, respectively. By having each button keep track of its own font, it is possible to create buttons with different font styles. The values for these components are passed to the constructor with the **S** and **F** parameters. The topmost data member, **Action**, points to the function that gets called when a button object is activated and is also set by the constructor.

In addition, the constructor is responsible for setting the border, frame, and color styles for a button. These components are assigned values using the **Ba**, **Fa**, and **Cp** parameters. The attribute options are the same as the window styles we've used in previous chapters. For instance, text buttons can be moveable, drawn with or without borders, and so on. The window color of the **ColorPak** parameter is used to draw the face of a button and its text. Also note that a text button is set to a default size of 25 by 25 pixels. This can easily be changed, however, by sending a message to the **SetSize()** member function.

Because selection buttons are more than just a rectangular window on the screen, we must override the **Draw()** member function in the **Wso** class so that it can display a button's text string.

The **Draw()** member function is responsible for sizing the string **Str** so that it is centered within the interior of the button. This task involves several steps.

First, using the dimensions specified by the **Panel.Interior** fields, in the **Text-Button** class, the font size is set using:

```
Rso *Pint = Panel->Interior;
setusercharsize(1,1,1,1);
setusercharsize(Pint->Wd, textwidth(Str),
                Pint->Ht, textheight(Str) * 4 / 3);
```

The following statements are used to clear a button's face, set the viewport to its interior, and write the text so that it is centered in the button:

```
Pint->Fill(0, 0, Pint->Wd, Pint->Ht, ' ', Panel->Colors.Wc);
// Write the text centered on the face of the button
setviewport(Pint->Xul,Pint->Yul,Pint->Xlr,Pint->Ylr,True);
setcolor(ForeGround(Panel->Colors.Wc));
settextjustify(CENTER_TEXT, CENTER_TEXT);
outtextxy(Pint->Wd/2+2, Pint->Ht/2, Str);
```

Finally, the view settings are restored to the full screen. Actually, the code would be more general if the current view settings were saved and restored, rather than resetting the clip region.

The **TextButton** class also contains the member function **ChangeText()** which repaints a button's text according to the font and string passed to it. If you want to use a different font on the button you must call **settextstyle()** prior to calling **ChangeText()**.

The key feature of a button object is that it has an action associated with it. We could derive different button classes and assign an action to each class, but this is an inefficient strategy. Why? Each derived class would have its own virtual function table that is almost identical to the other buttons' tables. In addition, because the button classes would be derived from the rather large **Wso** class, we'd be carrying around a lot of overhead in the virtual function tables. Is there a better approach available? Yes, we can use the same technique that was introduced in Chapter 8 when we assigned actions to menu objects.

To assign an action, **TextButton** allows us to pass a name, clothed as a parameter of type **ActionProc**, to its constructor. An **ActionProc** must have as parameters a pointer to a **Wso** object and a **MsgPkt** reference. The **Wso** parameter is used to pass in the object that is invoking the action. The **MsgPkt** is useful for sending back a return code. Typically, it will be set to **Idle**. However, if we are using an action that needs to perform an exit operation, for example, it could be set to **ShutDown**. For example:

```
void ExitAction(Wso *Src, MsgPkt &M)
{
  M.RtnCode - ShutDown;
}
```

This function is representative of the format you should use to define your own action routines. In the next section, an example is provided of how the **TextButton** class is used to create button objects.

Deriving Icons

An icon is another useful type of button. The major difference between a text button and an icon is that an icon has a figure drawn on its face rather than a text string, as shown in Figure 11.2. Most painting programs, for instance, use icons to provide the user with a palette of painting tools.

We can use several techniques to create icon objects. One way is to derive a different icon class for each object desired so that the object can have its own unique picture. However, this approach is wasteful. It is more efficient to use the same technique that we used to derive selection buttons. That is, create a generic icon class that is passed the name of a drawing procedure as a parameter. The

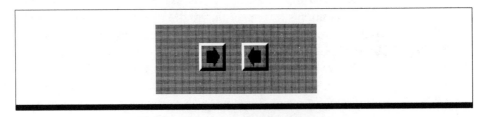

Figure 11.2 A pair of icon buttons

procedure will be responsible for displaying the icon's picture. Other than this, our icon class is similar to the **TextButton** class. Its definition is:

```
class IconButton : public Wso {
public:
  ActionProc Action;
  DrawProc DrawIcon;
  IconButton(DrawProc D, int Ba, int Fa, ColorPak &Cp, ActionProc A);
  virtual void Draw(void);
  virtual void Activate(MsgPkt &M);
};
```

Consider the new features that **IconButton** introduces. First, notice that its initialization routine is slightly different from **TextButton**'s. The **IconButton** is passed a draw function **D** that is of the type **DrawProc**. This parameter specifies the routine used to draw the icon figure on the button. **DrawProc** is defined in **gbutton.h** as:

```
typedef void (*DrawProc)(Wso *Src);
```

Typically the **DrawProc** functions are defined in an application. For instance, the following **DrawProc** routine might be used in a paint program to draw a rectangular pattern:

```
void DrawSquare(Wso *Src)
{
  setfillstyle(XHATCH_FILL, Foreground(Colors.Wc));
  bar(Src->Panel->Interior->Xul+2,
      Src->Panel->Interior->Yul+2,
      Src->Panel->Interior->Xlr-2,
      Src->Panel->Interior->Ylr-2);
}
```

As you might expect, the **Draw()** member function is also different for the **IconButton** class. Rather than writing out a text string as before, it now invokes the appropriate **DrawProc** function after the inherited **Wso::Draw()** function is called:

```
void IconButton::Draw(void)
// Draws the icon in the button's interior after calling
// the inherited version of Draw
{
  Wso::Draw();
  DrawIcon(this);
}
```

A Button Test Program

We'll now test the text and icon buttons that we've developed by using them in an application. Our next program, **gbutntst.cpp**, uses **gbutton.cpp** to display different text and icon objects. The output of the program is shown in Figure 11.3. As you can see, the buttons are of various sizes and styles. In addition, some of the windows are moveable, and others are not. One point to remember is that you can create buttons with close boxes so that they can be removed when the close box is clicked with the mouse. To quit the program select the "Exit" button or press the Alt-X key combination.

```
// gbutntst.cpp: Tests the graphics buttons.
// Press on Exit button to quit or type ALT-X key combination.

#include <string.h>
#include "grphscrn.h"
#include "gbutton.h"

void ChangeTextAction(Wso *Src, MsgPkt &)
// Changes the text on a button
{
  TextButton *Tb = (TextButton *)Src;
  if (!strcmp(Tb->Str, "Press"))
    strcpy(Tb->Str, "Press Again");
```

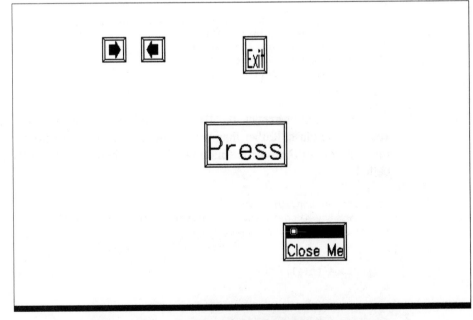

Figure 11.3   Output of the gbutntst.cpp program

```
      else strcpy(Tb->Str, "Press");
    Tb->ChangeText(Tb->Str, Tb->Font);
}

// ─── Some routines to draw icons ───

void DrawRightArrow(Wso *Src)
// Draws a right arrow icon
{
  int MidX, MidY;
  Mouse.Hide();
  MidX = Src->Panel->Interior->Xul + Src->Panel->Interior->Wd / 2;
  MidY = Src->Panel->Interior->Yul + Src->Panel->Interior->Ht / 2;
  setcolor(ForeGround(Src->Panel->Colors.Wc));
  moveto(MidX+6,MidY+6);
  lineto(MidX+6,MidY-6);
  lineto(MidX-2,MidY-6);
  lineto(MidX-2,MidY-10);
  lineto(MidX-8,MidY);
  lineto(MidX-2,MidY+10);
  lineto(MidX-2,MidY+6);
  lineto(MidX+6,MidY+6);
  setfillstyle(SOLID_FILL,ForeGround(Src->Panel->Colors.Wc));
  floodfill(MidX,MidY,ForeGround(Src->Panel->Colors.Wc));
  Mouse.Show();
}

void DrawLeftArrow(Wso *Src)
// Draws a left arrow icon
{
  int MidX, MidY;
  Mouse.Hide();
  MidX = Src->Panel->Interior->Xul + Src->Panel->Interior->Wd / 2;
  MidY = Src->Panel->Interior->Yul + Src->Panel->Interior->Ht / 2;
  setcolor(ForeGround(Src->Panel->Colors.Wc));
  moveto(MidX-6,MidY+6);
  lineto(MidX-6,MidY-6);
  lineto(MidX+2,MidY-6);
  lineto(MidX+2,MidY-10);
  lineto(MidX+8,MidY);
  lineto(MidX+2,MidY+10);
  lineto(MidX+2,MidY+6);
  lineto(MidX-6,MidY+6);
  setfillstyle(SOLID_FILL,ForeGround(Src->Panel->Colors.Wc));
  floodfill(MidX,MidY,ForeGround(Src->Panel->Colors.Wc));
  Mouse.Show();
}

main()
{
  TextButton *ExitButton;
  IconButton *LeftButton;
  IconButton *RightButton;
  TextButton *ChangeButton;
```

```
TextButton *CloseButton;
int Gd, Gm;

Gd = DETECT;
Setup(MouseOptional, Gd, Gm, "\\tcpp\\bgi", SANS_SERIF_FONT);
FullScrn->Panel->Clear(' ', 0x70);
LeftButton = new IconButton(DrawLeftArrow, Relief+3,
    Swappable, GrphColors, NoOp);
RightButton = new IconButton(DrawRightArrow, Relief+3,
    Swappable, GrphColors, NoOp);
ExitButton = new TextButton("Exit", "roman", Relief+3,
    Swappable, GrphColors, ExitAction);
ChangeButton = new TextButton("Press", "roman", Relief+3,
    Swappable+OutlineMove, GrphColors, ChangeTextAction);
CloseButton = new TextButton("Close Me", "roman", Relief+3,
    Swappable+OutlineMove+Closeable, GrphColors, NoOp);

LeftButton->Open(FullScrn, 20, 20);    // Buttons default to 25 by 25
RightButton->Open(FullScrn, 70, 20);   // pixels in size
ExitButton->SetSize(25, 40);
ExitButton->Open(FullScrn, 200, 20);
ChangeButton->SetSize(100, 50);
ChangeButton->Open(FullScrn, 150, 125);
CloseButton->SetSize(75, 25);
CloseButton->Open(FullScrn, 250, 250);
MainEventLoop();
CleanUp();
}
```

Windows with Scroll Bars

We'll now shift gears and build graphics windows with scroll bars. The scrollable windows that we'll present are similar to the ones created in Chapter 9. The object classes we'll use are shown in Figure 11.4.

We'll begin by developing a scroll bar class. Once we have it in hand, we'll be able to combine the scroll bar with a graphics window. In fact, we'll develop a special window class that has two built-in scroll bars—one on its right edge and the other on its bottom edge. Finally, we'll demonstrate how this new window class can be put to use. In particular, we'll derive a class that will allow us to interactively resize a rectangular figure drawn within the window's interior by moving its scroll bars.

Scroll Bars in Graphics Mode

Our graphics-based scroll bars will look different from those in Chapter 9 because they'll exploit the PC's graphics features. In particular, we'll use a combination of

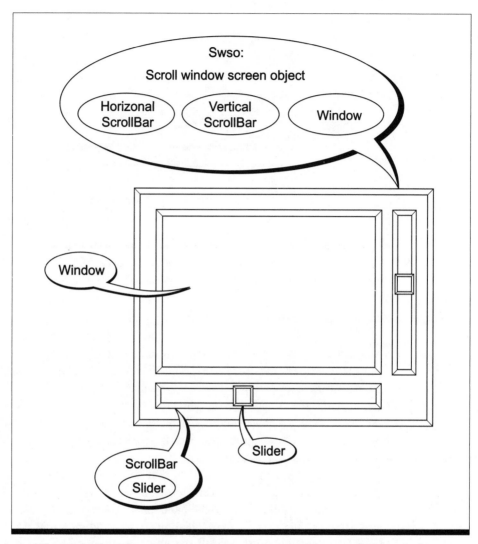

Figure 11.4   The classes used to create graphics scrollable windows

recessed and relief windows to create a three-dimensional looking scroll bar. Figure 11.5 presents an example of the new style of scroll bars.

We'll also take advantage of the ability of the mouse to change its cursor style. For instance, as the mouse moves over the scroll bar we'll modify its cursor style. We'll explore this feature later.

Other than these differences, the scroll bars are fairly similar to their text mode cousins. For instance, we will support both the mouse and keyboard and we'll use the same message passing system to allow the scroll bars to communicate with other screen objects.

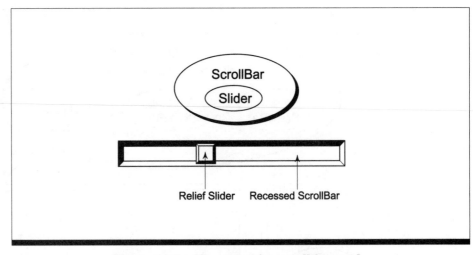

Figure 11.5   The graphics scroll bar style

Scroll Bar Overview

The graphics mode scroll bars are constructed using two classes derived from the **Wso** class: **Slider** and **ScrollBar**. The **Slider** class is used to create the slide button that the user can move with the mouse or the arrow keys. The **ScrollBar** class provides the foundation on which the **Slider** object moves. This is basically the same structure that we used in Chapter 9. The main difference is that we won't need a separate class to support a special frame design. Why? We won't be supplying scroll arrows at the ends of the scroll bars.

The other main feature added is that the mouse cursor style will change whenever the mouse crosses over the scroll bar or its slide button. In particular, the mouse cursor will change to the hand cursor (designed in Chapter 4) when the mouse moves over a scroll bar. This cursor will indicate that you can click the mouse at a location on the scroll bar and the slider will jump to that location. Similarly, the mouse cursor will change to a two-headed arrow cursor whenever the mouse is on the slider, thereby indicating that the mouse can drag the slider from side to side.

As before, we'll allow the scroll bars to have two possible orientations: horizontal and vertical. Note that unlike the text mode scroll bars, you can create scroll bars of different dimensions.

It's now time to start writing code. In the next few sections we'll develop a set of scroll bar and scrollable window tools and assemble them into **gscroll.h** and **gscroll.cpp**. These files are shown in Listings 11.3 and 11.4 near the end of this chapter.

The scroll bar slider is represented by the class **Slider**. Its definition is:

```
class Slider : public Wso {
public:
  Slider(ColorPak &Cp);
  virtual void Move(int X, int Y);
  virtual void OnMouseEnter(MsgPkt &M);
  virtual void OnMouseLeave(MsgPkt &M);
  virtual void OnMouseDown(MsgPkt &M);
  virtual void OnKeyStroke(MsgPkt &M);
};
```

The new **Slider** class provides two actions:

1. Moves the slider according to the position of the mouse

2. Changes the mouse cursor if the mouse is on the slider

We'll begin with the **Slider**'s constructor:

```
Slider::Slider(ColorPak &Cp)
// Initialize the object that represents the slider
: Wso(Relief+BorderWd, Swappable, Cp)
{
  return;
}
```

Notice that the **Slider** constructor simply chains back to the inherited constructor of the **Wso** class to initialize the slider object as a three-dimensional relief window that has a border width of **BorderWd**. The **BorderWd** constant is set to a value of three pixels in **gscroll.h**. The slider is defined to be **Swappable** so that it can be moved. You may want to add the constant **OutlineMove** to **Swappable** if you have a slow computer. This will prevent the slider from flickering as it is moved.

As stated in the summary of **Slider**'s features, the cursor style will change whenever the mouse is over the slider. This is accomplished by overriding the **OnMouseEnter()** and **OnMouseLeave()** member functions. All we need to do is change the cursor appropriately when **OnMouseEnter()** is called and restore it when **OnMouseLeave()** is invoked. These two functions are:

```
void Slider::OnMouseEnter(MsgPkt &M)
// Changes the mouse cursor when it is on the slider
{
  Wso::OnMouseEnter(M);        // Generally call this first
  if (((ScrollBar *)Base)->Orientation == HzOrient)
    Mouse.SetGCursor(LeftRightCursor);
    else Mouse.SetGCursor(UpDownCursor);
}
```

```
void Slider::OnMouseLeave(MsgPkt &M)
// Restores the mouse cursor when the mouse leaves the slider
{
  Mouse.SetGCursor(ArrowCursor);
  Wso::OnMouseLeave(M);
}
```

As shown, **OnMouseEnter()** changes the mouse cursor so that it uses one of the two double-headed arrows that we created back in Chapter 4 (**gcursor.cpp**). The double-headed arrow that is used depends on the orientation of the scroll bar on which the slider resides. Therefore, **OnMouseEnter()** must check the orientation of the scroll bar and set the cursor appropriately. Note that a slider assumes that its base window is a scroll bar.

The **OnMouseLeave()** member function restores the mouse cursor to its default arrow shape by calling **SetGCursor()** and passing it the **ArrowCursor** structure.

Before we move on, note how both **OnMouseEnter()** and **OnMouseLeave()** call their respective inherited member functions. In **OnMouseEnter()**, we call the inherited function first and then do additional processing, whereas in **OnMouseLeave()** we call the inherited function last. In situations such as this, where there are two functions that compliment each other, it's common for the order of the inherited function calls to be reversed. If you encounter a similar situation with your own code, check for this reversal. Chances are that if the inherited calling order isn't reversed, then you probably have a design error of some kind.

Another function in **Slider** is **Move()**. Recall that **Move()** is used to specify a new location for an object. In terms of the slider, this occurs when the mouse has caused the slider to move. We've overridden **Move()** so that the slider will send a message to its base window that it has been moved. We'll explore this more when we discuss how messages are used in the scroll bars. Notice that typecasting is used to access the scroll bar's **SendScrollPosn()** member function.

```
((ScrollBar *)Base)->SendScrollPosn();
```

The ScrollBar Class

Now that we have a slide bar we need to create the scroll bar that the slider will move on. The **ScrollBar** class has the following responsibilities:

1. Draws the scroll bar including its slider

2. Changes the mouse cursor whenever the mouse moves over the scroll bar

3. Sets the dimensions and locations of both the scroll bar and slider

4. Sends and receives messages to and from the base about the location of the slider

5. Moves the slider if it receives a message to do so

Its class definition is:

```
class ScrollBar : public Wso {
public:
  BarOrient Orientation;
  Slider *Slide;
  char InhibitMessage;
  ScrollBar(BarOrient Orient, ColorPak &Cp);
  virtual void SetSize(int W, int H);
  virtual void Open(Iso *B, int X, int Y);
  virtual void Redraw(void);
  virtual void OnMouseEnter(MsgPkt &M);
  virtual void OnMouseLeave(MsgPkt &M);
  virtual void OnMouseDown(MsgPkt &M);
  virtual void SendScrollPosn(void);
  virtual void RcvScrollPosn(float P, BarOrient Which);
  virtual void OnKeyStroke(MsgPkt &M);
};
```

The **ScrollBar** class presented here is similar to the text mode **ScrollBar** class created in Chapter 9. Basically, it is a derived **Wso** class with a nested **Slider** object. It can be either a horizontal or vertical scroll bar and it uses the same message passing system developed for text mode scroll bars.

Initializing Scroll Bars

The **ScrollBar()** constructor is used to initialize a scroll bar object and consists of two parts. First, it initializes a scroll bar object and then it initializes the slider object assigned to the scroll bar. Second, it sets three new flags that are introduced in the **ScrollBar** class. These flags will be examined in a moment.

Because **ScrollBar** is derived from **Wso**, its constructor chains back to the **Wso** constructor. Notice that the scroll bar's border style and frame attributes are hard coded so that it is recessed and is not moveable. This combination works well for scroll bars in graphics mode. You could pass these attributes as parameters to the **ScrollBar** constructor, however, if you want.

Next the constructor allocates memory for the **Slider** object that it contains. This is followed by a call to the **Slider**'s constructor.

Now examine the three slider bar flags that are needed. The first flag specifies the orientation of the scroll bar. It is passed as the parameter **Orient** and can either be set to **HzOrient** or **VtOrient**. Both **HzOrient** and **VtOrient** are enumerated values defined in **gscroll.h**.

The second assignment sets the **ClipToFrame** flag of the **Slide** object to **True**. Recall from Chapter 9 that this flag instructs the lower-level window management tools to allow objects drawn on the frame of the window, rather than clipping it to the window's interior. We're doing this so that we can overlap the slider on top of the frame of the scroll bar.

Finally, the flag **InhibitMessage** is set to **False**. A similar flag was used in the **ScrollBar** class in Chapter 9. Recall that it is used by the scroll bar to inhibit itself from sending unneeded messages to the base window.

One member function that is overridden in **ScrollBar** is **SetSize()**. It is overridden to handle the slider button as well as the scroll bar. The inherited **SetSize()** function is called first to set the size of the scroll bar, and then the size of the slider is set.

The size of the slider is dependent on the size of the scroll bar. Basically, we want to set the size of the slider to the width of a vertical scroll bar or the height of a horizontal scroll bar. This is the purpose of the statements:

```
if (Orientation == HzOrient)
  D = Panel->Frame->Ht - Panel->Bwd * 2;
  else D = Panel->Frame->Wd - Panel->Bwd * 2;
Slide->SetSize(D, D);
```

The calculation is a little tricky. Recall that **SetSize()** works with interior dimensions, so we must subtract from the border width of the scroll bar's frame to make the slider come out the right size.

Two other member functions that must be overridden to support the nested slider object are **Open()** and **Redraw()**. Like **SetSize()**, they must be overridden so that the slider object is opened and redrawn as well as the scroll bar. For instance, **Open()** calls the inherited function to open the scroll bar, and then follows this by opening the slider object on top of the scroll bar:

```
Wso::Open(B, X, Y);
Slide->Open(this, 0, 0);
```

Note that we set the initial position of the slider to (0,0), which is either the leftmost or topmost position of the scroll bar depending on whether the scroll bar is horizontal or vertical.

Scroll Bar Mouse Action

When we presented the **Slider** class we discussed how we had overridden the mouse event routines **OnMouseEnter()** and **OnMouseLeave()** so that they would switch between cursor styles when the mouse touches the slider. The same thing is going to be done in the **ScrollBar** class whenever the mouse touches the scroll bar. However, this time we'll switch between the default arrow cursor and the hand cursor. This is accomplished by calling the mouse member function **SetGCursor()** with the appropriate mouse cursor style in these two functions:

```
void ScrollBar::OnMouseEnter(MsgPkt &M)
// Changes the mouse cursor when it is over the scroll bar
{
  Wso::OnMouseEnter(M); // Generally call this first
  Mouse.SetGCursor(HandCursor);
}

void ScrollBar::OnMouseLeave(MsgPkt &M)
// Restores the mouse cursor when it leaves the scroll bar
{
  Mouse.SetGCursor(ArrowCursor);
  Wso::OnMouseLeave(M); // Generally call this last
}
```

ScrollBar Messages

Thus far we've described the various functions that must be added or overridden in order to create the mechanics of a scroll bar. However, now we need to discuss how the scroll bar interacts with other objects. As we did in Chapter 9, we'll tie into the event loop system provided by the **Iso** class discussed in Chapter 7. In particular, we'll introduce new event codes that the scroll bars will send to their base windows whenever they are moved. This will signal that they've been moved and that the associated windows should be updated as needed.

We won't discuss the intricate details of how the message passing works, because many of these details are identical to those in Chapter 9. (You may want to refer to Chapter 9 if you don't understand all of the code presented here.)

Basically, **SendScrollPosn()** and **RcvScrollPosn()** in the **ScrollBar** class are used to pass messages between the **Slider** and the base window. In particular, **SendScrollPosn()** uses the new event code **HzScrollMove** to return a message to the base window signaling when the horizontal slider has been moved. For example, if the scroll bar is horizontal, the following statements are used to send the message to the base window:

```
M.RtnCode = HzScrollMove;  M.Code = HzScrollMove;
M.Focus = Base; // Send message to base
M.Mx = floor(Rp * 10000.0); M.My = 0;
```

Note that the position of the scroll bar is passed in the **Mx** field of the message packet **M**. The message is actually sent by calling the base window's **Dispatch()** member function:

```
Base->Dispatch(M);
```

The only other thing to note is that we are using the same class of position encoding as we did in Chapter 9 to represent the position of the slider. That is, the ratio

```
Relative_Slider_Position / Scroll_Bar_Length
```

produces a real number between zero and one to indicate where the slider position is relative to the scroll bar. Similarly, **ScrollBar**'s **RcvScrollPosn()** function expects to receive a position command signaling where the slider should be moved to. This value is passed as the parameter **P**.

Windows with Scroll Bars

We'll combine the scroll bars we just developed with a window class. In Chapter 9 a scroll window class was written that was used to view a virtual buffer. In this chapter, we won't develop a comparable graphics mode virtual buffer. Instead, we'll develop the logic that ties together the scroll bars with the mouse and keyboard. Later we'll derive a specific example that enables us to change the size of a box within the window.

The new class that supports graphics windows with scroll bars is called **Swso**. It is also included in the files **gscroll.h** and **gscroll.cpp**. Like the **Slider** and **ScrollBar** objects described in the last several sections, **Swso** is derived from the **Wso** class. Some of the responsibilities of **Swso** are:

1. Set up and draw a window with slide bars

2. Capture scrolling messages from the scroll bars

3. Send scroll message from the scroll window to the scroll bars

The class definition for **Swso** is:

```
class Swso : public Wso {
public:
  ScrollBar *HzSlide, *VtSlide;
  Wso *Window;
```

```
Swso(int Ba, int Fa, ColorPak &Cp);
virtual void SetSize(int W, int H);
virtual void Open(Iso *B, int X, int Y);
virtual void Redraw(void);
virtual void SendScrollPosn(void) { ; }
virtual void RcvScrollPosn(float, BarOrient) { ; }
virtual void Dispatch(MsgPkt &M);
};
```

As you can see, a **Swso** object contains pointers to three nested objects: a horizontal scroll bar, a vertical scroll bar, and a display window, **Window**.

As always, we've provided a constructor for the **Swso** class. It is responsible for allocating memory for each of the nested objects and for calling their appropriate initialization routines. Note the nested display window, **Window**, is defined to be recessed and not swappable. This produces a nice looking three-dimensional effect.

Because **Swso** contains nested objects, **SetSize()**, **Open()**, and **Redraw()** are overridden. They all begin by invoking their corresponding inherited functions and then calling the corresponding member functions for each of the nested objects: **Window**, **HzSlide**, and **VtSlide**. The dimensions used in these member functions for the nested objects are calculated based on the size of the base window **Swso**. However, the width and relative location of the scroll bars and window are always the same.

Note that although we've been designing our scrollable window tools so that they pass messages back and forth corresponding to the position of the slider in the scroll bar, the **Swso** functions **SendScrollPosn()** and **RcvScrollPosn()** are simply empty stubs. Why? The reason is that many of the things that these two routines will do are application specific. Therefore, it will be the responsibility of any derived class of **Swso** to override these functions and handle the message passing as needed. An example of this will be shown in the next section.

A Sample Scrollable Window

The **Swso** class developed in the last section serves as a generic class for scrollable windows in graphics mode. It supplies us with all of the mechanics for creating a window that has two scroll bars. We must, however, derive an appropriate class that implements the specifics of a given application. In this section we'll show you how this is done by developing a simple program that displays a rectangle in the display region of a scrollable window. You'll be able to change the size of the rectangle by moving the scroll bars. This will also serve to test out **gscroll.cpp**. This new program will be called **bxstrtch.cpp** and appears at the end of this section. See Figure 11.6 for a sample of the output of this program.

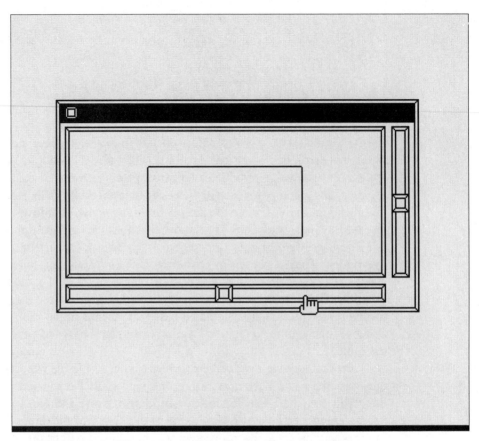

Figure 11.6   The output of the bxstrtch.cpp program

This new class, called **BoxStretcher**, is responsible for the following tasks:

1. Sets the dimensions of the box that is drawn

2. Draws the rectangle the appropriate size

3. Sends and receives messages to and from the slide bars

Its definition is:

```
class BoxStretcher : public Swso {
public:
  int BoxWd, BoxHt, MaxWd, MaxHt;
  BoxStretcher(int Ba, int Fa, ColorPak &Cp);
  virtual void SetSize(int W, int H);
  virtual void Draw(void);
  virtual void Redraw(void);
```

```
    virtual void SendScrollPosn(void);
    virtual void RcvScrollPosn(float P, BarOrient Which);
    virtual void OnKeyStroke(MsgPkt &M);
};
```

Let's take a look at the **BoxStretcher** class more closely. The **BoxStretcher** data members **BoxWd** and **BoxHt** specify the current width and height of the box that is drawn within the window. These variables are initialized to zero in the **SetSize()** member function. Similarly, the data member **MaxWd** and **MaxHt**, which correspond to the maximum width and height for drawing the box, are initialized in **SetSize()** to the interior width of **Window**.

The **BoxStretcher** class also overrides the **Draw()** member function so that the box can be drawn in its interior. The **Draw()** function uses the exclusive-OR feature to draw and erase the box figure from the rectangle. This will allow us to draw and erase the rectangle using the same function. We simply have to call it once to display the rectangle, and once again to erase the rectangle. This is the same approach we used in Chapter 10 to draw skeleton objects in graphics mode.

The **Redraw()** member function must also be overridden. The reason is tricky. The inherited **Redraw()** function causes the box to be drawn twice, but since the box is drawn by the exclusive-OR technique this effectively makes the box hidden. Therefore we must draw the box again in order for it to be visible. Thus the **Redraw()** function looks like:

```
void BoxStretcher::Redraw(void)
// Due to the inherited Redraw function drawing the box
// twice, and because it's drawn via XOR, we need to
// draw the box again to make it visible. That's the
// reason for the call to Draw below.
{
  Swso::Redraw();
  Draw();
}
```

Handling Keyboard Input

Recall that we've been overriding the **OnKeyStroke()** function in the **Slider** and **ScrollBar** objects so that they pass to their base windows any keypresses they detect. In this case, the base window is a **BoxStretcher** object. We want **Box-Stretcher** to trap the arrow keys. For this reason, we'll also override **BoxStretcher**'s **OnKeyStroke()** member function.

Pressing one of the arrow keys will cause the box to be drawn with a new size. This is accomplished by modifying **BoxWd** and **BoxHt**, which represent the current width and height of the box, according to which key is pressed. Then a message is sent to the **Slider** to command it to move appropriately. If a key other than the arrow key is pressed, the inherited version of **OnKeyStroke()** is called. This will effectively pass the keypress on to the lower-level window code. We used the keypresses in a similar way in the virtual window in Chapter 9. Take a look at what happens if the right arrow key is pressed:

```
case RightKey:
  Draw();
  if (BoxWd < MaxWd) BoxWd++;
  Draw();
  SendScrollPosn();
  break;
```

Here **RightKey** increments the box's width, **BoxWd**, each time it is executed—as long as it is already less than the maximum width allowed. Therefore, when **Draw()** is called it will use this new **BoxWd** value and cause the rectangle to be drawn a little larger. Note that because the box is drawn with exclusive-OR lines, the first call to **Draw()** erases it and the second displays it with its new size.

When you look at **OnKeyStroke()** you'll see that we've also captured the Shift-arrow key combinations. These are used so that you can make the box's size jump by increments larger than one. However, incrementing the dimensions of the box by one can be rather slow; therefore **OnKeyStroke()** allows you to press Shift-up arrow, Shift-down arrow, and so on, to alter the box's size in steps one-eighth the size of the maximum dimension allowed. Note, however, that the Shift-arrow keys were previously used to move windows on the screen. Since, we are trapping for them here, it will no longer be possible to move windows when a scrollable window is selected. For this reason, you may want to use other keys than the Shift-arrow keys to implement this feature.

Sending Messages

It is necessary to explain the functions **BoxStretcher** uses to send messages to and from the scroll bars. These messages are implemented in the overridden member functions **SendScrollPosn()** and **RcvScrollPosn()**. You've already seen how pressing a key causes the **BoxStretcher** class to invoke its **SendScrollPosn()** member function. This function sends the current position to the scroll bars so that they can update the slider locations. For simplicity, we'll always update both scroll bars each time a **SendScrollPosn()** command is issued by **BoxStretcher**. This is done by:

```
void BoxStretcher::SendScrollPosn(void)
// Sends message to slide bars to update their positions relative
```

```
// to the size of the box
{
  HzSlide->RcvScrollPosn(float(BoxWd)/float(MaxWd),HzOrient);
  VtSlide->RcvScrollPosn(float(BoxHt)/float(MaxHt),VtOrient);
}
```

Note that these statements call the **RcvScrollPosn()** functions in the scroll bars directly. We could have gone through the message packets and dispatcher, but this is far simpler. Also, notice that the position sent to the scroll bars is calculated as the box's dimension divided by its maximum value.

The **BoxStretcher**'s **RcvScrollPosn()** is only slightly more complicated. It is called by the scroll bars to update whatever is being displayed in the window in response to one of the sliders being moved. Therefore, **RcvScrollPosn()** has a call to **Draw()** to erase the box in its window and then another call to **Draw()** to redraw the box with its new size. Between these calls, the function recalculates the box's dimensions based on what value it is passed in the parameter **P** and which scroll bar is used. Recall that the **P** parameter is a real value between 0 and 1 representing the position of the slider in the scroll bar. For example, for the horizontal scroll bar the new box width is calculated by the statement:

```
if (Which == HzOrient)
  BoxWd = ceil(P * MaxWd);
  else BoxHt = ceil(P * MaxHt);
```

Before moving on, it's important to emphasize the difference between how the mouse and keyboard actions are handled. The mouse controls the slider directly. We are, however, overriding the slider **Move()** member function so that it sends a message to its scroll bar signaling the fact that it has been moved. This message in turn gets relayed to the scrollable window, which finally updates the size of the box.

The keyboard interaction is different. Keypresses are all serviced by the base window of the scrollable window. In other words, **BoxStretcher** updates the box's size based on which key is pressed, displays the box's new size, and then sends a message to the **Slider** to update its position.

The Main Program

Now that we've discussed how the **BoxStretcher** works, let's look at the main program of **bxstrtch.cpp** that puts **BoxStretcher** to use. The **bxstrtch** program displays a relief window, with a recessed window within it, that corresponds to the nested object **Window** and two scroll bars. When you run the program you can use the arrow and Shift-arrow keys to change the size of the box in the window. You can also use the mouse to click on and drag the sliders to alter the size of the box. Alternatively, you can use the mouse to click anywhere within the scroll bars to have the mouse slider jump to that location. To exit the program you can click on the close button or press the Alt-X key combination.

The main program is straightforward. The only odd statements are:

```
// Set size of box to quarter of window size
Bs->BoxWd = Bs->Window->Panel->Interior->Wd / 2;
Bs->BoxHt = Bs->Window->Panel->Interior->Ht / 2;
Bs->Draw();
Bs->SendScrollPosn();
```

These are used to force the box to initially be drawn so that it is half its maximum size. This is done by setting the **BoxWd** and **BoxHt** data members to half **MaxWd** and **MaxHt**, drawing the box with these dimensions, and then sending a message to the scroll bars to update their positions. We could have written **SetSize()** to use these dimensions by default, but we did it this way to show you how a program can interact with the scroll window.

```
// bxstrtch.cpp: Demonstrates scrollable windows in graphics mode.
// A scrollable window will appear that will allow you to inter-
// actively alter the size of a box by using the scroll bars.
// Alternatively, you can use the arrow and Shift-arrow keys
// to change the size of the box. To quit the program use ALT-X.

#include "math.h"
#include "gscroll.h"

class BoxStretcher : public Swso {
public:
  int BoxWd, BoxHt, MaxWd, MaxHt;
  BoxStretcher(int Ba, int Fa, ColorPak &Cp);
  virtual void SetSize(int W, int H);
  virtual void Draw(void);
  virtual void Redraw(void);
  virtual void SendScrollPosn(void);
  virtual void RcvScrollPosn(float P, BarOrient Which);
  virtual void OnKeyStroke(MsgPkt &M);
};

BoxStretcher::BoxStretcher(int Ba, int Fa, ColorPak &Cp)
// Initializes the box stretcher object
: Swso(Ba, Fa, Cp)
{
  BoxWd = 0; BoxHt = 0;
}

void BoxStretcher::SetSize(int W, int H)
// Sets the size of the window and the start and maximum dimensions
// of the box
{
```

```
  Swso::SetSize(W, H);
  MaxWd = Window->Panel->Interior->Wd;
  MaxHt = Window->Panel->Interior->Ht;
  if (BoxWd > MaxWd) BoxWd = MaxWd;
  if (BoxHt > MaxHt) BoxHt = MaxHt;
}

void BoxStretcher::Draw(void)
// Draws a rectangle centered in the interior of Panel
{
  Swso::Draw();
  Mouse.Hide();
  setcolor(3);
  setwritemode(XOR_PUT);
  Rso *Wi = Window->Panel->Interior;
  rectangle(Wi->Xul+Wi->Wd / 2 - BoxWd / 2,
            Wi->Yul+Wi->Ht / 2 - BoxHt / 2,
            Wi->Xul+Wi->Wd / 2 + BoxWd / 2,
            Wi->Yul+Wi->Ht / 2 + BoxHt / 2);
  setwritemode(COPY_PUT);
  Mouse.Show();
}

void BoxStretcher::Redraw(void)
// Due to the inherited Redraw function drawing the box
// twice, and because it's drawn via XOR, we need to
// draw the box again to make it visible. That's the
// reason for the call to Draw below.
{
  Swso::Redraw();
  Draw();
}

void BoxStretcher::SendScrollPosn(void)
// Sends message to slide bars to update their positions relative
// to the size of the box
{
  HzSlide->RcvScrollPosn(float(BoxWd)/float(MaxWd),HzOrient);
  VtSlide->RcvScrollPosn(float(BoxHt)/float(MaxHt),VtOrient);
}

void BoxStretcher::RcvScrollPosn(float P, BarOrient Which)
// Based on the value of P, which should be between 0 and 1,
// set the size of the box
{
  Draw();   // Erase old position of box
  if (Which == HzOrient)
    BoxWd = ceil(P * MaxWd);
    else BoxHt = ceil(P * MaxHt);
  Draw();   // Draw new box
}

void BoxStretcher::OnKeyStroke(MsgPkt &M)
// Resizes the box according to the keys pressed
```

```
  {
  switch(M.Code) {
    case UpKey:
      Draw();
      if (BoxHt > 0) BoxHt-;
      Draw();
      SendScrollPosn();    // Update bar position
      break;
    case DownKey:
      Draw();
      if (BoxHt < MaxHt) BoxHt++;
      Draw();
      SendScrollPosn();
      break;
    case LeftKey:
      Draw();
      if (BoxWd > 0) BoxWd-;
      Draw();
      SendScrollPosn();
      break;
    case RightKey:
      Draw();
      if (BoxWd < MaxWd) BoxWd++;
      Draw();
      SendScrollPosn();
      break;
    case ShiftRight:
      Draw();
      if ((BoxWd+MaxWd / 8) < MaxWd)
         BoxWd += MaxWd / 8; else BoxWd - MaxWd;
      Draw();
      SendScrollPosn();
      break;
    case ShiftLeft:
      Draw();
      if (BoxWd > (MaxWd / 8))
         BoxWd -- MaxWd / 8; else BoxWd - 0;
      Draw();
      SendScrollPosn();
      break;
    case ShiftDnKey:
      Draw();
      if ((BoxHt+MaxHt / 8) < MaxHt)
         BoxHt += MaxHt / 8; else BoxHt - MaxHt;
      Draw();
      SendScrollPosn();
      break;
    ShiftUpKey:
      Draw();
      if (BoxHt > (MaxHt / 8))
        BoxHt -- MaxHt / 8; else BoxHt - 0;
      Draw();
      SendScrollPosn();
      break;
```

```
      default: Swso::OnKeyStroke(M);
  }
}

BoxStretcher *Bs;
MsgPkt M;
int Gd, Gm;
main()
{
  Gd - DETECT;
  Setup(MouseOptional, Gd, Gm, "\\tcpp\\bgi", SANS_SERIF_FONT);
  FullScrn->Panel->Clear(' ', 0x70);
  Bs - new BoxStretcher(Relief + 3, Closeable, GrphColors);
  Bs->SetSize(301, 151);
  Bs->Open(FullScrn, 75, 75);
  // Set size of box to quarter of window size
  Bs->BoxWd - Bs->Window->Panel->Interior->Wd / 2;
  Bs->BoxHt - Bs->Window->Panel->Interior->Ht / 2;
  Bs->Draw();
  Bs->SendScrollPosn();
  MainEventLoop();
  CleanUp();
}
```

Code Critique

In this chapter we once again demonstrated the flexibility of inheritance by deriving several new graphics objects from our generic window tools. However, we could have used or added many other features. Some ideas for enhancements that you might consider are discussed in the following sections.

Merging Text and Graphics Scroll Windows

If you take a look at the code, you'll notice that many of the member functions used by the text and graphics mode scroll windows are similar. This suggests that we could have combined these common operations into a new generic base class and derived each of the specific implementations from them. This would parallel the approach we've taken, for instance, with the menuing tools.

Using Scroll Bars with Other Objects

As we did for our text scroll bars in Chapter 9, we designed the graphics scroll bars to communicate with their base windows. A more flexible design would have been to allow the scroll bars to send their slider position messages to any window.

You could accomplish this by modifying the **ScrollBar** class so that it is passed a pointer to the object that it will be communicating with. This pointer could then be used to direct messages to the target object rather than sending them to the scroll bar's base window.

Scroll Bars as Input Devices

In general, scroll bars are an excellent way of selecting an input from a range of acceptable values. For instance, you could easily build an application that uses a set of three scroll bars to interactively modify the color palette. In this program, each of the scroll bars would be dedicated to one of the three palette colors: red, green, and blue. The current setting of the color palette would be set according to the positions of each of these three scroll bars.

Listing 11.1 gbutton.h

```
// gbutton.h: graphics button class definitions

#ifndef H_GBUTTON
#define H_GBUTTON

#include "grphscrn.h"

typedef void (*ActionProc)(Wso *Src, MsgPkt &M);
typedef void (*DrawProc)(Wso *Src);

class TextButton : public Wso {
public:
  ActionProc Action;
  char Str[80];
  char Font[80];
  TextButton(char *S, char *F, int Ba, int Fa,
            ColorPak &Cp, ActionProc A);
  virtual void Draw(void);
  virtual void Activate(MsgPkt &M);
  virtual void ChangeText(char *S, char *F);
};

class IconButton : public Wso {
public:
  ActionProc Action;
  DrawProc DrawIcon;
  IconButton(DrawProc D, int Ba, int Fa, ColorPak &Cp, ActionProc A);
  virtual void Draw(void);
  virtual void Activate(MsgPkt &M);
};
```

```
// ————————— Some common button actions —————————

void NoOp(Wso *Src, MsgPkt &M);
void ExitAction(Wso *Src, MsgPkt &M);

#endif
```

Listing 11.2   gbutton.cpp

```
// gbutton.cpp: graphics button class implementations

#include <string.h>
#include "gbutton.h"

// ————————————— TextButton —————————————

TextButton::TextButton(char *S, char *F, int Ba, int Fa,
                       ColorPak &Cp, ActionProc A)
: Wso(Ba, Fa, Cp)
{
  strcpy(Str, S);
  strcpy(Font, F);
  SetSize(25, 25);  // Default size
  Action = A;
}

void TextButton::ChangeText(char *S, char *F)
// Redisplays the text on a button with the new string S and
// the new font F
{
  strcpy(Str, S);
  strcpy(Font, F);
  Draw();
}

void TextButton::Draw(void)
// Scales and writes the text within a button
{
  if (*Str == 0) return;
  Rso *Pint = Panel->Interior;
  setusercharsize(1,1,1,1);
  setusercharsize(Pint->Wd, textwidth(Str),
                  Pint->Ht, textheight(Str) * 4 / 3);
  // Clear out where text is to appear
  Mouse.Hide();
  Pint->Fill(0, 0, Pint->Wd, Pint->Ht, ' ', Panel->Colors.Wc);
  // Write the text centered on the face of the button
  setviewport(Pint->Xul,Pint->Yul,Pint->Xlr,Pint->Ylr,True);
  setcolor(ForeGround(Panel->Colors.Wc));
  settextjustify(CENTER_TEXT, CENTER_TEXT);
  outtextxy(Pint->Wd/2+2, Pint->Ht/2, Str);
```

```
  // Restore clip region to whole screen
  setviewport(0, 0, getmaxx(), getmaxy(), True);
  Mouse.Show();
}

void TextButton::Activate(MsgPkt &M)
// Performs the buttons action if the object is currently
// selected, else the button is deselected
{
  if (Active) {
    Wso::Activate(M);
    Action(this, M);
  }
  else Leave(M);
}


// ——————— IconButton ———————

IconButton::IconButton(DrawProc D, int Ba, int Fa,
                       ColorPak &Cp, ActionProc A)
: Wso(Ba, Fa, Cp)
{
  SetSize(25, 25);  // Default size
  DrawIcon = D;
  Action = A;
}

void IconButton::Draw(void)
// Draws the icon in the button's interior after calling
// the inherited version of Draw
{
  Wso::Draw();
  DrawIcon(this);
}

void IconButton::Activate(MsgPkt &M)
// Performs the buttons action if the object is currently
// selected, else the button is deselected
{
  if (Active) {
    Wso::Activate(M);
    Action(this, M);
  }
  else Leave(M);
}

// ——— Common button actions defined ———

void NoOp(Wso *, MsgPkt &)
// A sample action that doesn't do anything
{
  ;
}
```

```
void ExitAction(Wso *, MsgPkt &M)
// A sample action that causes the window system to shutdown
{
  M.RtnCode = ShutDown;
}
```

Listing 11.3   gscroll.h

```
// gscroll.h: provides classes to draw scroll bars and scroll bar
// windows in graphics mode

#ifndef H_GSCROLL
#define H_GSCROLL

#include "grphscrn.h"

const int HzScrollMove = 0xfe00;
const int VtScrollMove = 0xfe01;
const int BorderWd = 3;    // Border width is 3 pixels

enum BarOrient { HzOrient, VtOrient };

class Slider : public Wso {
public:
  Slider(ColorPak &Cp);
  virtual void Move(int X, int Y);
  virtual void OnMouseEnter(MsgPkt &M);
  virtual void OnMouseLeave(MsgPkt &M);
  virtual void OnMouseDown(MsgPkt &M);
  virtual void OnKeyStroke(MsgPkt &M);
};

class ScrollBar : public Wso {
public:
  BarOrient Orientation;
  Slider *Slide;
  char InhibitMessage;
  ScrollBar(BarOrient Orient, ColorPak &Cp);
  virtual void SetSize(int W, int H);
  virtual void Open(Iso *B, int X, int Y);
  virtual void Redraw(void);
  virtual void OnMouseEnter(MsgPkt &M);
  virtual void OnMouseLeave(MsgPkt &M);
  virtual void OnMouseDown(MsgPkt &M);
  virtual void SendScrollPosn(void);
  virtual void RcvScrollPosn(float P, BarOrient Which);
  virtual void OnKeyStroke(MsgPkt &M);
};

class Swso : public Wso {
public:
```

```
    ScrollBar *HzSlide, *VtSlide;
    Wso *Window;
    Swso(int Ba, int Fa, ColorPak &Cp);
    virtual void SetSize(int W, int H);
    virtual void Open(Iso *B, int X, int Y);
    virtual void Redraw(void);
    virtual void SendScrollPosn(void) { ; }
    virtual void RcvScrollPosn(float, BarOrient) { ; }
    virtual void Dispatch(MsgPkt &M);
};

#endif
```

Listing 11.4   gscroll.cpp

```
// gscroll.cpp: graphics scroll window class implementations

#include "math.h"
#include "gscroll.h"

// ——————— Slider type ———————

Slider::Slider(ColorPak &Cp)
// Initialize the object that represents the slider
: Wso(Relief+BorderWd, Swappable, Cp)
{
  return;
}

void Slider::OnMouseEnter(MsgPkt &M)
// Changes the mouse cursor when it is on the slider
{
  Wso::OnMouseEnter(M);        // Generally call this first
  if (((ScrollBar *)Base)->Orientation == HzOrient)
    Mouse.SetGCursor(LeftRightCursor);
    else Mouse.SetGCursor(UpDownCursor);
}

void Slider::OnMouseLeave(MsgPkt &M)
// Restores the mouse cursor when the mouse leaves the slider
{
  Mouse.SetGCursor(ArrowCursor);
  Wso::OnMouseLeave(M);
}

void Slider::OnMouseDown(MsgPkt &M)
// Moves the slider when the mouse is anywhere within the slider
{
  SwitchFocus(M);
  BorderHandler(M);
}
```

```
void Slider::Move(int X, int Y)
// Moves the slider to a new absolute coordinate
{
  Wso::Move(X, Y);
  ((ScrollBar *)Base)->SendScrollPosn();
}


void Slider::OnKeyStroke(MsgPkt &M)
// Sends keystrokes to slider bar
{
  Base->OnKeyStroke(M);
}


// ——————— ScrollBar type ———————

ScrollBar::ScrollBar(BarOrient Orient, ColorPak &Cp)
// Initializes a scroll bar object with a slider within it
: Wso(Recessed+BorderWd, 0x00, Cp)
{
  Orientation = Orient;
  Slide = new Slider(Cp);
  // Allow slider to overlap with the frame of the scroll bar
  Slide->ClipToFrame = True;
  InhibitMessage = False;
}

void ScrollBar::SetSize(int W, int H)
// Sets the size of the scroll bar and slider depending
// on whether it is horizontally or vertically oriented
{
  int D;
  Wso::SetSize(W,H);
  if (Orientation == HzOrient)
    D = Panel->Frame->Ht - Panel->Bwd * 2;
    else D = Panel->Frame->Wd - Panel->Bwd * 2;
  Slide->SetSize(D, D);
}

void ScrollBar::Open(Iso *B, int X, int Y)
// Opens the scroll bar and the slider within it
{
  Wso::Open(B, X, Y);
  Slide->Open(this, 0, 0);
}

void ScrollBar::Redraw(void)
// Redraw the bar and the slider
{
  Wso::Redraw();
  Slide->Redraw();
}
```

```
void ScrollBar::OnMouseEnter(MsgPkt &M)
// Changes the mouse cursor when it is over the scroll bar
{
  Wso::OnMouseEnter(M); // Generally call this first
  Mouse.SetGCursor(HandCursor);
}

void ScrollBar::OnMouseLeave(MsgPkt &M)
// Restores the mouse cursor when it leaves the scroll bar
{
  Mouse.SetGCursor(ArrowCursor);
  Wso::OnMouseLeave(M); // Generally call this last
}

void ScrollBar::OnMouseDown(MsgPkt &M)
// Moves the slider to the location where the mouse was just pressed
{
  if (Panel->OnInterior(M.Mx, M.My)) {
    Slide->Move(M.Mx, M.My);
    // Need to do this so you can leave the mouse button down
    // and still move
    Slide->OnMouseDown(M);
  }
}

void ScrollBar::SendScrollPosn(void)
// Sends a message to the base window to report the current
// location of the slider
{
  int Ip;
  float Rp;
  MsgPkt M;
  if (InhibitMessage) return;
  if (Orientation == HzOrient) {
    // Compute relative position of slider in slidebar
    Ip = Slide->Panel->Interior->Xul - Panel->Interior->Xul;
    if (Ip == 0) {
      Rp = 0.0;
    }
    else {
      int X = Panel->Interior->Wd-1-(Slide->Panel->Overall->Wd-1) / 2;
      Rp = float(Ip) / float(X);
    }
    // Send a message to base to update according to the new
    // location of the slider
    M.RtnCode = HzScrollMove;  M.Code = HzScrollMove;
    M.Focus = Base; // Send message to base
    M.Mx = floor(Rp * 10000.0); M.My = 0;
  }
  else {
    Ip = SubMgr->Top->Panel->Interior->Yul - Panel->Interior->Yul;
    if (Ip == 0) {
      Rp = 0.0;
```

```
      }
      else {
        int Y - Panel->Interior->Ht-1-(Slide->Panel->Overall->Ht-1) / 2;
        Rp - float(Ip)/float(Y);
      }
      M.RtnCode - VtScrollMove;  M.Code - VtScrollMove;
      M.Focus - Base; // Send message to base
      M.My - floor(Rp * 10000.0); M.Mx - 0;
   }
   Base->Dispatch(M);
}

void ScrollBar::RcvScrollPosn(float P, BarOrient Which)
// This function takes the number P, between 0.0 and 1.0, and
// cause the Slider to move to the appropriate position
{
   int NewPos;
   if (Which - HzOrient) {
     // Compute relative position to move slider within slidebar
     float Rx - Panel->Interior->Wd-1-(Slide->Panel->Overall->Wd-1)/2;
     NewPos - ceil(P*Rx);
     InhibitMessage - True;
     Slide->Move(Panel->Overall->Xul+NewPos,Panel->Overall->Yul);
     InhibitMessage - False;
   }
   else {
     // Compute relative position to move slider within slidebar
     float Ry - Panel->Interior->Ht-1-(Slide->Panel->Overall->Ht-1)/2;
     NewPos - ceil(P*Ry);
     InhibitMessage - True;
     Slide->Move(Panel->Overall->Xul,NewPos+Panel->Overall->Yul);
     InhibitMessage - False;
   }
}

void ScrollBar::OnKeyStroke(MsgPkt &M)
// Sends keystrokes to base window
{
   Base->OnKeyStroke(M);
}

// ———— ScrollBar window type (Swso) ————

Swso::Swso(int Ba, int Fa, ColorPak &Cp)
// Initializes a scroll window with two scroll bars
// and an interior window
: Wso(Ba, Fa, Cp)
{
   Window - new Wso(Recessed+BorderWd, 0x00, Cp);
   HzSlide - new ScrollBar(HzOrient, Cp);
   VtSlide - new ScrollBar(VtOrient, Cp);
}
```

```
void Swso::SetSize(int W, int H)
// Set the size of the Swso object and the nested scroll bars.
// Note: We have to relocate the scroll bars too. SetLocn has
// no way of knowing they need to be relocated if the window
// is resized.
{
  Wso::SetSize(W, H);
  Window->SetSize(W-Panel->Bwd*2-30, H-Panel->Bwd*2-28);
  HzSlide->SetSize(W-Panel->Bwd*2-30, 9);
  HzSlide->SetLocn(Panel->Bwd+2, Panel->Interior->Ht-
                  HzSlide->Panel->Interior->Ht-
                  HzSlide->Panel->Bwd*2-Panel->Bwd-2, Relc);
  VtSlide->SetSize(9, H-Panel->Bwd*2-28);
  VtSlide->SetLocn(Panel->Interior->Wd-Panel->Bwd-
                  VtSlide->Panel->Interior->Wd-
                  VtSlide->Panel->Bwd*2-2, Panel->Bwd, Relc);
}

void Swso::Open(Iso *B, int X, int Y)
{
  Wso::Open(B, X, Y);
  Window->Open(this, Panel->Bwd+2, Panel->Bwd);
  HzSlide->Open(this, Panel->Bwd+2, Panel->Interior->Ht-
                     HzSlide->Panel->Interior->Ht-
                     HzSlide->Panel->Bwd*2-Panel->Bwd-2);
  VtSlide->Open(this, Panel->Interior->Wd-Panel->Bwd-
                     VtSlide->Panel->Interior->Wd-
                     VtSlide->Panel->Bwd*2-2, Panel->Bwd);
}

void Swso::Redraw()
// Redraw the window, interior window, and scroll bars
{
  Wso::Redraw();
  Window->Redraw();
  HzSlide->Redraw();
  VtSlide->Redraw();
}

void Swso::Dispatch(MsgPkt &M)
// Traps messages from the scroll bar and sends them to RcvScrollPosn
// to interpret them
{
  if (M.Code == HzScrollMove) {
     RcvScrollPosn(float(M.Mx) / 10000.0, HzOrient);
     M.RtnCode = M.Code = Idle;
  }
  else if (M.Code == VtScrollMove) {
     RcvScrollPosn(float(M.My) / 10000.0, VtOrient);
     M.RtnCode = M.Code = Idle;
  }
  else Wso::Dispatch(M);
}
```

A Turbo C++
Survival Guide

C++ offers two types of extensions to the C language: those that make it a "better C" (such as stronger type-checking) and the object-oriented extensions. In this book, we've assumed that you are familiar with these extensions. In this Appendix, the object-oriented extensions are summarized. In particular, a review of the rules and syntax for doing OOP is provided, and we also point out those tips, tricks, and techniques that have been used in this book in developing sophisticated object-oriented programs. First, we start with the basics—defining classes.

Defining Classes

Classes are extensions to C structures. They define types of objects. In addition to having variables as members, classes can have functions as members. Also, with classes, you can restrict access to class members. Thus, there are three basic components to classes: variable declarations, function declarations, and access control declarations. These declarations can be listed in the class definition in any order. Classes are defined using the following general syntax:

```
<class-keyword> <class-name> {
  <access-control declaration>:
  ...
  <variable declaration>;
  ...
```

```
<function declaration>;
  ...
};
```

Here is a sample class that knows how to tally up numbers:

```
class Tally {
private:
  float Total;
public:
  void Reset(void);
  void Add(float Amt);
  float GetTotal(void);
};
```

Classes have two types of members: *instance variables* and *member functions*. Instance variables are the data portion of the object, and the member functions are used to act on the data. There is one instance variable in the **Tally** class, **Total**, and three member functions, **Reset()**, **Add()**, and **GetTotal()**. Note that the instance variables can be of any type, including other objects. This means you can have objects that are nested, just as you can have structures that are nested.

Our sample class is split into two sections having different access levels: *public* and *private*. Those members listed in the private section (in this case, the variable **Total**) can be accessed only by the member functions of the class. Those members listed in the public section (functions **Reset()**, **Add()**, and **GetTotal()**) are accessible outside the class.

The **Tally** class illustrates a typical configuration, with the instance variables private, and the member functions public. In that manner, the data portion of the class is kept hidden, and can be accessed only indirectly through the member functions.

Implementing Member Functions

The member functions can be implemented either inside or outside the class definition. In the first case, the functions are known as *inline member functions*. Here's the **Tally** class rewritten to have inline member functions:

```
class Tally {
private:
  float Total;
public:
  void Reset(void)       { Total = 0.0;  }
  void Add(float Amt);  { Total += Amt; }
  float GetTotal(void); { return Total; }
};
```

Inline functions are similar to macros, in that the body of the function is inserted inline into the code, with the appropriate parameter substitutions. Inline member functions should be used for very small functions, such as that shown for the **Tally** class.

In most cases, the member functions are implemented outside the class definition. The syntax used is adapted from normal function implementations:

```
<Return type> <Class name>::<Function name>(<arg1, ...>)
{
  // Code for member function goes here }
}
```

Note how the name of a member function header is composed of two parts: the class name and the function name. The **::** operator is used to join the two parts. By including the class name in the header, we tell the compiler which class the function belongs to.

Here is the **Reset()** member function for the **Tally** class if it were to be implemented outside the class:

```
void Tally::Reset(void)
// Resets the Total field
{
  Total = 0.0;
}
```

Creating and Using Objects

Once a class has been defined, objects of that type can be declared and used. Declaring an object is similar to declaring other variables: You specify the type followed by the object name. We can declare a **Tally** object in the following manner:

```
Tally T; // Declare Tally object T
```

You access the members of an object, that is, the instance variables and member functions, in the same way you access the members of a structure—by using the dot notation. For example, here's a code fragment that creates and uses a **Tally** object:

```
main()
{
  Tally T;     // Declare Tally object
  T.Reset();   // Reset total amount
  T.Add(4.0);  // Add some amounts to it
```

```
T.Add(17.0);
printf("The total is: %f\n", T.GetTotal());
}
```

In this example, we're accessing the member functions **Reset()**, **Add()**, and **GetTotal()**, through the object **T**. Note that we can't have any statements directly accessing the member **Total**, because it is a private variable. If we had declared **Total** public, we could have written statements such as:

```
T.Total *= 2; // Double the total amount
```

Understanding the this Parameter

Member functions have direct access to the instance variables of an object. Let's take another look at the **Add()** function of the **Tally** class:

```
void Tally::Add(float Amt)
// Add the amount Amt to the total
{
  Total += Amt;
}
```

It's easy to understand where **Amt** comes from—it's a parameter to the function. But how is it that **Add()** can use the **Tally** instance variable **Total**? From which object does **Total** come from? The secret lies in a special hidden parameter that is passed along with the parameters you supply. This hidden parameter is called **this**. It's actually passed as the first parameter and points to the object making the call. Take, for example, the function **Tally::Add()**. It's as though the function is coded as:

```
void Tally::Add(Tally *this, float Amt)
// Add Amt to the total
{
  this->Total += Amt;
}
```

Suppose you have a **Tally** object called **T**, and you make a call to the **Add()** function **T.Add(4)**. Internally, Turbo C++ translates this call to look like **T.Add(&T, 4)**. Here, **this** points the object **T**.

You usually don't need to be concerned with the **this** parameter because it's passed for you automatically. However, sometimes you must use **this** explicitly to remove ambiguities with other variables or when passing an object from within a member function.

Using Constructors and Destructors

Objects differ from other variables in that you can specify routines to be called when the objects are created and destroyed. These routines are called *constructors* and *destructors*.

Constructors and destructors are member functions declared in a special way. They have the same name as the name of the class (with destructors, that name is preceded by a ~ symbol). Also, they have no return type, and in the case of destructors, no arguments. Here is the general syntax for constructors and destructors:

```
// Syntax for constructors
<class name>::<class name>(<arg1, ...>)
{
  // Constructor body
}

// Syntax for destructors
<class name>::~<class name>(void) // Note ~ symbol
{
  // Destructor body
}
```

The code for a constructor and destructor can be defined inside or outside of a class body, just like any other member function. For example, here's how we might add an inline constructor and destructor to our **Tally** class:

```
class Tally {
private:
  float Total;
public:
  Tally(void) {
    printf("Powering up tally machine ...\n");
    Reset(); // Clear Total
  } // Constructor declaration, return type not allowed
  ~Tally(void) {
    printf("Powering down tally machine ...\n");
  } // Destructor declaration, return type not allowed
  void Reset(void)     { Total = 0.0;  }
  void Add(float Amt);  { Total += Amt; }
  float GetTotal(void); { return Total; }
};
```

Constructors are called when objects are declared and destructors are called when objects are destroyed. That is, if an object is declared inside a function, the constructor is called when program execution reaches the statement that the object is declared in. The destructor is called just before the function returns. For global objects (objects not declared inside any function), the constructor is called before

main() is executed, and the destructor is called after **main()** completes but before the program exits.

For example, if the following program were executed:

```
main()
{
  Tally T; // Constructor called at time of declaration
  T.Add(42.0);
  printf("The total is: %4.2f\n", T.GetTotal());
  // Destructor implicitly called at end of function
}
```

it would output the following:

```
Powering up tally machine ...
The total is: 42.0
Powering down tally machine ...
```

Unlike destructors, a class can have several constructors as long as the constructors have different argument types. The compiler distinguishes between the constructors by selecting the one that has argument types that match those used in the call. Here's how to declare a **Tally** object that has a constructor with one argument:

```
Tally T(42.0); // Create object, call constructor
```

It looks as though we're calling the function **T()**. Actually, we're not. Instead, we're calling a **Tally** constructor that takes one argument.

Creating Dynamic Objects

The **Tally** object **T** that we've been working with is a *static object*. Therefore, memory for the object is allocated in the data segment of the program. You can also create *dynamic objects*—that is, objects allocated off the heap. You do this by declaring a pointer to an object, then using the two special C++ operators **new** and **delete** to allocate and deallocate space for the object. For example:

```
main()
{
  T *TallyPtr;          // Declare pointer to object
  TallyPtr = new Tally; // Allocate object
  TallyPtr->Add(42.0);  // Call member function of object
  delete TallyPtr;      // Dispose object
}
```

Note how we reference the member function **Add()** using the -> operator, the same as we would for any member of a structure referenced by a pointer.

The operators **new** and **delete** take the place of the C functions **malloc()** and **free()**. These new operators are designed to call an object's constructor or destructor, respectively, if it has one.

It's important to understand the sequence of events when using constructors and destructors in conjunction with **new** and **delete**. For calls to **new**, the memory is allocated and then the constructor is called. For calls to **delete**, the destructor is called and then the memory is freed.

Our example used the **Tally** constructor taking no arguments. Its also possible to use **new** in conjunction with constructors that take arguments. For example, using the **Tally** constructor with one argument, you could write:

```
Tally *TallyPtr - new Tally(17.0);
```

which would allocate memory for a **Tally** object and initialize its **Total** field to 17.0.

You can also create arrays of objects on the heap. For instance, the following code allocates space for 10 **Tally** objects, then deallocates them:

```
// Allocate room for 10 tally machines
Tally *Parallel_Processors - new Tally[10];
// Deallocate the 10 tally machines
delete[10] Parallel_Processors;
```

Note how we had to tell **delete** how many **Tally** objects to deallocate. Otherwise, it wouldn't know, and would only deallocate one **Tally** object, even though **Parallel_Processors** points to 10 objects.

Deriving New Classes

Once you've defined a class, you can extend its capabilities by deriving a new class. The derived class can inherit all the capabilities of the old class, while providing new ones as well.

You derive a new class by using the same class definition syntax provided earlier, but with a slight addition. Following the name of the new class, you give the name of the old class, the names separated by a colon and a possible access control specifier:

```
class <derived-class> : <access-keyword> <base-class> {
  <new instance variable declarations>;
  <new function declarations>;
};
```

The class that's being inherited is called the *base*, *parent*, or *ancestor* class. The new class is called the *derived* or *child* class. To provide you with an example, we'll start with the **Tally** class and derive a new class that counts how many tallies are made, so that we can compute the average of the tallies. For now we'll use a simplified version of the **Tally** class, one that has no private members, and has no constructors or destructors.

```
class Tally {
public:
  float Total;
  void Reset(void)          { Total = 0.0;  }
  virtual void Add(float Amt); { Total += Amt; }
  float GetTotal(void);       { return Total; }
};

class SmarterTally : public Tally {
public:
  int NumTallies;                  // New data: number of tallies made
  void Reset(void) {
    Total = 0.0;
    NumTallies = 0;
  } // Overidden Reset() function
  virtual void Add(float Amt) {
    NumTallies++;
    Total += Amt;
  }  // Overidden virtual Add() function
  float GetAverage(void) {
    return NumTallies ? GetTotal() / NumTallies : 0;
  }      // New function to compute average
};
```

The **SmarterTally** class inherits all the instance variables and functions of the **Tally** class. This means it has the variable **Total**, and the functions **Reset()**, **Add()**, and **GetTotal()**. In addition, the **SmarterTally** class adds the variable **NumTallies** and the function **GetAverage()**. However, the **SmarterTally** class also adds new versions of the functions **Reset()** and **Add()**. These functions override the **Tally** class versions of **Reset()** and **Add()** in **SmarterTally** objects.

How can you distinguish between the two **Reset()** and two **Add()** functions? Recall that each function has a class name included in its definition. Thus, the two **Reset()** functions can be referred to as **Tally::Reset()** and **SmarterTally::Reset()**. Likewise, the two **Add()** functions can be referred to as **Tally::Add()** and **Smarter-Tally::Add()**. You'll see notation such as this whenever there is the potential for confusion between two functions with the same name.

There are actually three approaches to adding functions to a derived class:

1. Add a new function with a unique name.

2. Add a new function with the same name as one from the base class.

3. Add a new function with the same name as one from the base class, but make it *virtual*.

Approach 1 was used when we added the function **GetAverage()** to the **SmarterTally** class. Approach 2 was used with the function **Reset()**. And approach 3 was used with the function **Add()**. This approach involves the use of *virtual functions*—the true power behind deriving classes. But before we tell you what virtual functions are, you need to learn about *polymorphism*, a powerful feature of Turbo C++.

Polymorphism

The term *polymorphism* means to "take on many shapes." In the context of OOP, it means to have functions with the same name that take on different actions. Recall that functions with the same name are called overloaded functions. In our **SmarterTally** class, we overloaded the functions **Reset()** and **Add()**, since functions with these names existed in the base class **Tally**. Let's investigate how overloaded functions like these are called. In the following example, we declare a **Tally** and **SmartTally** object, and then call **Reset()** and **Add()** for both of them.

```
main()
{
  Tally T;       // Declare Tally object
  SmartTally S;  // Declare SmarterTally object

  T.Reset();     // Causes Tally::Reset() to be called
  S.Reset();     // Causes SmarterTally::Reset() to be called

  T.Add();       // Causes Tally::Add() to be called
  S.Add()        // Causes SmarterTally::Add() to be called.
}
```

The function calls to **Reset()** look the same for the two objects. However, the action taken is different, since different functions are actually being called. In particular, for the object **S**, **SmarterTally::Reset()** is called, causing both the **Total** and **NumTallies** variables to be reset, whereas for the object **T**, just the **Total** variable is reset by the **Tally::Reset()** function. A similar situation occurs for the calls to **Add()**.

There are actually two forms of polymorphism, static and dynamic, which has to do with how it is determined which overloaded function to call. In the next section we'll investigate the difference, and you'll see where virtual functions come into play.

Virtual Functions

The process used to link a function call with the actual code for that function is called *function binding*. In a normal procedure or function call, the compiler determines the address of the routine and uses that to create a jump to the routine's code. Since this is done statically at compile-time, the process is called *static* or *early binding*.

By default, the functions of an object are called using static binding. In our earlier example, the appropriate **Reset()** and **Add()** function is determined by looking at the types of the objects. For example, in the call **T.Reset()**, the compiler sees that the type of **T** is **Tally**, so it causes the **Tally::Reset()** function to be used. Likewise, since the type of **S** is **SmarterTally**, the call **S.Reset()** causes **SmarterTally::Reset()** to be used.

Suppose we changed our example to use pointers instead:

```
main()
{
  Tally *Tp - new Tally;
  SmarterTally *Sp - new SmarterTally;
  Tp->Reset();
  Sp->Reset();
  Tp->Add();
  Sp->Add();
}
```

When a normal member function is called through a pointer to an object, the compiler looks at the type of the pointer to determine what function to call. Thus, in **Tp->Reset()**, the compiler knows that **Tally::Reset()** should be called, since **Tp** is a pointer to a **Tally** object. Likewise, the compiler knows that, with **Sp->Reset()**, **SmarterTally::Reset()** should be called. Even though pointers are involved, the function binding is still determined at compile time, so the binding is static.

In contrast, the **Add()** functions use dynamic binding, since they are declared virtual. As a result, the addresses of the **Add** functions are found through a table lookup conducted at runtime. Each object has a pointer to such a table and, if the objects belong to different types (as is the case here), the objects point to different tables.

The table for the object pointed to by **Tp** is used in the call to **Tp->Add()**. This table contains the address for **Tally::Add()**, so that's the function called. A similar process happens with the call to **Sp->Add()**, except that, in this case, **SmarterTally::Add()** is called. In both cases, the call is bound dynamically, at runtime, and thus the binding is dynamic. Note that the decision to use static or dynamic binding is not based on whether pointers to objects are used. Instead, the decision is made based on whether virtual functions are used.

With virtual functions, the object itself always determines which function gets called. This makes polymorphism work correctly even when tricky pointer assignments are involved.

To achieve maximum flexibility with a class, all its member functions (besides the constructors, as you'll see later) should be declared as virtual. This way, any derived class that wants to override a function can do so easily, without need to modify the code of the base class. Also, the overriding process will work in both static and dynamic settings.

Using Parameters in Virtual Functions

A virtual function in a derived class must have the same number and type of parameters as its base class counterpart. Otherwise, the derived class won't work properly. The following code fragment shows an example:

```
class Lock {
public:
  int TumblerPositions[3];
  virtual void Setup(int A, int B, int C);
};

class PaddleLock : public Lock {
public:
  int Paddle;
  // What happens here?
  virtual void Setup(int A, int B, int C, int P);
};
```

In this example, the **Setup()** function in the derived class has an extra parameter. What happens in this case? Well, even though both **Setup()** functions are virtual, they are not related to each other. For example, in the following code, the **Lock::Setup()** function is called even though **L** points to a **PaddleLock** object.

```
Lock *L;
PaddleLock P;
...
L = &P;
L->Setup(1, 2, 3);
```

Looking Inside Objects

Using virtual functions assures you maximum flexibility for your classes. However, that flexibility comes at a price, since virtual functions have more overhead than normal functions, as you'll see next.

Virtual functions in C++ are implemented by way of a table of function pointers. Each class has such a table, which is known as a *virtual function table* (VFT). Each virtual function of a class has a corresponding pointer in this array.

Figure A.1 presents the VFT for the following class:

```
class Image {
public:
  char *Bitmap;
  unsigned Size;
  Image(unsigned S);
  virtual ~Image(void);
  virtual void Show(void);
};
```

To call a virtual function, C++ must be able to find the appropriate VFT. This is accomplished by including a pointer in each object that points to the VFT for that class of object. This pointer is hidden from view—you don't have to worry about it. When a virtual function is called, the VFT pointer is used to find the VFT. At this point, the VFT is indexed to the appropriate entry. That entry contains another pointer to the corresponding function. This pointer is then dereferenced to make the call.

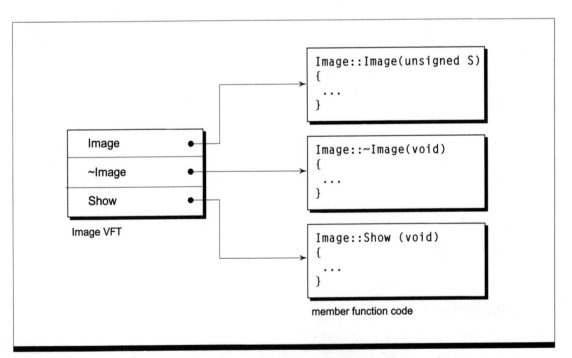

Figure A.1   The virtual function table for the Image class

Thus, to access a virtual function, two pointer dereferences take place. In most cases, this additional overhead is not noticeable. However, if you're calling a function in a time-critical loop, you may want to make the function nonvirtual so that the VFT doesn't have to be accessed.

It's important to realize that a class has only one VFT, regardless of the number of objects created from that class. Thus, the memory overhead incurred from using a virtual function (other than the additional code for the pointer dereferences) is one VFT per class, and one pointer per object.

Even though the VFT is shared between all objects of an class, each object has its own copies of the instance variables, including its own VFT pointer.

Just as there is only one VFT for any given class, there is only one copy of the member functions, too. The fact that objects created from the same class use the same member functions can lead to a few surprises. For instance, suppose you have a local static variable in a function. This variable will retain its value between function calls, regardless of which object calls the function.

Assignment Compatibility between Objects

You've already seen how it's possible to use a base class pointer to point to an object from a derived class, but it's worth investigating this technique in greater detail. Suppose we derive a **Circle** class from a **Location** class:

```
class Location {
public:
  float X,Y;
};

class Circle : public Location {
public:
  float Radius;
};
```

The following statements illustrate both correct and incorrect ways of performing assignments with pointers to objects of these classes:

```
Location *L;
Circle *C;
...
L = C; // Legal: base type pointer = derived type pointer
C = L; // Illegal: can't go the other way around
```

Note that the first assignment is legal, but the second assignment is not because a base class pointer can't be assigned to a derived class pointer. To see why, assume we've tried to execute the following statements:

```
C - L;          // Location pointer to Circle pointer }
C->Radius - 15; // Oops!!
```

The first assignment statement sets **C** to point to **L**. This means that the second statement, which accesses the instance variable **C->Radius**, is actually trying to access **L->Radius**. The problem is that the object pointed to by **L**, being a **Location**, doesn't have a radius!

Besides using pointers, you can also assign derived class objects to base class objects directly. For instance:

```
Location L; // No longer a pointer
Circle C;   // No longer a pointer
...
L - C;      // Copies data from C to L
```

When you do an assignment such as this, only the instance variables that were defined in the base type are copied. Thus, **C.X** and **C.Y** are copied to **L**, but **C.Radius** is not. As with object pointers, you can't make the assignment the other way around. You can't, for instance, assign **L** to **C** because **C** expects to have a radius copied to it, and **L** doesn't have one.

Passing Objects as Parameters

The assignment compatibility rule also applies to objects passed as parameters. That is, it's legal to pass an object of a derived class where a base class object is expected. In fact, it's quite common to do so. Suppose we have a routine that prints the coordinates of a **Location**. We could pass this routine either **Location** objects or **Circle** objects, because **Circle** is derived from **Location**:

```
void ShowLocation(Location L)
{
  printf("X - %f, Y - %f\n", L.X, L.Y);
}

Location L;
Circle C;
...
ShowLocation(L); // Print Location L's coordinates
ShowLocation(C); // Print Circle C's coordinates
```

If we had derived another class from **Circle**, such as a **Cylinder** class, we could pass a **Cylinder** object to our print routine also. This is true even if we hadn't thought of cylinders when the print routine was written. Thus, having assignment compatibility between base and derived class pointers is a major key in allowing us to write reusable code.

As you might expect, it's illegal to do the reverse. You can't pass a base class object where a derived class object is expected. In the previous example, we passed objects by value. That means a copy of the object was made and that copy was used in the function. As is the case when you assign a derived class object to a base class object, only those instance variables defined in the base class are actually copied.

Note that if you pass an object by reference or using a pointer no object data is actually copied; only the address of the object is passed to the functions.

Parameter Passing and Polymorphism

Apart from the fact that no data is copied when an object is passed by reference, there is a world of difference between passing an object by value and passing it by reference. That difference comes about when you're using derived types and polymorphism. The following program illustrates the difference:

```
// polypass.cpp

#include <stdio.h>

class GrandParent {
public:
  virtual void GiveAdvice(void) { printf("Learn to enjoy life!\n"); }
};

class Parent : public GrandParent {
public:
  virtual void GiveAdvice(void) { printf("Do your homework!\n"); }
};

void SayIt(GrandParent X)
// Uses pass by value
{
  X.GiveAdvice();
}

void SayIt2(GrandParent &X);
// Uses pass by reference
{
  X.GiveAdvice;
}

void SayIt3(GrandParent *X);
// Uses a pointer for pass by reference
```

```
{
  X->GiveAdvice;
}

main()
{
  Parent P;
  SayIt(P);   // Pass by value }
  SayIt2(P);  // Pass by reference }
  SayIt3(P); // Pass by reference with pointer
}
```

In our example, we have three procedures that are all passed a **GrandParent** object. The first procedure uses pass by value, the others use pass by reference. We create a **Parent** object and pass it to each of these three procedures.

Can you guess what this program produces when it's run? You might be surprised:

```
Learn to enjoy life!
Do your homework!
Do your homework!
```

You might think that, because **P** is a **Parent** type, in all three procedure calls the message printed would be "Do your homework." However, that only happens for the two pass by reference cases. Why doesn't it work right in the call to **SayIt**, which uses pass by value? When the copy of **P** is made, the copy is typed as a **Grand-Parent** object, since that's what **SayIt** thinks the parameter type is. Thus, the copy's VFT pointer, which points to **GrandParent**'s VFT, is used to make the virtual function call, and the message "Learn to enjoy life!" is printed. In the calls to **SayIt2** and **SayIt3**, no copy of **P** was made; instead, **P** was used directly. As a result, **P**'s VFT pointer, which points to the **Parent** VFT, was used and therefore "Do your homework!" was printed. Thus, an important rule about polymorphism emerges:

> *In order for polymorphism to work correctly for an object passed as a parameter, you must either use a pointer to the object as the parameter, or pass the object as a reference parameter.*

Typecasting Pointers to Objects

Although there is type compatibility between a base type pointer and a derived type pointer, you can also use an explicit typecast if you wish. For example:

```
main()
{
  Location *L;
  Circle *C;
  L = (Location *)C;
}
```

However, unlike the assignment compatibility rule, you can switch the order of the typecast:

```
C = (Circle *)L; // Be careful!
```

In this case, we assume that the **Location** pointer **L** actually points to a **Circle** object. In general, you should try to avoid such typecasts, since the assumptions being made might be invalid and can lead to many strange errors. Thus, when would you use such typecasts? A common situation occurs when you build generic data structures, such as stacks and lists. The window stacks developed in Chapter 10 are one example.

Calling Inherited Functions

The purpose of inheritance and derived classes is to allow you to reuse code from the base classes. When you override virtual functions, the overridden functions don't just go away.

Consider the **Reset()** and **Add()** functions of the **Tally** and **SmarterTally** classes. The **Reset()** and **Add()** functions of **SmarterTally** contain code from the corresponding functions of **Tally**—namely, the assignments to **Total**. Rather than duplicate this code, you can share it by calling the **Reset()** and **Add()** functions of **Tally** from within the corresponding functions of **SmarterTally**. Here's how:

```
void SmarterTally::Reset(void)
// Reset Total and number of inputs count
{
  Tally::Reset();  // Call Tally's version of Reset();
  NumTallies = 0;
}

void SmarterTally::Add(float Amt)
// Add to tally and keep track of number of inputs
{
  Tally::Add(); // Call Tally's version of Add()
  NumTallies++;
}
```

The process of using an inherited function such as this is sometimes referred to as *inherited function chaining*.

Note that you need to qualify an inherited function with the base class name only if the derived class has overridden it. Otherwise, just specifying the function name itself will do. For example, here is the **SmarterTally::GetAverage()** function, which calls the **Tally::GetTotal()** function using only the name **GetTotal()**, since the function is not overridden in the **SmarterTally** class:

```
float SmarterTally::GetAverage(void)
{
  // Note direct call to GetTotal();
  return NumTallies ? GetTotal() / NumTallies : 0;
}
```

Determining Which Inherited Function Is Called

One important question will surface when you start to use derived classes: What happens if a member function is called that isn't overridden, and that function calls another function that *is* overridden? Which version of the latter function is used—the one from the base class or the one from the derived class? The answer: The one from the derived class.

There's an easy way to keep track of which functions are called if you know how virtual function tables are created. When a class is derived, a new VFT is created for the derived class. By default, all functions pointers from the base class VFT are copied into the derived class VFT. However, if a function is overridden, the corresponding pointer in the new VFT is changed to reference the new function. In addition, new entries are created for any additional virtual functions defined in the derived class. It's important to note that nonvirtual functions do not have an entry in the VFT.

As an example, Figure A.2 shows the VFTs for the following two classes:

```
class Starship {
public:
  virtual void Build(void);
  virtual void Launch(void);
  virtual void ApplyThrust(void);
};

class Battlestar : public Starship {
public:
  virtual void Build(void);
  virtual void ApplyThrust(void);
  virtual void ArmPhasers(void);
};
```

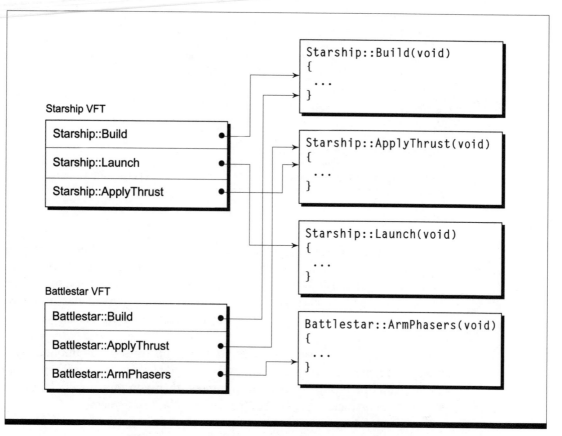

Figure A.2   Derived classes may share functions

Note how **Build()** and **ApplyThrust()** are overridden, but **Launch()** isn't. Also note how **ArmPhasers()** was added in the **Battlestar** class.

By examining Figure A.2, you'll see that it's easy to determine which virtual functions are called in derived objects. Just remember that, when a chain of virtual functions is called, the functions are always called from the derived object's VFT. This is true even for virtual functions that actually originate from the base class.

Using Constructors in Derived Classes

Let's rewrite the **Tally** and **SmarterTally** classes to have constructors. (We'll make **Reset()** virtual, and use function chaining in the derived class functions.)

```
class Tally {
public:
```

```
    float Total;
    Tally(void) { Total - 0; }
    virtual void Reset(void)      { Total - 0.0;  }
    virtual void Add(float Amt); { Total +- Amt; }
    float GetTotal(void);         { return Total; }
};

class SmarterTally : public Tally {
public:
    int NumTallies;
    SmarterTally(void) { NumTallies - 0; }
    virtual void Reset(void)    { Tally::Reset(); NumTallies - 0; }
    virtual void Add(float Amt) { Tally::Add(); NumTallies++; }
    float GetAverage(void) { return NumTallies ? Total/NumTallies : 0; }
    }
};
```

The **SmarterTally()** constructor looks as though it only does one thing, reset **NumTallies**. But it actually does more. Before the body of **SmarterTally()** is executed, the **Tally()** constructor is called implicitly, which causes **Total** to be reset. In this manner, the base class portion of an object from a derived class is always guaranteed to be initialized, and it is always initialized before the derived class portion of the object.

Since the **Tally()** constructor takes no arguments, this call is implicit—you don't have to make the call yourself. However, if you have a base class with all of its constructors requiring at least one argument, then you must make the call to one of those constructors yourself in the derived class constructor.

Also constructors cannot be declared as virtual functions.

Using Data Hiding with Inheritance

In almost all the examples in this book, we've made the members of our classes public. In only a few cases have we used private members. The reason is that specifying private members in classes adds to the complexity of defining the classes, since there are more rules to consider. This is especially true when you start using inheritance.

Sometimes its best to first wring out the design of your classes, determining what members to have in each, and then to go in later and "fine tune" the classes to use proper data hiding. One challenging project is to take the classes as developed in this book and split the members into private and public sections. It's educational to step back and see what happens when you make certain members private. You soon find the places where the details haven't been encapsulated as well as they could have been. (One example is where the **Wso** classes of Chapters 7 and 10 access the members of the nested **Panel** objects.)

Using Arrays of Objects

Just as you can have an array of structure variables, you can also have an array of objects. But an interesting case occurs when we have arrays containing pointers to objects. To use an array of object pointers, you must be sure to initialize each array element using **new**, and you must dispose of each element using **delete**. Of course, if your objects have constructors and destructors, they must be called, too.

As an example, consider the following class hierarchy, which consists of a generic bank account class, and then derived checking and savings accounts. We assume the difference between checking and savings is the interest that is accumulated on the deposits.

```
class Acct { // Generic bank account
public:
  float Amt;
  Acct(void) { Amt - 0.0; }
  virtual ~Acct(void); // Closes out the account
  virtual void Deposit(float A);
  virtual float WithDraw(float A);
};

class CheckingAcct : public Acct {
public:
  CheckingAcct(void); // Need new constructor
  ~CheckingAcct(void); // This destructor sends you a check to
                       // clear out your account
};

class SavingsAcct : public Acct {
public:
  float InterestRate;
  SavingsAcct(float Ir); // Constructor initializes interest rate
  ~SavingsAcct(void);    // Destructor computes final interest
                         // payment and sends you a check
  virtual void Deposit(float A);  // Handles interest
  virtual void WithDraw(float A); // Handles interest
};
```

Here's how you can initialize and destroy an array of pointers to generic **Acct** objects:

```
main()
{
  Acct *AcctPtr - new Acct[3]; // Allocate three bank accounts
  ...
  delete [3] AcctPtr;          // Deallocate the three bank accounts
}
```

Our array above uses pointers to the generic **Acct** class. Can we point to checking and savings accounts with our array? We certainly can, thanks to the assignment compatibility rule. But how do we initialize an array that has both the derived checking and savings accounts?

When creating the dynamic **SavingsAcct** and **CheckingAcct** objects, you can assign the result returned from **new** directly to **Acct** pointers.

```
main()
{
  Acct *Accounts[3];
  Accounts[1] - new CheckingAcct;
  Accounts[2] - new CheckingAcct;
  Accounts[3] - new SavingsAcct;
  // Use the array, then dispose of the elements
  delete[3] Accounts;
}
```

Note how we delete the accounts in the array collectively, by using the generic **Acct** pointer **Account**. Even so, the correct destructor for each object in the array will be called, since we declared the destructors virtual.

Arrays created in this manner can be quite powerful because the elements are of different types. Such arrays are called *heterogeneous* arrays. In Chapter 10, linked lists used as stacks for different-typed windows are defined in a similar fashion. When deleting the objects in an heterogeneous array, always be sure to use virtual destructors.

Using Composite Objects

Another way to group objects is to make *composite objects*. Such objects have other objects nested inside them. Composite objects are easy to define—just specify the objects to be nested as instance variables of the composite object. An example of a composite object is a scroll bar, which consists of a bar on which a button is moved back and forth. The two classes needed to define scroll bars might look like:

```
class ScrollButton {
public:
  int X,Y; // Position of button
  ScrollButton(int X1, int Y1);
  virtual ~ScrollButton(void);
  void Draw(void);
};

class ScrollBar {
public:
```

```
    ScrollButton Sbutton;
    int Wd; // Width of bar
    ScrollBar(int W);
    virtual ~ScrollBar(void);
    void Draw(void);
};
```

Note how, in the **ScrollBar** class, we've included the **ScrollButton** object **Sbutton**. We did this in much the same way we would if **ScrollBar** and **ScrollButton** were structures. The difference is that, since **ScrollButton** has a constructor taking arguments, that constructor must be called in the **ScrollBar** constructor. For example:

```
ScrollBar::ScrollBar(int W)
: Sbutton(0, 0) // Initialize Sbutton to be at (0,0)
{
  Wd - W; // Initialize scrollbar width
}
```

Different Types of Inheritance

You've seen where deriving a class from a base class allows you to inherit the members of the base class. You can think of the derived class as having a nested object—one that is of the base class type. In fact, nesting objects is actually another form of inheritance. Take our **Tally** and **SmarterTally** classes. Instead of deriving **SmarterTally** from **Tally**, let's have the **SmarterTally** class include a **Tally** object:

```
class SmarterTally {
public:
  Tally Tobj;        // Include nested Tally object
  int NumTallies;
  SmarterTally(void);
  virtual void Reset(void);
  virtual void Add(float Amt);
  float GetAverage(void);
};
```

By including the **Tally** object **Tobj** in **SmarterTally**, we have access to all **Tally** members. Let's compare the nested object approach with the derived class approach for the **Add()** function:

```
void SmarterTally::Add(float Amt)
// Using nested object approach
{
  Tobj.Add();   // Call function from nested object
  NumTallies++; // Do additional work
}
```

```
void SmarterTally::Add(float Amt)
// Using derived class approach
{
  Tally::Add(); // Call inherited function
  NumTallies++; // Do additional work
}
```

In both cases, the **SmarterTally::Add()** function is inheriting the **Add()** function from **Tally**. However, using class derivation is much more powerful than using nested objects, for three reasons:

1. With derived classes you can use the assignment compatibility rule. For example, derived **SmarterTally** objects can be assigned to **Tally** objects. However, if the **SmarterTally** class were defined using a nested **Tally** object, you couldn't do such assignments without using typecasting.

2. With derived classes you can exploit virtual functions.

3. With derived classes, you can directly access the inherited members. Using nested objects, you have to access the inherited members through the nested object.

Using Classes in Header Files

The main goal in OOP is to build a reusable set of class libraries that you can use in your applications. To use these class libraries, you'll want to implement them in separate files. Usually, class declarations go in header files, just as structure declarations do. The class implementation, that is, member functions definitions, are usually placed in a separate file.

Here is a sample header file for a window class, and a code file to implement the member functions:

```
window.h: The header file for the Window class

#ifndef H_WINDOW
#define H_WINDOW

enum Colors { Red = 0x40, Blue = 0x17, Green = 0x2e };

const int MaxWindows = 10;

class Window {
private:
  int Xul, Yul, Wd, Ht;
  Colors Attr;
```

```
      char *Image;
public:
   Window(int X, int Y, int W, int H, Colors C);
   virtual ~Window(void) { delete[Wd*Ht] Image; } // Inline function
   void Draw(void);
   void TypeInto(void);
   void Close(void);
};

#endif

window.cpp: Code file for Window class implementation

Window::Window(int X, int Y, int W, int H, Colors C)
{
   Xul - X; Yul - Y; Wd - W; Ht - H; Attr - Colors;
   Image - new char[Wd*Ht];
}

void Window::Draw(void)
{
   // Code to draw window
}

void Window::TypeInto(void);
{
   // Code to type into window
}

void Window::Close(void)
{
   // Code to erase and close window
}
```

The header file **window.h** illustrates five points: (1) that enumerated types can go in header files, (2) that constants can go in header files, (3) that class declarations can go in header files, (4) that inline functions can go in header files, and (5) how to protect from recompiling a header file using an **#ifndef** statement.

Note that constants can safely be placed in header files in C++. This is not true in C. The reason is that constants in C++ have local linkage, whereas in C they have external linkage. In C, including constants in header files can cause duplicate definition errors.

Also, inline functions can be placed in header files. Since they work much like macros do, you should use them the way you would use macros, and that includes when and where to put them in header files.

An important part of the **window.h** header file is the use of the **#ifndef** macro. This macro is used to avoid a header file from being compiled more than once if it happens to be included more than once, either directly, or indirectly, in a source file. This is to avoid compiler errors complaining of duplicate class declarations. The trick is to define a unique macro for each header using a **#define** statement. This macro gets defined the first time the file is included during compilation of a source file. For all subsequent inclusions of the header in the same source file, the **#ifndef** statement will cause the compiler to skip over all the code until the **#endif** statment, effectively eliminating the duplicate definition problem. As your class libraries grow and your header files become more complex, this trick can prove to be invaluable.

Index

A

ActionProc, 232
Allocating objects, 378–379
Arrays, 393–394
ArrowCursor, 103,106,113

B

BackGround(), 68,310
Background colors, 59,68
Base class, 16,380
Base window, 181–182
BGI, 306,319–320
bioskey(), 70
Border attributes, 148–149
BorderPrompt, 69,80,309
BoxStretcher
    BoxHt, 357
    BoxWd, 357
    definition of, 356–357,360
    Draw(), 357,359,361
    features of, 356
    keyboard input, 357–358
    messages, 358–359
    OnKeyStroke(), 357–358,361–362
    RcvScrollPosn(), 358–359,361
    Redraw(), 357,361
    SendScrollPosn(), 358–359,361
    SetSize(), 357,360–361
    using, 359–363
Button objects
    graphics mode, 339–346
    text mode, 201–204
button1.cpp, 201–204
ButtonStyle, 69
bxstrtch.cpp, 360–363

C

Chaining, 390
Child class, 380
class (keyword), 13
Classes, 5–6, *See also* Objects
    base class, 16,380
    declaring objects, 375
    defining, 373–374
    derived class, 16
CleanUp()
    graphics mode, 319–320,338
    text mode, 196,226
Clipping rectangles, 121–122
Closeable, 69,79,309
Close button, 151
CmndButton, 300
Color video card address, 28,58

ColorPak, 67–68,79
Composite objects, 394–395
Constructors
    example of, 38,377
    overloaded, 63
    syntax of, 377
    using in derived classes, 391–392
Converting to OOP, 10–20,35,55–56
Cycling through objects, 194,205,253

D

Dashed border, 68,79
Data hiding, 6,13,392
Data members
    accessing, 12–14,16
    definition of, 5
    example of, 12
Deallocating objects, 378–379
DefColors, 68
delete (keyword), 379
Derived class, 379–380
Destructors
    example of, 38
    syntax of, 377
    using, 377–378
    virtual, 394
Dialog boxes, 283–290
    general class, 284–284
    message box class, 285–286
    with options, 287–290
dialogue.cpp, 300–302
dialogue.h, 300
DlgBox, 284,300
Dmso, 247,255–256,261–262
Double-line border, 79
DrawProc, 343
Drop menus, *See* Pull-down menus
Dynamic objects, 378–379

E

Early binding, 382
EGA, 307,315
Encapsulation, 6–7,13
Event handling, 189–192

Event loops, 190,193
Events, 69–70,96–97
    keyboard, 190,192
    mouse, 190–192
Exclusive-OR, 317
ExitAction(), 365,367
Extended scan codes, 69–70

F

File browser,
    OOP version, 35–56
    standard C version, 21–35
ForeGround(), 68,79,310
Foreground colors, 59,68
Frame, 145
Frame attributes, 69,79–80
Framed screen objects, 120,143–145
Frames, 143,163
Fso, 144,164–165
    border attributes, 148
    Box(), 145,166
    Bstyle, 145
    Bwd, 145
    Clear(),
    Colors, 145,148
    constructor, 148,165
    default sizes, 146
    definition of, 145
    destructor, 164
    differences with Trso, 146
    DrawFrame(), 164
    DrawShadows(), 148
    Fattr, 145
    features of, 144–145
    Fill(), 145–146,166
    FillB(), 166
    Frame, 146–147
    frame attributes, 148
    GetImage(), 148
    HasShadow(), 165
    HzWrt(), 145–146,166
    HzWrtB(), 166
    Interior, 146–147
    OnBorder(), 147,165
    OnCloseButton(), 147,165
    OnFrame(), 147,165

OnInterior(), 147
Overall, 146–148
purpose of, 146,148
PutImage(), 148
Scroll(), 145,166
SetLocn(), 146,167
SetSize(), 145–146,167
ShadowXfr(), 148
Swap(), 148
TextHeight(), 156
TextWidth(), 156
Touches(), 147,166
using, 148,152
writing to, 146
fsounit.cpp, 165–167
fsounit.h, 164–165
FullScrn, 196–197,225,320
Function binding, 382

G

gbutntst.cpp, 344–346
gbutton.cpp, 365–368
gbutton.h, 364–365
General classes, 144,162–164,363
GetIm, 154,156
gmenutst.cpp, 322–325
Gfso, 119
    definition, 330
    description of, 305,313–314
    destructor, 315,331
    DrawFrame(), 315,332
    drawing, 315
    GetImage(), 316,333
    initializing, 314
    member functions, 313
    OnCloseButton(), 332
    PutImage(), 316,333
    SetLocn(), 315,332
    SetSize(), 315,331–332
    Swap(), 316,333
    using, 185
gfsounit.cpp, 330–334
gfsounit.h, 330
Graphics mode, 306–307,319–320
Graphics screen objects
    buttons, 339–346
    dimensions, 308

drawing frames, 311
hierarchy, 304–305
icons, 342–343
overview, 303–305
window styles, 305,309–310
Graphics skeletons, 316–317
Graphics windows
    backdrops, 326
    borderless, 305,309
    border styles, 309
    close box, 314
    example program, 320–321
    filling, 310
    fonts, 319–320,326
    frame styles, 309
    header, 314–316
    merging with text, 363
    moving, 316–317,326
    recessed, 312
    relief, 305,309,312
    scrollable, 346–363
    skeletons, 316–317
    styles, 305,309
    swapping, 326
    three-dimensional, 305,309,311–312
    with border, 305,309
    with close box, 305,309
    writing text to, 310
Grouping objects, 205
grphscrn.cpp, 319,337–338
grphscrn.h, 336
Grso, 119,145
    Box(), 311,329
    definition of, 307,327
    description of, 305
    Fill(), 310–311,326,328
    FillB(), 310–311,326,328–329
    initializing, 307–308
    HzWrt(), 310,328
    HzWrtB(), 310,328
    TextHeight(), 308,329
    TextWidth(), 308,329
    TxtHt, 308
grsounit.cpp, 327–329
grsounit.h, 327
gscroll.cpp, 368–371
gscroll.h, 367–368
Gskel, 119

definition, 317,330
description of, 305,316–317
DrawFrame(), 317,334
exclusive-OR, 317
moving, 317
Swap(), 334
gtest.cpp, 320–322
gwsounit.cpp, 335–336
gwsounit.h, 334–335

H

HandCursor, 103,106,113
Header files, 396–398
Hercules, 91–92
Heterogeneous arrays, 394
Horizontal extent, 229
Horizontal menus, 236–237,239
HzScrollMove, 275

I

IconButton
    definition of, 343,364
    DrawProc, 343
Icons, 342–343
Idle, 70,97
Inheritance, 8–10
    calling inherited functions, 389–391
    example of, 15–20
    extending objects, 8,15–16
    multiple, 127–128,251–252
    re-using code, 16–17
    sharing code, 17
    types of, 395–396
Inherited function chaining, 390
Inline member functions, 374
Instance variables, 5,374
Interior, 143,145
Iso, 181–192
    Active, 179
    Activate(), 181,190,192
    Base, 181–183
    BorderHandler(), 181,191,216
    ClippingRect(), 180,209
    closing, 186–187
    constructor, 180,185,209

definition of, 178–179,207
DeltaMove(), 180,188,211–212
DeltaStretch(), 180,188–189,212–213
destructor, 179,209
Dispatch(), 181,191–192,217
Draw(), 180,187
drawing, 187
DrawPanel(), 180,186,187–188,210
Enter(), 181,190,215
event handler, 189
features of, 176–179
functions of, 180–181
Hide(), 180,213
initializing, 183
IsClosed, 179,187
Leave(), 181,190,192,215
Move(), 180,188,211
MoveLoop(), 180,188,212
moving, 188–189
Obscured(), 180,217
OnClose(), 181,187,215
OnKeyStroke(), 181,192,216
OnMouseDown(), 181,190–191,215
OnMouseEnter(), 181,190,215
OnMouseLeave(), 181,215
OnMouseStillDown(), 181
OnMouseUp(), 181,191–192
OnMouseWithin(), 181
OnShiftArrow(), 181,216–217
Open(), 180,185–187,211
opening, 186–187
Over, 182–183
Prompt(), 180,192,214
Redraw(), 180,187–189
Remove(), 180,187,214
resizing, 188–189
Reopen(), 180,187,211
Select(), 180,190,192,214
SetLocn(), 180,185–186,188,209–210
SetSize(), 180,185,210
SetVisibleFlag(), 180,213–214
Show(), 180,213
Stretch(), 180,188–189,212
stretching, 188–189
StretchLoop(), 180,188–189,213
SubMgr, 182–183
Swap(), 180,213
SwitchFocus(), 181,191,214–215
TouchFlag, 179

Under, 182–183
UnPrompt(), 180,214
IsoMgr
    Base, 183
    Bottom, 183
    constructor, 217
    CycleForw(), 194,220
    CycleToSibling(), 194,219–220
    cycling, 194,205
    definition of, 193,208
    destructor, 217–218
    EventLoop(), 190,193,222
    EventStep(), 190,193–194,206,222–223
    features of, 176,193
    Marker, 194
    MoveToFront(), 218–219
    OnIso(), 221–222
    ProcessCycle(), 194,220
    purpose of, 192–193
    Push(), 218
    ResetTouchFlags(), 221
    SetTouchFlags(), 221
    Top, 183
    use in Iso, 182–183
isounit.cpp, 209–223
isounit.h, 207–208
IsShiftArrow(), 69,83

K

Keyboard events, 190,192
keybrd.cpp, 69,82–83
keybrd.h, 69,81–82
KeyEvent(), 69,82

L

LeftButton, 95,107
LeftRightCursor, 103,106,113
LineChar, 69,79

M

MainEventLoop()
    graphics mode, 319–320,337–338
    text mode, 196,226

mcursor.cpp, 103,113
Member functions
    accessing, 14,16
    calling inherited, 17
    defining, 374–375
    definition of, 5
    example of, 12
    inline, 38
    overriding, 16–17
Menu entry list, 234
Menu entry spacing, 229
Menus, *See also* Pull-down menus
    assigning functions to, 232–233
    class hierarchy, 229
    components of, 228–230,244
    drop menus, 246–247
    entries, 231–233
    example of, 241–243
    graphics mode, 230,251,322–325
    keyboard input, 247–248
    menu bar, 246
    menu entries, 231–232
    selecting mode, 230–231
    size of, 236–237
    steps in building, 244
    text mode, 227–263
    overview, 227–230
Meso, 230–233,256–257
    Activate(), 232
    definition of, 231,254
    features of, 231
MesoList, 233–234,257–258
    definition of, 234,254
    features of, 234
Message passing, 190
Method chaining, 17
Methods, 5, *See also* Member functions
mgrphtst.cpp, 103–105
Monochrome monitor address, 28,58
Mouse
    abstract, 105
    buttons, 94–96
    configuring, 90–91
    coordinates of, 92–93
    cursor, 92,103
    cursor masks, 100–101
    detecting, 89
    events, 88,96,106,190–192
    functions, 86

graphics mode, 93,100–105,319–320
Hercules mode, 91–92
hot spot, 102
interrupts, 88
Microsoft, 85
mouse.com, 86
moving, 93–94
object, 87
press count, 95
release count, 95
text mode, 93,196–197
MouseCursor, 102,106
MouseObject,
    ButtonStatus(), 94,110
    class, 87–88,107
    constructor, 89,108
    CursorMask, 102
    DriveExists(), 89,108
    Event(), 88,96–97,110
    Hide(), 88,92,109
    initialization, 89
    LowRes, 88,91,93
    MouseOff, 88,91
    Move(), 88,93,111
    Moved(), 93–94,111
    OK, 88–91
    Operating(), 91,112
    PressCnt(), 88,95,110
    ReleaseCnt(), 95,110
    ScreenMask, 102
    SetGCursor(), 88,102,112
    Setup(), 90,93,108
    SetupOK(), 89–90,109
    Show(), 88,92
    Status(), 88,94,109
    TextMode, 91,93
    TurnOff(), 91,112
    TurnOn(), 91,112
    using, 89
    WaitForAnyEvent(), 88,97,111
    WaitForEvent(), 88,97,111
MouseOptional, 196,320
MouseRequired, 196,320
mousetst.cpp, 98–100
MsgBox, 285,300
MsgPkt, 190,207,209,273
msgtst.cpp, 285–286
msmouse.cpp, 86,108–112
msmouse.h, 106–107

Mso, 234–240
    Activate(), 260
    Back(), 260
    constructor, 236,258
    CurrSeln, 235
    definition of, 235,254–255
    destructor, 236
    Entries, 235
    EntriesDrawn, 235
    EntryWidth(), 259
    features of, 235
    Forw(), 260
    IsHz(), 236
    IsVt(), 236
    Leave(), 260
    member functions of, 237
    MoveLoop(), 259–260
    Ncols, 235
    Nrows, 235
    OnKeyStroke(), 260
    Open(), 240,259
    overriding, 240
    SetSize(), 236
    SetupDim(), 236–237,258–259
    SetupEntries(), 259
    Spacing, 235
    using, 237
msounit.cpp, 230,256–263
msounit.h, 254–256
Multiple inheritance, 127–128,251–252

N

new (keyword), 378–379
No border, 79
NoMouse, 196
NoOp(), 365,366
NullMsg, 319

O

Objects, 5
    accessing data members, 12–14,16
    arrays of, 393–394
    assigning to, 385–386
    base class, 16,380
    combining, 127–128

composite objects, 394–395
constructors, 377,391–392
declaring, 13,374–376
destructors, 377–378,394
dynamic, 378–379
extending objects, 8,15–16
inheritance, *See* Inheritance
initializing, *See* Constructors
parameter passing, 386–388
pointers to, 388–389
polymorphism, 9–10,17–18,381–383,387–388
re-using code, 16–17
sharing code, 17
static, 378
typecasting, 388–389
using pointers, 382
VFT, *See* Virtual function table
Object-oriented programming
chaos to OOP, 2
components of, 5
converting to OOP, 10–20
definition of, 2–3
viewpoint of, 3–4
OptButton, 287–288
optexmpl.cpp, 288–290
OutlineMove, 69,80,309
Overall, 143,145
Overloading functions, 65

P

Parent class, *See* Base class
Pixels, 306
Pmeso, 246,255,262–263
PmesoAction(), 262
Pmso, 245,255,261
Pointers to objects, 382,388–389
Polymorphism, 9–10,17–18,381–383,387–388
private (keyword), 13,374
protected (keyword), 13
public (keyword), 13,16,374
PullDnBar, 246,255,261
Pull-down menus
assigning functions to, 232–233
classes used, 229
components of, 228–230,244
drop menus, 246–247
example of, 247–251

graphics mode, 322–325
keyboard input, 247–248
menu bar, 246
menu entries, 231–232
selecting mode, 230–231
size of, 236–237
steps in building, 244
text mode, 227–263
PutIm, 154,156

R

Recessed, 79,305,309,312
Rect, 119–120
class definition, 135
ClipDim(), 121,136–137
clipping, 121–122
ClipSize(), 121,136
constructor, 120,136
Contains(), 122–123,137–138
coordinates of, 122
destructor, 121,135
HzClip(), 122,137
initializing, 120
purpose of, 120
SetLocn(), 136
SetSize(), 136
Touches(), 123,138
VtClip(), 122,137
Rectangle screen objects, 124–125
Relief, 79,305,309,312
Resizing windows, 188–189
RightButton, 95,107
Rso,
class definition, 124,135
Contains(), 147
in hierarchy, 119
purpose of, 124
rsounit.cpp, 136–138
rsounit.h, 135

S

ScreenBuffer, 60
Screen colors, 59
Screen memory, 58
Screen objects

display modes, 117
framed, 120
hierarchy, 119,134–135
multiple, 175–176
overlapping, 123
overview, 57–58,116–117
rectangles (text mode), 124
rectangles (graphics mode), 307
scrnsty.cpp, 67,80–81,149
scrnsty.h, 67,79–80,149
Scrollable windows (graphics mode), 346–363
classes used, 347
components of, 347
mouse cursor, 348
overview, 348
scroll bars, 346–355
Swso, 354–355
Scrollable windows (text mode), 265–283
classes used, 266,291
generic class, 276–283
scroll bars, 267–276
Swso, 276–283
with one scroll bar, 290–291
Scroll bars
as input devices, 364
communicating with, 273–275,291–292
components of, 268,347–348
frame (text mode), 267–269
graphics mode, 346–354
slider, 269–270,349–350
text mode, 267–276
ScrollBar (graphics mode)
BarOrient, 367
communication with, 353–354
definition of, 351,367
features of, 350–351
HzScrollMove, 353
InhibitMessage, 352
initializing, 351–352
mouse action, 352–353
moving the slider, 354,357–358
OnMouseEnter(), 353,370
Open(), 352,369
RcvScrollPosn(), 353–371
Redraw(), 352,369
SendScrollPosn(), 353,370–371
ScrollBar (text mode)
BorderHandler(), 272,296

communication with, 273,291–292
definition of, 271,293
DelayCntr, 271
DelayLimit, 271–273
features of, 271
interior pattern, *See* ScrollFrame
mouse action, 272–273
moving the slider, 272
OnMouseDown(), 272–273,296
OnMouseStillDown(), 272–273,296–297
Open(), 271,296
RcvScrollPosn(), 273,275–276,292,297–298
Redraw(), 272,295
SendScrollPosn(), 273,297
ScrollFrame
definition of, 268,292
DrawFrame(), 268–269,294
orientation, 268–269
purpose of, 268
SetLocn(), 268,294
SetSize(), 268,294
Setup()
graphics mode, 319,337
text mode, 196–197,226
Shadows, 148,151–156
Shift keys, 69
Single-line border, 79
Skeleton windows, 160,316–317
sktest.cpp, 70–73
Slider (graphics mode)
constructor, 349
definition of, 349,367
features of, 349
mouse action, 350
Move(), 350
OnMouseEnter(), 349–350,368
style of, 349
Slider (text mode), 269–270
constructor, 270
definition of, 270,292–293
features of, 270
Move(), 270,272,295
movement of, 271–273,275
OnKeyStroke(), 270,295
OnMouseDown(), 270,295
Solid border, 79
Stack, 381–385
Static binding, 382

Static objects, 378
Stretchable, 80
struct (keyword), 11–13
Structured programming, 2
Swappable, 69,79,309
Swso (graphics mode)
    definition of, 354–355,367–368
    features of, 354
    Open(), 355,372
    RcvScrollPosn(), 355
    scroll bars, 355
    SendScrollPosn(), 355
    SetSize(), 355,372
    using, 355–363
Swso (text mode)
    definition of, 276–277,293
    Dispatch(), 278,299
    member functions of, 277
    Open(), 277
    Prompt(), 277,299
    RcvScrollPosn(), 278
    scroll bars, 277
    SendScrollPosn(), 278
    SetSize(), 278,298
    Stretch(), 298–299
    UnPrompt(), 278,299

T

Tear-away menus, 243
Texel, 59,73
TexelPtr, 73
TextButton, 340–342
    action, 342
    definition of, 340,364
    Draw(), 341,365–367
    drawing, 341
Text button objects, 201–204
Text cursor, 134
Text mode, 27–29,58–60,117–118,196–197
Text windows, 194–197
Tfso, 119,150–156
    Clear(), 170
    constructor, 152,168
    coordinates of, 152
    definition of, 151–152,167
    destructor, 168

DrawFrame(), 153,170
DrawShadows(), 153,155,171
example of, 151
features of, 150
GetImage(), 153,170
HzShadow, 152
OnCloseButton(), 170
parents of, 152
PutImage(), 153,170–171
SaveBuff, 152
SetLocn(), 152,169–170
SetSize(), 152,169
shadows, 151–156
ShadowXfr(), 153–155,171–172
Swap(), 153,155,171
swap buffer, 150
TextHeight(), 156
TextWidth(), 156
using, 152–153,156–159,185
VtShadow, 152
writing text, 156
tfsotst.cpp, 157
tfsotst2.cpp, 158–159
tfsounit.cpp, 168–173
tfsounit.h, 167–168
this (keyword), 376
tmenutst.cpp, 248–251
tmenu1.cpp, 241–242
Trso
    Box(), 129,140–141
    class definition, 125–126,138
    constructor, 126,139
    coordinate system, 129
    copying, 130
    destructor, 139
    Fill(), 126,129,140
    FillB(), 140
    HzWrt(), 126,128,139
    HzWrtB(), 129,140
    in hierarchy, 119
    multiple inheritance, 127–128
    Pic, 126
    purpose of, 125
    Scroll(), 126,141
    SetLocn(), 126–127,139
    SetSize(), 126,139
    Swap(), 130–131,141
    swapping, 130–131

test program, 131–133
using, 145,152
Xfr(), 130–131,141
trsounit.cpp, 138–141
trsounit.h, 138
trtest.cpp, 131–133
Tskel, 160–162
constructor, 162,172
definition of, 167–168
destructor, 172
DrawFrame(), 160,162,173
drawing a skeleton, 162
features of, 160–161
GetImage(), 162,173
PutImage(), 162,173
SetSize(), 172
Sides, 161
Swap(), 160,162,173
using, 195
twsounit.cpp, 223–225
twsounit.h, 223
TxBuff, 60–61,73–74,120,125–127
Aliased, 62
constructor, 62–63,74–75
destructor, 63,75
Fill(), 64–65,77–78
FillB(), 64–65,78
HzFill(), 65,74
HzFillB(), 65,74
HzWrt(), 65,78
HzWrtB(), 65,78
initialization, 62–64
member functions, 61
OrgPtr, 62,64,66–67
RelAddr(), 67,75
Scroll(), 67,77
SetRamPtr(), 63,75
SetLocn(), 63–64,76
SetSize(), 63,75–76
Swap(), 65–66,76
TxRam, 62–63
TxRamAddr(), 64,67,75
Xfr(), 66,77
txscroll.cpp, 293–299
txscroll.h, 292–293
txunit.cpp, 60,74–79
txunit.h, 60,73–74
Typecasts, 252–253,388–389

U

UpDownCursor, 103,106,113
User interfaces, 116–120

V

Vertical menus, 236–237
VFT, *See* Virtual function table
VGA, 307,315
Video attributes, 59
VideoModeType, 91,107
VideoPtr(), 64,78–79
virtual (keyword), 16
Virtual functions, 16,381
Virtual function table, 383–385,390–391
vw.cpp, 280–283
Vwso
constructor, 279
Draw(), 279
features of, 278–279
keyboard interaction, 279
OnKeyStroke(), 279
RcvScrollPosn(), 280
SendScrollPosn(), 280
using, 280–283
virtual buffer, 278–279

W

Windows, 115–133
borders, 128,148
combining text and graphics, 363
member access, 163
graphics, 117–118,303–338
hierarchy, 119
manager, 177
moving, 153–156
scrollable, 265–283,346–347
shadows, 148,151–156
skeletons, 160–161
stack, 181–183
styles (graphics mode), 305
styles (text mode), 148–150
text mode, 150
titles, 163

writing text to, 128–129
WindowStyle, 69
WithShadow, 69,81
Writing to windows, 128–129,206
Wso (graphics mode)
    constructor, 318,335
    definition of, 318,335
    description, 305,318
    features of, 318
    MoveLoop(), 335–336
    Prompt(), 318–319,336
    UnPrompt(), 318–319,336
Wso (text mode), 176,195–196
    constructor, 195,223
    definition, 195,223

    MoveLoop(), 195,223–224
    overriding functions, 200–201
    Prompt(), 195,225
    StretchLoop(), 195,224
    UnPrompt(), 195,225
    using, 197–200
wsotst1.cpp, 197
wsotst2.cpp, 198–199
wsotxscr.cpp. 225–226
wsotxscr.h, 225

Symbols

::, 12,17,316,375

Disk Order Form

If you'd like to use the code presented in this book but don't want to waste your time typing it in, we have a very special offer for you. We are making available a set of diskettes that contain all of the source code for the program listings in this book.

To order your disks, fill out the form below and mail it along with $19.95 in check or money order, or Visa/MasterCard (orders outside the U.S. add $5 shipping and handling) to:

Azarona Software
C++ OOP Disks
P.O. Box 13433
Denver, CO 80201

- -

Please send me _____ copies of the companion disks for *Object-Oriented Programming with Turbo C++* at $19.95 each. (Orders outside the U.S. add $5 shipping and handling. U.S. funds only.) Please make checks payable to Azarona Software.

_____
Name

_____
Address

_____
City   State   Zip Code

_____
Telephone

_____
Credit Card #   Exp. Date

_____
Name on card   Signature